FIXING THE FUTURE:
HOW CANADA'S USUALLY FRACTIOUS
GOVERNMENTS WORKED TOGETHER TO RESCUE
THE CANADA PENSION PLAN

In 1993, most Canadians believed that big government deficits were permanent and that the Canada Pension Plan (CPP) was in such deep trouble that younger Canadians would never collect a retirement pension. They believed too that Canada's politicians were incapable of dealing with either problem. Yet by 1998, both were essentially solved.

While the deficit battles have been recounted many times, the story of the reform that rescued the CPP has gone almost entirely untold. In *Fixing the Future*, Bruce Little explains the CPP overhaul and shows why it stands as one of Canada's most significant public policy success stories, in part because it demanded an almost unparalleled degree of federal–provincial cooperation. Providing an overview of the CPP's entire history from its beginning in 1965, Little pulls together both published and new unpublished material relating to the CPP reform, and interviews more than fifty politicians, government officials, and others who were deeply involved in the reforms, for their recollections, insights, and observations.

A superbly told history of one of Canada's most important public policy issues, *Fixing the Future* will be of interest to political scientists, historians, economists, and all those concerned about their retirement.

(Rotman/UTP Publishing)

BRUCE LITTLE has worked as a journalist and policy analyst, primarily as an economics writer and columnist at the *Globe and Mail*, and was most recently Special Adviser to the Governor of the Bank of Canada.

BRUCE LITTLE

Fixing the Future

How Canada's Usually Fractious
Governments Worked Together to
Rescue the Canada Pension Plan

UNIVERSITY OF TORONTO PRESS
Toronto Buffalo London

Rotman/UTP Publishing
Toronto Buffalo London
www.utppublishing.com
Printed in Canada

ISBN 978-0-8020-9874-0 (cloth)
ISBN 978-0-8020-9583-1 (paper)

Printed on acid-free paper

Library and Archives Canada Cataloguing in Publication Data

Little, Bruce, 1945–
Fixing the future : how Canada's usually fractious governments worked
together to rescue the Canada Pension Plan / Bruce Little.

Includes bibliographical references and index.
ISBN 978-0-8020-9874-0 (bound) – ISBN 978-0-8020-9583-1 (pbk.)

1. Canada Pension Plan.   2. Pensions – Canada.   3. Canada – Politics and
government – 1993–2006.   I. Title.

HD7105.35.C3L58 2008   368.4'300971   C2008-904079-1

University of Toronto Press acknowledges the financial assistance to its
publishing program of the Canada Council for the Arts and the Ontario
Arts Council.

University of Toronto Press acknowledges the financial support for its
publishing activities of the Government of Canada through the Book
Publishing Industry Development Program (BPIDP).

Contents

Foreword

In March 1999, the Canada Pension Plan Investment Board received $12.1 million from the administrators of the CPP in Ottawa. The money was immediately invested in a portfolio of domestic and foreign equities designed to track the performance of broad market indexes. This little-noticed event heralded the practical beginning of an exciting and closely watched public policy initiative: using capital market returns to help sustain the retirement, survivor, and disability benefits promised by a national pension plan.

For the benefit of current and future generations of Canadians, this book captures the demographic, economic, social, and political events and debates that led to increased funding of the CPP and the creation of the CPP Investment Board to invest the assets of the plan in the capital markets. Only if they know this story will Canadians be able to judge with confidence the success of a public policy initiative that was designed to meet the income security needs of multiple generations of Canadians over time horizons marked with risk and uncertainty.

This history covers the first three decades of the Canada Pension Plan from its inception in 1966 but focuses on the reforms of the mid-1990s – an overhaul that broke the mould of the CPP to date and set it off in a new direction. Increases in contribution rates were not new, but this time the federal and provincial governments legislated practical benefit reductions, innovative financing techniques, and trust-building governance practices for the CPP fund. These changes all but guarantee that CPP benefits will be sustainable across future generations, with a high level of confidence that future contribution rates will not materially exceed the currently legislated rate of 9.9 per cent.

Canadians can judge the past fairly only if history is presented fully, objectively, and candidly. By retaining Bruce Little to write this account, the CPP Investment Board has helped to ensure that Canadians have a complete and candid history of the events and debates that have shaped the CPP's benefit provisions, financing formula, and governance structure.

Bruce Little is a former economics reporter and columnist for *The Globe and Mail* and recently completed a one-year assignment as Special Adviser to the Governor of the Bank of Canada. He had complete freedom to research all available documents related to the 1997 reforms and interview the key people who participated in the reform process, including industry and national opinion leaders, federal and provincial politicians, their political advisers, and government officials. We encouraged Bruce to meet face to face with the people who were in the room when the key decisions were made – both those who advised and those who decided. Before taking the assignment, Bruce made it clear that his name would not appear on the cover of the publication if he believed that his views, observations, or conclusions were inappropriately influenced by the CPP Investment Board.

The Board thanks Bruce Little for his efforts. He has done a remarkable job. We also extend a special thanks to all those people who made themselves available to provide their perspectives and insights into the development of a sustainable Canada Pension Plan. In small and large ways, they have served the public interest – a noble calling.

Gail Cook-Bennett
Founding Chair
CPP Investment Board
15 July 2008

Foreword
Achieving Effective Pension Reform:
A Lesson from Canada

Post-work income provision has been an important economic challenge for people everywhere since the beginning of time. In the pre-industrial age, intergenerational 'pension deals' were family affairs. Mom and Dad took care of their children when they were young, and the children took care of Mom and Dad when they could no longer take care of themselves. In today's post-industrial age, intergenerational 'pension deals' have become significantly more complex multi-pillar affairs.

Typically, post-industrial societies provide all citizens with a basic Pillar 1 pension funded through a national tax and/or payroll deduction structure. Many employers supplement this basic Pillar 1 state pension through pre-funded supplementary workplace-based Pillar 2 arrangements. In some societies, Pillar 2 arrangements are voluntary; in others they are mandatory. Finally, states offer tax-related incentives to individuals without a Pillar 2 pension arrangement (or an insufficient one) to build their own Pillar 3 supplementary retirement savings nest eggs.

These 3-Pillar post-industrial pension systems are sustainable as long as the underlying design assumptions about productivity, workforce participation rate, wage growth, workforce entry and retirement ages, post-work longevity, and investment earnings continue to hold. If material negative gaps between any of these assumptions and experience develop, sustainability can only be maintained if appropriate course corrections (e.g., to pension eligibility and benefits, or to funding and/or investment policy) are made. Given that any country's initial pension system design assumptions are destined to become increasingly inaccurate with the passage of time, a country's ability to make 'appropriate course corrections' in a timely fashion is a critically important sustainability factor.

Acting decisively in a timely fashion is not an easy thing. Some historians blame the fall of the Roman Empire on its inability to continue to provide adequate pensions to its soldiers. Ironically, once again today, Italy is one of a number of post-industrial economies finding it increasingly difficult to sustain their generous universal Pillar 1 pension schemes in the face of the dual problems of an aging population and a low-productivity economy. The difficulty to make the necessary course corrections in these circumstances is not surprising, as it requires not only getting technical design changes right, but also addressing the evolving fairness imbalances between current and future generations of beneficiaries. Unfortunately, while current beneficiaries vote, future beneficiaries do not.

It is these realities that make the story by Bruce Little about how Canada was able to correct the unsustainable course of its Canada Pension Plan to a sustainable one so interesting. Yes, how Canada got the required technical design changes right is an important part of the story by Bruce Little. So, for example, the reform package required finding the right mix of benefit cuts, contribution increases, and investment policies that would re-establish the long-term sustainability of the CPP on the one hand, and would be politically saleable at the same time.

However, as Little ably shows us, successful reform involves a great deal more than just technical prowess. The political and human elements of the CPP reform story are equally important and compelling. The difficulty many politicians have thinking beyond four-year election cycles has been well documented. On top of that, Canada is a federation, implying that any acceptable solution also required maintaining a delicate balance between federal and provincial powers. Then there is the inevitable 'ego' factor. Some of the personalities in the CPP reform story thought themselves larger than life, and behaved that way. Yet, despite all of these formidable obstacles, Canada's politicians were able to reach consensus that CPP reform was essential, and that they were willing to spend political capital on taking the reform message to a skeptical electorate.

The response of ordinary Canadians to the CPP reform proposals may well be the most interesting part of Little's story. In short, the vast majority of Canadians coast-to-coast accepted the argument that reform was required, and that the proposed reform package offered a credible and fair solution. This remarkable achievement required meeting two conditions. First, the reform package itself had to be both understandable and credible. Second, Canadians had to be treated as adults in how the reform message was conveyed to them. In this book, Little lays out how the CPP reform project met both of these critical conditions.

So while, on the one hand, *Fixing the Future* shows why there have been so few instances of successful pension reform in the developed world, on the other, Little's book shows that it is not impossible. It requires sound technical design, broad political 'buy-in,' and a well-executed implementation strategy. Easy to say. Difficult to do.

Keith Ambachtsheer
Director, Rotman International Centre for Pension Management
University of Toronto
12 May 2008

Preface

This project began with a rather more modest objective. Originally conceived as an extensive monograph on the reforms to the Canada Pension Plan in the mid-1990s, it has turned into a much lengthier book that traces the roots of the CPP from the 1960s through to the 1990s before getting to the substance of the reform itself. The story could not really be told any other way. As I ploughed through books, articles, and reports on the CPP and interviewed about fifty people involved in the process, it became increasingly clear that much of what happened in the 1990s could not be understood without the perspective of the plan's entire history.

This is a history, but it is the work of a long-time journalist, not a professional historian who would doubtless have brought to the task a much different approach. Throughout this effort, I was struck many times by just how rich a vein Canada's retirement income system could be for scholars. There is plenty of running room left for further work by researchers in many disciplines – history, economics, political science, public policy, and sociology, to name just a few. I hope some will take up the challenge.

My thanks to the Canada Pension Plan Investment Board for commissioning what has been a deeply enjoyable and satisfying venture. Three years ago, long before this project came along, I remarked in a speech to economists that I regarded the latest CPP reform as one of the great untold public policy success stories of the 1990s. The CPPIB has given me a chance to tell that story. John Ilkiw, the CPPIB's senior vice-president, portfolio design and risk management, came up with the idea for this book in the first place. He provided enthusiastic support throughout and invaluable comments on all chapters as they were completed. Thanks also to Jennifer Arnold for her research assistance, especially on pension reform in other countries, and to Melissa Troemel for her fine work in tracking down the cartoons and photographs included in the book.

Thank you to those who read the manuscript and offered their insights on – and corrections to – what I had done: Keith Ambachtsheer, Bob Baldwin, Réal Bouchard, Rob Brown, David Dodge, Wayne Foster, Michael Gourley, Bruce Kennedy, Paul Martin, Jean-Claude Ménard, David Walker, and two anonymous readers for University of Toronto Press. They bear no responsibility for any remaining errors or omissions; that is all mine. Len Husband and Richard Ratzlaff of UTP made the transition from raw manuscript to finished product smooth and enjoyable.

Finally, my very special thanks to my wife, Ellen Richardson, who has willingly tolerated a delay in our many plans for semi-retirement while I carried out one last full-time project. I owe her big time for that. I could not have done this without her love and encouragement. She read it all, caught many errors, and often forced me to clarify the confusing, with results that I know will benefit the reader.

Prologue

In 1993, if you had told a Canadian that within a half-decade, the country would have both erased its federal deficit and put the Canada Pension Plan on a solid financial footing for the first time, you would have been greeted with hoots of disbelieving laughter and urged to bet some serious money on your obviously mad predictions.

Everyone 'knew' that Canada's fiscal problems were so grave and so intractable that big deficits and big debts would be part of the landscape for decades to come. Everyone 'knew' that the twenty-seven-year-old national pension plan was in deep financial trouble despite two substantial increases in contribution rates. Everyone 'knew' that when younger Canadians reached retirement age, a CPP pension would just 'not be there.' And everyone 'knew' that Canada's politicians were incapable of dealing with either problem.

Such was the national mood in those days. Yet by 1998, both problems had essentially been solved. The federal deficit was gone, replaced by annual surpluses that have persisted to this day, reducing the federal debt – relative to Canada's total economic output – by more than half. And the question of the CPP's future had been resolved so convincingly that the government's chief actuary gave it a clean bill of health, a view that also persists to this day.

The story of the deficit battles has been recounted many times; the story of the reforms that rescued the Canada Pension Plan has gone almost entirely untold. Yet the overhaul of the CPP stands as one of Canada's most significant public policy success stories, the more so because it demanded an almost unparalleled degree of federal–provincial cooperation. If the ingredients of a policy debate are tax increases, entitlements to social benefits, a large pot of money in the hands of governments, and federal–provincial relations, the resulting recipe is usually flavoured with rancour, rhetoric, posturing, and delay; in short, an unappetizing dish. There was some of that in the process that reformed the CPP, but very little. Over three years, ministers and officials in the federal and provincial governments worked together to produce a unique arrangement – one that raised CPP contributions, reduced benefits, and thus generated what has become a huge pool of capital at arm's length from the governments that created it. When needed, it will be there for future beneficiaries.

This is how it happened.

FIXING THE FUTURE:
HOW CANADA'S USUALLY FRACTIOUS
GOVERNMENTS WORKED TOGETHER TO RESCUE
THE CANADA PENSION PLAN

1 Gloomy Canada

Canada in the early 1990s was not a happy place. To a casual visitor, even a regular one, Canada would have looked as it always had – a country of magnificent vistas and bustling cities. But visitors, unless they come looking for such things, pay little attention to economic indicators or government finances. From an economic and fiscal perspective, Canada was a mess. Recession, unemployment, inflation, interest rates, and government deficits were daily fodder for thousands of disheartening headlines. And Canadians were getting angry at – and losing confidence in – their governments for allowing, even creating, the economic and fiscal wreckage that so upset them.

The country had rolled through the 1950s and 1960s with a booming economy that endured only brief setbacks. The politics of the 1960s were turbulent enough; minority federal governments in six of those years and persistent wrangling between Ottawa and the provinces attested to the turmoil. But it was also a period of strong economic growth and a burgeoning confidence that found its symbol in the Montreal World's Fair – Expo 67 – which was the focal point for Canada's centennial year celebrations.

It was also a period of high creativity and bold social policy initiatives from a federal government that seemed to stumble from scandal to scandal in a dysfunctional Parliament yet managed to craft a legacy that is today looked on with considerable pride by most Canadians. Under Lester Pearson, the federal government had – with the agreement of the ten provinces – introduced a national health insurance program, medicare, that paid the basic medical and hospital bills of all Canadians. And it created a national pension plan – again with the agreement of the ten provinces – that over time would reduce substantially the poverty rate among seniors.

The creation of either program would count as a high accomplishment. That both were proposed, negotiated, and finally launched during the same period – the first three years of a minority government in Ottawa – was utterly remarkable. With hindsight, 1966 stands out as a watershed in Canadian history for the launch of two programs that now stand as icons in the social policy firmament.

Two Decades of Failure

A quarter-century later, however, Canadians were looking back on two decades of what many regarded as – and no gentler words fit – abject failure.

The first oil shock of the 1970s, when the world price tripled in just fifteen months, set off a sudden increase in global inflation. After years of near stability, energy prices in Canada shot up by an average of 13 per cent annually from 1972 to 1977. Overall inflation had emerged as a concern in the late 1960s, when the usual 2 per cent increases in the consumer price index (CPI) rose to almost 4 per cent. But nothing had prepared Canadians for inflation of 11 per cent in 1974 and nearly as much again in 1975. In both the 1950s and 1960s, the consumer dollar had lost about one-fifth of its purchasing power in each decade; in the 1970s, when the CPI doubled, it lost about one-half. For people who tried to save their money by buying bonds, interest rates offered little protection. In rough terms, the earlier norm had been rates of 5.25 per cent (on a ten-year bond) that assured the investor a real annual return – after subtracting 2.25 per cent of annual inflation – of 3 per cent.

But in the middle years of the 1970s, the real return was a paltry one-tenth of 1 per cent annually as rising inflation galloped ahead of rising interest rates. On very short-term investments, it was even worse. A truly unwise investor who stuck some money in three-month treasury bills in late 1971 and kept rolling it over each time the notes came due would have endured seven lean years indeed. By 1978, his pool of capital would have been worth almost 10 per cent less in terms of purchasing power than he began with. The legacy of that decade is still with us in the financial markets, where the merest whiff of rising inflation is enough to send interest rates higher as investors with memories of the 1970s demand higher returns to protect themselves from potential losses.

In those days, high inflation appeared intractable – resistant both to higher interest rates from the Bank of Canada and to wage and price controls. Productivity growth, the foundation of any economy's long-term performance, was crumbling – from 3 per cent annually in the 1960s to 2 per cent in the 1970s. At the same time, the government was beginning to run substantial deficits, the biggest since the Second World War relative to the size of the economy. Each year, government spending outstripped revenues, and each successive annual deficit added to a growing federal debt. After falling steadily from over 100 per cent of gross domestic product (GDP) just after the war to 18 per cent in 1975, the debt climbed to 28 per cent at the end of the decade.

Political turmoil was part of the mix too – from the Quebec election in 1976 that brought to power the secessionist Parti Québécois (PQ) government to the rising influence of Alberta, a province whose confidence and wealth were fuelled by oil production from its large reserves of petroleum. At the federal level, voters replaced the Liberal Pierre Trudeau with a minority government under Progressive Conservative Joe Clark in 1979, only to turn around a few months later and give Trudeau another majority. 'Welcome to the 1980s,' he said on election night.

Deep Recession

The 1980s turned out to be anything but welcoming. The decade was just as tumultuous politically and even more disappointing from an economic and fiscal perspective. A rancorous and protracted federal–provincial battle over the Canadian Constitution transformed it from an act of the British parliament, a hangover from the days of empire, into a wholly Canadian document in 1982, albeit without the consent of Quebec. Running alongside that fight was a two-front energy dispute in which the federal government squared off against Alberta over the taxation of its oil and gas and against Newfoundland and Nova Scotia over the ownership and development of newly discovered offshore oil and gas fields. That issue, an old one, was brought to a head by the second oil shock, in which the world price of oil climbed by another two-and-a-half times through 1979 and the first half of 1980.

As those disputes played out, Canada plunged into its deepest recession since the one after the Second World War when the country was decompressing to a peacetime economy. With inflation already at 9 per cent, the Bank of Canada – the country's central bank – had begun raising interest rates in early 1978. Now, as the pace of rising prices climbed to almost 13 per cent annually, the bank pushed its benchmark interest rate, the bank rate, to a staggering 21 per cent in the summer of 1981, double its level three years earlier. It takes time for monetary policy to make itself felt in the real economy, but there was no mistaking the impact of the Bank's strong medicine when it hit. Over six consecutive quarters beginning in the summer of 1981, real economic output contracted by almost 5 per cent. The unemployment rate almost doubled from 7 per cent to 13 per cent, its highest level since the Great Depression of the 1930s; a staggering 615,000 jobs – one in every twenty – disappeared between June 1981 and November 1982. By the middle of 1984, inflation was down to 4 per cent, but the unemployment rate remained over 11 per cent, teaching Canadians a vivid lesson in just how painful a major disinflation can be. Grim as it all looked, no one would have guessed that the pre-recession jobless rate of 7 per cent in the summer of 1981 would be the lowest for another eighteen years.

The 1981–2 recession was a major reason (there were many others) for the trouncing that voters gave the Liberals in the 1984 election. Trudeau's successor, John Turner, had the second-shortest term of any Canadian prime minister. The new Progressive Conservative administration of Brian Mulroney inherited a rebounding economy but a government whose books were written in red ink. During the recession, Ottawa had run successive deficits equivalent to about 8 per cent of GDP a year and driven the federal debt to 43 per cent of GDP, half again as large as it had been five years earlier.

For the most part, the second half of the 1980s was a good period for Canada. The economy grew briskly (some regions even boomed), the inflation rate remained at about 4 per cent, and the jobless rate crawled back down to 7.5 per cent. Even so, productivity growth slipped again, to just over 1 per cent for the entire decade, one-third of its level in the 1960s. After a half-hearted attempt to reduce the deficit, the Mulroney government was content to let it coast along at about 5 per cent of GDP annually. As a result, the federal debt kept rising, to 51 per cent of GDP in the final years of the decade.

Other Priorities

The government had priorities other than deficit-fighting: a major tax reform initiative, free trade with the United States, and a constitutional agreement with the provinces that would allow Quebec to sign the document it had rejected in 1982. Tax reform and free trade – both highly contentious – passed, but the constitutional initiatives came to naught. The Meech Lake Accord, signed by the federal and provincial governments in 1987, failed its own ratification process in 1990. For the next two years, Quebec's future in Canada dominated the political agenda of the country as governments crafted a successor deal in the 1992 Charlottetown Accord; it was put to a national referendum that autumn and was defeated in six of the ten provinces.

While the politicians talked about the Constitution, the economy was heading onto the rocks and taking government finances with it. Towards the end of the 1980s, the Bank of Canada had decided that even a 4 per cent inflation rate was too high. As it had in the 1970s, inflation in the 1980s was on its way to eating away half of the purchasing power of the consumer dollar. In 1988, the Bank began to raise the bank rate, setting the mark for other short-term interest rates. Further steep increases followed in 1989 and early 1990, when inflation stubbornly kept rising as well – to almost 5.5 per cent in early 1990. The rising bank rate's companion was a rising Canadian dollar. The currency had begun a long slide in 1976, just after the election of the Parti Québécois, when it traded one-for-one with the U.S. dollar, and had bottomed out in 1986 at just over 71 cents (U.S.). By the time the central bank made its move on interest rates, the dollar was back over 76 cents. As the bank rate climbed from around 8.5 per cent in early 1988 to over 14 per cent in the spring of 1990, financial market investors found Canada was an increasingly attractive place to put their money. By then, the dollar had risen to more than 85 cents (U.S.) and Canadian exporters were beginning to feel the pinch; the higher dollar made them less competitive because their goods had become more expensive for foreign buyers.

Another Recession

The combination of high interest rates and a high dollar had a severe impact. In the spring of 1990, Canada ran smack into another recession, its second in less than ten years. The central bank began cutting interest rates, but the dollar kept rising, all the way to 89 cents before it too retreated. By comparison with the recession of the early 1980s, this one at first appeared shallow and short-lived; the overall decline in output amounted to only 3.4 per cent and the downturn lasted only four quarters, to the winter of 1991. When growth resumed that spring, many forecasters figured it was the beginning of a 1980s-style solid rebound.

'Here we go again,' pronounced one observer cheerily. Instead, it turned into a tentative, halting recovery in which the growth of economic activity barely matched the growing population. Real GDP per head stagnated through 1991 and 1992, crept up a bit in 1993 and 1994, and then flattened again in 1995 and early 1996, when the economy slowed in response to steep interest rate increases following the Mexican peso crisis and spending cuts by the federal and provincial governments as they tried to reduce their deficits.

The unemployment rate, which had declined to 7.5 per cent at the end of the 1980s, shot up once more to over 12 per cent. The 427,000 jobs lost in the twenty-four months after April 1990 fell short of the drop in the early 1980s, but this time it took longer to gain them back. Again, however, recession had worked its magic on prices. Once the short-term inflationary effect of the new goods and services tax (GST) was out of the way, the inflation rate fell to less than 2 per cent in early 1992 and stayed there, underpinned by Ottawa's new policy of inflation targeting to fight rising prices. In 1991, the government and the Bank of Canada had jointly adopted a formal target for inflation – 2 per cent annually after a transition period – that the Bank would strive to meet through its influence over interest rates. Though commonplace now, inflation targeting was then a novelty; Canada was the second country after New Zealand to embrace it.

The recession played havoc with government finances. Federal deficits worsened and the debt shot up from 51 per cent of GDP in 1989 to 67 per cent in the spring of 1994. The provinces were in the same bind; their combined debt ratio rose from around 15 per cent of GDP in the late 1980s to over 26 per cent in 1994. Internationally, Canada was running second in a race that no one wants to win – for biggest deficit and total debt relative to GDP. Only Italy fared worse on the lists of fiscal shame issued by the Organization for Economic Co-operation and Development.

In the fall of 1992, Canadians had also been given a vivid lesson in what can happen to highly indebted nations when world financial markets turn unruly. In early September, Canada was preparing for a national referendum on the Charlottetown constitutional accord, which looked set to pass in all provinces except Quebec, where opinion was more evenly divided. The Bank of Canada's benchmark rate was under 5 per cent – a nineteen-year low – and the dollar was trading at around 84 cents (U.S.). A more benign financial environment could hardly be imagined. Yet only four weeks later, the currency was down to 80 cents

(U.S.) and the central bank was frantically raising interest rates to fend off a further decline. On a single day, a massive sell-off of bonds and treasury bills – a market meltdown – had pushed short-term interest rates higher by two full percentage points. By 1 October, the bank rate was up to 7.6 per cent, and a week later it reached 7.9 per cent.

Canada had been caught in the backwash of a full-blown European financial crisis in which speculators were attacking almost every cur-rency in sight. In the weeks before France's September referendum that would either approve or reject the Maastricht Treaty on European unity (it passed narrowly), financial markets turned jittery and then panicky. Britain devalued the pound and dropped out of the European Mone-tary System, as did Italy. Throughout Europe, currencies plunged and interest rates soared. At one point, Sweden raised its key rate, very briefly, to 500 per cent. In mid-October, Standard & Poor's, a major rat-ing agency, downgraded the Canadian government's debt denomi-nated in foreign currencies – a small share of the total, but important nonetheless – and the dollar plunged again. Polls were turning against the Charlottetown Accord, which went down to defeat on 26 October. By November, the dollar would be down below 78 cents and the bank rate approaching 9 per cent. For Canadians, it was a sobering – even horrifying – lesson: a country with big debts and still borrowing heavily to finance its continuing deficits is at the mercy of its creditors.

Restive Voters

Markets eventually settled down, but the voters were becoming more restive – first over the recession and then over the dismal state of gov-ernment finances. When they got their chance to take it out on the pol-iticians, they did so. By 1993, attention had shifted to deficits and debt in almost all parts of the country. In Alberta, the governing Progressive Conservatives replaced their leader – and premier – with a successor who made deficit-cutting his top priority and who shortly won an elec-tion on that promise. Nova Scotians unloaded a Tory government that was widely seen as having created a fiscal mess in favour of a new Lib-eral government that vowed to correct it.

Maclean's magazine had explored the country's increasingly sour mood in June 1992 with a cover story by Mary Janigan that took a broad look at Canadians' angst and anger over everything they saw wrong around them. The headline captured the mood of the country: 'Mad as Heck: As their faith in the future erodes, Canadians are angry as never before.'[1] It spoke of Canadians' 'troubling erosion of faith in their economic future ... There is a sense across the nation that the economic rules are profoundly and permanently changing – and a fear that governments have neither the determination to help individuals nor the ability to protect them.' The 'fundamental belief in the inevitability of economic progress' was eroding, and Canadians were 'struggling to accept their reduced prospects, grasping for new certainties and new dreams.' They were scornful of politicians who raised taxes and cut services but who rarely reassessed their priorities. 'Canadians have developed an almost corrosive disdain for political leaders and a searing lack of faith in their ability to solve the nation's problems.' But while they were beginning to question many of the country's basic institutions, Canadians wanted 'to preserve their treasured social safety net.' They feared, however, that it was becoming unaffordable for debt-ridden governments. They recognized that the old 'safe and financially secure' world was gone for good, that their future would be more determined by market forces than governments, but they were ready for new approaches. 'Unfortunately, few Canadians believe that their political leaders have the will or the skill to lead them into the future – and to make that future less uncertain.'

In the spring of 1993, the *Toronto Star*'s astute columnist Richard Gwyn suggested that a 'click of consciousness' about the seriousness of deficits and debt had just occurred. 'Canadians have decided that the national debt matters. They are ready, I am convinced, to "do something about it."'[2] That conclusion may have been a little premature, but, beyond question, the tide of public opinion was moving quickly.

When a federal election came along in late 1993, voters were ready to pounce. Mulroney's most important economic policy achievements – free trade and tax reform – were good for the country in the long term but deeply unpopular at the time. Some blamed free trade for many of the job losses during the recession, while the new goods and services tax (GST) was loathed by most. Mulroney had stepped down that spring and the new prime minister, Kim Campbell, spent several months shaking up the government to demonstrate her fresh approach. It didn't work, and she wound up with the third-shortest term of any Canadian prime minister. In the election, the Conservatives were reduced to a humiliating two seats in the House of Commons as the Liberals under Jean Chrétien won a solid majority.

The new Parliament looked nothing like the old. The Progressive Conservatives had long been an uncomfortable coalition of Western, small-c conservative populists, eastern Tories with a small-l liberal bent (known as Red Tories), and soft Quebec nationalists, some of whom were supporters of the PQ in provincial politics. Mulroney's great political accomplishment had been to pull those three elements together long enough to win two elections – in 1984 and 1988. But the coalition shattered dramatically in the early 1990s. In Quebec, partly in response to Mulroney's failed constitutional initiatives, former Conservatives led in the creation of the Bloc Québécois – allied to the PQ – which won 54 seats in the Commons, second to the Liberals' 177. Suddenly, a party advocating the breakup of the country was Her Majesty's Loyal Opposition on the floor of the House. Nipping at its heels was the Reform Party, made up largely of one-time Western Conservatives, that, among other things, believed strongly in reduced deficits, lower debt, decreased taxes, and less government spending. The left-leaning New Democrats held onto a mere nine seats.

Facing the Deficit

The Liberals had won on a platform that included a woolly – and thus politically safe – commitment to reduce the federal deficit to 3 per cent of GDP by 1997. The job of finance minister was handed to Paul Martin, who was seen not only as the leading member of the Chrétien team, but also Chrétien's likely successor, and therefore rival.

Martin's first budget, in February 1994, initially won favourable reviews from the financial community but within months came to be seen as falling far short of what was needed. Rising interest rates in the United States were not just echoed in Canada, but amplified. For a government with a $550 billion debt, every rate increase added to the interest costs of carrying the debt; Martin had projected interest payments of $41 billion for the 1994–5 fiscal year, but $44 billion now looked more likely. By summer, the government's projections had been blown to shreds and the 1997 deficit target appeared out of reach. Martin, fully backed by Chrétien, froze spending on new programs. It was a prelude to his next budget and followed by a major review of all programs to identify the deep expenditure cuts needed to get the government's finances back on track.

If the government was going to cut its annual deficit, rising interest charges would have to be offset with deeper cuts to spending on programs. Martin also began preparing Canadians for what was coming in his February 1995 budget, setting the stage with a political sales job that became evident in the opinion polls. As two observers noted, 'In the summer, before the selling had swung into high gear, fewer than one in five Canadians had named the deficit when asked which issue should receive the greatest attention from Canada's leaders. By February, just in time for his budgetary assault, it had climbed to one in two in an Angus Reid poll, vaulting over unemployment to take over the top spot for the first time.'[3]

At the same time, Canadians were getting another devastating message from the world's financial markets about just how vulnerable the country was to swings of investor sentiment. It was a replay of 1992. On 20 December 1994, a long-overdue devaluation of the Mexican peso turned into a rout that spread to other countries whose currencies were also perceived to be on shaky ground. In the next month, the Canadian dollar fell by more than 1.5 cents to just over 70 cents and the Bank of Canada raised the bank rate from 5.5 per cent in December to 7.5 per cent in January and 8 per cent in February.

'Bankrupt Canada'?

During this turbulent period, the *Wall Street Journal*, read by everyone who is anyone in the U.S. financial community, suggested to its readers, in an editorial headed 'Bankrupt Canada?' that 'Mexico isn't the only U.S. neighbor flirting with the financial abyss. Turn around and check out Canada, which has now become an honorary member of the Third World in the unmanageability of its debt problem. If dramatic action isn't taken in next month's federal budget, it's not inconceivable that Canada could hit the debt wall and, like Britain in the 1970s or New Zealand in the 1980s, have to call in the International Monetary Fund to stabilize its falling currency.'[4] The final blow came on 16 February, only eleven days before the budget, when Moody's Investors Service announced that it had put Canada's debt 'under review' for a possible downgrade. The previous June it had cut the rating on Canada's $13 billion in foreign-currency debt from triple-A to double-A-one; now, it was looking to do the same for the $400 billion in Canadian-dollar debt. Bond rating agencies like Moody's and Standard & Poor's played a crucial role in those days. A lower credit rating translated into higher interest costs for governments; if they wanted to borrow money to finance their deficits by issuing new bonds, they had to offer higher interest rates to persuade would-be investors to step forward. If the government was wavering about deficit reduction, the financial markets had stiffened its spine for what Martin already had in store.

The budget was crucial because Martin had already said the government would meet its deficit target 'come hell or high water' and explicitly invited financial markets to judge him by what he would deliver that day. As one account put it on budget morning, it was a document 'that professional investors – the people who decide whether to buy Ottawa's bonds – will inevitably regard as a window on the soul of Prime Minister Jean Chrétien's government, the product of public consultations with the voters and private battles within the Liberal caucus.' In New York, Merrill Lynch's chief Canada watcher, vice-president Karim Basta, said Martin 'won't be given the benefit of the doubt again' as he was in 1994. 'They're not going to have a better opportunity to reduce the deficit. They're popular, the economy is strong and it's early in the mandate.'[5]

The Turnaround Budget

When the big day came on 27 February, Martin scored big with a seminal budget that utterly changed the direction of the government's finances, putting it on a course that would produce, in only three years, the first surplus since 1970. There were a few tax increases, but for every $1 in new levies, there were $7 in spending cuts. It was probably the toughest budget in Canadian history. All told, spending on programs would fall by 19 per cent. Some of the cuts, to departments and programs once deemed almost untouchable, were far deeper: agriculture, fisheries, resources, and environment – down 31 per cent; transport – down 50 per cent; industrial and regional development spending – down 38 per cent; business subsidies – down 61 per cent. The axe fell more gently on social programs like immigration, health, housing, and human resources – down only 8 per cent. But cash transfers to the provinces, at $27 billion one of the biggest items in the government's books, were in line for a 14 per cent cut. Karim Basta, who had flown to Ottawa for budget day, fired off a one-word summary to his colleagues in New York: 'outstanding.'[6]

It wasn't just the financial markets cheering; ordinary Canadians were giving a thumbs-up to the budget too. Opposition politicians, as well as provincial government leaders, had trouble gaining any traction for their critiques. When Martin rolled into Regina on his cross-country tour to promote the budget, the Saskatchewan government's finance minister, Janice MacKinnon, was waiting for him. In a private meeting at Queensbury Downs, where Martin was scheduled to make a speech, she protested the elimination of a century-old subsidy for transporting Prairie grains to market and other cuts to farm subsidies.

'I warned Martin that he would reap a prairie fire of protest when he came face to face with Saskatchewan farmers,' she recounted later. 'As I watched Martin leave our scrum [with waiting journalists] and head into the main auditorium, I realized that there were no prairie farmers protesting – only hundreds and hundreds of supporters, applauding his budget – and I knew it was all over.' She also realized that she and her colleagues had inadvertently prepared the ground. Two years earlier, when Saskatchewan was in such fiscal trouble that the province feared it might not be able to sell its bonds, she had brought down an extremely tough turnaround budget herself. 'Our budget cuts had taught Saskatchewan people that the deficit had to be defeated and everyone had to pay their fair share,' she observed ruefully. 'So what was the point of protesting? It had never worked when people protested against our government.'[7]

Dealing with Seniors

What was not known until later was that Martin had wanted even more: a radical reform of Canada's Old Age Security system. OAS is the bedrock pension program of income security for the elderly that goes to all seniors, though it mainly helps those with lower incomes. Uncertain over how far they had to go to appear credible to the financial markets, Martin and his officials thought the government 'needed one more demonstration of its resolve, a big-ticket item of such symbolic value that nobody would doubt that the government was on a track from which it would not retreat,' according to the vivid account by Edward Greenspon and Anthony Wilson-Smith in their 1996 book *Double Vision: The Inside Story of the Liberals in Power.*[8] Finance wanted to calculate benefits on a sliding scale based on family income, not individual income, so that well-off and middle-class couples with two pensions would see benefit reductions, while lower-income seniors would get more. In private meetings, Chrétien resisted, believing the budget would clear the credibility hurdle without touching seniors. Martin, in the *Double Vision* account, failed to read the signals that this was a battle he was not going to win. Martin's recollection is that he 'refused' to read the signals in what had become 'a huge battle between Jean Chrétien and me,' one that strained their relationship, the beginning of a rupture that would last for the life of the government.[9]

As he continued to press for pension reform, the deadlock between the two men, unknown to all but a handful of close advisers, grew more dangerous. According to Eddie Goldenberg, Chrétien's canny chief policy adviser and troubleshooter, Martin told Goldenberg 'that he was prepared to resign on a matter of principle,' a prospect that Goldenberg thought 'had to be avoided at almost all costs.'[10] Martin says he never made such a threat; had he been inclined in that direction, he would not have threatened, but simply quit.[11] Either way, the very possibility of a Martin resignation was extremely serious. Had he walked out on the eve of the budget under such circumstances, the government would have been thrown into a political crisis and the country into a financial crisis that would have sent the dollar plunging and interest rates rocketing higher. The message to markets and voters would have been simple and devastating: for all its talk, the government was not really committed to cutting the deficit. In the end, OAS reform was put off for a year, but Martin was able to say in the budget that it was coming – and the budget went ahead.

But the budget included another reference to pensions that went almost unnoticed that day. It involved not Old Age Security, which went to all seniors, but the Canada Pension Plan, a quite different matter. The CPP rested on earnings-based contributions, so its benefits went only to those who had contributed to it over their working lives. Three days before Martin's budget, the plan's chief actuary had released his latest assessment of the plan's finances, and it was a shocker – the CPP's fund would be exhausted within twenty years unless governments did something soon. The recession and other factors had knocked earlier projections far off track, and only a huge increase in premiums would get the CPP back on the rails.

The Finance Department had known this message was coming and was already working up options and talking with the provincial governments who were co-stewards of the plan. They were due to begin their regular review of the plan, which was required every five years under the CPP legislation, and it had to begin after the chief actuary released his full projection of the plan's finances, also required every five years; the job had to be done by the end of 1996. The CPP worked on the basis of a rolling twenty-five-year schedule of premium increases, and the current schedule covered the period from 1992 through 2016. The rules said governments had to review the schedule before the end of the first five years, decide whether or not it needed adjusting, and then extend it by another five years, which in this case would take it to 2021. There was no question that some adjustment was needed; the existing schedule of increases would generate too little revenue to keep the plan financially sound. This was not a problem that Ottawa and the provinces could duck, unpalatable as the prospect of raising contribution rates might appear. If they failed to agree, a much steeper path of higher rates would automatically go into effect under a powerful default provision in the CPP legislation. For the time being, Finance was content to get a two-sentence reference into Martin's budget speech: 'Concerning the CPP, the most recent actuarial report was released last week and it leaves no doubt that we will have to take steps to ensure that that plan continues to be sustainable. This we shall do when we sit down this Fall with the provinces to review the CPP.'[12]

The gun had just been fired on a debate that would preoccupy both the provinces and the federal government – Martin in particular – for the next three years.

A Patchwork of Programs

All forms of retirement income were under the microscope during this period, but the CPP was central to Canada's patchwork of income programs for seniors and the only one run jointly by Ottawa and the provinces. The federal government could do what it liked with the others – and indeed moved forcefully, though unsuccessfully, to reform Old Age Security – but it needed provincial support to change the CPP.

Canada's retirement income system consists of three tiers – public pensions financed out of general revenues, earnings-based pensions financed out of contributions from workers and employers, and private savings.

The first tier is the bedrock of the system – the federal Old Age Security program, introduced in 1952, along with its companion Guaranteed Income Supplement and Spousal Allowance for low-income seniors. OAS provides the most basic level of income security for the elderly – benefits that are available even to those who have never worked for money. Its primary objective is poverty reduction and it is financed out of the federal government's ordinary tax revenues. By definition, OAS involves some redistribution of income from higher-income to lower-income Canadians; the former group's share of income taxes paid is disproportionate to its numbers while the latter group's share of benefits is also disproportionate to its numbers. The annual benefit is worth about 14 per cent of average wages and salaries, and in the 1995–6 fiscal year, OAS cost $21 billion. Since 1989, some or all of the OAS benefit has been taxed back from those with higher incomes, and since 1996 the federal government has not even sent cheques to anyone whose full benefit had been taxed back in the previous year. The GIS, a component of OAS, is income-tested and is aimed at those with little or no income other than the OAS. Those at the very bottom of the income scale may also qualify for various provincial benefits and, in some cases, welfare.

The second tier takes in contributory pensions – both public and private. The Canada Pension Plan and the Quebec Pension Plan are the two public plans run by governments and offering benefits that are linked to the contributions paid over the years by workers and their employers. Workers and their employers make contributions that finance the benefits paid out to those who have contributed. The CPP covers people in all provinces and territories except Quebec, where the parallel QPP operates. From the beginning, federal and provincial policymakers have tried to keep the two programs in line; contribution rates are the same for both plans, and benefits are almost entirely the same. All recipients of CPP or QPP benefits have worked and contributed at some point in their lives. Both plans are explicitly designed to meet the objective of replacing a specified share of the pre-retirement income of those whose major source of income – work – dries up when they leave the workforce. Both plans replace about one-quarter of an average person's earnings in the final years before retirement and a steadily declining share for those with higher incomes. There is no attempt to redistribute income from the well-off to those with smaller incomes. As the reform process began, in the 1995–6 fiscal year, the CPP and QPP paid retirement benefits of $13.7 billion. (In addition to retirement benefits, both plans offer ancillary disability, survivor, and death benefits.)

The private plans in the second tier are employer pensions offered by companies, governments, and other organizations to their own employees. Though run privately, these Registered Pension Plans (RPPs) qualify for tax relief or, as some would put it, tax deferral. Contributions are not taxed, nor are the capital gains and other investment income earned on the pool of invested capital that accumulates, but the ultimate pension, when paid, is fully taxed. To a considerable extent, occupational RPPs have become integrated with the CPP, usually through normal collective bargaining arrangements between labour unions and employers. This integration, according to a 1995 federal analysis of the CPP, 'has meant that the C/QPP has become a cornerstone of the RPP system.'[13] RPPs may take the form of defined benefit plans or defined contribution plans. In the former, the expected monthly retirement pension is spelled out during the period of employment; the employer and employees contribute money that is invested to create a fund that will finance the eventual pension. In defined contribution plans, both the employer and employees contribute money on a regular basis, but the amount of the resulting pension is not specified in advance. Its size will depend on the condition of the investment portfolio at the time of an employee's retirement. In 1995, about 42 per cent of paid workers had a workplace pension;[14] union members were about three times more likely to have one than non-union members.

The third tier consists of private savings, which are just that – money set aside over a lifetime by individuals who put their extra cash in whatever investment vehicles they choose, which might be stocks, bonds, real estate, or a simple bank account. Some of this saving is sheltered from taxes through Registered Retirement Savings Plans (RRSPs) in much the same manner as RPPs; that is, contributions are exempt from tax, as is any investment income earned within the RRSP. Taxes are levied only when the saver begins to draw down the accumulated cash or reaches a specific age (71 now, but 69 in the mid-1990s), at which point he or she is required to turn the savings into an annuity or a Registered Retirement Income Fund, on which the income is fully taxable as ordinary income. For the self-employed and those without a workplace pension, this may be the only way to enhance retirement savings with support from the government. As a rule, RRSPs are used most extensively by those in higher income brackets.[15] In 1995, about 38 per cent of the labour force had an RRSP.[16]

All told, Canadians set aside almost $54 billion in contributions towards their retirement through government-run or tax-supported programs in 1995 alone, about 6.6 per cent of that year's gross domestic product. Contributions amounted to $20.4 billion in RRSPs, $19.7 billion in RPPs, and $13.8 billion in the Canada and Quebec pension plans combined. The 1995 assets of all those savings vehicles totalled $781 billion, almost 90 per cent of GDP. Most of that money – $526 billion – had been accumulated in private RPPs; since these plans were required to set aside enough money to meet all their long-term promises, this was hardly surprising. RRSPs held another $201 billion in assets. The CPP had almost $40 billion and the QPP almost $14 billion.[17]

Seniors may have other forms of income, of course. Some continue to work and some have private savings beyond what they hold in RPPs and RRSPs, savings that receive no special tax treatment; these, however, are outside the 'system' as defined by governments.

In its broad outlines, the system is similar to those in many countries. Retirement experts employ different metaphors to describe such arrangements – stools, pillars, and tiers are the most common – and even when they use the same ones, they use them differently. Usually, there are three parts to the system, as in the split set out above – a basic public pension, earnings-based pensions, and private savings. Some put the CPP-QPP with OAS into the first tier as government-sponsored systems and limit the second tier to employer-sponsored systems, with self-directed plans and earnings from work comprising the third and fourth tiers.[18]

The tiers metaphor best captures the cumulative nature of retirement income, since many people receive income from more than one source. Someone with access to only one tier almost always has a low income in retirement. Seniors with income from two or more sources have higher incomes and thus a more secure retirement. Extra tiers can be added at will, such as income from work.

Even in the 1990s, retirement was increasingly becoming a process of transition from full-time paid work to full-time leisure, or at least to full-time activity that involves no paid work. This trend has since intensified. Retirement is no longer a discrete event – watching the clock Schmidt-like[19] through that last day on the job, collecting the stereotypical gold watch and plaudits of colleagues, and then marching out the door to an utterly different life. Rather, the transition may begin as young as 55 and continue gradually until a person finally gives up all forms of paid work, which may be twenty years later.

Indeed, what is retirement? The answer is less straightforward than one might think. Dictionaries usually define it as the withdrawal from office, business, or active working life, or from one's occupation, usually because of age; someone who retires has concluded one's working or professional career. Statistics Canada publishes an average 'retirement' age, based on what Canadians tell interviewers from the agency's monthly labour force survey. The retirement age fell from about 65 for both men and women in the mid-1970s to about 62 for men and 60 for women in the mid-1990s and has since roughly stabilized. But even Statistics Canada is struggling to find a meaningful definition that will guide it through the coming decades when the baby boomers become senior citizens. As things stand now, the agency produces 'no regular statistics ... on the retired population,' partly because the need for retirement data is recent and partly because 'the concept of retirement is fuzzy, to say the least.' Retirement 'is both an event and a state of being,' the former marked by the retirement party, the latter by a new phase of life, it says. 'In reality, many people do not become retired overnight. Rather, a transition occurs as one moves from more intense labour market activity toward relative inactivity. At what point along this gradient should a person be considered retired?'[20]

As you move up through the tiers of retirement income, two things stand out. First (and this is so obvious it barely merits noting), the more tiers a pensioner can draw income from, the better off he or she will be. Second (and this is not quite as obvious), the retirement income sources of higher-income Canadians are clustered in the upper tiers. While those two observations are similar, they are not just two ways of saying the same thing. Those who arrive at retirement age with little in the way of savings or private pension rights – or none at all – can be assured of at least a basic income from OAS and from the GIS and Spousal Allowance, but that is all. Public policy will have delivered to them the most fundamental of policy goals – basic income security through the redistribution of income. Those who have worked – most Canadians, in other words – will also get a retirement pension from the Canada or Quebec Pension Plan, which is stacked on top of the OAS pension. If lucky, they might also have a pension from their workplace. Luck translates into choice of job; workplace pensions were much more common in the public than the private sector, and in the private sector, much more likely in large companies, which were also more likely to pay higher wages. Earnings-based pensions are the realm of income replacement, where the beneficiary's pension is linked to his or her work and income record through life. A person who has never worked outside the home (this is where the issue of poverty among elderly women arises) will not be eligible for CPP benefits. As a rule, people who have been better off before retirement will be better off after retirement, simply because their CPP contributions have given them the basis for additional retirement income. At the very upper end of the income scale are those who earned enough during their working lives to have saved substantial sums – often through RRSPs – and in retirement can draw on the investment income from those savings. For them, OAS benefits will probably be taxed back entirely (or denied based on their overall income) and CPP benefits might account for only a small portion of their total income. In 1992, for example, two-thirds of the income of the bottom quintile (one-fifth) of Canadian seniors came from OAS-GIS and another 17 per cent from the CPP-QPP; private pensions, investment income, and other income accounted for only 16 per cent of the total. For those in the top quintile, the OAS-GIS accounted for only 9 per cent of total income and the CPP-QPP another 9 per cent. Private pensions supplied 24 per cent of income and investment income another 36 per cent, while 18 per cent came from employment income and the remainder from other sources.[21]

Despite the broad range of potential sources of retirement income, though, no one seriously questions the value of the CPP. Ken Battle, one of Canada's leading social policy analysts, describes it – by comparison with the far more generous programs available in many European countries – as 'a relatively modest earnings-related social insurance program in terms of both its benefits and contributions.' But still, Battle says, the CPP

> constitutes a vital part of the country's retirement income system, especially for lower- and middle-income working people and their families in general, and women in particular. Canada's three-tiered retirement income system is for most people effectively a two-tiered system since the third tier of individual savings is largely the preserve of higher-income Canadians. Private pension plan coverage is the exception rather than rule for lower-paid workers, private sector workers and those employed by small or medium-size employers. Although the gap in coverage between women and men has narrowed somewhat over the years, the fact remains that most women (67 per cent of the female labour force) and indeed most men (66 per cent of the male labour force) do not belong to occupational pension plans. Moreover, the majority of women and below-average earners of both sexes contribute little if anything to RRSPs.[22]

In early 1995, however, it was apparent that the Canada Pension Plan – this 'vital part' of the whole system – had a problem that needed fixing.

2 The Creation of a Pension Plan

The chief actuary's *15th Report* in early 1995 was a bombshell for anyone who had not been keeping tabs on the finances of the Canada Pension Plan; which is to say the entire population save the handful of officials whose job it was to keep any eye on such things and another small group of social policy experts. News accounts of the report focused the public's attention: unless contributions to the plan almost tripled, the plan's fund would be exhausted – 'broke' in the headlines – in twenty years. Those with long memories recalled that the original architects of the CPP knew that their structure would not last forever but would need periodic adjustments to keep it financially sound. The federal and provincial governments that ran the CPP had indeed made adjustments, but they had enhanced the benefits paid by the CPP much more than they had increased the revenue stream needed to finance them. That pattern of government decision making, combined with demographic changes and economic reversals over thirty years, had undermined the long-term financial health of the CPP.

Building a Welfare State

Such developments were a distant concern in the 1960s, when the CPP was born. It was an era of optimism in which Canada was fully engaged in building a welfare state that would render the ravages of the Great Depression in the 1930s a thing of the past. Governments could do anything – or at least thought they could.

The development of more vigorous social programs that would provide a basic level of income security to Canadians had begun earlier.[1] In 1940, the provinces unanimously agreed to give Ottawa the constitutional authority to set up an unemployment insurance program that was further expanded in 1955. Another constitutional amendment in 1951 allowed the federal government to introduce the Old Age Security Act, which, beginning in 1952, delivered monthly pensions of $40 to Canadian seniors. The new system was universal, available to anyone aged 70 or more who had lived in Canada for at least twenty years. It replaced legislation from 1927 – by now discredited – under which Ottawa shared the cost of provincially run, means-tested old age benefits.

Pensions remained a hot political issue through the rest of the 1950s and into the 1960s.[2] In 1957 alone, the monthly benefit was increased twice. The first was a transparent attempt by the Liberal government of Louis St Laurent to win votes in the June election, but the $6 increase, to $46, was deemed by the opposition Progressive Conservatives as too stingy and mocked as the work of the 'six-buck boys.' The Conservatives, under John Diefenbaker, won the election and promptly raised the benefit to $55.

Though it may not have been apparent at the time, the first shoots of Canada's retirement income system – the three-tier system that we know now – were poking through the ground. By the late 1950s, bits and pieces of this structure were already in place or under consideration. Old Age Security was providing some rudimentary income security for the elderly. In addition, the Blind Persons Act of 1951 and the Disabled Persons Act of 1954 were providing payments to those with disabilities, but these were increasingly seen as insufficient. Diefenbaker's new Progressive Conservative government commissioned a study of the U.S. Social Security system, which was then a quarter-century old and which some thought offered a good model for Canada. The study rejected that notion but praised the inclusion of disability and survivor benefits in the American system, ideas that would soon come to Canada. Finally, a new income tax exemption allowed the self-employed to save for retirement through a Registered Retirement Savings Plan.

Canada was hardly at the forefront of providing social security for its elderly and others with low incomes. Britain launched a contributory pension plan in 1959, and its continental counterparts were close behind. 'By the mid-1960s, almost all Western European countries had introduced contributory, earnings-related pensions, and many included survivor and disability benefits, coverage for self-employed people and payment adjustments to counter inflation.'[3]

The political importance of pensions – and, more broadly, adequate incomes for the elderly – was grounded in the Great Depression of the

1930s and the Second World War. During the depression, Canadians endured five years in which the average real personal income – even after accounting for falling prices – dropped by almost 25 per cent. For most of that decade, Canadians spent more than they earned, making up the difference by running down whatever savings they might have built up. Incomes had almost recovered in 1939, when Canada went to war, bringing another six years of sacrifice and privation. By the 1960s, those born in the first two decades of the century were on the cusp of retirement – they now ranged in age from their early 40s to early 60s – and there was a widespread sense of responsibility for a generation of Canadians whose lives had been marked by a run of extraordinarily rotten demographic luck. Their prime earning years had been cut down by depression and war, and many had simply run out of time to recoup their finances. Now, however, the country was prosperous enough to do something to help, and politicians of all parties were determined to see that these people did not spend their final years in abject poverty.

Clashing Plans: Pearson, Lesage, and Robarts

By the early 1960s, the major parties were all promising to create a national, contributory pension plan to layer on top of OAS.[4] The Liberals had first committed themselves to such a plan in the 1958 election campaign – when it was called 'The Pearson Plan' – and further honed their thinking during their years in opposition. 'It became the firmest plank in the election platforms of 1962 and 1963.'[5] When the April 1963 election gave the Liberals 129 out of 265 seats, enough to form a minority government, they immediately set up an interdepartmental committee to turn the party's election promise into a concrete plan. The group, chaired by Joe Willard, the deputy minister of welfare, had to work rapidly; the Liberals had promised the voters 'Sixty Days of Decision' in which they would make good on many of their campaign pledges, including the proposed Canada Pension Plan. By mid-June, the government had sketched out enough details to put a resolution before Parliament. A day later, Prime Minister Pearson wrote to the premiers, suggesting that they meet 'as soon as possible' to discuss the federal government's proposal.

His letter set in motion one of the great public policy battles in Canadian political history – a high-stakes drama in which the governments of Canada, Quebec, and Ontario clashed over their competing pension visions against a backdrop of growing separatist sentiment in Quebec. Peter Newman called it 'a minor turning point in Canadian history,' not because of the pension plan itself, but because 'the accord that made it possible also prevented the Quebec administration from exploiting impulses and following directions that might eventually have led to the break-up of the country.'[6] Quebec's Quiet Revolution was in full flower, shucking off many of its old structures and attitudes in a spasm of modernization; the slogan was 'maîtres chez nous' and Quebec's role in Canada – if any – was constantly under review.

The policy differences over pensions were evident from the beginning, and the two key provinces were headed by strong, shrewd leaders – premiers Jean Lesage in Quebec and John Robarts in Ontario.

The federal government initially put forward a national pay-as-you-go Canada Pension Plan that would set contribution rates just high enough to pay each year's benefits. Full benefits would be paid after only ten years, a feature that implied 'a considerable redistribution in favour of older workers, in their fifties or so when the plan began, who had not been able to build up retirement savings in conditions of depression and war.'[7] This first iteration of the CPP was simply a retirement plan. The Liberals wanted to go further and include benefits like disability and survivor benefits, but the 1951 constitutional amendment that allowed the federal government to launch the Old Age Security program did not permit such measures. 'Non-aged' benefits remained in provincial jurisdiction; if they were to be part of a national pension plan, Ottawa would need provincial support for a further amendment to the Constitution.[8]

Quebec's first move was an almost reflexive warning to Ottawa not to press ahead before talking with the provinces. Lesage was a strong supporter of public pensions, but he was now moving in a very different direction. An interdepartmental committee within the Quebec government had been studying pensions for the past year, but most of its attention was devoted to following Ontario's new legislation, which extended and regulated private pension coverage. Pensions were low on the Quebec agenda until 'the federal initiative ... catapulted the matter to the highest priority.'[9] Asked for its views, the Quebec committee rejected the Ontario approach and said the federal proposal infringed on Quebec's jurisdiction. It said Quebec should set up its own plan 'with broader and more generous coverage and benefits and, most important, with a financing system that would build up a large fund to help channel Quebecers savings into provincial economic development.'[10] Cabinet endorsed the recommendation and told the committee to develop just such a plan.

Ontario was less than enthusiastic about the federal proposal. Canada's most populous and economically powerful province 'was promoting expansion of the private pension system as an alternative to introducing a contributory public pension plan'[11] and in 1963 had passed a Pension Benefits Act that secured the solvency of private pension plans and improved their portability and vesting provisions. Publicly, the government remained non-committal, but the province's large financial community did not. The life insurance industry, which favoured the Ontario approach, released a detailed attack on the federal plan. 'Criticism centred on the proposal's economic effects, its generosity, its effects on private plans, the likelihood of rapid cost increases, and the like.'[12] For the time being, the Roberts government was content to sit on the sidelines; it was philosophically inclined to agree with the financial community but politically disinclined (an election was looming) to appear to be a tool of the insurance industry.

The Competing Plans Take Shape

The lines among the major players were drawn. At a federal–provincial conference in July, the pension discussion was inconclusive, partly because many provinces were still learning about the issue and developing enough expertise of their own to be able to formulate a position. Lesage, however, said Quebec would go it alone. Tom Kent, Pearson's chief political aide and policy adviser, recalled that Lesage 'did not attack the federal pension proposal. He just said that it was irrelevant to Quebec, because he would have his own plan.'[13] Only if Quebec could opt out of a national plan would it agree to the constitutional amendment Ottawa needed to include supplementary benefits in a CPP. The conference concluded with a cheerfully worded communiqué, but 'the reality was different,' Kent observed. The first version of the CPP, he stated, 'was already dead in the water.'[14]

Lesage reinforced his position a month later with a resolution, passed unanimously by the Quebec Legislative Assembly, preparing the way for new pension legislation. It would be more generous than the federal plan – though full benefits would be paid only after twenty years, not ten – and it would not be strictly a pay-as-you-go plan. Instead, contributions would exceed paid benefits for many years, during which the plan would build a substantial fund that would be used 'to finance the great requirements of the new Quebec for social infrastructure – schools, roads and all the rest.'[15]

Ottawa was still wedded to pay-as-you-go financing as 'an entirely sensible prescription' for the CPP, in terms of federal finances. 'It was far better to start with low contribution rates, yielding relatively modest surpluses over the pensions paid in the early years, and then gradually increase the contributions as the payments of pensions increased.'[16] Sensible, perhaps, but Kent had already concluded that pay-as-you-go – or PAYGO, in the unlovely shorthand of the pension community – would not fly.

Quebec's idea for a fund that could finance new social investment, most of which was in provincial jurisdiction, would have far greater appeal to the provinces – as soon as they caught up to Quebec's thinking. 'Across Canada, the requirements were the same: new schools, universities, colleges, housing development, parks, highways, public buildings, municipal projects in all their variety.'[17] Kent argued that Ottawa should take the initiative at its next meeting with the provinces, set for early September; he thought the federal government should abandon PAYGO in favour of a partially funded system before being forced into what he regarded as an inevitable retreat.[18]

Pearson sympathized, but rejected the idea, for reasons of raw partisan politics. Ontario was in the midst of a provincial election campaign, and the provincial Liberals, lacking any other issues to use against Robarts's Progressive Conservatives, had latched onto the CPP as a centrepiece of their platform. The federal Liberals could hardly undermine their provincial brethren by changing the CPP proposal in mid-campaign, so it stood unchanged through the September federal–provincial conference, which was chaired by Health and Welfare Minister Judy LaMarsh, whose ministry had direct responsibility for the CPP.

The conference, unsurprisingly, produced little. Most provincial delegations were headed by officials or cabinet ministers, but Robarts showed up personally to declare his support for some kind of national contributory pension plan, as long as it was financially sound. Quebec attended as an observer only but supported the idea of public pensions and indicated its support of full portability between a Quebec plan and the CPP, which would allow people to move from province to province, and plan to plan, without losing credit for their contributions.

Robarts easily won his election and waited for Quebec to produce its plan, which was not expected until the spring of 1964, before he committed himself to any particular position. At the same time, various interest groups were weighing in on the pension plan question. Unions and other groups supported the plan, but they were not nearly as vocal as the insurance companies and chambers of commerce, who were conducting a vitriolic attack on the CPP. The most strident voice belonged to D.E. Kilgour, president of the Great West Life Assurance Company in Winnipeg, who travelled the country talking to government officials and urging the business community to unite in opposition to the CPP. 'Let's raise a storm!' he said. 'Let's make it a good one – the strongest, most lightning packed, angry wind that had blown around Parliament Hill for a long, long time ... Let's get militant ... There will have to be political pressure with teeth in it.'[19]

At the next federal–provincial conference in late November, this time with the prime minister and premiers attending, pensions were again on the table but were overshadowed by a wider battle over equalization and the sharing of tax revenues between Ottawa and the provinces. When the talk turned to pensions, Pearson said the federal plan would now build up a small fund and hinted that Ottawa might turn half of it over to the provinces. Since the other provinces had begun to figure out that a fund would represent a valuable source of financing for themselves, this option became increasingly attractive. Lesage continued to support public pensions but raised the stakes once more: Quebec would agree to a constitutional amendment only if the contribution rate for the federal plan was 4 per cent of contributory earnings, double the figure Ottawa was considering. Ottawa still had no provisions in its plan for non-aged survivors and the disabled but knew that if Quebec's plan had them, the federal plan would need them too, so Lesage's condition had teeth. Robarts continued to play his waiting game, asking sharp questions without sliding into hostility. The other eight provinces appeared sympathetic to the federal plan.

And so it stood through December and January as the federal government reworked its proposal, mainly with an eye to bringing Ontario on board. A new version – with reduced benefits, but a small fund, of which half would be loaned to the provinces – was attacked from all sides. The left-leaning New Democratic Party government in Saskatchewan thought it was a dreadful retreat, most provinces wanted access to much more of the proposed fund, and Ontario said Ottawa had done far too little to meet its concerns over costs and the impact on private companies. Even so, Ottawa decided to press on and in March brought the new proposals to Parliament in the form of Bill C-75.[20]

The High Drama of a Historic Deal

So it stood until the most dramatic – almost melodramatic – episode of all. The first half of April 1964 still stands as one of the most momentous periods in Canadian history. The federal–provincial conference that began 31 March in Quebec City opened in an atmosphere of crisis. Security was tight as thousands of students demonstrated on the lawns of the Quebec legislature, clearly audible to those inside. Ottawa was making no concessions to provincial demands for a bigger share of tax revenues, and the first ministers could not agree on other agenda items.

It was the pension issue, however, that delivered most of the fireworks. First, Robarts hinted that Ontario might develop its own pension plan if the federal plan did not include Quebec. Then, Lesage dropped his bombshell, spelling out the details of a pension plan that he had only just received from his officials; he had not even shared it with his own cabinet.

'The brain-child chiefly of Claude Castonguay [Quebec's chief expert on pensions], it was an excellent plan for its purpose,' Tom Kent wrote later. 'It would provide appreciably larger pensions than we proposed, and with the supplementary survivor and disability benefits that we did not have the constitutional power to include. It would generate, for many years, large investment funds. One could almost see the other provincial premiers licking their lips ... With such a plan in Quebec, Ontario would never go along with ours. That was dead.'[21] The Quebec plan even covered the self-employed and incorporated an element of income redistribution by exempting the first $1,000 of earnings from the requirement to pay contributions.

Everyone in the room knew that Quebec had delivered a stunning blow to the federal government. 'The Ottawa delegation just sat there, numb with embarrassment,' Newman writes. 'The Quebec plan was indisputably a better piece of social legislation than the federal version. Following the Lesage presentation, Pearson quipped weakly: "Maybe we should contract into the Quebec plan." Premiers Robarts, Roblin and Smallwood said as much without intending it as a joke.'[22]

The conference ended Thursday, 2 April, with no agreement and in a mood of deep gloom over what appeared to be a new low in federal–provincial relations. Quotations assembled by Richard Simeon give some flavour of the day. A federal official: 'We were on the brink of the abyss at that moment.' A federal cabinet minister: 'I think we suddenly realized that, by God, the country might break up.' A Quebec official:

'The questions were flying – would there be an election on the issue and might it lead to separation?' A Quebec journalist, writing in *Le Devoir*: 'Never at such a high and public level has Confederation seemed so menaced.'[23]

Over the following weekend, Kent and Gordon Robertson, secretary to the cabinet, wrote separate memos to Pearson. Kent's, fittingly, was the more political; Robertson, as the country's most senior civil servant and deputy minister to the prime minister, cast his arguments in much different terms. But the advice itself was the same: the threat to national unity was so great that Ottawa should move towards the Quebec position on pensions and commit itself to handing over more tax revenue to the provinces. Moreover, it should do so boldly and quickly.

Kent said the government needed a 'major coup' in federal–provincial relations to repair the rifts that had opened in Quebec City and reverse its own dwindling political prospects. 'We must make a deal with Quebec, but it must be one that all the provinces will welcome.' He outlined, as a 'first rough sketch,' a series of tax and equalization concessions to settle the fiscal impasse and proposed that Ottawa accept Quebec's pension plan with only one condition – that the province agree to a ten-year transition to full pension benefits, instead of its twenty-year period. The new CPP would generate more funds than the previous version, and these would be handed over to the provinces for investment. Kent continues: 'I concluded: "So it's worth a try, I believe." The "first rough sketch" turned out to be almost exactly what was agreed to in the following eight days, but that hardly seemed possible to hope for when I gave the memorandum to a very worried Prime Minister on the morning of 7 April.'[24]

That was a Tuesday. By evening, and in great secrecy, Kent was on a flight to Quebec City accompanied by Maurice Sauvé, the federal cabinet's most junior member, but the one with the best contacts in the Lesage government. Pearson had already invited a small group of senior ministers to meet Wednesday night at his residence, 24 Sussex Drive, so Kent and Sauvé had to move briskly. Both had already talked by telephone with Claude Morin, Quebec's deputy minister of federal–provincial affairs and knew the province was still keen to reach a deal. The three men spent Wednesday morning thrashing out the issues at the Chateau Frontenac hotel and in the afternoon went to see Lesage and two of his ministers, René Lévesque and Paul Gérin-Lajoie. Kent stressed that he 'had no negotiating authority from Cabinet,' that his mission was only 'an exploration on behalf of the Prime Minister,' that 'many federal ministers would dislike anything on which those present could agree.'[25] Those present, however, agreed to a tentative deal that could be presented to both cabinets.

To give themselves more time to reach a final deal, Lesage postponed by a week a provincial budget that was planned to include a blistering attack on the federal government. He also arranged for a government plane to fly Kent and Sauvé back to Ottawa in time for the 24 Sussex meeting. Kent had only a few minutes to brief Pearson before the ministers arrived, but the prime minister was convinced they were on the right track. 'Now the most delicate part of the whole operation began: persuading the federal cabinet to agree to a major shift in policy,' Simeon wrote. Pearson went to work on his cabinet colleagues and won them over, both the English-Canadian ministers who resisted a federal retreat and the Quebec ministers who resented having been left out of the discussions to date. 'The leading role in these internal discussions was played by Pearson himself. "He was the real hero of this period," said one minister.'[26]

On Friday night, Castonguay and Morin flew to Ottawa for another round of talks, this time with Kent, Sauvé, Joe Willard, and Don Thorson, an assistant deputy minister of justice who was a member of the federal interdepartmental committee on the CPP. But the details of meshing a CPP and a QPP defeated the group until mid-afternoon, when, Kent recalled, 'we turned to the more daring idea: could Parliament and the Quebec Assembly pass identical legislation, creating in law and in administration two plans, but in effect one plan?'[27] The group decided they could and set to work trading off changes to reach a compromise.

Quebec accepted Ottawa's ten-year phase-in period for full benefits. Ottawa accepted Quebec's proposal to exempt the first $600 of annual income from contributions,[28] a part-way move to the $1,000 exemption in the province's original outline of its own plan. The ceiling on annual contributory income – the income on which contributions would be levied – would be $5,000, higher than Ottawa's $4,500, but lower than Quebec's $6,000. Retirement pensions would amount to Quebec's 25 per cent of earnings rather than Ottawa's 20 per cent. Pensions would be adjusted for inflation up to 2 per cent a year, a form of protection that had been missing from the federal plan. Quebec would support the constitutional amendment allowing the CPP to include disability and survivor benefits. The plans would be less funded than Quebec originally wished but considerably more funded than Ottawa's initial scheme. Aside from a small float of cash to pay the monthly benefits, the fund would be lent to the provinces at an interest rate equal to that on twenty-year Government of Canada bonds; each province would be entitled to borrow in proportion to its share of CPP contributions.

'In my view, and subsequent events proved it to be a widespread view, we had indeed reconciled the best features of the two plans,' Kent wrote later.[29] The contribution rate – the premium paid by workers and employers on the $4,400 in earnings between the $600 exemption and the $5,000 ceiling – was set at 3.6 per cent. Employers and employees would split the cost of the premium at 1.8 per cent each; the self-employed would pay the full rate.

Events then moved swiftly. Kent and Morin spent the subsequent Monday and Tuesday hammering out a long statement incorporating all elements of the deal. Kent was briefly distracted on the Monday by the need to mollify LaMarsh, the minister officially responsible for the CPP. Inexplicably, Pearson had failed to tell her what had been going on during the previous week of frenetic meetings and phone calls. When she finally found out, it was through third parties. Furious, LaMarsh almost resigned from cabinet that day, but after a conversation with Kent, during which she vented her rage by smashing a framed photograph of Pearson on her desk, she stayed on and piloted the CPP through Parliament 'in fine style.'[30]

On Wednesday, the Quebec cabinet approved the deal. On Thursday, 16 April, a mere two weeks after the Quebec conference had broken up in such acrimony, the federal cabinet also endorsed the agreement. That evening, Ottawa sent telegrams to the other provinces informing them of the agreement, and the following Monday, Pearson and Lesage simultaneously unveiled the accord to the public. 'They were hailed as heroes,' Peter Newman wrote, quoting Paul Gérin-Lajoie's tribute to the deal in the Quebec Assembly: 'April 20, 1964, will become an outstanding date in the annals of Canada and the men who have taken part in these events will see their names in the pages of history.'[31]

Filling in the Details

It was not over, of course. Ahead lay months of intensive work on the details of the pension plan. The constitutional amendment sailed through by July, but the task of ironing out all the fine points and writing the legislation took several months, with a conference in July of officials from all provinces to review every small aspect of the plan before the bill was completely written. The bill was almost ready by the end of September, and Tom Kent best summarized its contents: 'The final outcome was a common text for all the elaborate provisions of the pension plan; in effect, the Quebec Bill was the French text of the Canada Pension Plan and our text, as written in English, was used by Quebec for the English version of their Bill.'[32]

The participants interviewed by Richard Simeon unanimously stressed the high degree of cooperation through the process. 'The reasons are clear: first, the political heads were strongly committed to protecting the agreement and, second, those working on the details saw themselves as pension experts sharing the same values and committed simply to preparing the best plans. Each side wanted its view to prevail, but on many issues there was complete agreement from the start, and on others both sides were willing to trade.' In a footnote, he cites a federal memorandum that said 'the constitutional and political facts are – as this whole business has shown – that federal freedom to move on pensions is limited by the provinces. The proposal merely recognizes facts.'[33] Simeon's account is remarkable for what it says about the staying power of the underlying forces that continue to drive the design of the Canada Pension Plan. As we shall see, each of those comments could be written with equal accuracy about the reforms of the mid-1990s.

Nevertheless, all was not sweetness and light. Kent recalled that Ontario was miffed at the fashion in which it had been outmanoeuvred in the Ottawa–Quebec deal. Ontario was caught between the fact that it could run its own plan as easily as Quebec and Robarts's stated preference for a national plan, so the province might have expected to play a substantial role in shaping it. 'From the viewpoint of Ontario, as of the insurance industry, we had used Quebec to turn the tables on them. For months, the Ontario government had been pressing us to scale down our proposals (and the insurance industry had been demanding that we abandon them) but the new plan went the other way and offered larger benefits.'[34]

Ottawa acceded to Ontario's desire for some provincial control over future amendments by agreeing that changes in the plan would require the agreement of two-thirds of the provinces with two-thirds of the population. This gave Ontario, with about 40 per cent of Canada's population, a veto over any redesign of the CPP. But the federal government balked at what was called Ontario's 'agency' proposal. A province could opt out of the CPP if it ran its own comparable plan, as Quebec was doing, but Ontario wanted a third option, under which the

Duncan Macpherson, 'Psst ... the fix is in,' 1964

federal government would administer a provincial pension plan that was identical to the CPP. Ottawa rejected that idea, fearful that the provinces would peel away one by one and leave the federal government administering a group of plans with no national advantages in terms of the labour mobility that portable pensions offered. Federal officials thought they had laid that idea to rest in June, but Robarts revived it in October, just as the legislation was about to be introduced in Parliament. It took some personal diplomacy by Pearson to cool the potential flare-up. The two met in early November and Robarts agreed to what Kent called a non-aggression pact: 'He would not attack the legislation while it was under detailed examination before a parliamentary committee, with extensive hearings of witnesses; he would maintain his non-commitment until he saw how the plan stood up to such scrutiny.'[35]

The legislation – Bill C-136 – was introduced 9 November and a week later was sent to a joint Senate–House of Commons committee for study. Over the next three months, the MPs and senators held 51 hearings and heard 116 witnesses, a list that looks impressive but belies the committee's impotence. Parliamentarians were getting a close look at the workings of executive federalism: what the federal and provincial governments had put together was not going to be unwound by members of Parliament and senators, especially when the measure had strong public support. Interest groups and opposition parties recognized this reality but did not like it. Gordon Aiken, the Progressive Conservatives' pension critic, complained during the hearings that the committee was 'sitting here to rubber stamp this Bill, and I am wondering if we are sitting here to any purpose.' The often combative LaMarsh soothingly replied that she could not 'imagine you being a rubber stamp for anything.'[36] Ontario appeared at the hearings as a witness and served up some further criticisms of the plan, but even that whiff of opposition died in mid-January when Roberts announced that Ontario would take part in the CPP. By then, the tide of public opinion on the CPP had shifted considerably. 'We were no longer defending it against the storm from the right,' Kent wrote later, 'but against the complaints, of Conservative MPs among others, that it did not go far enough.'[37]

The committee reported on 16 February 1965, recommending a few small changes, and the Commons began its clause-by-clause debate on 22 February. After twenty-five days of discussion, the bill passed on 29 March by a vote of 159 to 12; seven Social Credit members and five Progressive Conservatives opposed it. On 3 April, after a short debate in the Senate, the bill received royal assent. The debate in Quebec was much quicker. Bill 50, establishing the Quebec Pension Plan, was introduced on 21 May and passed on 23 June. Both the CPP and the QPP began operations on 1 January 1966.

Issues Then; Issues Later

Retrospectively, it is fascinating to tally the issues and concerns of the mid-1960s that foreshadowed both the reform process and the public debate three decades later. In terms of process, the most obvious item was the result of that last-minute change to appease Ontario – the rule that CPP amendments must be approved by a double two-thirds major-ity. In the mid-1990s, Ottawa had some firm ideas of what it wanted to do but needed widespread provincial support – vitally from Ontario – to go ahead.

The financing divide was also a factor in the 1990s: To what extent should the CPP be run as a PAYGO plan or be more fully funded? Despite the 1964 compromise that produced a fund to be lent to the provinces, the original CPP was still very close to its pure PAYGO roots; the fund amounted to a mere two years worth of benefits. Although there was a clear consensus in the 1990s in favour of greater funding, some voices were raised in favour of the status quo and of PAYGO itself. Closely related to the question of funding itself was the issue of how any fund would be managed. The insurance industry, the most vocal opponent of the CPP, raised fears in the 1960s about 'the concen-tration of a huge fund in the hands of the federal government.'[38] Those concerns became especially vivid in the 1990s, when governments decided to increase the size of the fund substantially and worked to put the money at arm's length from both the federal and provincial govern-ments. By then, however, there were enough large public sector pen-sion plans on the scene that there was little fear of a fund itself, only that it might be abused by governments. The insurance industry had mellowed since the 1960s and was no longer opposed to such funds.

The issue of intergenerational equity, so prominent in the 1990s, looked very different in the 1960s. No one expressed it in quite those terms in the 1960s, but the CPP was explicitly designed to favour the generation then in their forties and fifties. At the extreme, it would be possible for some people to contribute for only ten years and then retire with full CPP benefits for the rest of their lives, which might run for another twenty or thirty years. The contribution rate was high enough to cover those costs – for a couple of decades, at any rate. But it was so low that younger workers were not contributing enough to finance both the pensions of their elders and their own future pensions as well. This was never made clear in the debates of the day over a PAYGO plan versus a funded plan. In a pure PAYGO plan, the current generation of workers pays the benefits of the current generation of retirees. In a fully funded plan, contributors pay for their own pensions but must contrib-ute for about forty years before collecting full benefits, as is the case with private pension plans. Business might have liked the concept of a fully funded public plan, since it would adhere to the familiar business models, but the business community really preferred private occupational pensions. Organized labour went the other way, for obvious reasons; the current generation of workers, especially those within striking distance of retirement, would benefit most from a largely PAYGO plan.

Alan Jacobs, in his prize-winning 2004 Harvard University dissertation on pension development and reform in four countries, summarized the conflicting interests at play in the different options:

> PAYGO financing provides the first generation of contributors the best 'return' on their contributions: They pay in while the pension bill is relatively light because few retirees have yet earned significant benefits, but they get to take out the full benefits upon retirement. By comparison, funded financing of the same level of benefits would impose on current workers a double-payment burden: requiring them to pay contributions sufficient both to finance the pensions of the beneficiaries who retire before them *and* to accumulate funds for their own future pensions. The benefits of this arrangement would only accrue to the next generation of workers, who would enjoy lower contribution rates. The alternative path to funding would be to lengthen the maturation period for the scheme, more strictly tying pension levels to [the] length of the beneficiaries' contribution period. This option would avoid the double-payment problem but would largely exclude middle-aged workers from the benefits of the program. Only the youngest workers, and those too young to work (or vote), would benefit. By comparison to these policy investments, PAYGO financing offered the vast majority of union members the best deal over their life cycles, even if it would prove more costly for future generations.[39]

All this was fine by decision makers in the 1960s. They wanted to assure a secure retirement for the depression and war generations of Canadians, who were now middle-aged workers; that meant the plan would have to pay full benefits quickly. 'To abandon this objective would remove much of the objective of a public plan,' Pearson argued.[40] The prime minister, the premiers, and all their advisers could hardly have guessed that their solution would generate resentments in the 1990s and a fresh problem that would need different solutions.

There was a deeper financing issue as well. The 3.6 per cent contribution rate, as one analysis of the plan said later, 'was not an actuarially computed value, but was rather a compromise between the Federal preference of 2 per cent and the Quebec preference of 4 per cent.'[41] Policymakers of the day knew that the contribution rate was not high enough to finance the CPP forever; at some point, the rate would have to be raised. In a report dated 6 November 1964 (tabled in Parliament in 1965), the federal government's chief actuary projected that the costs of the CPP would not exceed 3.6 per cent of contributory earnings until the early 1980s under any one of several possible scenarios; and after that, the gradual depletion of the accumulated fund would continue to cover the costs until the late 1990s.[42] That was more than three decades off. As Bruce Kennedy put it in his 1989 doctoral thesis at the University of Victoria: 'How the plan would be financed over the long term was not resolved in 1964. It was left to future resolution.'[43]

But for the time being, the pension battles were over and the nation's politicians and policymakers moved on to other issues. Tom Kent's 1988 summary of the whole episode captures perfectly the storm of the day and the calm that followed:

> It is already almost impossible, barely a generation later, to appreciate what strong emotions, interests and political pressures in 1963–64 clashed around the idea of a comprehensive pension plan. It was denounced as a fraud and as certain to bring the ruin of the nation. It was caught so much in the tensions of changing federal–provincial relations that no sensible man should have been prepared to wager, in late 1963 or early 1964, that it would be achieved in foreseeable time.
>
> Nevertheless, as soon as it was legislated, the pension plan fitted into the fabric of Canadian society as if it had always been there. Few people have disappeared from public notice as quickly as those who, in their words, in 1963 'raised a storm' against the plan. Indeed, it is hard to think of anything of comparable significance to people about which there has been so little subsequent controversy.[44]

As he wrote, Kent was looking back on almost a quarter-century of the CPP's existence, during which it only occasionally came to the notice of the Canadian public. Indeed, for its first twenty years, very little happened to the CPP, aside from benefit enrichments, even though the broader issue of retirement income and pensions in general was one of the hotter public policy issues of the 1970s and early 1980s.

3 The Desultory Decades

From the late 1960s to the early 1980s, public debate over pensions – and, more broadly, retirement income in general – passed by the Canada Pension Plan entirely. Much of the CPP story during this period can be found in periodic reports of the plan's chief actuary, an official in what was then the federal Department of Insurance and is now the Office of the Superintendent of Financial Institutions (OSFI). The reports make for less-than-scintillating reading – actuarial reports are not written with an eye to attracting a wide audience – but they tell a vital tale all the same. Not even the actuary was pressing Ottawa and the provinces to make changes in the CPP.

True, problems were looming, but they always lay on the far horizon, where politicians could safely leave them for another day. While governments and the experts thrashed out the issues of private sector pensions, the adequacy of personal savings, and whether the elderly had enough income, the CPP remained largely untouched. Metaphorically, of course, it was always in the room, since most discussions of seniors' incomes and pensions rested on the permanent, if unspoken, assumption that the OAS and CPP would remain as the financial foundation for retired Canadians.

The CPP and the QPP reached a few milestones early – the first retirement pensions were paid in 1967, the first survivor pensions in 1968, and the first disability pensions in 1970.[1] The age of eligibility for retirement benefits was reduced during those early years. OAS benefits had previously gone only to those 70 and older, but the age requirement was reduced for both OAS and the new CPP, from 69 in 1966 to 65 in 1970. The politicians were not completely inactive. They recognized that many low-income seniors had been left out of the CPP altogether because they retired before making the contributions that would have made them eligible for benefits. So in 1967, the federal government launched the Guaranteed Income Supplement to top up OAS benefits for those at the bottom of the income scale.[2]

Tinkering with the Plans

Through the 1970s and early 1980s, governments tinkered with the CPP – always adding new benefits, but never new revenues. In 1974, they fully indexed benefits to the cost of living as measured by the consumer price index (CPI), rather than limiting increases to 2 per cent annually (Quebec had raised the ceiling to 3 per cent in 1973). The increase reflected the emergence in the early 1970s of rising inflation and the fumbling attempts of governments worldwide to manage it, a learning process that took two decades to produce lasting results. For politicians, protecting pensioners from rapidly rising prices was an obvious measure. In the decade before the CPP took effect, the inflation rate had averaged less than 2 per cent a year, but by 1973, it was over 7 per cent and climbing.[3] In 1975, a year after full indexing, the retirement and earnings tests were dropped for those between 65 and 70. Previously they had to show that they were retired from regular employment, and any other earnings were subject to a 50 per cent clawback once they reached a given level. As well, pensions for surviving spouses were extended to widowers as well as widows.

By 1976, the CPP was in full swing, paying full retirement benefits to anyone who had contributed since the plan's inception in 1966. During the first decade, the pension entitlement had grown in graduated annual steps – by 10 per cent of the full retirement benefit for each year between 1967 and the age of retirement – until reaching the full benefit in 1976. Now began a long spell in which the CPP and the QPP introduced, or matched, new measures to enhance benefits, regularly alternating the role of leader and follower.

In 1977, Quebec eliminated the retirement test from the QPP, thus matching the CPP move of two years earlier, and added another measure: in cases of divorce or marriage annulment, pension credits earned during a marriage could be split between the former couple. The CPP copied that a year later, and at the same time introduced a childrearing drop-out provision. The CRDO, as it became known, allowed a person to leave a job or reduce hours while caring for children under the age of 7 without a reduction in their future pension entitlement. Though legislated in 1978, it was five years before that change took effect; British Columbia withheld its approval until 1982 and Ontario until 1983, when the province withdrew its veto of the measure. Ontario's reluctance reflected in large measure its growing worries over the financing of the CPP.

In 1980, the definition of pensionable employment was extended to the employment of a spouse in an unincorporated family business, as long as the Income Tax Act regarded the spouse's pay as deductible from the business's income. Four years later, in 1984, Quebec brought in two further measures. One was yet another of those changes that affected only a small number of people: it removed the provision that survivor benefits would cease if the recipient remarried. The second change was much broader. Individuals could choose to retire early and still get retirement benefits as long as they were willing to accept a smaller pension. The benefit reduction amounted to 0.5 per cent a month before the age of 65 – 6 per cent a year. On the other side of the 65 age divide, the pension was increased by 0.5 per cent for every month of postponed retirement up to and including the age of 70. The CPP matched both in 1987.

Something, of course, was missing in all this action: any measures that addressed the question of how to finance all these new provisions for enhanced benefits. A federal–provincial committee examined financing issues in the early 1980s, partly because of Ontario's concerns. It was one of the few indications that governments were beginning to think seriously about how to pay for the CPP in the future, though the Economic Council of Canada devoted considerable attention to the matter in a 1979 report. The lack of a long-term financing plan for the CPP had always been apparent to those who understood its dynamics, but until the mid-1980s, there was no urgency about finding a solution. As Bruce Kennedy put it: 'For two decades the CPP remained in this ambiguous state with clearly transitory financial arrangements and no specific and viable long-term plan.'[4]

Thinking about the Long Term

Throughout this period, the government was getting periodic reports from the chief actuary, whose task it was to assess the financial condition of the CPP. The actuary produced two kinds of reports. Every five years, he was required to draw up a full actuarial projection of the plan's finances, looking ahead many years – thirty to begin with, seventy-five later on – to see where the plan would stand at any given point in the future. In addition, he was required to check his numbers every time Parliament passed a new piece of legislation affecting the CPP, no matter how trivial the new provision. The full reports ran seventy to eighty pages; the short ones fewer than ten pages.

Walter Riese, the chief actuary of the day, produced his first full assessment of the CPP in December 1970, setting the tone for the rest of the decade. Revenues would begin to fall short of expenditures by about 1985, but interest revenue from the fund built up by then would keep covering costs for a further ten years; only then would the fund begin to drop. If the government went ahead with proposals it had made in a white paper a month earlier, however, the CPP would hit those trip wires five years earlier – in 1980 and 1990 – and the fund would disappear entirely before the end of the 1990s unless contribution rates were raised to cover the additional costs. Riese, however, was sanguine when it came to stating his bottom line.

Those costs, expressed as a percentage of contributory earnings, would rise slowly, so 'the most orderly way of maintaining the Canada Pension Plan Investment Fund at an agreed level would be to raise contribution rates gradually in a series of steps.' But since it would be another fifteen or twenty years before the fund would begin to shrink, 'it may be somewhat premature to enact a definite schedule of increasing contribution rates which might be adjusted many times in the light of actual experience before being put into effect.'[5]

Premature it was and would remain for several more years, but the chief actuary was at least thinking about the issues, and in doing so, he influenced the thinking of policymakers about where the CPP was heading financially. He came up with projections for what he called Funds A, B, and C. Fund A simply extended the status quo with the 3.6 per cent contribution rate, and the latter two were hypothetical outcomes for the CPP – 'probable resolution scenarios,' Kennedy called them[6] – that would solve the long-term financing problem left by the CPP designers. The two hypothetical funds were a logical extension of Riese's thinking in the first report. Each involved those trip wires mentioned above, which the chief actuary soon labelled as the CPP's three critical points.

The actuary laid out the details of his three funds and the critical points in his second and third reports, each of which was triggered by legislation that amended the CPP. The second report, in November 1973, examined the effect of Bill C-224, the legislation that replaced the

2 per cent ceiling on annual benefit increases with full indexing to the CPI. The third report, only five months later in April 1974, took into account the impact of Bill C-19, the legislation that dropped the retirement and earnings tests and extended survivors benefits to widowers as well as widows.

Critical Point 1 was the year in which CPP expenditures would exceed revenues from contributions. (Figure 3.1 illustrates how the critical points worked in terms of revenues, expenditures, and the size of the fund. The projections from the chief actuary's *8th Report*, released in 1984, were slightly off; they put Critical Point 1 at 1985; it turned out to be 1983. The historical data, which were not published in the *8th Report*, were taken from a later report.) In the CPP's early years, revenues were much greater than spending on benefits. The plan was collecting the full 3.6 per cent on the contributory earnings of all workers, but the cost of benefits ramped up slowly. Few people were eligible at first, and it was not until the tenth year of the plan that new beneficiaries would get full benefits. In 1970, the fifth year of operation, the CPP's total costs amounted to less than one-half of one per cent of contributory earnings. That was the PAYGO rate for 1970, the portion of covered earnings needed to pay all benefits and expenses. By the tenth year, 1975, revenues from contributions had climbed to more than $1.4 billion, but costs were still only $561 million, for a PAYGO rate of 1.5 per cent. As expected – indeed, as planned – the CPP was piling up surpluses during the early years while the PAYGO rate – in effect, the CPP's annual cost relative to its revenue base – was climbing steadily towards the frozen contribution rate of 3.6 per cent.

And, as agreed, the growing surplus had accumulated in the CPP fund and been lent out to the provinces. Some day, though, the rising cost line on a graph would cross the line representing revenue from contributions. Relative to contributory earnings, the graph would show a flat line for contribution revenues – at 3.6 per cent – with a rising line representing the PAYGO rate. Once costs equalled revenues, and the lines met, net cash flow to the plan would drop to zero, and after that, there would be no new annual surpluses to lend to the provinces. The estimate that Critical Point 1 would occur in 1985, cited in the example above, was not new; it can be found, though not under that name, in the first actuarial report released in 1970.[7]

There was more to the CPP Investment Fund than that, however. The fund's growing assets – the sum of all those annual surpluses – were earning interest on the loans to the provinces, so the fund's total reve-

Figure 3.1 CPP benchmarks: The critical points

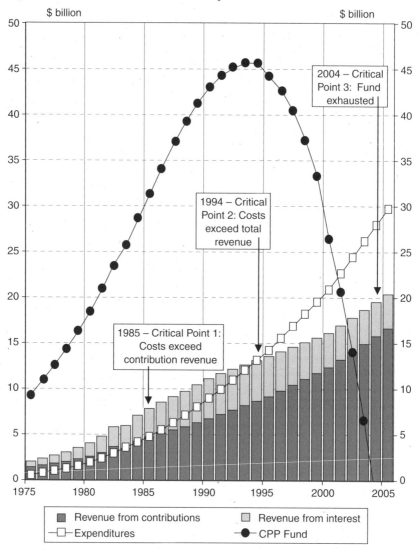

Source: Actual data for 1965–82 from chief actuary's *21st Report*, 2004; projections for 1983–2005 from chief actuary's *8th Report*, 1984.

nue each year was the sum of contributions from workers and employers plus interest revenue. That would give the CPP total annual
revenues that would continue to pay the bills for benefits until Critical
Point 2, the year in which this gross cash flow would drop to zero. After
that, the CPP would need to draw money from the fund to cover its
annual costs and the provinces would have to begin repaying their
loans. In the first report, Critical Point 2 was expected to be reached
between 1995 and 2000;[8] it turned out to be 1993.

Critical Point 3, to follow this to its arithmetic conclusion, was the
year in which the fund, having been steadily drained to pay the annual
bills, would run out of cash entirely. In the first such projection, it came
in 2004.

The Three Funds

The chief actuary's reports in the 1970s and early 1980s tracked the
progress of the three critical points through three separate actuarial
projections, called Funds A, B, and C. Projections – and this point cannot be stressed enough – are not forecasts or predictions. They do not
say 'This will happen.' They say: 'This will happen if ...' and there are
many 'ifs.' An economic forecaster who presents a view of future economic growth and inflation, for example, is saying: 'This is what I think
is most likely to happen.' That is not the case with projections, and the
actuarial projections of the CPP are a case in point.

The actuary makes a series of assumptions about the future course of
an array of factors: what birth and death rates will be; how many people will immigrate to Canada; what proportion of the working age population will have jobs; what the inflation and unemployment rates will
be; how quickly earnings (mainly wages) will rise; how many people
will make disability claims and how long will they remain too disabled
to work; what interest rates will be. For each of those factors, there is a
range of plausible outcomes. And for each, the actuary must choose a
firm number to plug into his computer model of the CPP, which then
generates a projection of the CPP's revenues and costs. (In the early
days, before computers, the calculations were done by hand.) If every
one of those assumptions is spot on, then the CPP's finances will unfold
the way the projection said it would. That is the biggest 'if' of all, and it
underlines the reality that no one can ever get every single assumption
exactly right, so no projection will ever get the future exactly right.

Riese's second report,[9] in 1973, set the template for several reports to come by laying out three alternative projections of how the CPP might unfold. That may not have been obvious from the second report, in which he made not three projections, but a dozen in all. First, he ran projections based on different outlooks for inflation, which was sensible because the new legislation would tie benefits to the CPI and also because he was working in an environment of rising inflation and deep uncertainty over how high it might go. He had projections using inflation rates of both 1 per cent ('reasonable stability') and 3 per cent ('moderate inflation'). Next, he produced projections for both the existing plan and the proposed plan under Bill C-224, so readers could compare the two and identify the added costs generated by the new legislation. And finally, he got governments thinking about how to get out of the box they were in as demonstrated through his Fund A status quo projection. He put forward two possible solutions, which he called Fund B and Fund C. Riese's third report in 1974[10] elaborated on the three-funds approach, but he dropped the 1 per cent inflation version, so there were only six projections this time. And by now, 1973's proposed plan had become the existing plan and the proposed plan reflected the new changes in Bill C-19.

Fund A was the projection for the status quo, with the 3.6 per cent contribution rate continuing indefinitely.[11] In 1974, the actuary figured that Critical Point 1, when costs would outstrip revenues from contributions alone, would arrive in 1982, only eight years away. Critical Point 2, when the fund would begin to need repayments of provincial debt, would follow in 1989, only seven years later. Critical Point 3 – when the fund would be exhausted – was 2000. That was still more than a quarter-century off, so no one was terribly concerned. Policymakers had every intention of making the kind of corrections that would avoid such an outcome. But as a measure of the generosity of the latest benefit enhancements, it is worth noting that the three critical points would arrive – compared with the estimate of only a few months before – three, six, and nine years earlier respectively. The status quo was beginning to look a little shaky.

Riese dismissed the assumption underlying Fund A as 'unacceptable,' of course. Theoretically, it might be possible to let the fund run down to zero and then cover the annual costs of the CPP by imposing a new contribution rate equal to the PAYGO rate, 'but such a discontinuity hardly commends itself, and in any event, the complete exhaustion of the fund would seem difficult to rationalize.'[12] Those unfamiliar with the language of actuaries might have glided past the term 'such a discontinuity' without realizing what it really meant: at some point, the Fund A path would require a sudden and very steep increase in contribution rates.

Now Riese rolled out the first of his possible solutions to the financing problem. Fund B assumed that when the CPP reached Critical Point 1, contribution rates would begin rising to match the PAYGO rate. In other words, annual revenues from contributions alone would rise in lockstep with the CPP's total benefits and expenses. There would be no new money going into the CPP investment fund – and thus to the provinces – but none would be removed either. The fund would keep growing, swelling each year as the provinces made their annual interest payments, which would then be rolled over into new loans back to the provinces. The actuary had a tart assessment of this option: 'It might not be easy to explain the significance of an ever increasing fund which had no effect on the rates of contributions.'[13] Kennedy put it more bluntly: 'In other words, the "loans" to the provinces would be clearly revealed as cash transfers not subject to interest or repayment.'[14] Indeed, the Fund B projection showed that in the four decades following 1982 (Critical Point 1), the contribution rate would have to double to over 7.2 per cent while the fund would grow to over $200-billion.[15] It took little political acumen to realize that Fund B was not a realistic solution.

Where Fund B would begin raising the contribution rate at Critical Point 1 in 1983, Fund C would postpone contribution rate increases for another five years or so, until Critical Point 2 was reached. Under Fund C, the contribution rate would remain at 3.6 per cent until the CPP's total expenditures were equal to total revenues from both contributions and interest payments on the fund. In effect, it would be the same as Fund A until Critical Point 2. After that point, contribution rates would have to rise steadily, but interest payments on the fund would be used to help finance total expenditures. The fund, rather than grow, would remain stable, so 'the loans to the provinces would never be repaid, but full interest would be paid in perpetuity.'[16] Contribution rates, though rising, would remain lower under Fund C than Fund B, but the difference – though substantial when cumulated over many decades – was small for any given year: by 2025, which was as far out as the actuary projected, the rate would be 7.79 per cent under Fund C, compared with 7.91 per cent under Fund B.[17]

Having dismissed his first two options as unacceptable (Fund A) and unexplainable (Fund B), Riese was not, however, prepared to give Fund C a strong endorsement. It 'may appear the most acceptable,' since it moved towards PAYGO contribution rates while preventing the fund from growing explosively, but he acknowledged that 'some other alternative may commend itself.'[18] The actuary's bottom-line advice in 1973 and 1974, however, was unchanged from 1970. Indeed, even the wording ('it may be somewhat premature')[19] was almost the same.

A Gentle Reminder

The chief actuary did not reappear with another full assessment of the CPP until 1978; his sixth report, released in December of that year, was based on data up to 31 December 1977, when the plan was a dozen years old.[20] Riese was by no means growing alarmed at the numbers coming from his new projections, but he nevertheless issued a gentle reminder that the day was approaching when Ottawa and the provinces would have to do something about the 3.6 per cent contribution rate.

'It was expected from the beginning,' he said, 'that this rate would be more than sufficient to meet current benefits and expenses for about fifteen years, that eventually it would have to be increased, and that the size of the required increases in contribution rates would depend on the experience of the Plan, the funding objectives and, of course, any amendments made to the provisions of the Plan.' In theory, it would be possible to devise 'an almost infinite number of scenarios involving increased contribution rate,' he added, but some of the more practical alternatives were already being studied by a sub-committee of the federal–provincial Continuing Committee of Officials on Economic and Fiscal Matters.[21] The committee he referred to – known in government shorthand as the CCO – consisted of the federal and provincial deputy ministers of finance. Below them were three sub-committees consisting of assistant deputy ministers: one dealt with taxation issues, another with fiscal arrangements like equalization and other federal transfers to the provinces, and the third with the Canada Pension Plan. The CPP sub-committee had been established in 1977 and at the time of the actuary's report was working on several issues relating to the impact of the CPP on the economy. To help the committee out, the actuary appended to his report six 'auxiliary' projections for the CPP based on different assumptions for inflation, investment yields, and earnings growth.

If the rate was left at 3.6 per cent indefinitely, the CPP was on course to run out of funds entirely (Critical Point 3) by 2003, three years later than the previous estimate, but Riese was not worried that governments would let that happen: 'It is difficult to visualize circumstances under which such a course would be followed as a matter of policy.' After all, if governments waited until the fund was exhausted before acting, they would have to raise the contribution rate to 5.4 per cent from 3.6 per cent in 2003 – a huge increase in relative terms – to cover the costs of the plan.[22]

Given the work already under way by the CPP sub-committee of the CCO, however, Riese confidently dismissed the periodic fears that had popped up in public over the future of the plan: 'Notwithstanding occasional comments reported in the news media to the contrary, there appears to be no reason why the Canada Pension Plan could not be operated in the indefinite future in the manner contemplated at its inception, which would involve a gradual increase in the contribution rate, beginning within the next decade or so.'[23]

Some flavour of these 'occasional comments' may be found in a column by Dian Cohen, a respected economics columnist, in the *Montreal Star* in late 1977. Cohen warned that the CPP 'will run out of money long before today's "prime age workers" reach retirement age' and added that 'a lot of this pension money [is not only] being invested at substandard rates, [but] there are suggestions that it isn't being invested at all, but is being used to pay for current expenses.'[24] Laurence Coward, a leading pension expert with the actuarial firm of William M. Mercer Ltd., described concerns that when people born during the baby boom retired after 2015, 'the burden on the working population would then be so great that the government might renege on its promises and cut back on CPP benefits.' For a variety of reasons, he added, 'a belief grew [during the 1970s] that the Canada Pension Plan was unsoundly financed and that a much larger fund should be built up from increased contributions.'[25]

These worries prompted calls for a deeper look at the finances of the CPP, which Riese was forced to address. Despite his comforting words in the sixth report, the chief actuary made one further calculation – of a number that would arise again and again and that would preoccupy some of those who took part in the 1990s debate over the CPP. At the behest of the federal auditor general, Riese took a stab at estimating the CPP's unfunded liability, which is the difference between the present value of the pension plan's liabilities and the assets held by the fund. In effect, if the CPP were to be shut down today, it was the sum that governments would have to pony up to meet the commitments they had already made to those who had contributed to the plan. This premise is highly unlikely, but measures of an unfunded liability are common in assessing the financial health of private pensions. The reason is simple: private pensions are required by law to be fully funded from an actuarial standpoint so that if the business promising the pension goes bankrupt, there will be enough funds set aside to meet the pension promise.

Riese tucked his estimate of the unfunded liability into a short appendix at the end of the sixth report. He began by noting that while the principles of 'actuarial funding' may be the cornerstone of security for a private pension plan, it is 'usually considered inappropriate' to apply them to social insurance.[26] He cited several reasons, some of which had been heard before and which would assume greater prominence in later years. The most important was that full funding 'would tend to concentrate overwhelming control of capital in the hands of governments or their agencies.' This argument arose in the 1960s during the original debate over the CPP and would return in the 1990s, when governments proposed a sharp increase in the size of the CPP investment fund through higher contributions. It is also the main reason why social security experts in other countries fear full funding of national pension plans.

He also said it was almost impossible to determine the extent to which actuarial funding would affect intergenerational equity. The point of full funding, of course, is to set aside the accumulated contributions of pension plan members in a separate pool of savings that can then be used to finance the retirement years. Across a whole society, however, the actuary implied that higher pension savings would almost certainly reduce other forms of saving, but with no certainty as to the overall impact. This passage may have been one of the first official uses of the term 'intergenerational equity,' though the concept had been part of the CPP from the beginning, when policymakers deliberately tilted the field to favour the generation then approaching retirement. Indeed, any pension plan that is not fully funded allocates its costs in such a way that some generations bear more than their share in relation to their benefits while others bear less. By now, however, a dozen years into the CPP's operation, some voices were beginning to question the plan's fairness to subsequent generations.

Bernard Dussault, a later chief actuary, says Riese's listing of such caveats should not be taken to suggest that he personally opposed the idea, though most actuaries do fall into this camp. 'He and I had several interesting discussions on technical (e.g., calculations) aspects of the unfunded liability, but at no time has he expressed any strong opinion in favour or not of the appropriateness of applying actuarial funding to social security programs.'[27]

Whatever the technical merits or demerits of the measure, Riese acknowledged that a calculation of the contribution rate needed for full funding 'is interesting' as well as requested by the auditor general.[28] He figured that if the plan were to be put on a full funding basis immediately, new contributors would have to pay rates of between 8 and 9.4 per cent, while the unfunded liability – the sum needed to ensure pensions for all previous plan members – would fall somewhere between $81 and $85 billion, depending on the inflation and interest rate assumptions used. The unfunded liability, he noted, 'may be expected to grow substantially.'[29]

With that observation in late 1978, the chief actuary went silent for the next five and a half years. It would be June 1984 before he re-entered the picture with his eighth report,[30] based on data up to 31 December 1982.

'The Great Pension Debate'

For almost everyone else with an interest in pensions, however, this was hardly a quiet period. Indeed, the late 1970s and early 1980s were marked by what soon became known as the Great Pension Debate, a discussion that ranged well beyond the CPP into private pensions, retirement savings, retirement income in general, and – in its broadest form – income security of all kinds.

The push to expand the welfare state through new income security measures had not ended with the launch of the CPP and QPP in 1966. The federal Department of National Health and Welfare (NHW) put forward the idea of a guaranteed annual income both in a 1970 white paper from John Munro and a 1973 green paper (though its cover was actually orange) from Marc Lalonde.[31] Neither proposal went anywhere – the Finance Department strongly opposed such ideas – but the tenor of the times was such that grand proposals for new social programs were still very much on the agenda.

In the mid-1970s, the Canadian Labour Congress launched a campaign for 'a massive expansion to the CPP,' recalls Bob Baldwin, who joined the CLC as a young economist in 1976 and spent most of the next three decades as the CLC's resident pension expert. 'Seniors' incomes were low and it was a period when expanding social programs was still on the table. The CLC proposal got a lot of support in the social policy community – labour, seniors, and women's groups. It was opposed by the financial services sector. But there was still an openness on these questions.'[32] Specifically, the CLC urged governments to raise the CPP retirement benefit from 25 per cent of earnings up to the average industrial wage to 50 per cent of earnings, with commensurate increases in contribution rates. The National Council of Welfare (NCW), a federal advisory group, was not quite so bold, but it pushed to increase the earnings replacement goal to 37.5 per cent. Ken Battle, the NCW's executive director at the time, says the main policy issue in those days came down to some simple choices: 'Do we expand the CPP or mandate private [occupational] pension plans or make incremental reforms to the existing system?'[33]

The next decade saw a blizzard of pension and retirement income reports that would bury anyone who tried to assemble and read them all. Everyone, it seemed, waded into the discussion and everyone called for some reform of the system, though they disagreed wildly on what kind of reform was needed. There were studies from governments, task forces, a royal commission, think tanks, pension supervisors, business groups, and labour organizations. Academics weighed in with learned papers on this or that aspect of the issue. Governments alone produced at least ten major reports.

In Quebec, there was a 1977 report from an advisory group to the provincial government known as Cofirentes Plus, a body whose full name, the Comité d'étude sur le financement du Régime de rentes du Québec et sur les régimes supplémentaires de rentes, invited the use of the acronym. The Economic Council of Canada produced a study (*One in Three*) in 1979, as did a Special Senate Committee on Retirement Age Policies. In 1980, the federal government's Lazar Task Force on Retirement Income Policy (so named for its lead author, Harvey Lazar) turned out a two-volume report. Ontario's Royal Commission on the Status of Pensions in Ontario, headed by Donna J. Haley, produced a ten-volume report in 1981. There were no fewer than four major reports in 1982: one from the BC government, another from the Ontario legislature's Select Committee on Pensions, a third from the Canadian Association of Pension Supervisory Authorities, and yet another green paper from the federal government, this one under the name of Health and Welfare Minister Monique Bégin. The House of Commons set up its own Task Force on Pension Reform under Liberal MP Douglas Frith that reported in 1983.

Non-government organizations were busy too. The Canadian Labour

Congress set out its views in a 1978 submission to the Ontario royal commission, while the Canadian Life and Health Insurance Association (which was generally on the other side of the issue from the CLC) issued a discussion paper in 1981. A year later came a policy statement from the Business Committee on Pension Policy, a group whose participants included the Association of Canadian Pension Management, the Business Council on National Issues, the Canadian Chamber of Commerce, the Canadian Federation of Independent Business, the Canadian Life and Health Insurance Association (again), the Canadian Manufacturers' Association, the Canadian Securities Industry Pension Reform Committee, the Finance Executives Institute Canada, and the Canadian Bankers' Association.[34]

No one disputed the range of deficiencies. 'In the private sector these include the large gaps in coverage of employer pension plans, restrictive vesting provisions, the lack of indexed pension benefits and frequently inadequate survivor pensions. Women are particularly hard hit by these deficiencies in the private system.' Private sector plans accounted for less than 10 per cent of total pension income, while 77 per cent came from public plans like the OAS, GIS, CPP, and QPP and just over 13 per cent from public sector employer pensions.[35]

Plenty of solutions were advanced to cure these ills, but there was little agreement on which were best. The advocates fell into three broad camps: 'The first recognizes the problem but sees no need for more government intervention. The second recommends the introduction of mandatory employer-sponsored pension plans and the third proposes the expansion of public plans. The approach chosen in different pension reports is often based less on technicalities of pension issues but more on *a priori* conceptions of the appropriate role of the private and public sectors.'[36] In short, pensions had turned into a left–right debate that pitted business interests against organized labour, with others ranged in between.

The focus on the quality of private pension plans reflected in part a growing uneasiness over the condition of the CPP, which for many Canadians offered the only prospect of a retirement income beyond the basic OAS and GIS. 'The Canada Pension Plan, alas, is not the sort of arrangement one can fall back on with confidence,' *The Globe and Mail* said in an editorial on 24 February 1981. 'It was ill-conceived in the first place, evidently intended to generate large sums of money to which the provinces could have easy, low-interest access. They dipped in to build hospitals, universities, and high schools, which, splendid as they might have been, were not investments that returned money to the fund. If the premiums (with interest) are to be returned to the fund, the provinces must tax us over again for what we have already paid – our Canada pensions. We are rapidly moving into the demographic doldrums, the depletion phase in which retirement payout exceeds premium income – the sort of circumstances that would, in private business, unmistakably spell approaching bankruptcy.'[37] Those notions – a financially shaky CPP, a free ride for the provinces, and a looming demographic reckoning – would become a central part of the debate over the CPP for the next fifteen years.

In the middle of all this ferment, the federal government convened a National Pensions Conference in March 1981. Would-be pension reformers approached the conference with high hopes. With delegates from industry, labour, government, women's, and pensioners' groups, the conference had all the earmarks of being a highlight of the Great Pension Debate. Prime Minister Pierre Trudeau opened the conference with a 'promise of major pension reform during his government's mandate.'[38] Trudeau was then only a year or so into his final term, so it appeared there was plenty of time for action.

There wasn't. By the summer of 1981, Canada had entered a recession that would last for a full eighteen months – the worst since the Great Depression of the 1930s – and pension reform simply dropped off the table. Even when the recession ended and the economy embarked on a strong expansion that lasted for the rest of the decade, the appetite for major pension reform remained dulled. 'Federal and provincial politicians, their advisers and certain business groups [were reluctant] to accept the need for *sweeping* change.'[39] Some improvements were made, but 'most ... were modest, and none of them addressed the major problems that were known to all the experts.'[40]

In the 1984 budget, the federal government advanced a three-pronged reform that affected all pillars of the retirement income system. First, it proposed tougher new standards to regulate private pension plans in areas under federal jurisdiction (banking, transportation, and communications plus the civil service itself and Crown corporations). There were measures to 'tackle the classic private pension problems of inflation, vesting, portability and survivor benefits.'[41] Second, the budget revised and enriched the tax incentives under which contributions to both occupational Registered Retirement Pension Plans and personal Registered Retirement Savings Plans were tax exempt, as was any investment income earned on the funds in those plans. Finally, it increased payments under the GIS and said it would ask the provinces for some small changes in the CPP. Although the Liberal government lost the election before its proposals could be made law, most were adopted by the Progressive Conservatives under Brian Mulroney, who took over in September 1984.[42]

Other ideas generated by the Great Pension Debate were left until later or died altogether. One of the latter was a proposal to create a homemaker pension that would address the fact that 60 per cent of elderly single women in Canada were poor. Proposals for a homemaker pension had first appeared in the mid-1970s but remained dormant until the early 1980s. The idea was fully fleshed out in 1983 as an add-on to the CPP and QPP. While the idea won some support among politicians and women's groups, it was opposed by even more organizations, including many that represented women and many others that were in the forefront of advocating greater income support in general.[43] Though the issue of a homemaker pension stirred far more talk than action, it represented a lasting legacy of the National Pensions Conference, in which women's groups participated actively in the pension debate for the first time. Newly alert to the question of income security for older women, women's groups would continue to play a strong role in future pension debates.

4 Finally, Some Action on Financing

The Canada Pension Plan was about to return to the federal–provincial agenda, but any thoughts of a greatly expanded package of retirement benefits – along the lines of the CLC and NCW proposals – were off the table entirely. 'Finance dumped it,' says Ken Battle. The department had two key objections. First, Old Age Security and the Guaranteed Income Supplement were already accomplishing the anti-poverty objective, and second, the earnings replacement goal might not be met because people would simply contribute less to their RRSPs. 'The same arguments are true today.'[1]

Now the chief actuary re-entered the debate with his eighth statutory actuarial report based on the data up to the end of 1982. His report – later than usual – was tabled in the Commons on 5 June 1984, just as Parliament was winding down for the summer, which turned out to feature an election campaign. The government changed hands less than three months later.

But it was time, finally, to do something about the finances of the CPP. Critical Point 1 – the year in which the plan spent more than it took in from contributions – had already arrived.[2] In 1983, contribution revenues dropped for the first time while expenditures kept growing, and the result was a $124 million shortfall that had to be covered with interest income. In part, the revenue stream was suffering from the effects of the 1981–2 recession; the economy and employment both grew in 1983, but slowly, and the jobless rate kept rising. The revenue decline was also a bit of a fluke. In the previous year, almost all contributions relating to 1982 earnings had actually been collected in 1982; normally, some slopped over into the next year. While that inflated 1982 revenues, and produced a higher-than-expected surplus, it automatically depressed 1983 revenues.[3]

The actuary's projections were not much different from those made in the sixth report, which were based on hard numbers to the end of 1977. Once more, he set out projections for Funds A, B, and C; once more, he said the key question was 'how soon and at what pace the contribution rate should begin to rise to its ultimate level.' But again, 'this matter is expected to be resolved fairly soon in the course of federal–provincial negotiations.'[4] If governments were going to hew to the principles of the CPP 'envisaged at the outset,' governments would have to begin raising the contribution rate by 1994 'at the latest.' If they were to stick to the 3.6 per cent rate, and wait until the fund was run down to zero, the money would run out in 2003 and the contribution rate would have to be pushed suddenly up to 6.1 per cent (not the 5.6 per cent rate projected in the sixth report) in 2004.[5]

With that warning hanging over their heads, the federal and provincial finance ministers went to work. In January 1985, the new finance minister, Michael Wilson, and his provincial counterparts quickly agreed that the CPP contribution rate would have to rise soon, though they could not quite agree on how to characterize the size of the likely increase. Coming out of the meeting in Montreal, Wilson told reporters that 'the increases that are in the cards are significant increases.'[6] Two days later, however, Ontario Treasurer Larry Grossman (who was campaigning to succeed Premier William Davis as leader of the Ontario Progressive Conservative Party) said he 'wouldn't have called it substantial,' though he added later that the differences were 'just phraseology.' He thought the rate might have to rise to between 4.5 and 5 per cent over a period of six to nine years, but he rejected a suggestion that the CPP was in any financial difficulty. 'The plan is solid and secure,' he said.[7]

The CPP, however, had to wait until after Wilson weathered the separate pension firestorm that followed his first full budget on 24 May. In an effort to reduce the government's large deficit, Wilson announced that he would partially de-index large chunks of the federal revenue and spending machinery. The proposal would remove some of the inflation protection from personal income tax brackets and exemptions and from the benefits paid under the family allowance and Old Age Security programs. The Guaranteed Income Supplement and the CPP remained fully indexed, but OAS benefits would remain frozen if the annual inflation rate was 3 per cent or less.

This was not an easy sell at a time when the prices were rising by about 4 per cent a year, and the new government quickly got a lesson on the dangers of tampering with benefits for the elderly. For weeks, the old, the young, labour unions, business organizations (even though they strongly supported deficit reduction), and the provinces pilloried the government over its plans. It was described as a 'put the boots to granny' budget[8] that would reduce seniors' purchasing power by 3 per cent a year beginning the following year. It did not help the government that Wilson personally had opposed the Liberal government's move in 1982 to limit OAS benefit increases to 6 per cent in 1983 and 5 per cent in 1984 under its anti-inflation '6-and-5' program, nor that the Conservatives had promised in the 1984 election campaign to restore full indexing of the OAS benefit.[9]

Goodbye Charlie Brown

Wilson and Prime Minister Brian Mulroney gamely held their ground until 19 June, when Solange Denis, a diminutive 63-year-old, confronted Mulroney at a demonstration on Parliament Hill. 'You lied to us. You got us to vote for you and now it's goodbye Charlie Brown,' she told the prime minister. 'I think, Madame ...' Mulroney began before she cut him off. 'Madame is mighty angry,' Denis said.[10] The episode, caught on film, became a media sensation, played and replayed on television newscasts in the days that followed. On 27 June, the government buckled and restored full indexing to the OAS benefit. The money that would no longer be saved from the OAS would be made up by extending a temporary corporate surtax and raising the tax on gasoline.

As he returned to the CPP file after this bruising lesson on the power of pension politics, Wilson was preparing a federal position paper with every expectation of provincial government support. In April, Quebec released a white paper that proposed sweeping changes in both public and private pensions, including a near doubling of QPP contribution rates over the seven years beginning in 1987. Other provinces appeared equally receptive to higher contribution rates. But both levels of government were also looking at ways to sweeten the medicine of rate increases with a package of benefit enhancements. In mid-September, Health and Welfare Minister Jake Epp, whose department administered the CPP, announced that he had given his provincial counterparts – usually designated as ministers of social services – a new proposal for homemaker pensions and that all had agreed to recommend to their governments a set of what he called modest improvements to the CPP. The changes would allow for the splitting of pension entitlements on marriage breakdown, the continuation of survivors' benefits even if a surviving spouse remarried, better disability benefits, and more flexibility in the age of retirement.[11]

The homemaker pension idea once more went nowhere (several provinces were opposed), but the 'modest improvements' already agreed on were part of the bigger deal that governments were working toward. At a federal–provincial finance ministers meeting in Halifax on 26 and 27 September 1985, there was a broad consensus – but no firm decision yet – on enriching benefits while raising premiums. Wilson released a twenty-three-page booklet, jointly issued with Epp, that was 'intended to inform all interested Canadians about the CPP's financial condition.'[12] The booklet laid out an extended explanation of the planned increase in contribution rates and was clearly designed to forestall criticisms of what some would regard as a tax increase. It made only passing reference to the proposed benefit enhancements, which were unlikely to draw much fire, if any. Not so curiously, it also laid out a set of proposals that was very close to the package that Ottawa and the provinces announced several months later. Clearly, officials and ministers had done plenty of homework and were close to a deal.

The booklet is revealing in that it illustrates the change in thinking about the CPP that had taken place since the mid-1960s and hints at how thinking would change further over the decade to the mid-1990s. It also set the tone for how the federal government would handle its communications of CPP issues over the next decade.

Selling Pension Reform to the Public

The paper opened with a brief description of the CPP and some bare facts of the kind that would be familiar to anyone who had been reading the chief actuary's reports. Revenues from contributions had exceeded costs until recently and the fund had grown to about $30 billion 'because the great majority of people who have paid into the plan have not yet retired.' Most of the money had been lent to the provinces, which 'have used this money for economic and social programs.' The provinces' interest payments had become 'an important secondary source of revenue for the plan.'[13]

The very neutrality of the language is interesting, especially in the reference to provincial borrowing. When the CPP was created, loans from the fund would be used – in the rhetoric of the day – to finance nation-building through much-needed infrastructure – schools, universities, colleges, housing, roads, and bridges. In the 1960s, the CPP fund was touted in the positive, uplifting language of investing for the future. Now in the 1980s, the use of the fund was cast in the language of mere government spending – 'for economic and social programs' – which, given the tenor of the times, was beginning to look like plain old government spending of any kind, a concept that seemed far less inviting.

The context, of course, had changed hugely. In the 1960s, Ottawa and the provinces were financially strong enough to launch grandly ambitious programs like the CPP and medicare. By the mid-1980s, the eleven governments were running annual deficits of more than $40 billion a year, and their total debt load of $280 billion amounted to almost 58 per cent of gross domestic product, nearly triple the level of twenty years earlier. Grand ambitions – at least of the sort that involved big spending – had disappeared from the political toolkit.

Next came the projections for the CPP out to 2003. Benefits would nearly double in the next five years and more than quadruple in the next fifteen years. Contributions and interest income would cover the costs until 1994, at which point the CPP would have to begin drawing down the fund, which would be 'completely depleted around the year 2003 – in only 18 years' time.'[14] There were three reasons for this outlook, the first two of which were not surprising.

First, the population was aging; Canadians were having fewer children and were 'healthier and living longer than they used to.' There were now six working-age Canadians (those aged 20 to 64) for every Canadian 65 and older. In fifty years, there would be only three. The baby-boom generation would contribute to this trend, but the booklet made a key point that would continue to elude many people who would enter the CPP debate over the next decade. Population aging was not a temporary phenomenon that would end once the baby boomers passed from the scene. 'It is a long-term trend caused by Canada's continuing lower birth rate.'[15]

Second, spending would continue to increase faster than revenues because the CPP was only twenty years old and still maturing. Many of those who were retired in 1985 were people who had either stopped working before the plan was created, so they had not paid into it and were thus not eligible for benefits, or who had retired during the plan's first ten years, so they contributed for only a short time and received only partial benefits. That would change as a steadily rising proportion of the newly retired would have contributed for enough years to have earned full benefits; 'more funds will be required to pay for these benefits.'[16]

Third, benefits had been enriched several times in the previous twenty years with no corresponding increase in contributions. The paper reeled off the list: inflation indexing, elimination of the retirement test and the earnings test, the childrearing drop-out provision. All these had increased the long-term costs of the CPP significantly, by over 2 per cent of contributory earnings, one learned from a footnote, which did not make the more vivid point that this compared with a contribution rate of only 3.6 per cent. At 3.7 per cent of contributory earnings, the cost of the CPP was already higher than the 3.6 per cent contribution rate; it was projected to reach 6.1 per cent by 2000 and 11 per cent by 2035.[17]

Now, in a string of strongly worded paragraphs that collectively amounted to a projection of looming economic disaster, the booklet hammered home the consequences of doing nothing and thus allowing the worst-case scenario to unfold. With no increase in the contribution rate, the CPP could meet all its commitments until 2003, but to do so in 2004 would require an increase in the contribution rate to 6.4 per cent from 3.6 per cent, with further increases in subsequent years to meet the rising costs. 'Such an abrupt and dramatic increase in contributions would face workers with a significant cut in their take-home pay, and employers with a sharp increase in labour costs. This in turn could have a potentially serious impact on the economy.' Next came the intergenerational equity argument. Future contributors – 'our children and grandchildren' – would pay more for their pensions than people today. Current contributors should pay a greater share of the benefits they will one day get. Another problem: if the CPP fund were allowed to run down quickly, the provinces would have to pay back about $45 billion in the decade from 1994 to 2003, forcing most to raise taxes or borrow elsewhere to foot the bill. 'Raising taxes would cut into people's disposable incomes, while borrowing on such a large scale could put upward pressure on interest rates and disrupt capital markets.' And finally, if the fund were completely emptied, there would be no reserve to deal with unexpected events and 'no way to cushion the impact of the baby boom.'[18]

This was not stuff for the faint of heart. It was the chief actuary's Fund A, but written now in very non-actuarial terms. The language was dramatic and emotive. It was easy to see why the actuary had been so confident that governments would avoid the Fund A option. What politician wants to be tagged as the author of that litany of woes?

The federal booklet then set out the logical (especially after that analysis) objective of 'putting the CPP on a firm financial footing for the future in the fairest and least disruptive way.' The way to do that is through gradual increases in the contribution rate – of 0.1 to 0.2 percentage points a year – that would lift the rate to about 11 per cent at some point in the next fifty to seventy-five years. An accompanying numerical example acknowledged that a rate increase of 0.15 percentage points a year would double a worker's cash contribution over the next decade. But – an attempt here to soften expected attacks on such a sharp increase – wages would increase over the same period, so the rise in contributions as a share of earnings would be lower; and because contributions are tax-deductible, the final impact on take-home pay would be even less.[19]

Three Key Issues

Three other related issues came next in the government's paper. First, it defended the practice of lending CPP funds to the provinces at what some critics said were unusually low rates that undermined the CPP's finances. That, said the paper, is 'a frequent misconception.' True, the provinces' borrowings carried an interest rate lower than they could get in the private capital markets, the paper conceded. But the differential for large provinces was between one-third and three-quarters of a percentage point, and for smaller provinces it was about one percentage point, too small to have much effect on the CPP's long-run finances.[20]

Second, governments had to decide how big the fund should be in the future. The fund was then about six times annual expenditures, but the ratio was falling quickly as the CPP matured and costs rose. A two-year fund, the paper suggested, would be about right. A one-year reserve might lead to sudden rate increases to pay the bills during periods of rapid economic and demographic fluctuations. But a reserve much higher than two years could not be justified on those grounds alone. Here, the paper revived the old arguments over full funding versus PAYGO. 'A large fund would give rise to a need to manage large public sector funds, and it is not needed to ensure that benefits that have been promised to Canadians will always be paid.' Private plans need full funding to ensure that funds are always available to cover the eventual costs of the members' pensions. 'Companies can go bankrupt,' the paper said, a possibility that does not apply to the CPP. 'Countries like Canada do not go out of business.' The CPP has behind it 'the resources of the entire country.'[21]

Finally, the government set out an issue that attracted very little attention at the time but that would – again, almost unnoticed – become a central feature of the CPP's governance. It was a purely mechanical issue, one of those 'process' matters that often seem to preoccupy governments at the expense of more substantive policy issues. This one was different. After twenty years, the time had come to resolve the long-term financing question that had been left to future resolution. The proposal was simple: governments should set a long-term schedule of contribution rates and review it every five years; at those times, they would either confirm the rates for the next five years or revise them. They should also revise the long-term schedule as needed and on each occasion extend it by another five years 'to ensure that a "rolling" 25-year schedule always existed.'[22] This idea had been floated two years earlier in the report of the Commons task force on pension reform under Doug Frith, though the idea probably came from the Finance Department.

Higher Rates, Sweetened with New Benefits

A deeper read into the details of the paper suggests that the federal government was leaning towards the lower end of the possible rate increases. In an appendix, the paper set out twenty-five-year projections under four possible scenarios – rate increases of 0.1 per cent, 0.15 per cent, and 0.2 per cent a year, plus a stepped increase of 0.1 per cent for the first ten years to 1996, 0.15 per cent for the next five years to 2001, and 0.2 per cent for the final decade to 2011. Both the 0.2 per cent and the 0.15 per cent rate increases would produce funds well in excess of the two-year reserve Ottawa deemed sufficient – 5.6 years and 3.5 years respectively in 2011. A series of 0.1 per cent increases would produce too small a fund – only 1.2 years – while the stepped increase would lead to a 2.3-year reserve.[23]

One Ontario official[24] recalls that the big debate in 1985 was over the rate of increase in the earlier and later periods. Ontario and a few other provinces pushed for increases that were 'steeper, earlier and longer,' but Ottawa would not buy into higher rate increases. Wilson did not like payroll taxes in general, and politically, the CPP contribution was 'seen as a federal payroll tax for which Ottawa would take the heat.' Alan Eastwood, a BC official in those days, remembers that his province and Alberta wanted full funding of the CPP, but since the unfunded liability was already at around $100 billion,[25] the cost of moving to full funding would be so high as to make that prospect unrealistic. They instead pushed to keep the fund as a constant percentage of the unfunded liability.[26]

In the end – at a 13 December 1985 meeting at a hotel near Toronto's Pearson International Airport – the finance ministers settled on increases of 0.2 per cent for the first five years (the rate would go from 3.6 per cent in 1986 to 4.6 per cent in 1991) and 0.15 per cent for the subsequent twenty years (pushing the rate to 7.6 per cent in 2011). One option discussed, but rejected, would have involved 0.2 per cent annual increases for the first twenty years, so the rate would reach 7.6 per cent in 2006. A steeper path like that would have produced a bigger fund that would automatically lead to more provincial borrowing. The provinces had to tread carefully here, the Ontario official said, because they had a clear conflict of interest. As stewards of the plan, they had to support bigger rate increases that would improve the finances of the CPP, but as borrowers from the CPP fund they stood to gain substantially because it would create a bigger fund from which they could borrow. They were not inclined to invite accusations of self-interest.

The benefit enhancements first flagged by Health and Welfare Minister Jake Epp went through much as planned. CPP disability benefits were brought up to the more generous levels of the QPP. The CPP, like the QPP, would allow a person to retire at 60 with a reduced pension or delay retirement until 70 and get a larger pension. Credit-splitting was made mandatory on divorce and optional on separation, so pension credits – or entitlements to future benefits – would be split between former spouses; previously, it had been optional for all. Widows and widowers of CPP beneficiaries would no longer lose their survivors' retirement pension if they remarried. Homemaker pensions did not make the cut because there was no consensus, only an agreement to study the matter further.

'The changes we are proposing will ensure the financial health of the CPP in the decades to come,' Wilson told reporters. 'They will also result in each generation of working Canadians contributing fairly to the cost of the benefits they themselves eventually receive.'[27]

In one sense, Wilson was overstating his case. His 'decades to come' became less than a single decade, and he personally would participate in another rate increase as finance minister only five years later. Yet in another sense, his comment was utterly prescient for reasons that very few people appreciated at the time.

The Key Measures

A key feature of the deal from the financing perspective was that governments had adopted the twenty-five-year 'rolling' schedule of rate increases floated in the September booklet. They laid out five years of firm increases followed by a further twenty years of potential increases; at the five-year mark, they would review the projections and set another five years of firm increases and another twenty years of potential increases. The finance ministers had, in effect, scheduled for themselves a visit to the CPP negotiating table every five years. Never again could they let the financing issue slide for twenty years as they had done since 1966.

That alone was a hugely significant change, as would become apparent over the next decade; without it, the reforms of the mid-1990s might never have occurred. But tucked into the federal–provincial deal was a little-noticed twist in the form of a powerful default provision. If ministers could not agree on a new schedule of rate increases after each review, their failure would trigger a formula that would mandate rate increases large enough to generate, over fifteen years, a fund equal to two years of the following year's expenditures. Having agreed to a two-year fund, the ministers had, in effect, committed themselves to rate increases (or, hypothetically, cuts to benefits) that would deliver a fund that large.

The fifteen-year rule turned out to have another function, one that was of more practical import than just being on hand if future ministers could not agree to raise rates when needed. Even if ministers were heading towards a decision, officials used the rule as a benchmark to assess the CPP's current financial conditions and any new schedule they were discussing. 'We used that formula to see how far off track we were,' says Réal Bouchard, the federal Finance Department's long-time pension expert who was deeply involved in CPP issues from the 1980s until his retirement in 2007.[28]

Bouchard is quite proud of the formula: 'I designed it.' It had begun as a twenty-year rule that he had developed and used in the discussions leading up to the 1985 deal. He wanted to assess whether various scenarios of contribution rate increases were consistent with the objective of creating a fund worth two years of benefits and to make rate assumptions beyond twenty-five years. At first, he recalled, the 'provinces paid little attention' to it, though he found it 'an extremely useful tool.' In the discussions, policymakers began to pay more attention to the period beyond twenty-five years, and the formula became even more helpful. 'Then the issue of [a] "default" provision got on the table and it was then that people realized that we had the perfect "ready-to-use" formula to be the "default" provision. The discussion then focused on whether to use a shorter period than 20 years and we settled on 15 years.'[29] The formula proved so powerful that it drove the thinking of policymakers and the reports of the chief actuary for the next decade.

Provincial officials recall the appeal of the default clause in terms that are more political. Alan Eastwood calls it 'a neat clause' that 'got [the politicians] off the hook.' Even if they had a technical escape hatch (they could simply eliminate the provision with a legislative change), the politicians could gain some cover from opposition attacks by saying: the chief actuary tells us we have to raise rates, so we're doing it. 'We thought it was a master stroke,' says Eastwood. An Alberta official of the day, Gail Armitage, says the motivation was less crassly political than that: 'The introduction of the five-year review reflected the fact that politicians in the 1980s were more long-term in their thinking than they are now (though less so than in the 1970s).'[30] There was probably a mix of these motives. Either way, they had institutionalized a rare form of discipline on their successors.

The 1985 deal met with broad approval from opposition members and the media. The *Ottawa Citizen* editorialized that 'the baby boomers are going to start paying for their own old age.'[31] This was a bit of a stretch, as subsequent events would demonstrate, but the boomers were at least paying a bit more for their own old age than previously; they would wind up paying much more.

If the CPP itself was a winner from the 1985 deal, in that it was guaranteed both higher revenues and the regular reviews that would keep it on track, there were other winners too – the provinces. 'It is clear that the provincial governments did well in the latest round of negotiations to perpetuate a revenue source that many observers believed would be temporary,' Bruce Kennedy concludes in his study.[32] Before these talks, the chief actuary's Fund C appeared to be the most likely outcome of the CPP, and under that projection the provinces not only would lose their access to new funds after 1994 (since there would be none) but would also have to keep paying interest on a $47 billion fund so that the CPP could pay its annual bills. The deal assured them of a steadily rising source of new loans from a growing CPP fund, one that would swell to $74 billion, according to the chief actuary.[33]

Important as it was to the provinces, however, the CPP fund was not widely regarded among pension experts as a source of security for future beneficiaries. 'The major role of the CPP fund seems to be that it supports the savings imagery that surrounds the CPP,' Kennedy observed in a subsequent article. 'Public pensions have effectively socialized an ancient system of within family, inter-generational support. Whether or not they personally have raised any descendants, all Canadians now enjoy a claim on the earnings of the next generation. The notion that we each fund our future pensions through our own contributions is simply a convenient myth, one that is difficult to sustain without a fund.'[34]

By the end of June 1986, the legislation to enact the deal, Bill C-116, had cleared Parliament, and the new provisions – the higher contribution rates and enhanced benefits – went into effect 1 January 1987. As a front-line issue for the politicians, the CPP went back into hibernation.

At the same time, there was a sense of unfinished business. 'In pensions, sooner is always better,' the Ontario official said. The experts who ran the numbers knew that higher rates now always generated lower rates later. The provinces would have supported a steeper schedule of rate increases, he said, but this was the most that Wilson and the federal government would accept. They would simply have to return to the question another day. 'There was no sense at the time of having "done it,"' the former Alberta official said. 'These policy issues never go away.'

5 Finance Takes Over the File

Once more, the CPP disappeared from public view, but the officials kept plugging away. In Ottawa, a new dynamic was developing in terms of who controlled the plan. Before 1987, the National Health and Welfare Department (NHW) took care of the benefit side – running the day-to-day administration of the plan and examining new policy proposals, which usually involved improved benefits – while the Finance Department took care of the financing side. Now that financing had emerged as a more important concern, Finance began looking more closely at the benefit changes. As Réal Bouchard recalls, there was a growing recognition that the benefit and financing sides of the CPP were not integrated.[1]

Beginning in 1987, a federal–provincial working group carried out a thorough review of the CPP's survivor benefits. It was led by NHW, working with provincial social services departments, but in many provinces, Finance Department officials began to play a key role. Gradually, the Finance officials – who were mainly concerned with financing issues – shunted the social services departments into a secondary role; the same trend was soon evident in Ottawa as well. By the early 1990s, the people on the federal–provincial survivors' committee were the same as the people on the financing committee. Very little came of the review of survivors' benefits, but by the time of the next five-year review of CPP financing, in 1990 and 1991, the two streams – benefits and financing – had merged almost completely. The working group headed by NHW disappeared, and Finance, no longer willing to make benefit decisions in isolation from financing issues, took over.

This shift in bureaucratic influence had been building for some time. Ken Battle and Sherri Torjman,[2] in a 1995 paper whose title featured an apt bit of wordplay (*How Finance Re-Formed Social Policy*), argued that 'the ascendancy of the Minister of Finance and his officials in social policy' was a key development during Michael Wilson's stint as finance minister from late 1984 to early 1991. 'Traditionally, power over federal social policy had been shared between the Ministers of Health and Welfare, and Finance. This made sense, since social programs constitute a large – and growing – portion of federal spending. However, the influence of the Department of Finance increased during the 1970s ... During the Wilson era, Finance came to rule decisively over social policy-making, outflanking and overshadowing Health and Welfare.'[3]

One reason, according to a former federal official who specialized in social policy, was that the income security division was 'weak on pensions' during this period, both when it was lodged in National Health and Welfare and later in Human Resources Development. 'The horses weren't there' in terms of strategic policy analysis. By the mid-1980s, the Finance Department's Réal Bouchard 'knew as much about the CPP as anyone in HRDC. Part of the Finance takeover was the HRDC vacuum.'[4]

Finance was moving on other retirement income issues as well. In the late 1980s and early 1990s, Ottawa changed the rules to provide some rough equity between tax assistance to RPPs, which affected only the members of workplace pension plans, and RRSPs. The latter affected everyone and were especially important for those with no workplace pension plan, a group that included the growing number of self-employed Canadians. It was a key piece of social policy, but because the issue was highly technical, it attracted little attention. One change allowed taxpayers who contributed less than the allowed maximum to their RRSP in one year to carry forward any 'unused room,' as it was called, into later years. The change meant that younger people, who might be buying a house and unable to make the maximum contribution, could preserve their RRSP room until they were better able to afford it.

Several provinces, increasingly jittery about the CPP's finances, had no objection to this shift in power to Finance, which paralleled a similar trend in provincial governments, where social services departments were losing sway. Many provinces were beginning to push hard for a look at CPP financing. They understood the tendency to increase benefits as well as premiums – the same thing happens in the private sector, one former Alberta official said – but it was time for a little more balance. The federal Finance Department 'realized that Health and Welfare officials were not hearing the message that everyone was shouting at them' and finally just grabbed 'all the reins of the CPP. Federal Finance just pushed Health and Welfare aside.'[5]

The Low-Key 1990–1991 Review

In public, at least, the 1990 review went through with remarkable ease. There was none of the nervousness that was reflected in the 1985 booklet, which was full of careful explanations of the need for rate increases and reassurances that the CPP was not going broke. But some participants recall that, in private, the negotiations were somewhat more difficult.

The numbers that mattered were far from comforting. In January 1990, the chief actuary had released his *11th Report* on the CPP, and his projections – based on year-end 1988 CPP data – were decidedly more negative than his previous outlook. His *10th Report*[6] had been based on year-end 1985 data and reflected the new, steeper schedule of contribution rates. The *11th Report* said that if governments followed their twenty-five-year schedule right through to 2011, then the subsequent pace of rate increases would have to quicken substantially. Instead of rising from 7.6 per cent in 2011 to 10.1 per cent in 2020 and 11.65 per cent in 2030, as the *10th Report* had projected using the fifteen-year formula,[7] the actuary was now saying in his *11th Report* that the rate would have to leap to 11.93 per cent in 2020 and 13.62 per cent in 2030.[8]

The *10th Report* had said the fund would reach $128 billion in 2012, equal to 2.3 years of benefits; the *11th* said it would be only $17 billion, or 0.32 years. Two years later, in 2014, it would fall to a low of 0.25 years – a mere three months – 'much below the ratio of 2 which is the aim of the Act.'[9] The actuary had changed a number of his assumptions for the *11th Report*; he scaled back his growth estimates for the earnings on which contributions rested and took account of higher-than-expected early retirement rates, lower mortality, and lower fertility, which would raise costs. Relative to previous assumptions, the new outlook called for fewer workers supporting more seniors over more years as a result of people living longer and retiring earlier. The existing schedule called for what the pension experts referred to in their own shorthand as five 20s and twenty 15s, which is to say five years of annual 0.20 percentage-point increases followed by twenty years of 0.15 percentage-point rises. If ministers did nothing, the actuary's report said, the CPP would need

Danny Pritchard, 'Just checking to see how big it is,' 1991

increases of 57 points a year for the 2012–16 period – *almost quadruple* the 15-point yearly increases of the previous two decades – *plus* further increases of 37 points annually from 2017 through 2021.

It was just the kind of disruptive lurch in rates that the 1985 booklet had worried about. The longer-term outlook was worse too. Instead of stabilizing at around 11.8 per cent in the early 2030s, as spelled out in the *10th Report*, the *11th Report* said the contribution rate would stabilize only when it reached 13.7 per cent. That was more than triple the 4.4 per cent rate that was in effect in 1990 as the governments sat down to talk. Across the board, the chief actuary was projecting contribution rates that were roughly two percentage points higher than previously. It took little imagination for politicians and policymakers to envisage the howls of opposition that would greet their successors in the second decade of the twenty-first century if they allowed that prospect to unfold.

The idea of raising contribution rates once more was not quite as daunting as it had been five years earlier. 'They had been pretty nervous in 1986,' the Ontario official said of the finance ministers, but after twenty years of doing nothing, they had succeeded in making some major changes and been pleasantly surprised 'when we got away with it.' The main response from the public and their political opponents had been praise, not criticism. As they reviewed the actuary's numbers in 1990, they knew the 1987 rate schedule was insufficient for the task, 'but they figured they could go back and do it right this time with little risk. They had a comfort level with making changes.'

Happily, the fifteen-year formula offered a way out. If put into force immediately – that is, beginning in 1992 – governments could bump the contribution rate increases by only 22 points a year – 0.22 percentage points – and escape the actuarial train wreck that was lying just over the horizon. Since they had already scheduled annual increases of 15 points a year, a series of 22-pointers did not look all that damaging. The actuary's projection featured fifteen years of 22-point annual rises, followed by five years of 23-point increases and another five years of 24-point rises. The rate for 2011, the end of the CPP's first twenty-five-year schedule, would be 9.05 per cent rather than the original 7.6 per cent; and in 2016, the end of the new twenty-five-year schedule, the rate would be 10.25 per cent.[10] Over the longer term, the rate would stabilize at around 13.1 per cent.

In the end, the finance ministers did almost exactly that, making only minor tweaks to the rate schedule implied by the fifteen-year formula. Instead of 22-point increases in each of the first fifteen years (1992 through 2006), they endorsed a schedule of five years of 20-point rises, followed by ten years of 25-point increases. The rate in 2006 would be 8.1 per cent rather than the actuary's 7.9 per cent. But for the next ten years (2007 through 2016), they moderated the rise to 20 points a year from the slightly faster pace set out in the actuary's report. In 2016, the contribution rate would be 10.1 per cent, not 10.25 per cent.

Once more, Wilson reassured Canadians that when they were ready to retire, their CPP benefits would be ready for them. 'The important thing is that people, with the decisions that we've agreed on today, can be assured that their pension benefits are secure and that the fund is sound and it's financially able to meet its obligations.'[11] As far as some officials were concerned, the 1991 deal did not constitute a major reform, unlike the previous round that included the first rate increase and the new twenty-five-year schedule. This time, the changes were seen merely as an adjustment to the schedule.

A Notable Omission

But in one key respect, the federal–provincial agreement reached on 28 January 1991 was a very different deal than the previous one – not for what it did, but for what it did not do. Missing was the sugar-coating of major benefit enhancements that had helped the earlier rate increase go down with both the ministers and the public. Aside from a small improvement in benefits for the children of disabled or dead contributors, there was nothing new.

Not that some of those involved in the talks had not tried. At least two provincial officials from the West – both from their respective finance departments – said that, early in the process (probably in early 1990), a team from National Health and Welfare proposed a substantial improvement in survivors' benefits, which had been the subject of much study in the previous few years. Several provinces, already uncomfortable with the finances of the plan as it was, resisted. 'There were some fairly strong views expressed at the time,' one official said. Another recalled the reaction in more colourful terms: 'What planet are you from?' Ontario, Saskatchewan, Alberta, and British Columbia all opposed adding new benefits; 'enough is enough' was the response to even more benefits. Rather, they wanted a higher contribution rate to ensure the financial integrity of the CPP with no further benefits at all. The NHW people, who thought they were proposing 'good social policy,' were shocked, the official said. 'It was an eternal struggle between the spenders and those who recognized a problem, who saw that unless changes were made, the financing would lead to the demise of the CPP. We said "no more of this social stuff" and they figured we were the bad guys. That may have been the true beginning of dealing with deficits.'[12]

Indeed, governments from coast to coast were beginning to turn deadly serious in their efforts to control government deficits, which were worsening by the month as the 1990–1 recession killed off jobs and sent the unemployment rate climbing towards 10 per cent. But whatever the portents for the future, the ministers' January 1991 deal appeared once more to have wrenched the CPP onto – or at least closer to – the path of financial integrity. In November 1991 the chief actuary released his *12th Report*, the first to take full stock of the new agreement.[13] In it, he projected that under the new, higher rate schedule, the fund would keep growing fast enough to preserve at least a two-year reserve until 2019, a full two decades later than he had reckoned in his previous report. Beyond 2016, the life of the new twenty-five-year schedule, the contribution rate would have to keep rising beyond 10.1 per cent, but it would top out at 13.2 per cent around 2040 and stay there.

The deal evoked little public comment. Indeed, a scan of newspaper accounts at the time unearths only a handful of routine accounts of the new arrangement and surprisingly little analysis. Perhaps Canadians were simply too preoccupied with what was going on around them at the moment to worry about higher CPP premiums in the future. The recession was almost a year old, jobs were disappearing, the unemployment rate was climbing past 10 per cent, and average personal incomes – adjusted for inflation – had been falling for almost a year. If people wanted to grumble about new levies, the federal government's 7 per cent goods and services tax, which had just gone into effect, was a much more inviting target.

Through 1991, Ottawa wrote the legislation to enact the new rate schedule and introduced it in October as Bill C-39 in Parliament. At the same time, two developments were unfolding that would strongly influence the next review of the CPP. One was all too visible – the recession; the other was evident only to the officials who monitored these things – a rapid increase in the cost of the CPP's disability benefits.

The Disability Explosion

The CPP's provisions for disabled contributors had undergone several changes in the previous few years. The more generous provisions for the disabled that were part of the 1985 agreement went into effect in 1987. Before, a claimant for disability benefits had to have contributed to the CPP in five of the past ten years; now, it was two of the past three years. Before, claims could be made retroactive for twelve months; now, it was fifteen months. Before, the flat-rate component of the disability benefit was $91 a month; now, it was $233.[14]

The federal and provincial governments had endorsed all those changes. Over the next six years, however, the federal government alone – because it administered the CPP – carried out a series of innovations that were 'all in the direction of the liberalization of benefits, rules, supports and services.'[15] A 1988 decision by the Pension Appeals Board, which adjudicated disputes over CPP benefits, opened the door to change. In 1989 Health and Welfare Canada walked through it with directives that recognized, as Ken Battle put it, 'additional disability-engendering conditions such as stress, environmental hypersensitivity and chronic fatigue.' In addition, 'non-medical factors (such as the regional unemployment rate, availability of certain jobs, and applicants' skills) were taken into account for older applicants (aged 55–64) who typically find it harder to find work.' In effect, Battle argued, the CPP disability benefit was now being 'used as a *de facto* method to encourage earlier retirement – a practice also then common in several European countries.'[16]

In 1992, Bill C-57 carried the process further by lifting the time limit on people making late applications for disability benefits. The legislation had originated in a private member's bill whose rationale was 'that many potentially eligible candidates had not applied for the disability benefit because they were unaware that the CPP paid such a benefit.' A year later, the auditor general chided the government for not making the CPP's disability provisions better known. In response, the Department of Human Resources Development Canada – to which income security programs had migrated in a 1993 government reorganization – carried out a major information program to plug the knowledge gap. This led not only to more applications from individuals but to a rise in referrals from provincial government programs like workers' compensation and social assistance and from private insurers as well, 'all of which reassessed their respective caseloads and referred to the CPP any candidates deemed possibly eligible.' Ontario, New Brunswick, and British Columbia made special efforts; Ontario even helped 16,000 people prepare their applications.[17] Provincial governments had a special incentive in that all were struggling with large deficits; any costs they could shuffle off to the CPP would help them with their own finances.

The effect on the CPP's caseload and finances was powerful, but unsurprising. From 1986 to 1994, the number of disability beneficiaries almost doubled from 153,000 to 281,000, and the cost of disability benefits almost quadrupled from $681 million to $2.6 billion. The recession triggered some particularly steep increases in the early 1990s, as many newly unemployed people applied for – and got – disability relief from the CPP. Tellingly, the numbers were very different in Quebec, where there was no possibility of unloading the costs of disability from the books of the provincial government; the QPP's disability caseload was lower in 1994 than it had been in 1986.

The federal government, beginning to worry about its own deficit, moved to stifle the trend. As Ken Battle outlines:

The rapid rise in the caseload in the first half of the 1990s sparked measures to tighten access to the Canada Pension Plan disability benefit.

Administration was sharpened (e.g., regarding reassessments and tracking of clients, administrative data-linking to detect recipients who were
receiving benefits from other programs), tougher guidelines were issued
for determining medical eligibility (including an end to the use of socio-
economic factors), and the appeals system was made more formal and
toughened. Back-to-work efforts were increased. These changes contributed to a decline in the number of Canada Pension Plan disability beneficiaries after 1995.[18]

The CPP Outlook Worsens – Again

In April 1993, the chief actuary – Bernard Dussault now – was back
with another full projection of the CPP's finances. Since it took into
account all hard data up to the end of 1991, this *14th Report*[19] reflected
some of the damage done by the recession. Dussault flagged higher life
expectancy and projected a steeper decline in the account-expenditure
ratio because the recession of the early 1990s resulted in reduced contributions (from lower employment), increased disability payments, and
a higher proportion of people retiring before 65, especially at the age of
60 itself. Still, he said the long-term contribution rate 'is not materially
different than that of the previous report.'[20] The contribution rate
would be somewhat higher – 13.04 per cent in 2030, rather than 12.73
per cent, but the outlook for the two-year reserve was more troubling. It
would not last until 2019, as previously projected, but fall below that
mark in 2003, a mere decade away.[21] The contribution rate, 5 per cent at
the time, was already scheduled to double by 2016 to just over 10 per
cent. It now appeared that a double-digit contribution rate would be
needed well before then.

For those who knew their pension arithmetic, the conclusion was
inescapable. The new contribution rate schedule was barely sixteen
months old, but unless the economy improved sharply and quickly,
governments would be looking at another rate increase beginning in
1997. Twice, Ottawa and the provincial governments had agreed to
steeper contribution rate schedules; twice, they had discovered very
quickly that the new revenues would not be enough to cure the CPP for
the long term.

In two years, the CPP would be back on the front burner, and it was
already evident that yet another new schedule – with even steeper
increases in contributions – would be needed. Governments seemed to
be on a treadmill. They had made two fixes, but no real progress. The

finances of the CPP still needed work. Unless they found something very different this time around, officials and their political masters could expect this pattern to repeat every half-decade. Among the officials, at least, there was a growing mood that the next round should indeed be different.

6 Public Fears, Proposed Solutions

The sense among pension officials that it was time to break the mould and try something different reflected a broader attitudinal change in the country. The public – at least the public that understood something about pensions – was stirring to the idea that the CPP needed a thorough repair job. And some were beginning to suggest that reforms should go well beyond simple contribution rate increases to more radical alternatives.

Beginning in 1992, just after the latest rate schedule had gone into effect, Canadians were increasingly treated to studies, reports, newspaper stories, and magazine articles that articulated their growing anxiety over the recession, falling incomes, government deficits and debt, high government spending, high taxes, politicians in general, and the apparently shaky outlook for financial security in their retirement years. The drumbeat continued right through until 1995, when governments settled down, as scheduled, for their next review of the CPP.

For the young – and indeed many older people as well – the world of work, the work they needed not just for current income but for future pension rights, had taken a turn for the worse. Not only was the unemployment rate higher, but average spells of unemployment were longer as well – eighteen weeks in 1989 compared with fifteen weeks in 1980.

The structure of the labour market has changed as well. The available work is being polarized increasingly into 'good jobs' and 'bad jobs.' 'Good jobs' refer to high-skilled employment that pays decent wages and provides benefits, such as pensions or disability insurance. 'Bad jobs,' by contrast, pay low wages and have few associated benefits, such as employer-sponsored pensions, and health and dental plans. The growth of bad jobs is not the only problem. It has been accompanied by a rise in 'non-standard employment.' Many new jobs are part-time, term, casual or contractual in nature. Even former full-time jobs are being converted to non-standard work. Both good jobs and bad jobs are assuming non-standard forms.[1]

'Good jobs, bad jobs' entered the lexicon of economic and social policy debate, as did another phrase – Generation X, from Douglas Coupland's 1991 novel of that name. They were the generation that reached adulthood in the late 1980s, only to find themselves facing a more insecure job market and much bleaker economic prospects than their parents. The boomers, following a generation thinned out by depression and war, had joined a welcoming labour market eager for new hands and minds. The Gen-Xers entered a labour market already filled with boomers, still relatively young, holding down the best spots and likely to stay put for decades to come.

'Are Pensions Safe?'

The opening volley of the new pension debate arrived in a March 1992 *Maclean's* magazine article with the ominous heading: 'Are Pensions Safe?: Why Canadians cannot count on government to secure a golden retirement.'[2] Coupland's Gen-Xers featured prominently. A 24-year-old business student in Halifax had been saving for retirement since he was 20 because 'I don't even think about the CPP being there when I retire.' A mutual fund executive figured government retirement benefits would one day be taxed back from all but the very poorest: 'The system is bankrupt. Nobody under 30 today will ever collect Old Age Security and CPP benefits unless they are destitute.' The possibility of intergenerational conflict was raised by a 20-year-old microbiology student in Vancouver: 'I don't think there will be an anti-CPP revolt. But if things don't change, will my generation refuse to pay their taxes?' It quoted an actuary who noted that anyone born in 1920 who retired in 1985 would get back $7 in benefits for every $1 contributed, while someone born in 2000 could expect no more than 80 cents on the dollar.

Two months later, an article in the *Ottawa Citizen* posed the question, 'Can you afford to retire?'[3] and the answer was clearly 'no.' Baby boomers with no occupational pension plan or tax-sheltered Registered Retirement Savings Plan (RRSP) 'could face destitution.' And since that description fit six of ten Canadians, the prospects looked dire. Solutions offered by the experts to the specific problem of the CPP ranged from the National Council of Welfare's proposal for an even more generous CPP financed by much higher premiums to the Fraser Institute's suggestion to limit benefits to those most in need.

Articles of this nature continued to appear through 1993 and 1994, enriched by periodic public opinion surveys that chronicled Canadians' attitudes to retirement income and pensions. The first two months of any year were (and remain) a popular season for such polls. Typically, the surveys were commissioned by financial institutions that wanted their existing clients – and any new clients whose attention they could attract – to invest in an RRSP. Tax rules allow people to add money to an RRSP in the first sixty days of the new year and claim a tax credit on the contribution when they calculate their previous year's taxes. Opinion surveys were part of the January-February marketing effort and usually probed Canadians' fears and hopes for their financial future.

In January 1993, one such survey found that only 29 per cent thought the CPP would be available to everyone when they retired, while 88 per cent – a huge-looking figure – thought they could not depend on government for adequate retirement support.[4] The first revealed the extent of Canadians' worries that the CPP was in deep trouble, but it is difficult to figure out what to make of the second finding. The CPP has never promised to replace more than 25 per cent of a person's pre-retirement earnings, while Old Age Security, for a person with an average income, might replace another 15 per cent. Governments had never promised to replace more than about 40 per cent of income in total, a sum no one regarded as 'adequate income support.' This was deliberate; governments wanted to retain incentives for Canadians to do some of their own retirement saving. So it was not clear if the 88 per cent were truly fearful or were simply agreeing to a truism – that if they wanted an 'adequate' retirement income, usually defined as about two-thirds of pre-retirement income, they had to save in other ways too. Still, over half of those surveyed worried they would not be financially self-sufficient in retirement – worried enough, the financial institutions hoped, to invest in the RRSPs offered by those same institutions.

Such polling data would not have surprised anyone in the federal government, which had been commissioning its own surveys. According to one done for the Department of Health and Welfare, almost every Canadian had heard of the CPP, but 'only 13 percent of Canadians

Brian Gable, 'Pension mirage,' 12 April 1993

believe it will be available to all Canadians in the future; 50 percent of the respondents believe it will be limited at some point and 28 percent believe it will not exist at all.'[5]

Some of the fears exposed by the surveys were justified. In March, Statistics Canada released a study[6] showing that one-third of those aged 45 to 64 in 1991 – the generation then facing imminent retirement – were running out of time to get their finances in order. Two-thirds had 'reasonably solid financial security' based on mortgage-free homes, RRSPs, and private pension plans, but for the rest, 'their "golden years" may be tarnished.'[7] Canadians were also seeing hard evidence of just how dreary the 1970s and 1980s had been for their own finances. Another StatsCan report reviewing seven decades of wage changes – from 1920 to 1990 – revealed that the latest two decades had been the worst of the seven. Average real wages – actual wages adjusted for the effects of inflation – had grown by 42 per cent in the 1950s and 37 per cent in the 1960s, but the advance had slipped to 8.5 per cent in the 1970s and a scant 2 per cent in the 1980s, when men's wages actually fell slightly. Even during the 'dirty thirties' of the Great Depression, wages had grown faster – by 10 per cent.[8]

Reminders and Warnings

StatsCan had a sharper warning for policymakers involved in health and pensions. The population aged 65 and older would double by 2036,[9] and without a major restructuring of government programs, both the public pension and health care systems could buckle under the load.[10] The report, designed as 'a reminder' and planning aid for policymakers and individuals alike, was an unusually pointed lesson in demographics. 'The aging of the population is a slow and unobtrusive process, the consequences of which can be formidable for those taken unaware and for those who only recognize the seriousness of events after they have come to pass,' the report said.

It too raised the possibility of intergenerational conflict, to the point of suggesting, none too subtly, that the boomer generation – because it did not have enough children – might be to blame for a future in which the young reneged on support for the old. 'After being hampered in entering the job market by their numerous elders, will tomorrow's workers be able to honour the generous social and political contracts consented to by their parents at a time of rapid population growth – a growth, furthermore, which they themselves interrupted through a much lower fertility schedule?' The CPP's PAYGO nature was based on a formula that required wage earners to support the retired at all times. 'There is some doubt as to whether the formula can remain operational. The sustainment of retirees by wage earners won't be possible without, at the very least, a careful and thorough rearrangement of policies.'

That warning was reinforced by David Dodge, the federal deputy minister of finance, in a speech to the Canadian Association for Business Economics in Ottawa in May 1993. At this point, a federal election was at most six months away. Dodge said the public pension system, including Old Age Security and the CPP, needed reform if it was to remain sustainable, and the reforms must start after the election.[11] 'We can maintain the system today, but the problem is [that] it doesn't look very good when you get out 20-odd years,' he told reporters after the speech. 'It doesn't look very sustainable.' Without changes to the CPP, workers might be paying almost triple the current rate in CPP premiums within twenty years. 'That's a big problem,' he said, adding that workers would never voluntarily join a pension plan with rates that high. He also floated another idea that had a wide following – raising the normal retirement age from 65 to 67.[12]

Provincial finance ministers and their officials had heard this before from Dodge at federal–provincial ministers' meetings after he took over as deputy minister in the summer of 1992. At one meeting, as a former Ontario official[13] recalls with admiration, ministers had been arguing over an agenda item when Dodge observed that it was small beans when compared with the really important long-term issues facing all governments. Dodge, this official remembers, almost 'hijacked' the meeting for two hours, during which he delivered a wide-ranging, university-style lecture laying out the major challenges ahead that were just over the horizon: fixing the CPP, dealing with Native land claims, and paying for health care costs after the baby boomers retired. His essential message was: 'These are huge things coming at us reasonably fast and if we don't turn our minds to them, they'll kill us.' A senior official from another province, though he does not recall this specific episode, says it was not out of character. 'David delivered more than one lecture to ministers and certainly he raised the CPP issue, and the general issue of aging demographics for nation's finances, while Maz [Donald Mazankowski] was still minister [of finance] and long before the 1995 actuarial report.'[14]

A Proposal with Legs

Clearly, a public debate over the future of the Canada Pension Plan had begun in earnest. However, a pension party is never complete until the actuaries show up, which they did during the fall of 1993. As the actuaries began to publicize the issues and lay out their views, the discussion that would occupy policymakers, private sector experts, interest groups, and the public over the next four years began to take shape. Like most good contests in the marketplace of ideas and public policy, the CPP debate of the 1990s involved assembling a factual foundation, analysing the strength and weaknesses of the CPP, promulgating long-held views, developing new solutions, and indulging in no little amount of myth-busting.

First up was, unusually, the Metropolitan Toronto Board of Trade, whose employee benefits committee, chaired by actuary Ian Markham, had been studying the CPP. In late September 1993, the board fired off a letter to Bernard Valcourt, human resources development minister in the cabinet of Prime Minister Kim Campbell, whose new, and short-lived, government was fighting the election campaign that reduced her

Progressive Conservative party to two seats in the House of Commons only a month later. It is likely that Valcourt never even saw the letter, which – when the politicians returned to Ottawa from the campaign trail – would have awaited his successor, Lloyd Axworthy.

The board of trade's warning was familiar: if the CPP were to remain viable for future generations, it needed reforming now. Otherwise, Markham told *The Globe and Mail*, 'at some stage in the future somebody is going to start saying "To hell with this, we won't pay these big pensions to our parents."'[15] The group made three suggestions. First, raise the retirement age from 65, though it did not propose a number. Second, levy the CPP contribution rate on the entire average wage, then $33,400 annually, rather than only 90 per cent of it. (The first $3,300 was exempt, which helped very-low-income earners.) Third, put a limit on the automatic indexing of CPP benefits to the consumer price index. If those three ideas wouldn't fly, there was a fourth, fallback, proposal: 'Speed up the increases in contribution rates for the next 10 to 15 years to put more money in the CPP kitty and then invest the money the way a private pension fund would.'

In retrospect, the letter is almost spookily prescient. The first three ideas were indeed found wanting by governments when they turned to the issue in 1995, but the fourth was adopted in almost exactly the form suggested by the board of trade. The idea of a bigger CPP fund invested in the financial markets rather than lent to the provinces had doubtless been drifting around for some time at this point, but the board's letter appears to have been the first time it was raised in public.

Educating the Public

In addition to suggesting how the politicians could fix the CPP, however, the actuarial community performed another valuable service – that of public education. It was all too easy for the debate to veer in the direction of apocalyptic talk, and it was often the actuaries who restored balance by injecting some realistic analysis that neither understated the problems nor overstated the perils.

The Canadian Institute of Actuaries (CIA), the actuaries' national organization, joined in two months later, in November 1993, when it released the report of a task force on the future of the CPP. At their press conference, Christopher (Kit) Moore and Rob Brown, both former presidents of the institute, wasted no time in dealing with what they regarded as the public's three main fears about the CPP.[16] The first was that the CPP was going broke. Not so, said Brown; the real question was how much more future workers would willingly pay to finance benefits for a growing population of retirees. The second fear was that the government might 'claw back' future CPP benefits as it was doing with Old Age Security benefits to upper-income recipients. Highly unlikely, Moore said; the OAS was financed from general tax revenues, while the CPP was a contributory plan with an account for each person. Clawing back benefits through special personal income tax provisions would be 'entirely inconsistent' with pension philosophy. The third fear was that Canadians could not or would not pay the sums needed to keep the CPP. Brown said several 'relatively small but important modifications' could prevent too rapid or great an escalation in contribution rates. The contribution rate, then 5 per cent of covered earnings and scheduled to double by 2016, was heading towards 13.25 per cent by 2035 (consistent with the chief actuary's *14th Report*), but the task force said three changes could cut that substantially.

First, push the normal retirement age to 70 over the next two or three decades, a change that would also cut the cost of Old Age Security and other support programs. People could still collect at an earlier age, but with lower benefits, a prospect that would encourage them to save more on their own. This proposal would, they acknowledged, be a 'tough sell' at a time when the recession was pushing thousands into early retirement, but they foresaw a trend towards later retirement taking hold when employers would be struggling to fill all the jobs held by aging baby boomers. That one change would knock three full percentage points off the projected 2040 rate. (If the new retirement age were applied to OAS and GIS benefits as well, the federal government would save a further amount equal to about 1 per cent of all industrial wages. That would not affect CPP financing.)

Second, eliminate the basic $3,300 exemption and levy CPP premiums on all covered earnings. True, the task force noted, the additional $165 in premiums would hit lower-income workers harder, but in the long term it would make them eligible for higher benefits. Someone earning $3,400 or just over the minimum, it noted, would contribute based on $100 of earnings but earn benefits based on $3,400 of earnings, while someone earning $3,200 or just under the minimum would make no contributions and earn no benefits.[17] Eliminating the exemption would reduce the 2040 rate by another two percentage points.

Third, change the general drop-out provision, under which 15 per cent of a contributor's lowest-earning years are not counted in calculating retirement benefits. The provision meant that some people could get full benefits after working for only 35.7 years rather than the 42 years they would need in the absence of the drop-out. The task force suggested full benefits should be available only to people who had worked and contributed for at least 40 years. That would take another 0.5 points off the 2040 rate.

The CIA task force made a fourth proposal, but did not attach a value to it. It suggested cutting the survivors' benefits that then accounted for 14 per cent of all CPP outlays. Brown explained to the media that those benefits were rooted in the 1960s family, which had only one breadwinner and more children than the typical family of the 1990s. To understand why this idea held so little appeal to politicians, you merely have to remember that 'survivors' is another way of saying 'widows and orphans.' And while the bill for widows indeed amounted to only 14 per cent of all benefits paid (their dependent children brought the total to 16 per cent), they also accounted for almost one-quarter[18] of all the people getting CPP benefits of one kind or another. No politician was likely to risk reducing benefits for 765,000 widows and orphans, no matter how dire the CPP's finances were.

Finally, the CIA rejected the idea of turning the CPP into a private-sector-style pre-funded pension plan. 'Fully funded public plans have seldom proven successful. In fact, fully funded plans' susceptibility to inflation destroyed a number of such European plans during the first half of this century. In most cases, government control of such large amounts of capital accumulating under fully funded plans has also proven to be a major area of concern.'[19]

Not only would a fully funded plan require a startling increase in contribution rates soon, but it would lead to rising pressure for more benefits. Besides, the provincial governments could just use the money to increase their own spending and run ever-larger deficits.[20] That latter point underlines a reality of the day. Canadians were not just turning against big deficits by all governments; they were also growing chary of instruments like loans from the CPP that made it easier and cheaper for governments to run deficits.

The CIA team had a final word for those who were growing sceptical of the CPP itself and beginning to endorse the path taken by some countries of winding down or limiting national defined benefit pension plans like the CPP in favour of mandatory personal accounts similar to Canadians RRSPs. Don't forget the CPP's four big advantages, they said: almost all workers are covered; benefits are portable from job to job and province to province; benefits are protected against inflation; and the cost of running the plan is low.

A few weeks after that report, Statistics Canada underlined the CIA's argument that raising the retirement age would be a tough sell because the recession had forced so many people into retirement well before they had planned. In a short study, StatsCan compared early retirements during the recession (1990–2) with those in the previous three years (1987–9).[21] Between those two periods, the number of people who retired earlier than planned increased by 10 per cent, from 190,000 to 211,000. But the number who retired for economic reasons (layoffs, company closings, or the offer of an early retirement plan or incentive) shot up by 63 per cent, from 54,000 to 88,000. The number retiring because of illness or other reasons actually fell between the two periods from 137,000 to 123,000.[22] 'Economic' early retirees had accounted for 28 per cent of the total when the economy was strong, but 42 per cent during the recession. 'Freedom 55,' a notion popularized by a major life insurance company as the goal of its savings plans for individuals, was attractive as long as it was voluntary and came with financial security. But in the first half of the 1990s, early retirement was more associated not with freedom but with an involuntary and financially insecure straitjacket.

In the same publication, StatsCan published an interview with Laurence E. Coward, widely regarded as one of Canada's most influential pension thinkers. Coward waded into the question of whether or not future generations would balk at paying substantially higher premiums to support the CPP, an issue that would receive much attention in the next few years. 'In *The Prince*, Machiavelli said that the public could stand any burden or hardship so long as it was imposed gradually. We are subject to high rates of taxation and contributions for benefits, far beyond what would possibly have been acceptable 30 years ago. The price of our security may go higher still. But since it comes in slowly, we grin and bear it.'[23] Machiavelli aside, Coward said the CPP would have to reduce costs, and the most painless route lay in raising the retirement age at which people would get full benefits. A decade earlier, the United States had done just that – lifting the age from 65 to 67 in a delayed and very long transition period that would begin in 2000 and continue until 2027. There would, he said, be pressure for a similar move in Canada.

Kill the CPP?

All those players were talking about how to repair the creaking CPP. But now another argument was popping up: the CPP should be killed altogether. In an editorial, *The Globe and Mail* asked why the government should be planning Canadians' retirement at all. Providing for the very poorest through the Guaranteed Income Supplement was acceptable, but Old Age Security and the Canada Pension Plan were not. 'The premise behind the OAS and CPP – that the government must force Canadians to save for their own retirement – is a paternalism we have surely outgrown ... Rather than try to hold these programs together with safety-pins, maybe it would be better to scrap them outright, plough part of the proceeds into an enriched GIS, and give the rest back to Canadians, to save and invest as they see fit. Maybe it's time to privatize pensions.'[24]

Seniors, who knew a threat when they saw it, responded. Two weeks later, *The Globe* published a rejoinder from Jean Woodsworth and Andrew Aitkens, of One Voice, a seniors' organization. Their comments focused on the OAS but applied equally to the CPP. Seniors had paid taxes all their lives with the understanding that they would get their OAS benefits when eligible, they wrote. 'We planned our retirement around them; our company pensions were negotiated around them. And we expected our children and grandchildren would eventually benefit from them as well ... It is unfair and heartless to change the rules when seniors have practically no flexibility to change their income sources.'[25] That, in turn, prompted a letter to the editor from Toronto actuary Frederick J. Thompson, who said the 'profligate spending' of the older generation had left behind 'a national debt that is at an obscene level ... Unfortunately, we seem to be rapidly approaching a time when ... succeeding generations must say: "Sorry, you are on your own."'[26] Canadians were suddenly getting a whiff of intergenerational conflict and it was not pretty.

The Globe wasn't finished with its frontal attack on the very existence of the CPP. Editorial writer Andrew Coyne returned to this theme in August 1994 with a four-part 8,000-word series that trashed the federal and provincial governments for running a plan that charged too little, offered too much, gave away the CPP fund to the provinces as a government 'slush fund ... a private no-questions asked line of credit that saves them the bother of facing either their legislatures or the capital markets,' and in the process, ran up an unfunded liability of $656 billion (according to figures from the Fraser Institute, which included the QPP), a figure almost the equal of the national debt.[27] 'Had the first generation of contributors paid a higher rate,' Coyne continued, 'had they not lavished more and richer benefits on themselves, had the surpluses in the CPP fund not been squandered on the provinces, the plan would not now be in deficit, and we would not now be facing 50 years of rising taxes.'[28]

So much for the spirit that imbued the CPP debates of the 1960s, with its concern for the generation that had endured depression and war. All that mattered now was the future and the punitively high contribution rates that younger Canadians would have to pay to make up for the errors or the greed – or both – of their elders. In place of the CPP, Coyne proposed a system of basic income support at a modest level for the poor, a kind of seniors' guaranteed annual income. Anyone who wanted more would be encouraged to save additional funds both through their workplace pension plans and through RRSPs that would set much higher limits on annual contributions. Individuals would make their own investment decisions and live with the consequences.[29]

Newspapers west and east picked up on the idea of what became known as super-RRSPs to replace the CPP; everyone would have to contribute to a private savings plan approved by the government. The Vancouver *Province* approvingly cited an article in *The Economist* that 'makes a strong case for mandatory private pensions,'[30] while the Halifax *Daily News* carried a commentary on the 'scandalous mess' of the CPP. 'The people will not allow the government to take 14 per cent of salary to perpetuate a doomed Ponzi scheme.' Dismantle both the OAS and the CPP, it said. 'Model social security on the brilliant RRSP system.'[31]

The 'Aging Paper'

As the public debate heated up, the federal government was gearing up for some real action. Little had been accomplished – or even initiated – during the final two years of the Progressive Conservative government. As its popularity sagged during the recession, it spun out its term almost to the maximum five years hoping its political fortunes would turn. Now, the new Liberal government of Jean Chrétien, which took office in November 1993, was preparing to review all social policies. Much of that responsibility came under Lloyd Axworthy, the minister

Alan King, 'Oops, sorry,' 1 May 1994

of human resources development (HRD), but the CPP fell to the minister of finance, Paul Martin. In his first budget on 22 February 1994, Martin promised 'a paper that looks at what an aging society will need in terms of services and what changes are required to the public pension system to ensure that it is affordable.' The review would take in the CPP, OAS, private pension plans, and RRSPs; Finance and HRD would jointly prepare a discussion paper that would be published by summer and followed by public hearings.

Almost immediately, Axworthy fanned the flames of the intergenerational fairness debate with an unwise answer to a reporter's question. Asked to elaborate on the upcoming review, he said pension costs would rise dramatically and the government faced a key question: Should it use its limited funds to maintain the pension levels of those about to retire or reallocate some of the money into creating jobs for the young? Within twenty-four hours, he was being attacked by seniors' groups for 'pitting the older generation against the younger generation.'[32] The Liberals, like Mulroney almost a decade earlier, were learning not to mess with seniors.

Summer arrived, but no paper on aging, which was by then due for publication in the fall. Then it was expected in time for the February 1995 budget, then in the fall of 1995. In the end, it never appeared at all, and even today some people still wonder what happened to that paper. Social policy got reviewed all right, but the aging paper disappeared along the way. Axworthy focused on the social programs directly under his control, notably unemployment insurance, and in October 1994 produced a discussion paper on social security. It explicitly noted that the OAS, GIS, CPP, and health care were 'outside the scope of this review.'[33] His job was to promote a more knowledgeable and skilled workforce to enhance Canada's competitiveness, income support for the neediest, and a social security system that was both affordable and efficient. Everything else stayed with Finance, which was quietly working on an overhaul of the OAS and GIS that it called the Seniors Benefit. One former HRD official, who had been assigned to work on the aging paper, recalls hearing in December 1994 that the new benefit would be in the 1995 budget. 'Finance had written off the aging paper,' he said, and since 'Finance had all the power,' that was the end of it. As noted in chapter 2, Martin could not win Chrétien's approval for the Seniors Benefit that time around, but it appeared in the 1996 budget.

The aging issue was now on two distinct tracks – one that would carry reforms to the OAS and GIS through a new Seniors Benefit and a second that would carry the CPP review. Ottawa would do the first on its own. The federal–provincial overhaul of the CPP, wherever it went, would not be weighed down by any baggage that might come from being linked to other reforms that were purely matters of federal jurisdiction.

A Global Affair[34]

Pension issues were not just a Canadian preoccupation. Around the world, pressure to reform retirement income programs had increased in many countries, a trend driven mainly by shifting demographics. In October 1994, the World Bank issued a seminal report, *Averting the Old Age Crisis*,[35] that attracted much attention. The massive study, the result of a two-year research project, argued that redistribution, savings, and insurance should be the main goals of retirement income policy.

Its analysis was largely based on developing countries – its direct clientele – but its prescriptions were offered more broadly. Canada's demographic trends were much the same as those in the rest of the world. The number of retired people was growing (or would soon be growing) faster than the general population, a result of declining fertility and rising life expectancy, which in turn was a result of advances in medical science. Developing countries had a second problem that Canada had largely gone through already – a weakening of the extended family support systems that had previously been a main source of support for the aged. Urbanization, increased mobility, war, and famine all reinforced that trend as young people left home to work in cities or to fight in wars. Finally, there was a growing recognition that the government-backed pension plans currently in place could not be sustained over the long run.

The World Bank report advocated pension reforms based on three 'pillars' – a publicly financed safety net for the poor; mandatory saving by workers, partly through occupational pension plans, but mainly through individual pension accounts; and voluntary savings. In Canadian terms, the first would be like the Old Age Security program, with its Guaranteed Income Supplement. The second would, in effect, privatize the CPP and QPP, replacing them with compulsory Registered Retirement Savings Plans (RRSPs) and, to a lesser extent, employer-based Registered Pensions Plans (RPPs). The third would be up to the individual. The bank's advice for countries like Canada was first to overhaul the redistribution pillar by raising the retirement age and reducing benefits and then to downsize earnings-based pensions like the CPP gradually while making the transition to mandatory individual savings plans.[36] Chile, which had introduced reforms along these lines in 1980 under the military government of Augusto Pinochet, was the leading example of how such a World Bank–approved pension system could work.

The World Bank report has acquired a curious status in Canada. Even now, it is periodically demonized by those on the left who see it as the intellectual fountainhead of anyone who would tamper with any public pensions. Yet it never had much influence on government policy in Canada. After it was published, the *Averting* report, as it was called, acquired a small base of adherents in Canada, mainly a few conservative think tanks, the Reform Party, and *The Globe and Mail* editorial board. But among federal and provincial policymakers alike, it gained no traction at all. The World Bank model never made it onto any government list of options, and it was barely mentioned in the ensuing public debate over the CPP.

Fans of the World Bank approach often cited Chile as a model to emulate, even though the *Averting* report noted that the administrative cost of its system per member amounted to 2.3 per cent of income per capita, compared with a 0.05 per cent rate for both the Canadian and U.S. systems. In another reference, it said the total administrative costs came to 2.3 per cent of total pension assets.[37] Even so, there were early indications that the reform was delivering on many of its promised benefits. Subsequent reviews have been less favourable. In 2004, *The Economist* reported[38] on a new World Bank study[39] that pension privatization had modestly boosted economic growth by improving labour and capital markets but had left many workers outside the pension system altogether. 'Excessive charges have been a persistent complaint since the earliest days of reform' and plans were subject to political risk from governments that directed pension plans to invest in government bonds; some incurred big losses, as when Argentina's government defaulted on its debts. The World Bank contributed to the 1990s idea that pension privatization would work anywhere, *The Economist* noted, 'so this book is a salutary correction. The uncomfortable truth is that Latin America's pension reforms – like the pensions themselves – were oversold.'[40]

In a 2006 examination of the reforms in Chile and other Latin American countries, Alberto Arenas de Mesa and Carmelo Mesa-Lago concluded that while the reforms helped to develop capital markets in the region, they not only reduced national savings, but after a quarter-century had produced other negative results: 'Administrative costs are high and stagnant; capital returns are fair but declining ... labour-force coverage has declined in all ten countries, and gender and income inequalities have expanded.'[41]

The International Monetary Fund and the Organization for Economic Co-operation and Development (OECD) also turned their attention to pensions during the mid-1990s. In 1996, an IMF study suggested that most countries' public pension systems could cope with population aging by reducing benefits and introducing what it called a sustainable contribution rate. 'By levying a constant projected contribution rate through time – the sustainable contribution rate – this system preserves the compact between the generations that is at the core of a [PAYGO] system, as it distributes equally the burden of meeting pensions across the generations. Advance funding has the further advantage of strengthening fiscal discipline if the publication of regular reports on the actuarial status of the pension system heightens awareness of the future cost implications of today's pension benefit promises.' The study also said the fiscal costs of shifting to a fully funded scheme 'may be very high.' Unless there were other gains – like a stimulus to total saving – 'it may be preferable to fix the [PAYGO] system instead of shifting to a fully funded system.'[42] This idea, as we shall see, had more appeal among Canadian policymakers. The OECD published a series of reports, including one that examined where the public pension plans in twenty OECD countries were heading over the next seventy-five years. (In Canada, the report covered OAS as well as the CPP.) In the G7 group of leading industrial countries, only the United States and Canada seemed well positioned to meet the challenges ahead, mainly because both countries were facing only a moderate rise in pension spending and each had a solid underlying budget position.[43]

In addition to Chile, both Sweden and Britain had reformed their pension systems just before Canada began to move. Each faced its own unique circumstances, but the overriding trend was the same – a shift from defined-benefit to defined-contribution schemes as a way to increase transparency and accountability. Sweden's reform had two major components financed by a contribution equal to 18.5 per cent of earnings, far higher than anyone in Canada was willing to contemplate. Most of that – 16 per cent – was earmarked to pay benefits to those already retired but was also used to calculate each worker's pension on retirement. The other 2.5 per cent of earnings went into an individual premium pension account.

In Britain, reforms to the system were carried out in 1985 and 1995. It consisted of a flat-rate PAYGO basic state pension, which has always been kept low, but supplemented with additional income-tested benefits for the very poor. Superimposed on that is mandatory membership in an earnings-related pension, which can be a state earnings-related plan, an approved occupational scheme, or an individual account. In 2004, Britain was once more in the throes of pension reform, the existing system having been criticized by a review commission as too complex.[44]

Reforms elsewhere were all very well, but retirement income systems are vastly different in almost every country, even though they share some common characteristics and problems. Most countries had a panoply of programs that tried to accomplish the same combination of ends as Canada, but the Canadian system was firmly rooted in its own alphabet soup of retirement income support – the Canada and Quebec Pension Plans (C-QPP); Old Age Security and the Guaranteed Income Supplement (OAS-GIS); and Registered Retirement Savings Plans (RRSPs) for individuals on their own and registered pension plans (RPPs) for the workplace.

The issues may have been similar across borders, but the peculiarities of the Canadian system dictated purely Canadian solutions. There may have been some national pride at work here too – and not just in Ottawa. As one Alberta official put it, 'no one was prepared to believe we had one of the best pension plans in the world.' But almost all the policymakers believed it, and they were ready to fix it as best they could.

7 The Bombshell Report

In early 1995, the federal and provincial officials who monitored the Canada Pension Plan were awaiting the chief actuary's *15th Report*, which would become the basis for their next review of the CPP. They knew it would be grim reading, but even so, it still came as something of a shock when it was released quietly on 24 February 1995, the Friday before Paul Martin's big turnaround budget. For the CPP, it was the proverbial 'straw that broke the camel's back,' according to one federal Finance official.[1]

Bernard Dussault, the chief actuary, wasted little time in getting to his bottom line. Costs had risen so quickly since his previous report that the reserve fund would no longer be equal to 1.65 years worth of benefits in 2016, the final year of the current contribution rate schedule. 'The CPP account would be exhausted by the end of 2015.'[2] If ministers decided to apply the fifteen-year formula beginning in 1997, the contribution rate would have to increase by 0.39 percentage points a year, rather than the scheduled 0.25 points, from 1997 through 2001. The existing rate schedule of a slow progression to a 10.1 per cent rate in 2016 would not be enough; the contribution rate would have to reach 11.8 per cent by then.

'These differences from the previous (fourteenth) report are very significant,' said Dussault in a classic bit of actuarial understatement. Most striking of all in the report was the CPP's astonishing deterioration in a single year. The projections in the *14th Report* for 1992 had been almost dead on, but for 1993, the year-end CPP account had been 'overestimated by $805 million,' a sum equal to almost 2 per cent of the fund. Actual contributions had fallen short of the projection by $427 million while actual expenditures had been $378 million higher.

There were two main reasons for the variance: 'the greater than expected effect of the recession of the early 1990s on employment earnings for 1993 (and hence contributions) and ... higher than expected disability benefits.' In 1993, the number of new CPP disability cases had increased 'at a very high and unforeseen rate' from 1992. 'At the same time, the proportion of CPP disability recipients coming off benefits has been declining steadily since 1988, and the average duration of disability benefits has consequently been gradually increasing.' More ominously for the future, the actuary based his new report on the assumption that this new pattern of disability would be permanent.

'Some Revision'

The twenty-five-year schedule, he concluded in another massive understatement, 'requires some revision.' Some revision, indeed. In remarkably short order, the projections based on the 1992 rate schedule had simply fallen apart. The actuary's new *15th Report* was based on data to the end of 1993, when the new rates had been in place for only two years. The *14th Report*, released a mere twenty-two months earlier, had figured that the CPP fund would keep growing, albeit slowly, as the new, steeper rate schedule kicked in. The *15th* said the fund had contracted in 1993 and was on track to keep declining until it was gone. Not only was the provinces' source of new funds gone, but those governments would have to pay back some of what they had already borrowed.

Unsaid, but known to anyone familiar with public finances, was the brutal fact that some provinces would have trouble paying off those loans. They were already deeply in debt. Collectively, the provinces' net debt amounted to almost $210 billion, or more than 25 per cent of Canada's gross domestic product, about double the 1990 level. The message of the federal government's 1985 booklet, cited earlier, had returned in full force a decade later. Faced with the prospect of paying back their $41 billion in loans over the next two decades, the provinces would now have to either raise taxes or replace their CPP loans with more expensive borrowing on the capital markets. As the 1985 booklet had put it: 'Raising taxes would cut into people's disposable incomes, while borrowing on such a large scale could put upward pressure on interest rates and disrupt capital markets.'[3]

The projection that the fund would be exhausted in 2015 grabbed plenty of public attention, but 2015 was not the key number in the report. That honour went to 14.2 per cent, which became almost a

Brian Gable, 'Pension Fund collapse,' 19 January 1996

touchstone in the debate over the next two years. It was the projected PAYGO rate for 2030, and it compared with just under 13.2 per cent in the previous report.

The PAYGO rate is a shorthand measure of the CPP's costs. It is the cost of the CPP as a percentage of the earnings base – a simple ratio – and it conveys instantly what the plan needs to pay its bills in any given year. The *15th Report* figured that in 1994, contributory earnings, the wages and salaries on which premiums are based, amounted to just over $200 billion, while the total cost of CPP benefits and administration came to $15.38 billion; that gives a PAYGO rate of 7.68 per cent. By 2030, the PAYGO rate would climb to 14.22 per cent, which everyone soon rounded to 14.2 per cent. (See figure 7.1.) Because it became so important in public discussion, and because it was tossed around so sloppily, this 14.2 per cent rate requires a short explanation that readers should keep in mind. It was the projection for the CPP's *cost* in 2030. The projected *contribution rate* for that year was 13.9 per cent, and the 0.3 percentage point shortfall from the 14.2 per cent cost would be paid for out of earnings on the CPP investment fund. In the debate that followed, many participants referred to 14.2 per cent as the projected contribution rate in 2030. The confusion is understandable because 14.2 per cent was also, by coincidence, the projected contribution rate for 2040.[4]

As usual, the chief actuary offered two projections for the fund itself. The first was the do-nothing scenario – which would lead to the empty CPP coffer in 2015 if the federal and provincial governments failed to revise the twenty-five-year schedule in the review they were about to begin. The second scenario was the default projection used in previous reports. If the fifteen-year rule were put into place beginning in 1997, revenue would again exceed spending by 1999 and the CPP's annual accounts would be back in the black. Subsequent annual surpluses meant the fund would begin growing again and there would be enough money to pay the bills until 2100. But for that to work, the contribution rate would have to rise from the current 5.4 per cent to 13.9 per cent in 2030 and 14.2 per cent in 2040.

The Disability Assumption

Strikingly, the assumptions underlying the projections were – with one huge exception – unchanged from the *14th Report*. Inflation, earnings growth, interest rates, the unemployment rate, immigration, and fertil-

Figure 7.1 How the CPP looked in 1995

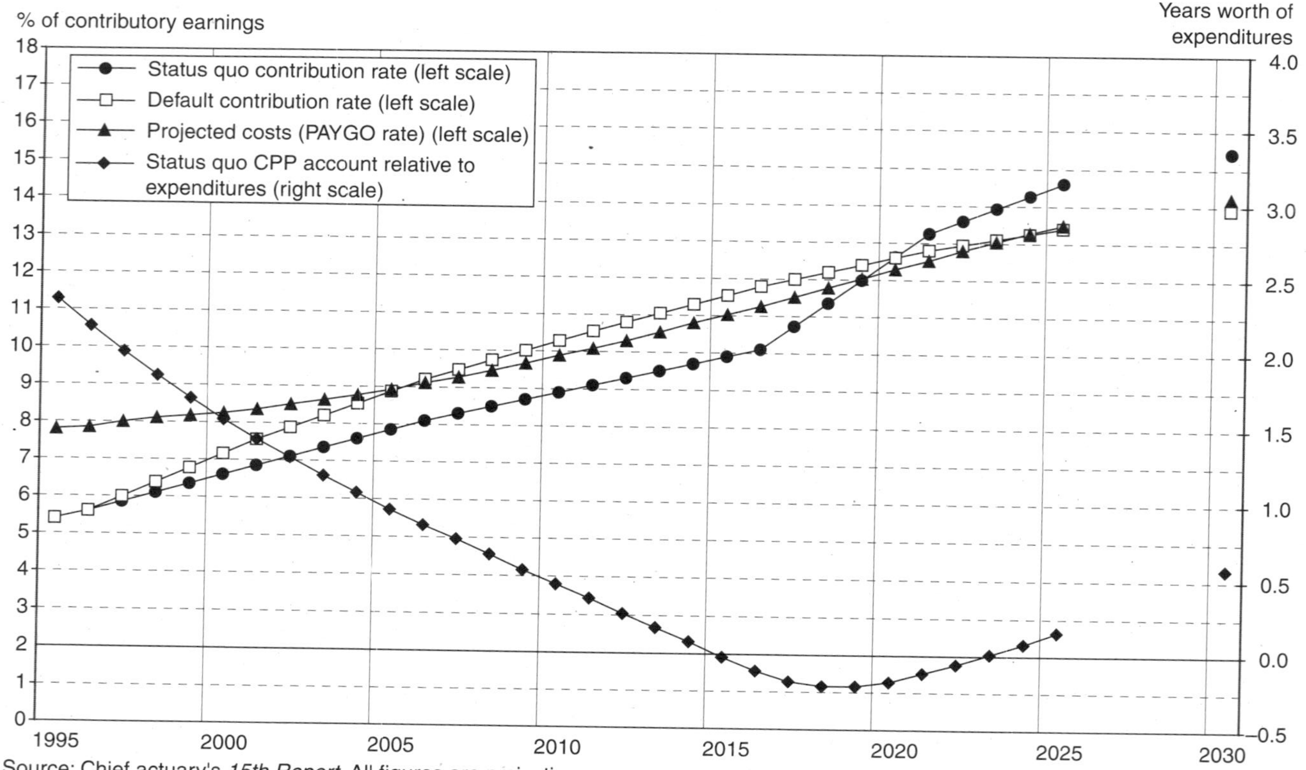

% of contributory earnings

Years worth of expenditures

Legend:
- ●——— Status quo contribution rate (left scale)
- □——— Default contribution rate (left scale)
- ◀——— Projected costs (PAYGO rate) (left scale)
- ◆——— Status quo CPP account relative to expenditures (right scale)

Source: Chief actuary's *15th Report*. All figures are projections.

ity were all assumed to be the same. The exception was disability, where Dussault was now assuming a sharply higher rate of 5.5 disability cases for every 1,000 workers for 2000 and all subsequent years; the rate would be even higher between 1994 and 1999. In his previous report, he had assumed rates of only 4.19 for men and 2.14 for women from 2000 on.[5]

The decision to change the disability assumptions so radically was not taken lightly. Not only had the number of new disability cases (the incidence of disability) been rising since 1980, but the number of people going off disability benefits (termination) had been falling; that meant an increase in the length of time people remained on disability assistance (the duration of disability).

'Our studies of benefits statistics indicate that the observed increases in the incidence of disability over the years are quite uniform by age, sex, province, elapsed duration and cause of disability,' the actuary's report said. 'The CPP disability patterns of both incidence and termination appear to track closely, since 1980, the U.S. experience with its Old Age, Survivor and Disability Insurance program. On the other hand, the Quebec Pension Plan has not shown any corresponding increase in either the incidence or the duration of disability since 1988.'[6] Dussault said he had 'discussed all these findings with relevant officers responsible for the administration of the CPP in the Department of Human Resources Development Canada' and taken account of 'their view that the current levels of disability incidence are not expected to return to their previous levels'[7] in deciding to make the new assumptions.

The importance of the new disability assumptions stands out vividly in a particularly useful table in the report. To help readers understand the differences between the projections of the *14th* and *15th Reports*, the chief actuary included a reconciliation table that bridged the gap between the PAYGO rates in the two reports for selected years. For 2025, to take one example, the PAYGO rate had increased from 12.40 per cent to 13.49 per cent, a difference of 1.09 per cent. Improvements in valuation methodologies, on their own, would have reduced the rate by 0.29 percentage points. An 'experience update,' in which projected values for the most recent years were replaced with actual values, would have reduced the rate by a further 0.12 per cent. The demographic and economic assumptions, mostly unchanged, would generate a reduction of 0.02 percentage points. Together, these items would have *reduced* the 2025 PAYGO rate by 0.43 percentage points. But the new disability assumptions alone *added* a stunning 1.52 percentage points to the 2025 rate. In effect, the disability component of the CPP account was the sole driver of the increase in the PAYGO rate.[8]

Liabilities and Returns

There were more horror stories buried in the actuary's report, for anyone who cared to read that deeply. Two are pertinent. First, the unfunded actuarial liability of the CPP was $487.5 billion as of 31 December 1993, up from the previous report's estimate of $420.4 billion as of 31 December 1991. The liability would keep growing, the actuary said.[9]

Second, the chief actuary provided fodder for the debate over intergenerational fairness by calculating the contributions made and benefits received by different age cohorts. The luckiest were those born in 1911, who would have been 55 in 1966 when the CPP began and could have earned the full CPP retirement pension by making a full decade of contributions – at the old 3.6 per cent contribution rate – before retiring at 65 in 1976. All told, they contributed $107 million to the CPP and drew $5.107 billion in benefits – or $47.70 in benefits for every dollar contributed. For them, the CPP was a spectacular investment, giving them a net internal rate of return on their savings of 31.1 per cent a year.

The returns for subsequent cohorts of Canadians fell steadily. Those born in 1948, around the time the baby boom began, could expect to get back $11.70 in benefits for every dollar contributed, for a 9.0 per cent rate of return. Those born in 1988 or later would get back about $5.40 on the dollar for a return of 5.2 per cent. The actuary did not present the numbers for the real rate of return on contributions, but it was easy enough for anyone to subtract his assumed inflation rate of 3.5 per cent. For the 1988 cohort, youngsters who were still more than a decade away from joining the labour force, the real return ahead of them was a scant 1.7 per cent.

Martin Promises Action

The focus of newspaper headlines on stories reporting the chief actuary's conclusions was inevitable: 'Pension Plan could be exhausted in 20 years';[10] 'Canada Pension Plan going broke';[11] 'Canada Pension Plan can't keep pace';[12] 'Wiped-out pension plan seen by 2016.'[13] Yet the problems of the CPP were overshadowed three days later, on 27 February, when Martin brought down his second budget, the one whose deep spending cuts launched the federal government's remarkably short journey from deficit to surplus over the next three years. The promised aging paper was missing, but Martin signalled his intention to overhaul the Old Age Security program in his next budget and to overhaul the CPP. 'Concerning the CPP, the most recent actuarial report was released last week and it leaves no doubt that we will have to take steps to ensure that that plan continues to be sustainable. This we shall do when we sit down this Fall with the provinces to review the CPP.'[14]

Questioned after the budget, Martin promised not to abandon the elderly, but the issue of how an aging population would affect both the OAS and the CPP was clearly on the front burner. 'We're going to deal with the problem. The problem is one that is growing with every passing year. We're not going to pass on to the next generation the need to deal with a problem that is going to occur in 2001 and 2002.'[15] His horizon might have been a little short, but there was no mistaking his determination, which he repeated in subsequent speeches and interviews.

Four days after his budget, Martin was in New York selling the financial community on Canada's new fiscal direction and promising action on public pensions. The cost of Old Age Security was soaring, and an unreformed CPP would need a substantial increase in premiums. 'And that's not acceptable,' he said. 'The problem does not exist with the current elderly. The sustainability ... is in terms of those people who are middle-aged who will be facing either very heavily increasing premiums over the course of the next 15 years or declining benefits.'[16] Three weeks later, he was in Vancouver on his cross-country tour to promote the budget. 'We've got a big problem with the CPP,' he told a *Vancouver Sun* reporter. 'For 15 years we've known about it and we've sat on our duffs and done nothing. If we don't deal with it in the next three to five years, we've got big trouble.'[17]

The same article in the *Sun* carried a quote from an unnamed 'high-handed' Finance Department official. 'The Parliament of Canada can confer benefits and take them away. I'm not aware of any legal precedent saying this is a binding contractual obligation. Someone had to pay for the generosity of our forefathers.' As for the contributions already made by baby boomers: 'That money has been spent. The money is gone.' The comment was doubtless intended as a mere reminder of the legalities of the CPP and indeed all legislation not covered in the Constitution. But remarkably, it was ignored by critics who worried that the politicians were bent on dismantling the CPP. The critics could easily have portrayed the line as a government threat to withdraw pension benefits in the future or, at the very least, consider such a draconian step.

Some were quite happy to contemplate the end of the CPP, like *The Globe and Mail* and the Reform Party. Shortly after the budget, *The Globe* came out in favour of mandatory RRSPs along the lines of the system introduced in Chile in 1980. Contributions would still be deducted from paycheques but would 'go into your own RRSP, to be invested as you see fit (subject to prudential regulations).' Instead of one big PAYGO pool to pay pensions to the currently retired, 'there would be millions of individual, fully funded plans,' which would 'generate an enormous stream of private savings for productive investment, as it has in Chile.' Even better, 'an RRSP-based plan would also offer substantially better rates of return.'[18] The Reform Party had already been toying with the Chilean model, which would soon become the centrepiece of its own proposals for the CPP.

The Disability Assumption Revisited

The Finance official quoted by *The Vancouver Sun* was not the only news story that could have become a political flashpoint. Another such episode later in the year centred on the chief actuary's assumption that CPP disability rates would remain at a very high level. In mid-September, Southam News reporter Eric Beauchesne wrote a story that raised questions about the entire basis of the gloomier projections in the chief actuary's *15th Report*. His article appeared in at least nine newspapers. The *Calgary Herald* ran the item on its front page under the provocative headline, 'Ottawa hid fact CPP's future is not so grim.' A sub-head drove the point home: 'Disability claims are on the decrease rather than on the rise.'[19]

'The federal government knew the outlook for the Canada Pension Plan was not as grim as claimed when it issued a report early this year that the pension fund was in danger of going bankrupt,' the story said, referring to the actuary's report. 'An unexpected surge in CPP disability payments, which threatened to help drain the fund, had already been reversed, documents obtained under Access to Information and interviews with federal pension officials reveal. But what sounds like good news may not be for a debt-burdened government seeking justification to gut the public pension plan in order to save money.'

That latter highly charged line was questionable. The notion that the government was looking for reasons to 'gut' the CPP would have come as news to the officials who were working to rescue the CPP, and the accounting rationale was simply wrong. Since the CPP is kept in an account entirely separate from the government's public accounts, it had no effect on the government's debt burden whatsoever. In another exaggeration, the story said the report in question had been 'presented by Finance Minister Paul Martin,' creating the impression that Martin himself – rather than the chief actuary – was directly responsible for its contents. However, the article correctly cited the actuary's *15th Report* in blaming higher-than-expected CPP disability claims for the rising long-term costs of the CPP, and it specifically quoted the line that higher disability costs were now assumed to be permanent.

'But only two weeks before that report was released, an internal government memo claimed just the opposite was happening,' the newspaper article continued. It went on:

'Over the next two to three years we can expect a significant downward trend to be exerted on the CPP disability case load and expenditures,' the internal memo stated. 'Finally, you should know that the number of applications appears to have declined significantly over the last six months.' No mention of that contrary finding was included in the report that the government made public or in an accompanying news release. The internal memo offered a variety of explanations for its conclusions that disability claims were falling and would continue to do so. It pointed to more stringent enforcement of eligibility rules, closer scrutiny of existing beneficiaries and initiatives to reduce barriers to employment among the disabled. It noted that other measures to reduce costs were in the works, and the decline in claims, which began in mid-1994, has continued, the author of the memo said in an interview.

The Beauchesne article quoted Pierre Fortier, HRDC's director-general of policy and legislation, as saying 'the numbers are coming down,' so that disability payments over the long term should be 20 per cent less than projected by the actuary. The CPP was still struggling because of population aging, the article continued, but that trend had already been taken into account in making earlier CPP projections and setting contribution rates. 'Rather, it was the unexpected surge in disability payments that sparked fear over how deeply CPP benefits would have to be cut or how high premiums would have to be boosted to keep the fund solvent.' The story acknowledged that disability payments had soared in recent years, 'but the government's decision not to publicize evidence indicating that those payments were in fact declining suggests it may have been looking for justification to introduce measures to cut CPP costs.'

Another HRDC official, quoted near the end of the original story in a passage that most papers did not run, deflected any potential blame away from the government itself. In the view of Wayne Ganim, assistant director of program delivery services, 'it was federal actuaries who wanted more evidence of a reversal in disability pension costs before including it in their report,' the article said.[20] 'If I can't give them concrete information, they're going to go on the most conservative estimate,' he said. But he figured the big increase in disability claims was already over. His 'gut feeling' was that the outlook for the CPP was not as grim as the one set out in the actuarial report.

Dussault fired off letters to the newspapers that carried the article defending himself against the implicit charge that his actuarial report had been tilted to serve some hidden – and quite nefarious – agenda of the government. 'The report was prepared independently by myself and my officials using the most recent available evidence and in accordance with the stringent professional standards of the Canadian Institute of Actuaries,' he wrote, going on to say:

> While officials from the Department of Human Resources Development quoted by Mr. Beauchesne may have honestly believed that evidence existed indicating disability payments were declining, an extensive analysis by my staff reached a different conclusion. A thorough actuarial and statistical study of relevant CPP experience data showed no evidence of such decline. These data showed that over the period 1989 to 1994, the incidence of new disability cases grew by about 50 per cent for men and about 90 per cent for women. The disability assumptions in the actuarial report were appropriately based on this information. I stand by the conclusions I reached. The report shows that CPP projected costs are considerably higher than previously expected. If the existing schedule of contribution rates is not increased and benefits continue as now legislated, the CPP fund is expected to be exhausted by the year 2015.[21]

With hindsight, the disagreement between two arms of the federal government looks like an honest one. The disability numbers were just beginning to turn when HRDC and the chief actuary were preparing their reports in late 1994 and early 1995. In 1993 and 1994, both the number of disability beneficiaries and the cost of benefits increased by more than 30 per cent, but that turned out to be the final gasp of the surge. In June 1995, HRDC official Elizabeth Wills told a conference that in the 1994–5 fiscal year, which ended 31 March 1995, a month after the chief actuary's report was released, there had been 90,000 new applications for disability benefits, down significantly from 110,000 the previous year.[22] 'While it is too early to tell, it is possible that this could be the beginning of another trend,' she said. In recessions, people who have reached the end of Unemployment Insurance benefits often apply for CPP disability benefits. When a recovery begins, the number of applications usually falls. 'We are seeing something we have seen in the past,' she stated. Later data would show that the cost of benefits began to fall in 1995, while the explosion in the number of beneficiaries peaked in 1995 and 1996 at just under 300,000. Both measures remained flat for the rest of the decade.

The government had begun cracking down on disability payments in early 1994 after the auditor general found that between $120 and $220 million had been paid to people who did not deserve benefits, mainly because of ineffective procedures for monitoring the program.[23] By September 1995, HRDC had reassessed 10,000 cases and stopped payments to 4,000 people, for an estimated saving of $40 million. The department was planning to review another 25,000 cases by March 1997, and an official figured one-quarter of those people would be ruled ineligible because they were either capable of working or already had a job.[24]

But though the chief actuary's aggressive disability assumption in the *15th Report* was central to his new projection of the CPP's costs, and though it would form the basis for the CPP reforms to come, the controversy attracted little attention. Neither the opposition parties in Parliament nor the many private sector experts on the CPP picked up on the dispute between HRDC and the actuary. There was plenty of public debate over the CPP during 1995, but none of it questioned the actuarial projections themselves. Beauchesne's story was a one-day wonder.

8 The Outside Debate

In the months following the chief actuary's report, activity on the Canada Pension Plan quickened noticeably. Outside government circles, the media were replete with predictably apocalyptic articles. After all, the government itself had declared a crisis, and there are few things the media like better. It is difficult in ordinary times to grab the attention of the public for a discussion of big public policy issues. This time, however, the CPP mattered: it was in trouble, and the government had declared its intention to act. It was time for the experts to explain and analyse, time for the advocates of different viewpoints to battle out the issues in the media. Throughout 1995, the factions skirmished to define the issues and advance their causes. Inside government circles, a part of the story we will leave to the next chapter, the action was quite different and quite divorced from the noise in the media.

The CPP was something of an also-ran in the great public policy debates of 1995. Far more attention was focused on the federal budget and its aftermath, and all policy questions were overshadowed by Quebec's expected referendum on sovereignty. The Parti Québécois had won a provincial election in September 1994 and under Premier Jacques Parizeau was heading for a vote on the sovereignty question on 30 November 1995.

Even so, the pension debate continued. It would be easy to get an impression from newspaper articles from that year that a higher retirement age was the single biggest solution to the CPP's woes, almost to the exclusion of other possible ways of rescuing the CPP. Raising the retirement age from 65 to 67 over a period of decades – as the United States was already doing – had long been discussed in public by actuaries and in private by federal and provincial officials. Most of them liked the idea. People were retiring earlier, but living longer, so they faced the prospect of basing more years of retirement income on fewer years of earnings and savings. It seemed logical to push the age of eligibility higher, which would add a couple of more years of work and earnings while subtracting a couple of retirement years. The University of Waterloo's Rob Brown noted that if the CPP had adjusted its normal retirement age (and the associated benefits) to account for increases in longevity since 1996, the retirement age would have risen to 68.4 in 1991 and would keep rising – to 69.9 in 2011 and 70.7 in 2031.[1] Such an adjustment would have kept constant the number of years between retirement and death and the number of years in which the CPP paid retirement benefits.

The issue gained visibility in January 1995, when rumours circulated that a higher retirement age would be part of the forthcoming budget. Finance greeted the stories with the usual 'neither confirm nor deny' responses, and HRDC Minister Lloyd Axworthy, while repeating the usual line that existing seniors would not be affected, rather boldly said 'there have been some countries trying it, but our feeling was first that we would like to have a good discussion with Canadians.' Some, of course, took this as a yes. 'Consider it a go,' *The Globe and Mail* noted in an editorial.[2] The idea was vigorously attacked by seniors groups and social policy analysts, one of whom said it would 'boot' the poor onto provincial welfare rolls at 65.[3]

The retirement age issue is difficult to sort out because it was discussed separately in the context of overhauling first the OAS-GIS and then the CPP. Réal Bouchard recalls three streams of policy development. First, the age of entitlement for OAS-GIS benefits was an issue before the 1995 budget but disappeared after that. Second, the government's 1996 proposal for a Seniors Benefit to replace OAS-GIS excluded any reference to the age of entitlement, a fact that reflected its earlier disappearance. But third, the 'normal' retirement age of 65 re-emerged during the CPP debate in 1996, when it was an option that governments held up for public consideration.[4]

Later retirement was a favourite option of academics and officials, but it was loathed by anyone who had to face a voter. In the CPP debate, Quebec and Ontario both opposed it, as did Manitoba. So did Jean Chrétien, though he did not say so publicly. Indeed, the prime minister left the issue open (though it was not clear if he was thinking about OAS-GIS or the CPP, since the government was moving on both fronts during this period) even when challenged by the separatist Bloc Québécois in Parliament during the referendum campaign. In September, Bloc leader Lucien Bouchard accused the government of hiding plans to cut the OAS until after the referendum. Chrétien dismissed the charge as baseless fear-mongering, but aside from promising to protect existing seniors, he carefully foreclosed no other avenues when it came to pension reform.[5] 'We want to ensure that the system is adjusted, not only for this year and next year, but good healthy administration requires that we be in a position to forecast what the situation will be for individuals who reach retirement age in the year 2005 and 2010,' he said. 'If we aren't cautious, then perhaps at that time, retired individuals will no longer have the same (pensions) that people have now.'[6]

Chrétien's caution was typical of the man. He never liked to back himself into a corner on any issue until he was ready to make a final decision. But at some point, he let it be known to his aides that raising the retirement age was just not on, for at least two reasons. According to his long-time senior policy adviser Eddie Goldenberg, Chrétien did not want to mess with seniors, especially in the period around a sovereignty referendum on Quebec. To a greater extent than the young, seniors vote, and in Quebec, 'they vote federalist.'[7] Goldenberg personally favoured raising the retirement age but 'got nowhere' with his boss, whose political instinct was to reject anything that could be portrayed as an attack on existing seniors. 'We did not want to create even an opening for the opposition.' Chaviva Hosek, who worked under Goldenberg as director of policy and research in the Prime Minister's Office, recalls the proposal under consideration – raising the retirement age to 67 over twenty-four years at a rate of one additional month per year – but Chrétien was 'not willing to do that.' A few extra months of work might be easy for educated professionals in offices, she said, but for some people, it would mean extra months of carrying bricks up a ladder. 'We were all nervous about it.'[8]

In the end, it was a non-starter, but in the first year or so after the actuary's report, later retirement became – in the public mind – the single biggest issue in CPP reform.

The Experts Weigh In

There were two particularly useful discussions of aging and the CPP during 1995. One appeared in January, when the Canadian Institute of Actuaries published *Troubled Tomorrows*,[9] a 120-page report that received considerable media coverage. The other came from a one-day conference in early June run by the Caledon Institute of Social Policy and sponsored by Human Resources and Social Development Canada. Billed as a roundtable on the country's aging society and retirement income system, it featured a range of experts on the issues that the federal government had under review. Since it was not covered by the media, it had no impact on public opinion, but Caledon published the papers a year later.[10] Both the CIA and Caledon contributions went well beyond the CPP – the CIA covered all aspects of an aging society, including medicare, and the Caledon conference dealt with all forms of retirement income – but they stand as the year's most thorough canvass of the major issues.

Both began with demographics, and the message might have startled anyone who thought that the aging of Canada's population was a here-and-now problem or that Canadians had suddenly become very old. The opening line of the CIA report put it bluntly: 'Canada is a young country with a young population.'[11] In 1990, only 11.3 per cent of Canadians were over 65, the lowest proportion of any G7 country.[12] The next youngest was Japan at 11.9 per cent, and the oldest was Britain at 15.7 per cent. Population aging 'is neither surprising nor alarming. The process is well understood and essentially irreversible: declining fertility rates, slow population growth, healthier lifestyles, medical advances and longer life expectancies. The transition from a young population to an old one will be gradual – almost imperceptible to those who experience it. But the consequences are profound, and will reshape our society and institutions.'[13]

It was a timely reminder to a country that was paying increasing attention to intergenerational tensions and to the financial strains that the baby boomers would one day put on their children and grandchildren. At the Caledon conference, the lead-off speaker also dealt with demographics, but he shifted attention away from the boomers. 'The real issue is not the proportion of one group but changes in the overall age structure,' demographer Michael Murphy argued.[14] 'The reason we understand aging so well and the reason it is so predictable is that in a modern population it is the fertility rate [the number of children a woman will bear in her life] that, in the long run, determines the age structure. Changes in mortality, change in immigration and even baby booms have only short term and relatively minor effects. The Canadian population is getting older because Canadian fertility is low.'[15] The key

Brian Gable, 'There is no Easter Bunny,' 8 February 1996

fact was that the fertility rate had dropped from 3.63 in the two decades before the CPP was launched in 1966 to 1.65 in the most recent twenty years.

A population's age structure is usually graphed as a triangle in which horizontal bars show the number of people in each age group, with men on the left and women on the right and with the bars arranged top to bottom from oldest to youngest (see figures 8.1a–c). Traditionally, the result has been the familiar pyramid with a handful of old people at the top and increasing numbers going down the age scale to plenty of children at the bottom. That is how Canada looked until 1966; indeed, that is how all societies looked historically, when people had few elders and plenty of children. But in 1991, the widest bulge in Canada's 'pyramid' was not at the bottom but in the middle, where the boomers were in their 30s and 40s. Beneath was the baby-bust generation, forming a much smaller base. By 2031, Murphy emphasized, the pyramid would become a 'vase,' still narrow at the top, then spreading quickly to encompass the boomers, by now in their 70s and 80s, and finally tapering gradually to a slightly smaller base.

'This vase shape is the age structure of modern low-fertility populations,' Murphy said. 'Europe has already experienced the kind of age structure towards which Canada is moving ... The society of the population vase is a different society from that of the population pyramid, but it is not necessarily an unworkable society.'[16] Don't blame the baby boom for the aging population, Murphy said. 'In fact, it delayed the inevitable. Baby booms, like everything else, shall pass away,' he added, and when they do, Canada will be left with an aged population structure caused by low fertility.[17]

The demographic lesson from both the CIA report and the Caledon conference was at once both reassuring and dire: no, the apocalypse is not just around the corner, but yes, we face major problems; Canadians must act to deflect those problems, but there is time to do it properly. Important as it was, that message never truly got through to the broad public. Governments and the media kept up the drumbeat of simple baby-boom numbers – seven workers supporting each senior in 1966, five now, and three in 2030. The arithmetic was easier for politicians, the media, and the public to understand.

A Ruinous Debt Load?

The CIA's *Troubled Tomorrows* report got plenty of attention for its esti-

Figure 8.1a Canada's population: 1966

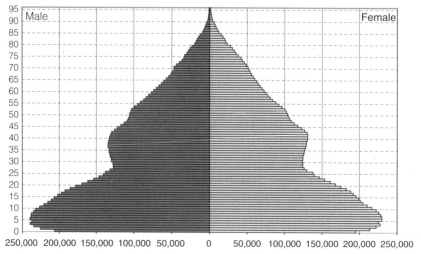

Source: Statistics Canada

Figure 8.1b Canada's population: 1991

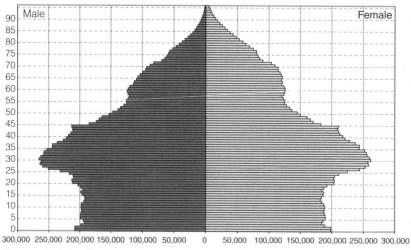

Source: Statistics Canada

Figure 8.1c Canada's population: 2031 (projected)

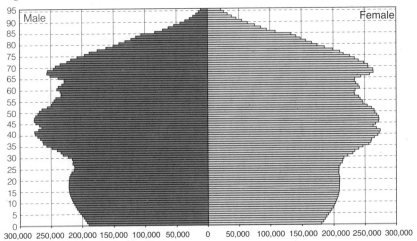

Canada's population structure in 1966 was close to the classic pyramid shape, except for the effects of the Great Depression in the 1930s among those aged 27 to 36, and the first signs of the baby bust began after 1966. In 1991, the baby-boom generation is clearly visible among those ranging in age from their late 20s to early 40s. By 2031, the pyramid will be replaced by what Michael Murphy called a 'vase.'

Source: Statistics Canada, actual data for 1996 and 1991; projection for 2031.

mates of what an aging society might cost Canadians in that still-distant future. The actuaries calculated the unfunded liabilities in 1991 for all of Canada's major programs for the aged – the CPP and QPP, OAS, and medicare – and came up with a figure of more than $1.2 trillion. When they added in the federal and provincial governments' total debt, their estimate of the 'financial burden on future generations' was close to $1.8 trillion, more than two-and-a-half times the country's gross domestic product. 'The debt is, of and by itself, not a problem ... But the cost of carrying the debt is significant – perhaps ruinous to a small generation bequeathed a troubled economy.'[18]

And how might all this be paid for? Numbers in the trillions are almost beyond human comprehension, but no one had trouble with the figures when the CIA translated that future burden into tax rates. Take your choice, the report said: raise personal income taxes by 70 per cent; or quintuple the goods and services tax to 35 per cent from 7 per cent; or increase all payroll taxes by about 17 per cent of pay. 'Apocalypse soon?' read one newspaper headline.[19] As well as crunching the numbers with uncommon authority, the CIA report was unusual and refreshing in another respect – it did not ask anything of the government except that it get moving quickly on the issues so that Canadians would get a better idea of where they stand. 'This is not a lobbying paper. We're trying to elevate the level of debate,' said Malcolm Hamilton, who had chaired the task force writing the report.[20]

At the June Caledon conference, panelists roamed the field of retirement issues almost as widely. Grant Schellenberg of the Canadian Council on Social Development explored the increasingly varied pathways to retirement, some voluntary and some not – like job loss and early retirement incentives. People who retire in their mid- to late 50s might have trouble making ends meet until they qualify for public pensions like CPP and OAS.[21] Bob Baldwin, the Canadian Labour Congress's respected pension expert, noted that the proportion of low-income seniors had fallen to less than 20 per cent from about 30 per cent fifteen years earlier, partly because of 'a significant maturing of the CPP.'[22] He criticized the 'strong pro-market bias' of the current political environment which favoured workplace pensions and personal RRSPs 'that don't work very well for most people.' But he was sanguine about the condition of the CPP: 'I don't see us being in serious trouble.' Many countries had social security contribution rates as high as 20 per cent, and many Canadians paid 15 per cent of their pay for workplace pensions on top of their CPP premiums. Hysteria over double-digit premiums did not appear justified.

'Devastating Consequences'

Monica Townson, a leading pension expert with a left-of-centre tilt, dealt with the question of retirement incomes for women but noted almost wearily that she had been making many of the same arguments since the 1981 National Pensions Conference.[23] Women are disadvantaged for two reasons: they take time out of the paid workforce to bear and raise children, which disrupts their lifetime work pattern; and their earnings are well below those of men, which reduces benefits from their earnings-based pensions, including the CPP. The CPP is the best pension for women because it allows for childrearing time, but even so, it still replaces only one-quarter of pre-retirement earnings, so cutbacks 'would have absolutely devastating consequences for women.' She recognized, though, that there was 'very little public support' for higher benefits. She took a whack at *The Globe and Mail*'s promotion of privatizing the system through mandatory RRSPs in which workers, but not employers, would contribute 10 to 20 per cent of their pay. 'I find the suggestion so outrageous I can hardly treat it seriously. I hope no one is really thinking of that.'

After sessions on RRSPs and OAS, the roundtable got to the issue of financing the CPP. Here the tone changed quickly when Rob Brown spoke. Brown's prominence in the entire CPP debate reflected both his expertise and his communications skills. As a professor of statistics and actuarial science at the University of Waterloo who had published extensively on pension issues and as a former president of the Canadian Institute of Actuaries, Brown had been deeply involved in preparing the CIA's *Troubled Tomorrows* report and its position papers on the CPP. And he was popular with the media, because he could speak clearly, forcefully, and knowledgeably about the complex issues involved.

The Essence of Security

What, he asked, 'is the essence of the *security* of retirement income security?'[24] It was a question few asked, but he had two answers. One was a healthy economy, because in a PAYGO system like the CPP, 'you are essentially talking about transferring wealth and before you can transfer wealth, it has to be created.' Second, people have to believe the promised pension – whether the CPP, OAS, or GIS – will be there when they need it; otherwise, there is no security. All this was attainable, but Canadians needed to prepare for some surprises. More seniors would work in the future, he said, so earnings from work would supplement their income from government-sponsored systems (like OAS/GIS and CPP), employer-sponsored systems (RPPs), and self-directed savings (RRSPs). Higher contribution rates for the CPP were also in the cards because in 1966, the CPP had been based on the demographics of the baby boom, 'which just happened to come to an end' the year the CPP began.

The key financing issue, he said, was the intergenerational question: Will the next generation pay the high contribution rates needed to keep the CPP working? Brown had an impassioned answer:

We have a generation that is the tail of the baby boom and the entire baby bust generation. We have promised ourselves pay-as-you-go pension plans, Old Age Security and prescription drugs. We have loaded this cost on their backs and then [said to them] don't ever whine because we will call you the 'me-generation.' They are not facing all that nice a life. When they entered the labour force, it was tough to find a job. By the time they got to buy a house, the prices had already been booted up by the baby boomers. The interest rates that they are able to earn [on the proceeds] from [selling] their homes are not going to bring the windfall benefits of the previous generations. Their house will not be a retirement nest egg, it may be egg on their face, and now they are worried about whether they can get their social security benefits ... Today, we have been talking about whether we can do more for the elderly. Well, there is a generation out there that doesn't think you have done very much for them, and when you send them the bill, they might just send it back.

To reinforce his point, Brown pulled out an October 1994 Gallup poll result that was widely circulated throughout the CPP debate. The pollster asked people if they were confident that they would receive retirement benefits from the OAS, the CPP, and the QPP. Among those 65 and over, 85 per cent said yes, as did 47 per cent of those aged 50–64. Among those under 50, however, the figures were all under 30 per cent – 29 per cent among those in their 40s, 23 per cent among those in their 30s, and 29 per cent among those 18–29.

Brown took on some other popular notions as well, including fellow actuaries who thought the CPP should have been fully funded from the beginning. First, full funding would increase security only if it raised gross national savings, he said, and the jury was out on that question. Second, the savings generated by full funding would have to be invested in a way that raised national productivity; again, there was no clear evidence that would happen. Some people argued that Canada's dependency ratio – the number of young plus the number of old relative to the number of working-age people – did not matter because the rising number of seniors would be offset by the falling number of children and the total would be no higher than before. 'But this is not the story of public wealth transfer.' Transfers to the young, for things like education, do not equal transfers to the old, for pensions and health care. 'We transfer $2.50 to the elderly for every dollar transferred to the young.'

Go Big?

Brown's tough message aside, the Caledon roundtable was in some ways a last gasp of the Great Pension Debate of fifteen years earlier.

Many of those involved had been talking about retirement income issues for most of the previous two decades, and for them retirement income was a big box with many compartments. They wanted – as they always had – policies to enhance all elements of the system. In the vernacular, many wanted government to go big. The presentations were very good – learned, thoughtful, provocative, and complete. But as far as the governments involved were concerned, much of it was beside the point. They were not at all inclined to go big. They were not out to save the world. As a group of ministers and officials, they simply wanted to put the CPP on a sound financial footing. The federal government was not ignoring other components of retirement income. Finance Canada was working on an overhaul of the OAS and making changes to the rules governing RRSPs, both of which were entirely within federal jurisdiction. Ottawa did not need to consult with provincial governments over those programs. But the CPP was very much a joint program and governments had to act in concert. Whatever their level of interest in broader retirement income issues, they approached the CPP negotiating table with a clear focus on the CPP. What they had in mind was ambitious enough.

Reform's Reform – Chile North

The Reform Party formally jumped into the CPP debate on 11 October 1995 with a plan to scrap the CPP altogether and replace it with a system of mandatory do-it-yourself 'super-RRSPs.' The plan was explicitly modelled on Chile's retirement savings system, launched in 1981 by the dictator Augusto Pinochet after the country's former pension system collapsed. The Reform proposal, unveiled in Toronto by Calgary MP Jan Brown, the party's critic of the Human Resources Development Department, had several strands. Super-RRSPs would be tax-sheltered and government-regulated, but individuals would choose where to invest the money they had contributed. The plan would guarantee all benefits to existing seniors; current contributors, when they retired, could redeem their already-paid premiums with special recognition bonds. Ownership of a super-RRSP could be transferred to the elderly widows of contributors. 'Increases in total investment wealth is the key to our plan,' she said. Canadians 'will no longer depend on the management skills or the financial well-being of the government.'[25]

In a television interview, Brown said 'CPP contributions currently would be moved into this super-RRSP account so that you would have something at the end of your working life upon retirement that would be your own, and it would be an investment that you would be able to draw on in the course of your retirement. And it would give you certainly a level of security that CPP is not going to give you now.'[26] The idea was not new, Brown said. Singapore and Britain had already moved away from a PAYGO system. 'And Chile is really the model on which our program is based. So, we are looking at renewing the Canada Pension Plan.'

The Reform plan was immediately attacked from several sides. Maurizio Bevilacqua, parliamentary secretary to Human Resources Development Minister Lloyd Axworthy, said it would 'place all risks on the backs of individual Canadians.' From the left, François Dumaine of the National Anti-Poverty Organization said that if the government broke away from the CPP's collective risk-sharing in favour of everyone going their own way, 'then those who don't invest wisely (will be penalized).' Brown's concession that CPP contribution rates would probably continue to rise until the CPP was phased out entirely drew fire from the right. Garth Whyte of the Canadian Federation of Independent Business said higher payroll taxes would make Reform's plan difficult for employers to support.[27]

The toughest critique of the Reform plan had actually come more than three weeks earlier. Versions of the proposal had been circulating in September and one fell into the hands of James Daw, the *Toronto Star*'s pension and personal finance columnist. For an analysis of Jan Brown's proposal, Daw called on the University of Waterloo's Rob Brown,[28] who said an obvious disadvantage was that millions of super-RRSP plans would be far more costly to administer than the single CPP, and those additional costs would reduce the eventual benefits.

Rob Brown went much further: replacing the CPP would raise three other absolutely crucial problems, he said. First, the Reform plan failed to deal with the $500 billion in entitlements for which Canadians had already paid. 'If we are going to ask this generation to both save for itself and pay off that liability, then this generation is going to have to pay twice.' Second, Reform's individual RRSPs would have no inflation protection, whereas CPP was fully indexed to the cost of living. 'So we would be throwing the inflation risk on to the shoulders of the individual, rather than passing it across 29 million shoulders as is now the case.' Third, Reform's plan made no provision for any redistribution of wealth, as there was – at least to a modest extent – in the CPP. 'In other words, similar to the Chilean plan, the poor in their working lives would be guaranteed to be poor in their retirement years, and the rich in their working lifetime are guaranteed to be rich in their retirement years.' He challenged Reform to deal with any of the three problems. 'I don't think they have got answers to any of them.' Each problem on its own is crucial. 'The three of them in total are crushing.'

In December, Jan Brown's language had become even more alarmist. 'The system will collapse. It will be unsustainable,' she told the *Calgary Herald*.[29] 'There will be no CPP for anybody. This is not fear mongering. There's a window of opportunity here where we can make some change, but it is closing.' She cited as major problems the CPP's unfunded liability, which the article pegged at $650 billion (the estimate in the chief actuary's *15th Report* was actually $487.5 billion, but the liability was growing fast enough that no one was inclined to quibble with estimates like $650 billion), and the prospect of substantially higher contribution rates. The old, she argued, would suck the CPP dry before the young would even get close to it. 'My own kids have said to me: "Sorry, Mom, don't expect me to pay this ... Don't expect me to take care of the problems your generation created,"' she said. 'Young people will not honor the rules of the game any longer if they see they have this kind of a liability.'

Pension experts were divided on the Reform proposal, their views ranging from 'the cautiously positive to strongly negative,' the *Herald* noted. It turned first to University of Toronto economist James Pesando, a noted pension expert. 'This isn't some sort of flaky idea that one should just dismiss out of hand,' he said. 'Under the Canada Pension Plan as it's currently structured, those people who are currently retired will do extremely well, those people currently 45 to 50 will do okay, and anyone under 25 is going to be screwed ... If I were a spokesperson for 21-year-olds, I'd probably be very anxious for that type of alternative to be honestly aired.' And for the contrary view, the *Herald* went to Rob Brown, who reprised his earlier view that younger workers could not escape the need to pay more for their elders' retirement. 'We now have $650 billion of unfunded promises. Who is going to pay for them?' he asked. 'One generation is going to have to pay twice. If we adopt Reform's plan, they are going to have to pay for their own defined contribution Reform plan and pay off the $650 billion unfunded promise. So if the concern is the next generation paying too high a contribution rate, this (Reform plan) cannot possibly be the solution.'

9 The Reform Takes Shape

While the pension debate swirled outside government circles, the federal and provincial officials who devote large chunks of their careers to thinking about pensions spent 1995 coming up with options for their political masters to consider.[1]

Collectively, this was – and remains to this day – about as unsung a group of public servants as you can find. Their work was highly technical and, to most people, epitomized the word 'boring.' Outsiders, including the politicians, took an interest in what these people thought and did only when a problem needed solving or a crisis was perceived or when the public grew fearful that it might lose its expected pensions. But there was, among these low-profile officials, a shared interest in the issue and something approaching a sense of camaraderie. Since their expertise was specialized and arcane, most dealt with pensions over a long period in their careers. They got to know each other through regular federal–provincial meetings and phone calls to discuss issues small and large as they arose. The federal and provincial deputy ministers of finance often met – usually just before meetings of their finance ministers – and for years had operated under the bland rubric of the Continuing Committee of Officials (CCO). Under it was a sub-committee of assistant deputy ministers devoted to the CPP that met as needed. 'There is a real stability in the CCO and the CPP sub-committee,' one federal official said. 'It is not a revolving door; there is a lot of corporate knowledge on the CPP among the people involved.' These were the people who knew the CPP cold – its history, its strengths, its weaknesses, and its technicalities.

Unfinished Business

Among this group, there was a sense of unfinished business. They thought the CPP was a good program and had little time or regard for the more radical proposals – either from the left or right – that they saw in the media. But they knew their previous two 'fixes' to the CPP had not worked, and this time the plan needed a more thorough repair job. They came to this view gradually. 'Awareness is a slowly dawning thing,' said one federal official. The realization 'that your basic assumptions are no longer valid doesn't happen overnight.'

Much later, in the fall of 1997 when legislation to implement the CPP reforms came before the Commons Finance committee, Liberal MP Mark Assad asked when the Finance Department realized that the problem was growing quickly and that the hour of decision was at hand. 'That's a fascinating question,' replied Susan Peterson, the department's assistant deputy minister responsible for CPP policy. 'Repeated actuarial reports' kept showing the impact of lower productivity and changing demographics until 'it became clear there was a problem here.' Other countries faced the same problem, she said. 'It's not unlike an analogy with deficit financing in the sense that it takes a while for people to come to a collective sense that this just can't go on. There is a real problem here. It's the same thing with pay-as-you-go public pension plans.'[2]

The chief actuary's report automatically put the CPP on the agenda of the federal and provincial finance ministers. The rules required it. As one official put it, 'we had to have reports from the chief actuary, we had to have five-year reviews and we had to have meetings with the provinces, so we had to deal with this issue again.' In government, 'a lot of things happen because they have to,' not because someone decides it is time to act. This was one of those things, but although the need to do *something* was dictated by the five-year review schedule, the need to do *something better* was driven by the officials and politicians involved.

If they did not do something better, or at least something different, the default mechanism to which they had agreed a decade earlier would come into play. The fifteen-year rule said the fund must be equal to two years worth of benefits in fifteen years according to the chief actuary's most recent report. If the finance ministers tried to duck the issue or failed to agree on a new schedule of contribution rates – as they had done in 1985 and 1991 – the actuary's schedule of rate increases that would meet the fifteen-year test would take effect. That, of course, was the schedule leading to the dreaded 14.2 per cent contribution rate at some point in the future.

Having been given some indication of the chief actuary's conclusions, the federal Finance Department was already kicking around ideas for longer-term solutions. This would be Peterson's third round of CPP talks. This time, she and her team were looking for that elusive 'better' solution and the authority to pursue a more thorough reform that would break the seemingly endless pattern of new, ever-steeper schedules of rate increases every five years. Luckily for them, their deputy minister, David Dodge, needed no persuading; he had long believed that the CPP needed a more permanent fix. When the opportunity arose, he was ready to grab it.

Dodge was perhaps the federal government's most powerful and respected official, having just steered the Finance Department through the 1995 budget that turned around Ottawa's finances and put them on the road to surplus after a generation of deficits. Even at this stage of his career – he later went on to become governor of the Bank of Canada from 2001 to 2008 – Dodge was one of Canada's more unusual public servants. He was an economist by training, with a PhD from Princeton University, and his résumé was more varied than that of most federal officials. From the late 1960s to the early 1980s, he had taught at Queen's University and Johns Hopkins University, headed the international economics program at the Institute for Research on Public Policy, and taken on increasingly senior positions in four federal government departments and agencies. In government, he had worked on policies as varied as taxation, housing, inflation, and labour market development. At Finance in the 1980s, he had been assistant deputy minister first for economic and fiscal policy and subsequently for tax policy before moving up to associate deputy minister, where he was Canada's G7 deputy, responsible for dealing with Finance and central bank counterparts in the other Group of Seven leading industrial countries.

The CPP was one of his interests well before he assumed the job of deputy minister. Economist Jack Mintz, then at the University of Toronto, was seated by happenstance next to Dodge on a flight from Paris to Toronto during Dodge's spell as G7 deputy, and the two discussed economic policy for much of the trip. Both were policy wonks with wide interests, so this was a conversational natural.[3] Mintz had been on a World Bank mission to Eastern Europe and Dodge was returning from one of his many meetings with foreign officials. During the flight, they talked at length, and Mintz remembers Dodge's concern over the big liabilities that Canada was leaving to future generations. He worried not just about government deficits and debt, but about the CPP as well, which he put in the same category. When Dodge became deputy minister after 1992, Mintz says, 'he drove that [theme]. He fought hard on deficits and debt and the CPP. That's why he was successful; he was so focused.'[4]

A Question of Credibility

It is not clear when the finance minister, Paul Martin, signed on to his officials' thinking about the need for a major overhaul of the CPP. One recalls that Martin was not initially keen on a big reform – it would mean adding another important and controversial initiative to an already daunting agenda – though another says he readily accepted that the job had to be done right this time around.

Martin himself says he had begun to think about the fiscal and pension issues as similar problems as early as 1994 during his first full year on the job.[5] When he had arrived at Finance after the October 1993 election, he was committed only to the new Liberal government's vague promise of cutting the fiscal deficit to 3 per cent of GDP over three years. His first budget in early 1994 was initially well received, but the reviews soured in the following months as interest rates climbed, pushing up the cost of servicing the federal debt and forcing on Martin the need for more drastic measures. He had also discovered just how meagre was Canada's reputation with its lenders, the people who bought all the bonds the federal government needed to keep selling to finance its annual deficits. As he toured the world's key financial markets – New York, London, Tokyo – after the 1994 budget, 'I saw the extent to which Canada and its finance minister had no credibility,' he said later. Bond buyers simply did not believe the federal government would ever deal with its deficit. He was also worried about forecasts that the U.S and Canadian economies would both slip back into recession in 1995 or 1996; for Canada, with its 'terrible balance sheet,' there would be downward pressure on the Canadian dollar in world markets and interest rates would rise.

'So we faced a recession and we had no credibility. We'd still be able to borrow, but only at very high interest rates. I returned from that trip vowing to increase confidence and deal with the debt; and part of that had to be the CPP unfunded liability.' He had paid little attention to the CPP while in opposition, but as finance minister, he said, he became preoccupied with what he called the 'real unfairness between genera- tions. We were borrowing to pay for current expenditure, not infra- structure, so we were asking our grandchildren to pay for us. And this applied to the CPP as well as the debt.' For him, a key date was 2011, when the first of the baby-boom generation would reach 65 and begin to retire in large numbers; they would put increasing pressure on not just the CPP but the Old Age Security program as well. Confidence, though, was key. The capital markets had little confidence in Canada's ability to reduce deficits and debt, while Canadians appeared to have lost all confidence in the CPP and – perhaps worse – in their govern- ments' ability to save it.

In a 2007 speech, Martin recalled his surprise at the lack of real out- side pressure on the government to resolve the CPP's problems. While the fiscal deficit 'was the stuff of headlines, there was virtually none of this in terms of the CPP. Nor was there any pressure from the financial markets, not even after the chief actuary's 1995 report. This always amazed me.' The absence of political pressures, he said, was important because 'it meant [that] when Canada's governments sat down to repair the CPP, they did so not with an eye to the electoral cycle, but to the generational cycle.' The loss of confidence in the CPP was so severe that the young regarded it as 'a dead horse ... not even worth flogging ... No one, it seemed, thought we as politicians could muster the will to fix the CPP, so they didn't bother to press hard for changes. This lack of confidence went to the heart of government, and we could not let that stand.'[6]

There was more to the question of retirement incomes than the CPP. The cost of Old Age Security was rising as well. Finance had wanted to overhaul OAS in the 1995 budget by putting it on a household income rather than individual income basis and taxing back some of the bene- fits from higher-income households. When Chrétien rejected that move (it would return in the 1996 budget as the proposed Seniors Benefit), the department turned its attention once again to putting the CPP on a more sustainable footing. 'What drove the 1990s fix was that we were all aware of the terrible fiscal situation – general federal–provincial def- icits and debt,' David Dodge said later. 'People had very low confi- dence in the CPP and the federal and provincial governments realized that if the CPP couldn't pay, the money would come out of their hides. They would be on the hook for any shortfall.' Since the CPP was kept in a separate account, it was not part of the budgets of either the federal or provincial governments; in government parlance, it was off-budget. But if the CPP failed, both Martin and his officials realized that governments would somehow have to meet the promises made to seniors and to contributors who were still working. Such a rescue, even one that might not be needed for another couple of decades, would be very much on-budget – not a legacy any politician or public servant wanted to leave. 'That's when CPP reform came alive,' Dodge said.

Sorting Out the Options

Within Finance, issues of this magnitude were rarely left to one unit alone. Senior officials met regularly to review all the department's initiatives, partly to ensure that the left hand knew what the right was doing, partly to bounce ideas and plans off people who might bring a fresh perspective. The meetings were called DMOs, for deputy minister and others; the deputy and the assistant deputy ministers would be there, along with other senior officials invited according to the agenda of the day. When the CPP hit the agenda, officials talked about options like lifting the retirement age to 67 and raising the contribution rate now with an eye to reducing it later on. At first, 'things were muddled,' one said later. Everything was on the table – from the status quo (which meant adopting the fifteen-year formula) to full funding (which meant creating a massive fund that would finance all future costs). Officials at Human Resources Development Canada, who were consulted even though all the policymaking authority was at Finance, were on the side of the status quo, but in Finance, some economists were willing to go to the other end of the spectrum and ask why the government could not just fully fund the CPP.

Early on, Dodge asked the department's economic studies and policy analysis division to examine the pure economics of both extremes of CPP financing – PAYGO and full funding. The economic studies team, then under Munir Sheikh,[7] was an in-house policy research shop – 'almost a consulting group for the whole department,' one official said – that specialized in this kind of dense economic research and analysis. The result was a paper that came down squarely on the side of fuller, but not full, funding.[8] It argued that future benefits are determined in a PAYGO system by the growth of real (i.e., inflation-adjusted) wages but in a fully funded system by the rate of return on pension contributions, which should be the real rate of interest. The economic cost of a PAYGO system, then, was the difference between real wage growth and the real rate of interest. In the 1960s and 1970s, when real wage growth exceeded real long-term interest rates on government bonds, PAYGO 'thus appeared to make eminent sense.'[9] But in the 1980s and 1990s, real interest rates had been higher than real wage growth, so this argument no longer held; PAYGO was imposing real economic costs on Canadians. Indeed, these costs were probably even larger than suggested by the commonly used differential between the interest rate on risk-free government bonds and wage growth.

'One should instead compare real growth with the average real cost of funds across all assets, which comprises aggregate risk in the economy,' the paper said. 'Making this correction reveals that the economic costs of PAYGO are even larger than [those] given by the differential between real wage growth and real interest rates on risk free government bonds, and have existed since the introduction of the CPP,' because the real cost of funds was almost always higher than real wage growth.[10] In short, PAYGO had probably been a bad choice from the beginning; it only looked good in the early years because the CPP had to lend its money to the provinces at lower-than-market rates of interest. There was another argument for fuller funding. Over the long term, 'significant economic impacts will be realized through reducing debt or funding public pensions since aggregate savings in the economy would increase, thereby increasing investment and output.'[11]

The High Ground – Fuller Funding

For any government already bent on getting rid of the deficit and reducing government debt, this was powerful stuff. 'The economics of fuller funding was the same as the economics of paying down debt,' one official said later. Once people understood that link, fuller funding was 'seen as the high ground' in the discussion of CPP financing. It was an argument with two advantages: not only was it supported by some solid analysis – one official called it 'one of the best pieces of research we did' – but it would appeal to finance ministers, both federal and provincial, who were already committed to fiscal budgets that did away with deficits and reduced debt.

The status quo was out – the study said it would be 'very costly in economic terms for future generations.'[12] But just as no one advocated trying to pay down the entire national debt – then about $525 billion, or 68 per cent of GDP – no one in federal Finance suggested that absolute full funding was the way to go. Even though the research said that was the most efficient solution from a pure economics perspective, meaning it would generate the biggest increase in the economy's productive potential, it was not practical from a political perspective. A full-funding solution would mean rapidly building a CPP fund equal to about two-thirds of GDP within about forty years, which would have pointed to very steep increases in contribution rates, much steeper than Canadians appeared ready to accept.

The unfunded liability in the CPP was a major problem, a legacy of the millions who, over three decades, had contributed too little to the plan to cover the cost of what they were entitled – or at least expected – to receive. Full funding would pay off the liability, but at a cost no government could accept. Another possibility was to carve out the liability and finance it separately as a dead-weight burden, an explicit admission of an error that had to be financed somehow. A CPP contribution rate of about 6 per cent would cover the cost of future pensions and other benefits, but some officials wondered if the liability could not be financed separately through a new payroll tax or other tax instrument. That idea immediately ran into a wall: a new payroll tax with no associated benefits would be constitutionally impossible and a new tax with no benefits would never win public acceptance.

'Steady-State' Financing

Finance began to gravitate towards an idea that Réal Bouchard's social policy division injected into the discussion – something called 'steady-state' financing. The contribution rate would rise faster than it would under the fifteen-year formula included in the chief actuary's report, something everyone knew was needed. But if the rate could be pushed high enough quickly enough, it could then be flattened permanently at the new higher level within a decade. The steeper rate increase would create a much larger fund, well over two years worth of benefits. The larger fund would then generate enough investment returns to cover part of the cost of future benefits, eliminating the need for a contribution rate that kept rising until the 2030s, when all the baby boomers would reach retirement age.

Steady-state financing became the central idea for the eventual reform. As a middle ground between the status quo and full funding, it would involve the short-term pain of a much higher contribution rate but quickly get to a rate much lower than the chief actuary was projecting and leave it there permanently. As a bonus, it would produce 'fuller funding' of the CPP, thus achieving some of the efficiency gains revealed by the department's economic research. The steady-state idea came from the social policy division, but no one appears to know exactly where the concept originated, though Bernard Dussault recalls discussing it in the late 1980s. One Finance official said later that it was 'hard to pinpoint the moment of birth' for the idea, but it quickly became the focus of the department's thinking.

The benefit side of the CPP appears to have received less attention at this point, beyond the talk about raising the retirement age, but a list of possible cuts was under consideration. The federal officials knew benefit cuts would likely be needed to make a reform work – Alberta was already letting it be known that it would push for reductions – but benefits were familiar ground, easier to deal with than the newer concepts of steady-state financing and fuller funding.

By July 1995, 'the policy seems to have been born,' one official recalls. Contribution rates would rise and some benefits would be cut. The CPP would once more begin to run annual, and growing, surpluses that would reverse the decline in the fund, now in its third year of decline from the 1992 peak of $42.3 billion. But the prospect of a bigger fund raised an even larger issue – what to do with the money. The answer lay in what became the single biggest innovation of the reforms to come. The money would go into a fund that would invest its burgeoning pool of capital in the public capital markets; it would be used to buy stocks, bonds, and other investments that would earn a higher return than loans to the provinces. When needed, the earnings on this much larger fund would help finance CPP benefits through the years when the baby boomers were all retired. These three elements – higher contributions, lower benefits, and an investment fund resembling occupational pension plans – became the tripod on which governments would rest their reform of the CPP. All raised major problems for the policymakers.

The Big Questions

First, how big a contribution rate increase would Canadians swallow? People were already grumbling about high taxes and turning their political support to parties that advocated smaller government and tax cuts. Nationally, the Reform Party was a growing force and Ontario delivered a vivid example of the public mood as Finance was examining its options for the CPP. In the June 1995 Ontario election, the Progressive

Conservatives under Mike Harris staged a powerful come-from-behind victory on a platform of lower taxes, deep spending cuts, and smaller government. At this point, the CPP contribution rate was 5.4 per cent of covered earnings. Under the existing schedule that had gone into effect in 1992, the one ministers were now required to review, it would almost double to 10.1 per cent by 2016, and under the chief actuary's new default projection, it would rise to 11.8 per cent by 2016 on its way to a peak of 14.2 per cent by 2040. Now there was something entirely new on the table – a very rapid increase that was far steeper than anything previously suggested. Finance ministers, federal and provincial alike, were certain to cringe at putting such an increase in front of both their own cabinet colleagues and their respective voters, especially at a time when all payroll taxes were increasingly fingered as job-killers in an economy that some feared was teetering on the edge of another recession.

Second, what kind of benefits could be cut, and how? Existing benefits for seniors were deemed politically untouchable, though some argued for a partial de-indexing of CPP retirement benefits that would have removed some of the inflation protection enjoyed by recipients. Survivor benefits – widows and orphans, that is – had roughly the same status. The death benefit was a possibility, but it was not big enough to deliver a major financial difference. Disability benefits, which had risen so quickly in the early 1990s and which – according to the chief actuary – were the main reason for the CPP's deteriorating finances, were already being reined in through administrative measures by the federal government.

Third, could a big investment fund be sold to the public, and if so, how would it work? This idea had been raised before, discussed but dismissed in both the mid-1960s when the CPP was established and in the mid-1980s when the first contribution rate increase was endorsed. Financially, it made sense; public sector pension funds were by now a familiar part of the landscape and they had a track record of earning better returns than the CPP. Politically, however, it looked like a radical and risky course; governments would control a capital fund that would soon become one of the biggest in the country, and the investment track record of governments was not encouraging. Yet there was no longer any appetite for lending CPP money to the provinces. Most provinces were either running surpluses or heading quickly in that direction in response to public pressure for greater fiscal responsibility. Their need for fresh CPP funds had dwindled; indeed, the CPP had dried up as a source of funds in 1992 and provinces had been repaying some of their

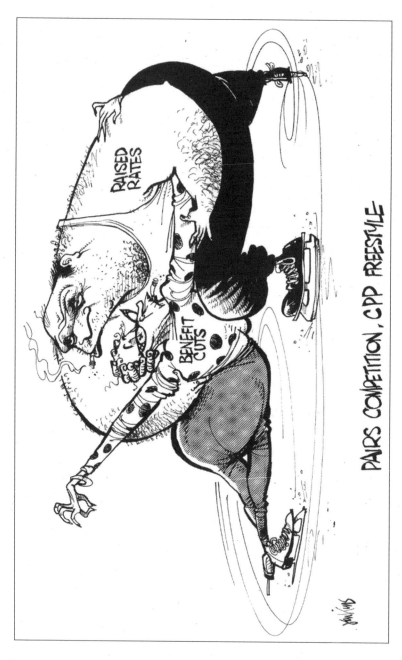

PAIRS COMPETITION, CPP FREESTYLE

Anthony Jenkins, 'Pairs competition,' 12 February 1996

loans for the previous three years. If they still harboured a hankering for such cheap and easy money – borrowing from the CPP, unlike issuing bonds in the financial markets, involved little paperwork and no brokerage fees – they were becoming a bit embarrassed to admit it. Too many critics were ready to say CPP loans would just encourage more deficits and slack financial management, and by the mid-1990s no government wanted that kind of labelling.

The possibility of setting up a major investment fund raised issues beyond the experience of the social policy division, so the department's financial sector policy division was brought in to explore those issues. Since the CPP fund had always been lent to the provinces, this was a first for the financial sector officials, who set about figuring how a big investment fund might work, how big a return it might earn, and what impact it might have on Canada's capital markets.

Investing in Markets

The Finance officials spent much of the spring and summer of 1995 doing some preliminary thinking about and analysis of the implications of creating a major investment fund. As long as CPP funds were lent to the provinces at the interest rate on the federal government's twenty-year bond, the task of forecasting the return on the fund was fairly straightforward. Now they had to figure out what returns could be expected from a diversified investment portfolio that included stocks as well as bonds. And it would presumably be investing some of the money outside Canada as well – in both stocks and bonds. The comparison was complicated, as one official recalled, by the fact that the CPP's returns under the old policy were actually quite good, despite the widely held belief that the provinces were getting cheap money. Yes, the federal rate of interest was lower than what they would have paid for the same funds had they gone to the open market, but the CPP had invested a lot of money in provincial notes in the late 1970s and early 1980s when bond rates were quite high. In 1995, the CPP portfolio was earning a yield of more than 11 per cent on those twenty-year obligations. Since inflation was running around 2 per cent by that time, the real rate of return was about 9 per cent, which was not at all shabby. 'We looked at what the portfolio returned and what it might return,' one federal official said. 'We looked at all the moving parts – looked at an all-bond portfolio and then at other portfolios. We used the major pension funds as examples.'

By the fall of 1995, Finance had produced a paper on the subject for provincial officials to review. A publicly invested fund would mark a huge change for the CPP; both the provinces and the federal government needed time to become comfortable with the idea. Some provinces, notably those on the east coast which had borrowed CPP funds at rates well below their own, were reluctant to give up their privileged access to the fund. This would remain an issue that needed fine-tuning, but for the most part all were willing to see this kind of fund put forward as an option.

That was the least of the problems that federal and provincial policymakers had to consider. If they were going to allay the old fears about government control of a vast pool of capital, they were going to have to think long and hard about such a fund. What exactly would be its mandate – to invest solely for the highest returns or pursue other goals as well, like financing specified government projects? Would governments dictate how the fund would allocate its investments? Would they, for example, insist that the fund be invested in each of the provinces according to its share of the contributions? What governance rules would they put in place for the fund? How would directors and officers be appointed? How much of the money could be invested abroad at a time when other investors were limited to 20 per cent? Indeed, would there be one big fund or several smaller ones? None of these questions was easy, yet the answers to each might very well make the difference between success and failure of this part of the venture.

A Prescient Paper

Several times during 1995, Finance sought advice from pension consultant Keith Ambachtsheer. Based in Toronto, Ambachtsheer was well known in pension circles around the world, with an international clientele for whom he wrote a regular advisory letter of commentary on pension governance, finance, and investments.[13]

He came to the task with some clear opinions about what kind of solution the governments should consider seriously, views that he had laid out in mid-April 1995, less than two months after the chief actuary's *15th Report*. In one of his advisory letters to clients, he set out what he called a 'bold proposal' for saving Canada's social security system, specifically the Canada Pension Plan, and it was remarkably prescient.[14] Using the CIA's *Troubled Tomorrows* report as a jumping-off point, Ambachtsheer argued that Canada had to increase its rate of savings, and to do that it would have to move from a PAYGO system to 'a pre-funding form of financing.' That financing should also equalize intergenerational contribution rates to achieve intergenerational fairness. 'In short, the best solution ... is not so much benefit curtailment as it is increased wealth creation through a credible increased funding and productive investment programme.'

Ambachtsheer wrote that there were four legitimate objections to such a plan, which he developed specifically in the context of the CPP, but some compelling answers to each. First, Canadians would not 'jump with joy' at a rapid increase in contribution rates from 5.4 per cent, which took in about $16 billion a year, to the 10 per cent needed to stabilize the system. But he was convinced that Canadians would also 'respond very positively' to the argument that it was intergenerationally fair.

The additional $10 billion in CPP revenues that such an increase would generate would lead to the second objection: governments would just spend the money through loans to the provinces, as they had done since 1966. His answer took the form of a 'yes, but ...' Canadians would not pay higher rates – which he thought they would rightly see as higher taxes – unless (it was an important 'unless') there was 'a credible mechanism to turn excess CPP contributions into productive investments.' That was now possible because 'we have learned how to create legitimate arms-length pension investment agencies in Canada ... Good made-in-Canada operating models already exist.' As an example, he pointed to the $35 billion Ontario Teachers Pension Plan Board, which the public not only accepted but admired.

Even if such an agency could be set up for the CPP, there would be a third objection – that there would be no guarantee as to what the pension fund could earn in the way of a long-term investment return. True enough, Ambachtsheer said, but there was a 'reasonable expectation' that a well-diversified asset pool could earn a real return (after inflation, that is) of between 5 and 6 per cent, roughly double the expectations of real economic growth. 'Thus economics clearly favour saving and investing today over pay-go spending as the surer path to wealth accumulation.'

But even if you accept that point, he said, there might be another problem: Why stick with the CPP's defined benefit (DB) pension model rather than convert to 'its defined contribution (DC) cousin?'[15] There were prominent advocates of the DC approach, like the Reform Party and *The Globe and Mail*, but they 'miss three important advantages which DB systems have over DC systems,' Ambachtsheer said. 'First, DB systems are much better at pooling actuarial risks such as mortality and long term disability. Second, DB systems will earn higher investment risk premiums than individualized DC systems which have a pronounced low-risk bias. Third, economies of scale and operational simplicity make large DB systems much less costly to operate than large DC systems.' Operating expenses for Chile's DC system were about 2.3 per cent of assets, compared with 0.1 per cent for a large Canadian DB plan. Since an additional one percentage point annually of long-term return generates about 20 per cent of additional pension, Ambachtsheer continued, the DB pension would produce a level of pensions more than 40 per cent higher than a DC system.[16] ('The math is just devastating,' he said in a later interview.)[17]

There was a final objection to a CPP investment agency: that the pool of funds would grow so large so quickly that it would 'swamp Canada's capital markets and become an inordinately large owner of Corporate Canada.' Ambachtsheer countered that 'the idea of a purely Canadian capital market is a myth. Increasingly, there is only a single global market for capital' and Canada's suppliers and users of capital alike must think in those terms. 'Many already do.' Canadian pension funds invest abroad just as Canadian governments borrow abroad, just as investors and borrowers in other countries do.

Ambachtsheer's short advisory letter – it was only four pages long – anticipated almost exactly the course governments chose to take and the arguments that would be advanced in the course of the CPP debate that was about to begin. He said in a subsequent interview that his proposed fix for the CPP was not 'rocket science.' He had been involved in the Ontario public sector pension reforms of the late 1980s that led to the creation of the Teachers plan, 'so by 1995, I was already an "old hand" at stating political pension problems and proposing solutions.'[18] A year later, he would be advising federal and provincial policymakers on the options for a sound investment policy. And he would still be talking about the issues almost three years later, when he appeared before a Senate committee on the question of pension plan returns and governance.

The Ministers' First Big Decision

Martin and the provincial finance ministers finally got down to the business of the CPP at a December 1995 meeting tucked in between the

Quebec referendum and Christmas. Over dinner on the evening of 12 December and through a full day session on 13 December, they discussed the state of the economy, taxes, federal transfers to the provinces (which Ottawa was cutting substantially through its new Canada Health and Social Transfer program), and the CPP. At this point, plenty of CPP options were on the table, but no firm plan, and the public had not yet begun to see the real shape of what would emerge. 'About 15 options have been put on the table, some from the federal government and some from the provinces,' one provincial official told *The Globe and Mail* at the time.[19] Martin's caution as he approached the meeting was evident in the comment of one of his aides: 'The federal government is not coming down with a set of proposals.'[20]

There was no specific federal proposal, perhaps, but Finance was ready to talk about elements of the package it had been developing. Unlike the 1991 tweaking of the contribution rate that governments endorsed quickly, however, the Finance Department's proposed solution this time was far too big for ministers to swallow the first time they saw it. This was not just another stopgap that would get them (or their successors) through to the next review five years hence, but a major change in the whole structure of contributions and benefits. They had done higher contributions coupled with enhanced benefits in 1985 and higher contributions unaccompanied by significant new benefits in 1991. Now they were looking at a particularly steep rate increase alongside reduced benefits. Moreover, the fund itself would be transformed into something very new and somewhat risky.

Most ministers were nowhere near ready to make decisions. For almost thirty years, the CPP had been for some provinces what one official called a 'side-of-the-desk' issue. They had to deal with it periodically, but most provinces simply could not devote much in the way of analytical firepower to the issue. They did not initiate policy; they just responded to policies designed by Ottawa. Now they were being drawn more closely into the process. Ottawa was asking them to make much more fundamental decisions, and take much bigger chances, than in the past. They decided they needed to get the issue out in the open for a much wider discussion that would allow them to gauge public opinion before acting.

'We have to put these options out to the public,' Saskatchewan Finance Minister Janice MacKinnon told the media after the meeting. 'We shouldn't be doing this behind closed doors any longer.'[21] Her BC counterpart, Elizabeth Cull, said Canadians needed to debate the tradeoffs between raising contribution rates and cutting benefits, but more important, they needed 'to have confidence that the plan will be there for them when they retire.'[22] Looking back recently, MacKinnon said the Prairie provinces and New Brunswick, which had been the first to reduce their fiscal deficits, had learned that getting the public onside was a key to success in this kind of venture. 'We could not do this from on high and say that the actuary's report tells us to do this, so we must do this.' She argued that 'the provinces understood this a lot better than the feds.'[23]

Paul Martin would take issue with the idea that only the provinces understood the value of consultations. He had just pulled off his own big deficit-cutting budget, and his view of consulting the public was close to MacKinnon's. Consultation was not just a way to 'prepare the public,' he said later, but to deal with issues on which people hold strong views. 'Success comes from the greatest degree of consultation possible ... When people understand the issues and they see that governments face these choices, they may not like it, but they find it understandable.'[24]

'Difficult Choices'

Ontario's finance minister, Ernie Eves, said the CPP should come up with administrative savings as a first step towards curing the plan's financial ills and warned that one of the 'difficult choices' ahead involved cutting disability benefits. Contribution rates would have to rise, but not to the extent that the economy might be damaged by rising payroll taxes.[25] When he talked about payroll taxes, Eves was thinking about Unemployment Insurance premiums as well as CPP contributions, as Martin and the others would discover. But his support for higher contribution rates was significant, given his government's antagonism to higher taxes of any kind.

Alberta came in with several concerns. The province objected to what one official called 'easy cheap debt for the provinces.' Investments should earn income, so 'the notion of putting the CPP on a proper investment footing was consistent with that philosophy.' Jim Dinning, the Alberta treasurer, was also keen to reduce benefits by raising the retirement age and partially de-indexing benefits. 'We were on an anti-indexing kick at that point,' the official recalled. The province's pension benefits to its own employees had actually risen faster than inflation between 1971 and 1993, and the government had just de-indexed several programs. Alberta also argued for a single-purpose CPP: death and disability benefits should be carved off into a separate program, leaving the CPP strictly as a retirement program. 'But Ontario and Quebec ministers said early – don't touch disability benefits. They were more open to increasing the retirement age, but they were also pretty negative about a major [de-indexing] hit. They saw it as arbitrary.' Alberta had staked out some strong ground that marked it as the toughest province in the early stages of the CPP negotiations. It was a clear sign that this round of talks would not be like the previous ones.

The December ministers' meeting was notable for one other factor. While they squabbled over harmonizing the federal goods and services tax (GST) with provincial sales taxes and over federal transfers to the provinces, their approach to the CPP was far less partisan, almost non-political. The voices from the right that wanted the CPP dismantled in favour of mandatory personal savings through individual accounts or super-RRSPs were not heard in the room. 'The extremist option of abolishing the CPP was never on the political table,' Ken Battle of the Caledon Institute observed later.

> Even if the federal government wanted to take the enormous political risk and contend with the incredible transition problems of winding down a 30-year-old program that has promised many billions of dollars worth of pensions to the entire Canadian workforce which pays into the plan, it probably would not be able to do so because of opposition from at least some of the provinces ... It seems unlikely that Quebec would agree to the CPP's abolition. Parliament must approve changes to the CPP; there certainly would be opposition to abolishing the CPP from most Liberals as well as the Bloc Québécois and the NDP, though the rightist Reform Party favoured replacing the CPP with super-RRSPs.[26]

The ministers talked about raising the retirement age to 67, and at least one province – Alberta – raised the possibility of moving away from the PAYGO model to a fully funded CPP. There was little enthusiasm for either idea – several ministers described the higher retirement age as a 'last resort' and Martin called it 'my last choice'– but even a discussion of such options indicated the extent to which the finance ministers were willing to entertain new ideas.

10 Clarifying the Choices

During the two months after the ministerial meeting, officials worked to put their proposals on paper in a form that the public could understand. They needed a discussion paper that explained the roots of the problem and laid out the options for solving it. Federal Finance officials 'held the pen,' as the saying in government circles goes, but provincial officials were consulted along the way and their favourite options were included. Midway through the writing process, on 12 January 1996, the officials got together in Ottawa to sort through the options that would and would not go into the paper. Over dinner on Thursday evening, 8 February, the finance ministers signed off on the paper and released it to the waiting media the next day during the ministers' all-day meeting.

Some ministers made their own preferences very clear. Alberta's Jim Dinning was on the side of benefit reductions. 'Let's not ask Canadians to pay more and put money into a big, black sinkhole,' he said on his way into the Friday session. 'Clearly, the benefits are too rich.'[1] Ontario's Ernie Eves, despite his opposition to payroll taxes, was resigned to higher contribution rates. 'Everyone acknowledges that the premiums are going to go in excess of 10 per cent, even under the current plan,' he told reporters. 'The question is, how can we best limit that growth and keep it within a reasonable figure.'[2] One newspaper account of the meeting noted that most ministers stressed the need to put CPP reforms in place by 1 January 1997, the federal government's preferred deadline, but there was at least one dissent: 'British Columbia's Elizabeth Cull warned that it's premature to pick options until the federal government releases long-awaited proposals for reform of the entire pension system, including CPP, Old Age Security, RRSPs and company plans.'[3] She was probably referring to the notorious aging paper, the federal government's often-promised but always-delayed overview paper on all programs affecting seniors; it was never written.

Still, the document the governments produced that day – though narrower in scope – was quite ambitious on its own. It carried the blandest of possible titles – *An Information Paper for Consultations on the Canada Pension Plan*[4] – but it utterly changed the public debate. Suddenly, CPP reform had a focus – a rationale for the reform itself, a sense of urgency about resolving the issue now, a detailed listing of the choices at hand, and a clear sense of the governments' preferred outcome. The governments were asking Canadians what they wanted, but the debate would be circumscribed by the issues and options laid out in this sixty-two-page paper. Parts were similar in tone to the 1985 booklet that preceded the first overhaul of the CPP, but it served a very different purpose. In 1985, the governments had already decided what they were going to do and the booklet laid out that plan; in the end, what Canadians saw in the booklet was very much what they got in the 1985 deal. This time around, the governments were still not agreed on many of the big questions, let alone the details, so the 1996 paper set out more choices. But it did so in a way that tightly framed the discussion, giving it a coherence that had been lacking in the public debate so far.

The paper, issued in the name of 'the Federal, Provincial and Territorial Governments of Canada,' set in motion a federal–provincial road trip of public consultations that covered eighteen cities – Toronto twice – over the period from 15 April to 10 June, ending just before the finance ministers' subsequent meeting in Fredericton.

The *Information Paper* opened with a two-page trumpet blast that homed in on the key themes of CPP reform – confidence, fairness, and sustainability. Anyone who read only those two pages would understand how their governments saw the issues. The CPP was set up to provide Canadians with retirement income and financial help in cases of death or serious disability. 'It is a vital part of Canada's retirement income system. All generations – young and old alike – deserve to have confidence that the CPP can be sustained and will be there for them when they need it.'[5]

But the cost of the plan was rising faster than expected when the CPP was created and 'will escalate dramatically' when baby boomers begin to retire. The architects of the CPP in 1966 thought the top contribution rate would never go higher than 5.5 per cent of contributory, or covered, earnings.[6] It was already legislated to reach 10.1 per cent in twenty years' time, but 'costs are now expected to mount to 14.2 per

Table 10.1 Projected CPP costs in 2030

	Costs as a percentage of contributory earnings
Costs in 2030 projected when CPP started	**5.5**
Changed demographics (lower birth & death rates)	2.6
Changed economics (slower productivity growth)	2.2
Enrichment of benefits	2.4
Disability (more people for longer periods)	1.5
Costs in 2030 as now projected	**14.2**

Source: Department of Finance, *An Information Paper for Consultations on the Canada Pension Plan*, 20.

cent of earnings in the future if nothing is done.' The 8.7 percentage point increase in the projection of long-term costs was a result of changed demographics (2.6 points), changed economics (2.2 points), benefit enrichments since 1966 (2.4 points), and higher disability costs (1.5 points).[7] (See table 10.1.)

The core of the argument occupied only four paragraphs:

The basic challenge facing Canadians today is one of fairness and equity. If no changes are made to the CPP and the way it is financed, our children and grandchildren will be asked to pay two to three times more than we are paying for the same pensions from the CPP. For the past 30 years, we have not paid our way. Even today, we are not paying our way. Today's CPP pensioners have paid much less than their benefits are worth. In contrast, future generations will be asked to pay considerably more than their benefits are worth.

Will they be able to do so? Will they be willing to do so?

To ensure the sustainability of the CPP, steps must be taken to be as fair to future generations as possible.

The Government of Canada and the Governments of the provinces are joint stewards of the Canada Pension Plan. They believe that all reasonable steps should be taken now to ensure that future generations are not faced with unreasonable burdens. They do not believe that Canadians wish to be faced with this problem yet again at the next review of the CPP in five years' time. If the problems of the CPP are faced squarely now, fairness can be restored, and the CPP can be sustained not only for today's seniors, but for tomorrow's as well.[8]

It would be difficult to write a tighter summary of the CPP's financial problems while conveying a blend of crisis, urgency, and optimism. The bottom line came through clearly: bigger problems loom if we fail to act, but 'reasonable' steps now can prevent 'unreasonable' burdens in the future; there is a way forward that is fair to all; and if we do it now, we can do it right.

What's the Problem?

The paper quickly affirmed the fence that governments had already put around the CPP debate. They were not interested in radical alternatives to the CPP of the kind endorsed by the Reform Party and other conservative critics. They wanted to fix the CPP, not kill it. 'Canadian governments have been strongly committed to the CPP since its beginning. Governments today maintain that commitment.'[9] The paper would set out facts, address concerns over the CPP's sustainability, and lay out choices for change, but the bottom line was clear: governments were looking for public input to 'help determine what needs to be done to make the plan sustainable, so that working Canadians – particularly those now in their 20s and 30s – can be sure that the plan will be there for them in their retirement.'[10]

It dismissed the popular notion that the CPP's financial problems were caused by the policy of lending the reserve fund to the provinces. 'This is incorrect. The reserve fund has earned a very good rate of return because investments made in the high interest years of the 1980s have been locked in. Earning an even higher rate of return on a structurally "small" fund – just two years worth of benefits – would have a minimal impact on escalating contribution rates.'[11]

After describing how the CPP worked, the paper set out the reasons why the plan was in trouble in a chapter beginning with yet another reassurance that 'the CPP is today and will continue to be a key pillar of Canada's retirement income system.'[12] The problem was rising costs – more than expected in the past – with even more dramatic increases ahead. Four factors had driven the cost of the CPP up faster than the plan's architects had expected.

Changed Demographics

Canadians were 'living considerably longer' because lifestyle changes and medical advances had improved their health.[13] On average, life expectancy at 65 was another 15.3 years in 1966, 18.4 years in 1995, and heading for 19.8 years in 2030. As a result, the CPP was already paying benefits for a longer period – three years longer than in 1966, and by 2030, four and a half years longer.[14]

Even more significantly, the baby-boom generation would begin to retire in 2011, leaving behind relatively fewer younger workers – because of the baby bust – to pay the rising pension bill. Currently, there were five working-age Canadians to support every senior; by 2030, this would fall to three. (There had been seven in 1966, but this was not mentioned.) And because each working generation pays for the pensions of previous generations, 'today's youth will need to pay much more into the CPP than their parents paid, yet receive no more in the way of benefits. More than anything else, this is why Canadians are concerned about the future sustainability of the CPP.'[15]

Intergenerational fairness was there, but the idea of intergenerational conflict was soft-pedalled – not young-versus-old or us-versus-them, but something much closer to home: youth and their parents. The young were less likely to take out any anger on their parents than 'the old' and the old were less likely to fear their kids than 'the young,' though parents were perhaps more likely to feel guilty about handing their children a raw deal. But the lower birth and death rates that lay behind those changed demographics, though they had been a large part of the public discussion to date, account for just under one-third of the 8.7 percentage point increase in the long-term costs of the CPP, 2.6 points to be exact. Other factors were not only involved, but also very important.

Changed Economics

Almost as important, but tougher to explain, were the changed economics of the CPP, which accounted for 2.2 points of the cost increase. In plain language, the paper laid out the view that PAYGO made sense when the CPP was set up – and through the 1970s – because of rapid wage growth and low interest rates; it made less sense in the 1980s and 1990s when wage growth slowed and interest rates were much higher. The foundation of a PAYGO pension plan is its contribution base, the wages and salaries of all working Canadians; when those earnings grow, so do the plan's revenues from contributions. A fully funded pension plan, on the other hand, rests on its pool of investment; it grows fastest when interest rates are high.

In the early years of the CPP, the *Information Paper* explained,

> total wages and salaries were growing rapidly because both output per
> worker and the number of workers were growing rapidly. This meant that
> total contributions could grow fast enough to cover growing expenditures
> without needing large increases in contribution rates ... Such strong
> growth in aggregate wages and salaries was assumed to continue. For this
> reason, few thought that workers in the future would need to pay much
> higher contribution rates to finance the same benefits ... At the same time,
> real interest rates were low in 1966. This meant there were few advantages
> in building up a substantial reserve fund. Because of low interest rates, a
> large fund would not have been much help in paying for benefits.'[16]

For a PAYGO system, that was nice while it lasted. Real wages and
salaries (earnings adjusted to remove the effects of inflation) grew by an
average of 5.1 per cent a year in the 1960s and 4.8 per cent annually in
the 1970s. Real interest rates (nominal rates minus the rate of inflation)
averaged 2.4 per cent in the 1960s and 3.6 per cent in the 1970s. It was
obviously better to have earnings in the driver's seat for CPP revenue
growth than interest rates.

It did not last, of course. Growth in the size of the labour force slowed
dramatically in the 1980s and early 1990s, and productivity growth –
output for every hour worked – did the same. In the 1980s, real total
wages and salaries slowed substantially to an average growth rate of
only 2.1 per cent a year, and in the 1990s growth disappeared altogether. 'In a pay-as-you-go system, this demands rapid contribution
rate increases to compensate for the slower-than-expected growth of
the contribution base.' At the same time, real interest rates jumped to an
average of 6.3 per cent in the 1980s and 4.6 per cent in the early 1990s.
'This means that building up a larger fund can substitute for the slower
economic growth that Canada is experiencing. A larger fund earning a
higher rate of return could help to pay for the rapidly growing costs
that will occur once baby boomers start to retire.'[17] This justification for
a bigger CPP fund in the changed economic environment allowed a
shrewd reader of the paper to see where this analysis was leading – to a
proposal for a bigger fund.

Enrichments to the CPP since 1966

Benefit enrichments had added 2.4 percentage points to the CPP's

PAYGO rate – its long-term costs relative to contributory earnings – a bit more than the changed economics and a bit less than the changed demographics. The paper listed the most important additions to CPP benefits: full indexation of benefits to inflation (1975); the payment of survivor benefits to widowers as well as widows (1975); discontinuation of the retirement and earnings tests (1975); the childrearing dropout provision (1978); higher disability benefits and easier eligibility (1987); and survivor benefits for widows and widowers who remarried (1987).[18] A sharp reader might have noticed something in this list that was germane to the current reform effort: benefit enrichments had ended almost a decade earlier.

Disability Benefits

Finally, the paper laid out the rising cost of disability benefits as the source of a further 1.5 percentage-point increase in the CPP's long-term costs relative to covered earnings. Costs had more than doubled between 1987 and 1994 because more people were getting disability payments and more people were getting benefits for longer. The main causes were higher unemployment, administrative guidelines that gave 'greater weight to non-medical factors such as the rate of unemployment,' more referrals from provincial social assistance programs and private insurance companies, and legislative changes that had 'increased benefits, reduced the number of years of contribution required for coverage, and allowed late applicants to qualify for benefits.' All of this was true, but the paper essentially put most of these problems in the past. 'Since 1993,' it said, 'measures have been put in place which have improved the plan's administration and guidelines: these have helped curtail the growth of disability claims.'[19]

An annex[20] to the *Information Paper* went even further in explaining the reasons for higher costs. The 1987 CPP amendments had lowered the threshold for getting disability benefits – from at least five years in the plan to two of the last three years, or five of the last ten. The non-medical factors allowed in the 1989 administrative guidelines went beyond the unemployment rate and availability of certain kinds of jobs in a region and a person's skills. Those over 55 were considered disabled if they could not do the particular job they had, as opposed to any job. A further change in 1992 had given more latitude to late applicants for disability benefits.

But since mid-1994, the annex said, the government had deployed a variety of measures to contain costs. 'These have taken place at all points in the system – initial applications; appeals; reassessments; communications with clients; removal of work disincentives and encouraging return-to-work efforts.' By the end of 1995, and partly because of all these measures, 'the growth of the disability caseload had nearly ceased by the end of 1995.'[21] Most significantly, new guidelines for determining medical eligibility now eliminated socio-economic factors in judging applications. Officials had also launched a 'vigorous program of reassessments ... to identify beneficiaries whose medical condition has sufficiently improved to make them no longer eligible for benefits.' Beneficiaries had also been contacted and told that 'they have a responsibility to report any improvement in their medical condition or a return to work.' The new rules made it easier for beneficiaries to go back to work by allowing them to engage in full-time volunteer work, go back to school, or try out a new job for three months without jeopardizing their benefits.[22]

Setting Out the Issues

Now the *Information Paper* moved into the guts of the rescue plan that policymakers were considering. There was no discussion of any major alternatives to what they had in mind; they were not seeking big new ideas for CPP reform. Any expansion of benefits of the kind usually promoted by social advocacy groups and those on the political left was simply not on the table. If anything, benefits would be cut. Neither was there even a nod in the direction of those on the right who wanted to kill the CPP and replace it with Chilean-style individual savings plans.

Instead, the paper went straight to the broad package that governments had already chosen, setting it out plainly in the first two paragraphs of the fourth chapter, which was modestly titled, 'CPP: An Approach to Strengthening the Financing':

> The financing of the CPP can be strengthened by ensuring that today's working Canadians pay a fairer share of CPP costs. Raising contributions more quickly now would ease some of the contribution burden that will otherwise be passed on to future generations of workers. This would not only be fairer across generations – it would also make the CPP more sustainable for future participants.
>
> To strengthen CPP financing would require both fuller funding and a new investment policy. Together with benefit reductions, these actions

could help to keep future contribution rates from rising to levels which may be beyond the capacity and willingness of future generations to pay.[23]

It was all there – higher contribution rates, a bigger investment fund with a new investment policy, and benefit cuts. This trio of measures would prevent excessive increases in future premiums, ensuring both fairness and sustainability.

The contribution rate would rise quickly from the current 5.6 per cent 'to a higher level which can then be maintained without further increases. This contribution rate would cover the costs of each contributor's own benefits, plus a share of the burden that has built up because both current and past contributors have paid far less than their benefits are worth. This rate can be called the 'steady-state' contribution rate.'[24] That in turn would lead to fuller funding and a reserve fund containing not two years of benefits, the existing target, but six years of benefits. A fund that big could earn enough money to 'help pay for an increased share of CPP benefits,' and that, in turn, 'would make a major contribution to lowering contribution rates in the future.'[25]

How High a Rate?

Then came a key question: how high might the contribution rate have to go? That would depend on the answers to several questions, the paper said. How much money could a more fully funded plan earn from sound investments? How quickly could a steady-state rate be phased in? How much would long-term CPP benefits cost? As an example, it said the current structure of benefits could be afforded with a steady-state contribution rate of about 12.2 per cent indefinitely as long as two conditions were met. First, the CPP fund would get a real rate of return (the actual return minus inflation) of 3.5 to 4 per cent over the very long term, and second, the contribution rate increases were fast enough to get to the steady-state over a period of six to eight years. Under those circumstances, the contribution rate would never have to go to 14.2 per cent.

But – and here, the paper's sense of urgency was on display – 'the window of opportunity for fuller funding of the CPP is rapidly closing. If the current contribution rate schedule were maintained for another five years, the opportunity for fuller funding would be significantly curtailed. The longer that higher contribution rates are postponed, the less the degree of funding that can be achieved. This would put the steady-state contribution rate that much closer to the pay-as-you-go rate, with the sustainability and intergenerational fairness problems that this would entail.'[26] Among pension experts, that is a bread-and-butter argument, one they often use on people who hope to delay tough decisions. In dealing with pension problems, they will tell you, 'sooner is always better.'

Higher contributions and an investment fund might not be enough, though. The contribution rate might be held to 12.2 per cent if benefits remained at their current level, but it could be reduced if benefits were reduced as well. A 7 per cent cut in benefits would bring the steady-state rate down to 11.3 per cent; and cuts of 10 per cent or 15 per cent would lower the steady-state rate to 10.9 per cent and 10.3 per cent respectively.[27] This quick reference to benefits cuts was merely a warning shot of what would come later.

Better Returns

The new investment policy was explained carefully, but there was a clear tilt in favour of major change. Returns on the CPP had been comparable to those of other pension funds over the previous three decades, but that was largely attributable to high returns earned in the early to mid-1980s, when the fund's lending to provincial governments had locked in that period's high interest rates. 'There have nonetheless been criticisms that the current CPP investment policy does not maximize returns. This issue should therefore be addressed, particularly in light of the possibility of building a larger CPP fund.'[28] The paper had to tread cautiously here. Critics of the policy usually pointed their fingers at the provinces as the culprits in this area. The provinces, after all, had insisted in 1966 on access to the fund and the provinces had borrowed most of the money at the federal government's cost of funds, which was lower than their own.

Governments could choose to continue that policy but charge the full market rate to each province, the paper suggested. If provinces did not need the money (most were then busily reducing their deficits and thus their borrowing needs), any excess could be invested in the financial markets. Another option – and here the tone became more enthusiastic – was to invest 'most or all' new funds in the market. 'Increasingly, pension plans in Canada sponsored by governments as employers have their assets professionally managed and invested in the interest of pension plan contributors and beneficiaries. Federal and provincial legislation regulating private sector pension plans in Canada and recent reforms of pension plans in other countries have followed a similar principle. Pension funds managed on the basis of this principle are generally invested in a diversified portfolio of assets which enhances returns and prudently limits risks.'[29]

The world had indeed changed since the 1960s, when many Canadians – politicians and businesspeople especially – feared the prospect of a large, government-controlled fund rampaging through the country's relatively small financial markets. By 1996, the country had more experience with government pension funds that were no longer limited to investing only in non-marketable government bonds. The Ontario Municipal Employees Retirement System (OMERS) had been investing all its new funds in marketable securities since 1975 and the Ontario Teachers Pension Plan (Teachers) had followed suit in 1990. In addition, the Caisse de dépôt et placement du Québec had been investing the funds of the Quebec Pension Plan in the financial markets since the QPP began in 1966.

Still, the *Information Paper* recognized that this option raised several important issues, 'including how such a fund should be governed and the implications that a larger CPP fund would have for Canada's capital markets.'[30] It was a major issue – one with implications far bigger than the average reader might have thought – and it would preoccupy government officials and people in the pension industry for the next two years. It was bigger, perhaps, than even some of the government officials realized at the time. One federal official recalled that it was easy to persuade the provinces to put the two big options into the *Information Paper*. 'We got no strong signals from any of them.'[31]

The Sensitive Exemption

One more question of the CPP's design had to be addressed – what to do with the Year's Basic Exemption (YBE). The issue was technical but involved impacts on the poor and companies that employ low-income workers, and, as such, it was a sensitive one for politicians.[32]

In 1996, the Year's Maximum Pensionable Earnings[33] level (YMPE) was $35,400, meaning that the 5.6 per cent contribution rate was levied on income only up to that amount. But employers and employees were also exempted from paying contributions on the first 10 per cent of those earnings, which worked out to $3,500 because all sums were rounded to the nearest $100. Someone making $35,400 or more in 1996, then, paid contributions only on the $31,900 of earnings between the exemption and the maximum. This was often referred to as contributory earnings or covered earnings. (Pensionable earnings – the PE in YMPE – was defined as everything from zero up to $35,400, since the retirement benefit was calculated on this amount.)

In terms of CPP financing, the exemption was important because while the first $3,500 generated no contribution revenue, CPP benefits were paid on these earnings. The presence of the basic exemption introduced 'an element of progressivity into the CPP – since lower income earners are exempted from contributions on a larger proportion of their earnings than are higher income earners,' the paper said.[34] But to generate enough revenue to cover benefits to those very-low-income earners, the overall contribution rate had to be about 15 per cent higher than it would otherwise. It was not just the poor who benefited from this arrangement. So did the employers of 'workers with only a marginal attachment to the workforce,' because they did not have to pay premiums for casual workers they might employ for only a few days or weeks a year.[35]

If the basic exemption were to be reduced or frozen, the contribution rate could be cut substantially 'because contributions would be levied on a broader earnings base,' that is, a larger proportion of the full $35,400 rather than the more limited $31,900. If the YBE was only 5 per cent of the YMPE rather than 10 per cent, the long-term PAYGO rate could be reduced by 1.1 percentage point. Although the paper expressed all its proposals in terms of their impact on the PAYGO rate – the cost of the CPP relative to earnings – it was clearly understood that a lower PAYGO rate translated almost completely into a lower contribution rate. In the case of reducing the YBE, this one move alone would cut the steady-state contribution rate from 12.2 to about 11.2 per cent.[36] The proposal to reduce or eliminate the YBE was clearly attractive to policymakers. A one percentage point cut in the contribution rate was a big number, as we shall see. Few other measures could deliver that big a punch.

A Bit of Economics

Fuller funding of the CCP – moving the plan further away from its PAYGO roots – was the whole point of the argument for raising contribution rates quickly and creating an investment fund that would earn enough to stabilize the contribution rate quickly. But the governments recognized that fuller funding would also affect the entire economy. In the longer term, these effects would be positive, as argued in the Finance Department's working paper issued three months earlier.[37] The *Information Paper* boiled all its analysis and equations down to a simple list. Fuller funding would generate 'increased national savings, more investment, higher capital stock [and] reduced foreign indebtedness – all leading to higher national income. This would provide a sounder economic base to sustain the CPP down the road when there will be many more seniors than today.'[38]

The short term, which preoccupies politicians more than distant horizons, was a different matter. Higher contribution rates would reduce overall spending in the country, but the impact 'would likely be small enough' that any slowdown in growth could be 'ameliorated' by easier monetary policy (lower interest rates being a likely, though far from guaranteed, result of slower growth) and reductions in unemployment insurance premiums. Higher contribution rates would also reduce federal and provincial tax revenues, because individuals get a credit on their tax returns for CPP contributions, while companies can deduct them in calculating the corporate income tax they owe to Ottawa and the provinces. These short-term negatives were important, the *Information Paper* concluded, but 'as stewards of the CPP, the federal and provincial governments must weigh them against the longer-term benefits of fuller funding and lower contribution rates. Canadians deserve to have confidence that the CPP can be sustained and will be there for them in the future.'[39]

The Toughest Issue: Cutting Benefits

Now the *Information Paper* had to address the toughest – and for politicians, the most delicate – questions of all. Policymakers knew some benefit cuts would be needed to come up with a politically acceptable contribution rate – meaning something under 10 per cent, a rate some provinces had already pegged as the upper limit. After three decades in which benefits had only been enhanced, benefit cuts represented an unsavoury option for many politicians whose entire careers had been spent promising and delivering more for their constituents. But in an era of large deficits, huge debt, and a public that appeared suddenly willing to accept less, the paper set out a range of options for reining in the CPP.

Only one option was easy – saving money by tightening and streamlining the administration of the CPP. The federal government was already improving its computer systems to provide better and more timely service to seniors while saving $1.5 billion over the next fifteen years.[40] The rest were far more difficult.

Retirement Pensions

The central problem was paying for an additional four and a half years of retirement benefits, which was the increase between 1966 and 2030 in life expectancy at age 65. There were four ways to do it. Governments could cut pensions for new pensioners, increase the number of years required for a full pension, raise the age of entitlement, or provide only partial protection against inflation. Any of these on its own, or a combination, was possible.[41]

First, for new retirees only, the pension could be reduced to about 22.5 per cent of earnings from the current 25 per cent,[42] meaning that future seniors would get about 10 per cent less throughout their retirement years from the CPP. This measure on its own would reduce the 14.2 per cent long-term PAYGO rate by 1.25 percentage points to 12.95 per cent, making it a high-impact option.

Second, workers could be required to contribute longer before getting the full pension. The longer contribution period would finance the longer retirement period before death, and, again, only future retirees would be affected. The existing system allowed workers to drop from their earnings record 15 per cent of the years between 18 and 65 when their earnings were lowest or when they were not working at all. Cutting from 15 to 10 per cent would reduce the drop-out period from about 7 years to 4.7 years. To get a full pension, people would have to work 2.3 years longer.[43] Failing that, the additional 2.3 years of low earnings would be included in their record and their pension would be lower. The saving in terms of the long-term PAYGO rate would be 0.31 percentage points. There was also the childrearing dropout provision which allowed contributors to lop off the years caring for children under the age of 7. One option would be to limit to fifteen the total number of years dropped from the record of earnings.

Third, the age of entitlement could be raised. If people were living four and a half years longer after they reached 65, raising the retirement age to almost 70 'would be another way of dealing with the costs of rising life expectancy, but many would consider this excessive.'[44] A 'less drastic' alternative would be to raise the retirement age gradually to 66 or 67 and delay eligibility for early retirement pensions to 61 or 62 from

60. Governments would have to give notice of such a move – five to ten years – and the higher retirement age would have to be phased in gradually, but it could be done by 2011, when the baby boomers would begin to retire. The saving would amount to 0.63 per cent of covered earnings, so it would take that amount off the long-term PAYGO rate. The higher retirement age option might have been politically dead, given the number of key politicians already opposed, but it still had fans and had to be included, if for nothing else than the sake of completeness. Besides, politicians always like to have a highly controversial benefit reduction to reject, so that their choice of less onerous cuts looks reasonable by comparison.

Fourth, the governments could take away full indexing of CPP benefits. Instead of automatically rising at the same rate as inflation, as measured by the consumer price index (CPI), benefits could instead be indexed at the rate of inflation minus one percentage point. This would reduce future PAYGO rates by 1.28 percentage points – making this another very high-impact option. The *Information Paper* proposed a variation: benefits would be partially indexed only for the next ten years. 'This would allow current seniors, and those about to retire, to make a contribution to lessening the burden which CPP will impose on younger generations.'[45] Such a move would, of course, run counter to the promises of many federal politicians not to touch the pensions of current retirees, but some provincial governments were only too happy to consider such a proposal and their views had to be reflected in the paper.

Disability Benefits

The disability issue was trickier to explain to people because it was mainly a technical matter understood only by pension experts and advocacy groups for the disabled. Only the administrative cures taken to suppress the explosion in disability claims were simple to get across. The measures already taken were enough to shave 0.22 percentage points off the long-term PAYGO rate, and there were more to come. 'Efforts to improve the administration of CPP disability benefits will continue so as to ensure that benefits are provided only to those who are truly incapacitated and must rely on the CPP for income support.' But other changes to disability benefits – which would not affect current beneficiaries – could also 'further reduce costs and ensure the sustainability of this part of the CPP.'[46]

The first issue was the stacking of disability benefits from the CPP and provincial Workers' Compensation Board (WCB) programs. In provinces where the disabled could get benefits from both programs, the paper suggested that part or all of the WCB benefits could be subtracted from CPP benefits. This would be 'consistent with Workers' Compensation principles that the employer – not the CPP – should bear the cost of a work injury. Such a move would align the CPP closer to Quebec Pension Plan policy in this regard, and it would reduce disincentives to return to work.'[47] However, it would contribute little to the CPP's bigger financing problem. If future CPP disability benefits were reduced by an amount equal to one-quarter of workers' compensation payments, the reduction in the PAYGO rate would amount to a scant 0.08 of a percentage point.

Second, governments could tighten eligibility requirements. Contributors could now claim benefits if they had contributed to the CPP in two of the last three calendar years or five of the last ten calendar years before applying for benefits. If that period was changed to four of the last six years, the long-term PAYGO rate could be trimmed by 0.17 percentage points.

Third, the *Information Paper* suggested changing the way in which retirement pensions are calculated for those who were getting a disability pension before reaching 65. Disability pensions, which were indexed to the CPI, were automatically converted to retirement pensions when the recipient reached 65. But the retirement benefit was calculated on the basis of average wages when the beneficiary reached 65. In effect, the retirement benefit was indexed to wages for the period of the disability. Other CPP benefits, however, were based on average wages at the time of the event giving rise to the benefit, such as death or retirement. The paper suggested getting rid of this anomaly with an amendment under which the retirement pension of disability pensioners would be based on the average wage at the time of disablement, with subsequent price indexing. At age 65, the benefit would have the same purchasing power as it had at the time the person became disabled. 'This would link the retirement pension more closely to the work history of the disability recipient.'[48] The impact of such a change was not large – it would reduce the PAYGO rate by only 0.15 of a percentage point.

Finally, the governments proposed getting rid of another oddity that meant disability pensioners who reached retirement age did much better than people who had taken an early CPP retirement pension. The early retirement pension was reduced – by one-half of a percentage point per month – to reflect their fewer years of contributions and more years of anticipated benefits. For someone who retired at age 60, the CPP benefit was reduced by 30 per cent, so the monthly cheque was only 70 per cent of that received by someone who waited until age 65 to begin drawing the benefit. Few disability recipients chose the early retirement pension for obvious reasons. In 1996, an early retiree at 60 would get 70 per cent of the full $727 monthly pension, or $509. Someone who qualified for the disability pension at 60, on the other hand, would get $871 a month for the next five years, and then the full retirement pension. 'Disabled Canadians, therefore, receive, when they reach 65, more generous retirement benefits than workers who retire early and receive reduced benefits.'[49] Putting the two on an equal footing by converting the disability pension to a retirement pension that matched the reduced early retirement pension would treat the two groups alike. It would also reduce the long-term PAYGO rate by 0.39 of a percentage point.

Survivor Benefits

Survivor benefits were another thorny area that the governments wanted to address. Benefits for the widows (and widowers) and orphans of CPP contributors 'were designed in an era when most women did not work outside of the home. As such, when a contributor died, the plan provided the spouse at home, typically the wife, with a basic amount of income. Today, when 68 per cent of working-age women are in the work force, consideration could be given to redesigning CPP survivor benefits so that they reflect the changing realities and needs of today's families.'[50] That, however, was as far as policymakers were prepared to go at the time. 'Fundamental reform would be complex and time consuming ... [and] beyond the timeframe of the current review,' though they would return to it later.

Still, there were a couple of things that might be done immediately. Some people were entitled to two kinds of benefits, such as survivor and disability pensions and survivor and retirement pensions, but combined benefits of this kind were subject to a ceiling. Someone getting the combined survivor/retirement benefit was limited to the maximum retirement benefit of $727 monthly. A person under 65 getting the combined disability/survivor benefit was limited to the maximum disability pension of $871 a month plus one-quarter of the maximum retirement pension, which worked out to $182 a month. One cost-cutting measure would limit the combined disability/survivor benefit to the maximum disability pension alone. Another possible change would reduce the 'stacking' of earnings-related benefits. Such change could reduce the long-term PAYGO rate by 0.17 percentage points.

The death benefit was another target. The CPP offered a one-time death benefit (capped at 10 per cent of the year's maximum pensionable earnings, or $3,540 in 1996) to help pay the funeral costs of a contributor or pensioner who died. In 1966, the paper argued, 'when many elderly Canadians had few assets, this benefit filled a real need. Today, after three decades of rising incomes among the elderly and a need to limit escalating CPP costs, this benefit might be eliminated.' Eliminating it completely would knock 0.21 of a percentage point off the PAYGO rate.

As a final aid to readers, the paper summarized the financial effects of all the key options in a table. It was accompanied by the caveats that 'these savings cannot be simply added up because there is interaction among some of them ... [and] some measures are alternatives to others.'[51]

Questions for Canadians

The *Information Paper* closed with a set of questions for Canadians.[52] Public consultations would begin soon, and the ten governments were looking for feedback on all the major issues.

- How high can contribution rates go before they become unaffordable or go beyond the limits of fairness?
- How should governments strike a balance between higher contribution rates and reduced benefits?
- Are the benefit cuts listed in the paper the right ones or do others exist? And of the ideas outlined, which are most appropriate and least appropriate?
- If a much larger CPP fund is created, should the money be invested to earn maximum returns and how could this be done?
- Finally, are there other important considerations that governments should consider in making their decision?

A Debate with Focus

No matter what anyone thought of the contents of the paper, there was

Table 10.2 Financial impacts of possible CPP measures

	Savings in 2030	
	As % of CPP expenditures %	As reduction in PAYGO rate %
Retirement benefits		
Reduce income replacement rate to 22.5%	8.8	1.3
Reduce drop-out to 10 % over 5 years	2.2	0.3
Raise age of entitlement to 67	4.2	0.6
Index benefits in pay by CPI minus 1%	9	1.3
Disability benefits		
Tighten administration	1.5	0.2
Lower benefit by 25% of workers' compensation	0.6	0.1
Stronger labour force link	1.2	0.2
Convert pension at age 65 to actuarially reduced pension	2.7	0.4
Base retirement pensions on YMPE at time of disablement	1.1	0.2
Survivor benefits		
New rule for combined benefits	1.2	0.2
Eliminate death benefit	1.5	0.2
CPP earnings base*		
Cut YBE to 5 % and index	−0.1	1.1
Freeze YBE at 1997 level	−0.2	1.6

* Savings as a per cent of CPP costs are negative because more people would be brought into the system, thus increasing expenditures. However, the PAYGO rate would decline because the earnings base on which contributions are paid would expand.

Source: Department of Finance, *An Information Paper for Consultations on the Canada Pension Plan*, 43.

no doubt that it set the debate over the CPP's future off in a new direction. 'There was a paradigm shift,' said pension consultant Keith Ambachtsheer.[53] After years in which CPP discussions and proposals had wandered all over the map, Canadians suddenly had a clear idea of where this issue was heading – towards higher contribution rates, a big investment fund, and cuts to benefits. For the next year, that is how people would talk about the CPP.

The paper was smartly done. It not only informed Canadians of the choices, but established a framework for thinking about the issues. The men and women at the negotiating table were not yet agreed on an outcome – sharp divisions remained on many key questions – but they had set the parameters of their own discussion and wanted Canadians to do the same. One Ontario official recalled, 'we wanted to focus the debate, but not drive the conclusion.'

The *Information Paper* came under severe criticism from the left throughout the year for creating a 'crisis' where none existed and for failing to propose a more ambitious agenda for the CPP that would, of course, expand benefits even further. But for the most part, it was seen as a good effort. It contained a reasonable range of options, Ken Battle of the Caledon Institute of Social Policy recalled. 'It was short, but there was real meat to it.'[54] One senior Ontario official described the paper as taking the middle ground on the key issues: 'That may have been the only place where there was solid footing.'

Before the month was out, the politicians got an early glimpse of reaction to their proposals from a public opinion survey. The poll, conducted by the Angus Reid organization for Southam News, contained some encouraging news for those working to overhaul the CPP. By a very wide margin, Canadians favoured saving the CPP and QPP (70 per cent) over scrapping them (just under 30 per cent). Even among Reform Party supporters, 53 per cent wanted to save the CPP compared with 43 per who supported their party's proposal to kill it. Asked what kind of solution they preferred, 62 per cent of all respondents supported higher premiums compared with 26 per cent who preferred to see benefits cut.[55]

For politicians of every persuasion and in every government, the poll contained an early – and sobering – warning from the public as they considered how to fix the CPP. The stakes were high and Canadians had some firm views on the issue; they would be watching closely. If the policymakers did not understand this already, they were about to conduct major surgery on a very popular patient.

11 Consultations – Of All Kinds

Now the CPP reform was moving on two tracks. Behind the scenes, federal and provincial officials continued to work through the particulars that made up the broader reform plan. Even where they agreed on the basics of an item in the reform, there were plenty of devils in the detail. The public track involved something entirely new. Governments had consulted the public before on major issues, but never in quite the way the CPP ministers ran their show – as a joint federal–provincial effort. It took longer than hoped to get the public consultation process rolling, but by the end of March 1996, the governments were ready to go.

Heading the consultations was David Walker, the Liberal member of Parliament for Winnipeg-North Centre and Paul Martin's former parliamentary secretary. In late February, Jean Chrétien had carried out a routine shuffle of all MPs just below cabinet level, in the process shifting Walker from Finance to become chairman of the Commons industry committee. He was, he admits, 'sulking' about the move and, when approached to run the consultations process, leapt at the chance. As a former politics professor at the University of Winnipeg, he had 'the sort of policy-wonk credentials usually associated with such a thankless task.'[1] Even better for this purpose, he had taken an interest in the CPP while working with Martin and was a long-time believer in what he called participatory consultations. His formal title in this new role was Chief Federal Representative on the federal–provincial–territorial panels that would visit all ten provinces and both territories for public consultations on the CPP. The panel in each province or territory would comprise Walker and another MP from that province plus one or two elected representatives from the respective provincial or territorial governments.[2]

Walker pushed hard for a format that would force people of different views to talk with, rather than past, each other. Typically, when parliamentary and legislative committees hear from the public, the different groups and individuals appear in sequence, presenting their views, answering questions, and leaving. The CPP panel tried something new, inviting groups with disparate views to sit down for a morning or afternoon around a table, where they would present their views and then discuss the issues with the others. 'Each hearing was balanced by having protagonists and antagonists at the same table,' said one federal official[3] who sat through most of the hearings. 'It was a roundtable – not one after the other. This was key.' Walker was skilled at hearing people out but tried to focus people on making choices. 'He drove people to the issues.' Walker would end each session by summarizing the views of each group. As this official recalled it, he was 'not like a commissioner; more like a facilitator.'

Martin figured Walker brought two attributes to the task – the 'right personality' and his experience with the consultations leading up to the 1995 budget. As Martin saw it, public consultations offered two benefits. One was the legitimate seeking out of the views of Canadians. Second, consultations prepared the way and began selling the ultimate end product, something a government could do if it knew what its ultimate end product was likely to be. 'In most public policy areas, if you have debated the policy internally and you are doing it for the right reasons, people will come to the same conclusion.' That becomes easier 'if you put all sides at the same table and people can see that your decision was not made for Machiavellian reasons.' Walker, having been through that process with the budget, understood that, Martin said.[4]

The Road Show

From 15 April through 10 June, the panels held thirty-three sessions in eighteen cities – five in Ontario, two each in Alberta and Manitoba, and one each in the other seven provinces and two territories. Toronto was visited twice, once to hear general submissions and another time for a session that focused solely on the investment issues. A hearing in Waterloo was limited to disability issues, while another in Ottawa dealt with youth. By the time it was over, the panels had heard from 219 organizations and 59 individuals in their public hearings and received 144 written submissions; the list of participants filled 26 pages of their final report.

Media coverage of the hearings was low-key. Local newspapers and radio and television stations covered the panels when they visited town, but no one consistently followed the consultations across the country. For the national media, the hearings rapidly turned into one of those stories that produced little real news because the story was almost the same every day. In Winnipeg, the fourth stop, a Canadian Press report summed up the discussion this way: 'So it went. There is no crisis/yes there is. The CPP needs minor tinkering/major surgery. Employers should pay more/less/nothing.'[5]

A small CPP secretariat prepared daily summaries of the sessions each evening and fired them off to key officials in Ottawa and the provincial governments so they could follow the debate on a regular basis despite the lack of consistent media coverage. For advice on technical issues that arose, Walker could turn to Finance officials Hal Hanes and George Marshall from the social policy division, at least one of whom was at each session.

By mid-June, when the finance ministers were ready to meet again – this time in Fredericton – the secretariat had produced a ninety-two-page report[6] on the consultations that summarized the views heard on all the options raised in the *Information Paper*, plus a few more that some participants wanted added to the list. There were other consultations as well. The Ontario government organized its own hearings under two provincial Conservative MPPs, who went to ten communities, seven of which had not been on the tour of the national panel. The Caledon Institute of Social Policy – as it had done a year earlier on behalf of the Human Resources Development Department – ran two more one-day seminars, one at the behest of the Finance Department and a second for the federal Status of Women agency.

Five Themes

The CPP secretariat's report pulled from the panel hearings five themes that 'emerged at almost all of the sessions no matter where in Canada they were held or who was around the table.'[7]

First, Canadians wanted the CPP preserved and protected because of its key role in the retirement income system. 'The consultations panels heard over and over that Canadians are deeply attached to the CPP and believe it is well worth keeping. Canadians want the plan's current problems fixed quickly and fixed for good. The majority of Canadians participating in the consultations urged governments to put the CPP on a sound financial footing now. Strong support came from organizations as well as individuals who said the plan is important to Canadians because it provides full coverage, portable benefits, inflation protection, low administration costs, and a major source of income to the elderly.'[8]

Second, the panels found a deep lack of confidence in the CPP, especially among the young, and a willingness to see governments make substantial changes in the plan, particularly to cure the plan's unfairness to future generations. In Toronto, one person said that if governments failed to overcome that problem, 'it is an act of cowardice.' At the same time, there was mistrust of governments, especially from some unions and social advocates, who said governments and the media had stirred up a 'crisis' that did not really exist. Some faulted the CPP *Information Paper* 'because it is alarmist and attacks the principles of the CPP. They also disputed assumptions in the paper and deplored the lack of impact analysis, gender in particular.'[9]

Third, the notion of privatizing the CPP found little support; there was a 'strong desire' to keep it as a public pension plan. Bankers, actuaries, unions, and social groups all took that view, for several reasons: not everyone would be able to invest their funds wisely in a private plan and would still need retirement pensions; the cost of administration would rise; it would not deal with the existing unfunded liability, valued in 1995 at $556 billion; and it would not allow for the pursuit of social objectives, like supporting childrearing. Support for privatization came only from conservative organizations like the Fraser Institute and the Canadian Taxpayers Federation and some young people.[10]

Fourth, the issue of disability benefits commanded a great deal of attention, though 'the intensity of the debate varied from session to session.' The panels stumbled on a wider debate over moving disability benefits out of the CPP altogether, though for different reasons. Some thought the disabled would be better served by a separate national program, while others saw this as a means of sustaining the CPP through lower costs. Groups representing the disabled were divided on the issue.[11]

Finally, many participants chided governments for not keeping Canadians fully informed of the CPP's workings and its deteriorating financial condition. 'It was suggested throughout the consultations that the CPP has been misunderstood and taken for granted by Canadians over the years. A good number of people said they would have been more concerned about the future of the CPP had they been aware of the Plan's current financing and investment structure. Some presenters blamed governments for the lack of public understanding about what the Plan is and how it works.' In Yellowknife, one person said he thought 'bad communications and ignorance has contributed to the general malaise over the CPP. Lack of information is causing intergenerational rivalry between those who benefit and those who must pay.'[12]

Fault Lines and Alliances

The hearings exposed some unsurprising fault lines. Intergenerational conflict was never far from the surface and occasionally broke through quite vividly. In Vancouver, a theology student asked if there were 'seniors who are getting money and are wealthy enough to take care of themselves who are selling out younger generations for a house and a golf membership.' To this, a senior in the audience retorted: 'I paid for your university, for God's sake. You paid $3,000 and it cost $10,000.'[13] Business groups were wary of steep increases in contribution rates and urged that the rate be held to less than 10 per cent by reducing benefits, while labour unions and social policy groups preferred to maintain benefits even if it meant substantial increases in the contribution rate.[14]

But there were some surprising alliances as well. Business groups and labour unions alike strongly supported the CPP's retirement pensions. Business, labour, and seniors' groups favoured the idea of investing the CPP fund in the market to maximize returns, though some labour representatives wanted the fund to pursue other investment goals as well.[15] David Walker observed later that while the Canadian Labour Congress wanted an investment policy that included economic development goals, 'regional labour groups were telling us to invest solely for the purpose of maximizing pensions.'[16] Social policy groups found common cause with some pension professionals – like pension funds and actuaries – in suggesting that the CPP should not be examined in isolation from other social programs or other elements of the retirement income system.[17] Labour and social policy groups, not surprisingly, opposed cuts to benefits, and all disability groups opposed cuts to disability benefits in particular.

Key Questions, Key Answers

The *Information Paper* had posed four broad questions for the consultations: What is affordable? What is the right balance between rate increases and benefit 'changes' (read: cuts)? Which options for reducing the cost of benefits seem most and least appropriate? How should a larger CPP fund be invested?

The affordability of the 14.2 per cent contribution rate was hotly contested. The majority said it was not, but labour groups and a few others said it was. After all, other countries were paying that much for their public pensions and had higher payroll taxes than Canada. The response: other countries paid higher benefits as well and many were also worried about affordability; Canada's payroll tax load might be low, but the overall tax burden was higher in Canada than in its three major trading partners – the United States, Japan, and Britain. The Canadian Labour Congress argued an arithmetic point: because the contribution rate was levied only on earnings between the basic exemption and the maximum, the contribution rate as a percentage of the maximum was lower than 14.2 per cent; and the average contribution would be less than 9 per cent. Hardly a 'sustainability crisis,' the CLC sniffed.[18]

Benefits also came in for scrutiny on a broad scale, as different groups focused on intergenerational accounting. The first generation – people who retired in the 1970s – got a 30 per cent return on their contributions while future generations might expect a slender 1.5 per cent return. Philip Connell, a retired chartered accountant from Toronto, made a memorable presentation, one that some observers recall to this day for its rarity: he thought his own benefits were too rich. He figured he and his employers had contributed $18,607 to the CPP, but in his seven years of retirement, he had already received $54,287, a 'scandalous' overpayment. Had he used the funds to buy an annuity at 65, he would have gotten only $14,317.[19]

Affordability popped up in the debate over a steady-state contribution rate and fuller funding. Most liked both ideas, but again, the CLC favoured the PAYGO status quo over a new financing system, as did pension consultant Monica Townson. They got support on that point from the University of Waterloo actuary Rob Brown, who had already been active in the public debate over the CPP. The report said 'they presented a number of arguments to support their positions: a pension system cannot be pre-funded because in the end, all benefits must be paid out of national income; increased contributions would not raise national savings and thus be ineffective and self-defeating; real growth will again exceed real interest rates so there is no need to act; and, a large pension fund could be misused.'[20] One of the more imaginative suggestions came from the Canadian Institute of Actuaries. Under its proposal for 'smart funding,' the CPP would set a funding target that varied with the real rate of interest; at a rate of 6 per cent or higher, the CPP would aim for full funding, but at a rate of 2 per cent or lower, it would run as a PAYGO plan.[21]

The Question of Balance

Through the thicket of conflicting views, the consultations secretariat discerned a clear bottom line on where Canadians stood regarding the balance that should be struck between higher contribution rates versus benefit reductions. 'The predominant view ... was that comparatively more action should be taken on the contribution side than on the bene-. fit side.'[22] Only a handful of the participants pressed for more generous pensions, but most were willing to accept some benefits cuts. No matter how deep their weariness with rising taxes in general, however, Canadians appeared willing to accept the higher CPP contribution rate as a price worth paying to cure the financial ills of the CPP. For policymakers seeking a balance that would be politically acceptable, that was an extraordinarily useful finding.

There was more to potential CPP revenues than contribution rates alone. There was the earnings base on which the rate is levied – the income between the $3,500 Year's Basic Exemption (YBE) and the $35,400 Year's Maximum Pensionable Earnings (YMPE). If the former was cut or eliminated or if the latter was raised (not an option included in the *Information Paper*), the earnings base would expand and each percentage point of the contribution rate would raise more revenue. Reducing the YBE was touchy because it primarily affected the poor, where women accounted for a disproportionate share. This was perhaps the only element of the CPP that made it even mildly progressive. Hypothetically, a person could spend a lifetime earning $3,600 a year and earn a retirement pension based on that sum, despite making contributions on only $100 a year of that income, the difference between the actual income and the $3,500 YBE. The business community largely favoured a cut, with the notable exception of the restaurant and food service industry, a major employer of part-time workers, many of whom were young. Some social groups pressed for an increase in the YMPE, which would generate more revenue from upper income earners. But the federal and provincial governments argued that this could also undermine the existing link between contributions and benefits.[23] Under most such proposals, higher earners would make bigger contributions, but there would be no immediate increase in benefits.

Cutting Which Benefits?

But there was still the third big question – how to cut the cost of benefits? – and there, the answers were more complex, simply because there were so many options. For retirement pensions alone, there were four choices, and only one of those received even a modicum of public support from the hearings. Cutting the pension to 22.5 per cent of earnings from 25 per cent was widely rejected, as was reducing the number of years worth of earnings that can be dropped from the earnings record when calculating a pension. Thumbs went down too on raising the age of entitlement – the normal retirement age – to 66 or 67, though some said it was probably inevitable. The CLC argued that because almost all private pension plans were built on the assumption that CPP benefits would begin at 65, any increase 'would have a massive impact on private pension plans.'[24] Indeed, most private pension plans, many of which had been the subject of labour–management bargaining, were so closely integrated with the CPP that they would have to be substantially redesigned.

The only option to find some favour was the partial de-indexing of pensions to the inflation rate minus one percentage point; on that question, participants were evenly split. Proponents said it would contribute to intergenerational equity, since it would affect those already getting a CPP pension. A few suggested that it could be temporary, so its impact would be limited to the first generation that had done so well out of the CPP. But there was plenty of opposition as well, especially from women's groups, who noted that since women generally live longer than men, they had more to lose from a steady decline in the real purchasing power of their pensions.[25]

The cool reception to this cluster of options for trimming retirement pensions was clearly going to make it harder for policymakers to cut costs on the backs of retired Canadians, either then or in the future. Of all the options laid out in the February *Information Paper*, the four dealing with retirement pensions included several with the biggest impact in terms of reducing the long-term contribution rate. Cutting the replacement rate to 22.5 per cent of pre-retirement income from 25 per cent or partially de-indexing pensions would each, on its own, reduce the rate by about 1.25 percentage points, while raising the retirement age would have half that effect. If those went off the table, cuts to disability and survivor benefits would have to be larger.

Disability questions had stirred some of the most emotional debates

Thomas Boldt, 'Parachute,' 1996

of the whole consultation, from the small details to the biggest question of all: Should disability benefits even be part of the CPP at all or should they be carved off into a separate program? But there was little agreement on any of the options. In almost all parts of the country, unions, workers' compensation boards, advocacy groups for the disabled, and private insurers engaged in a vigorous debate over the interaction among the CPP, WCBs, and private insurers over who should be the 'first payer' of disability benefits and who was trying to offload costs onto some other payer. Provincial WCBs and insurance companies were usually seen as encouraging clients to apply first to the CPP so that they could reduce their costs; provincial WCBs, not surprisingly, believed the CPP should indeed be the first payer. For all the talk, however, there was little consensus on the key issues raised in the *Information Paper* or, in the case of the more technical items, little discussion at all. Nor was there any consensus on what to do with survivor benefits.[26]

The death benefit was another matter. Everyone, it seemed, even those 'who opposed almost all reductions in benefits were willing to see death benefits eliminated, or subjected to a means test in order to target those in need.'[27]

Putting the Money to Work

Finally, there was the matter of an investment policy for the CPP. If policymakers could raise the contribution rate fast enough, the increased revenues would generate in short order a substantial pool of capital that would need investing. If it were large enough and invested wisely enough, its earnings could help finance future pensions, especially in the 2020s and 2030s, when the vast majority of baby boomers would be retired.

The consultations with the general public produced a strong consensus on the broad features of the investment policy. 'There was near unanimous support ... for a better investment strategy for the CPP fund,' with most endorsing the idea of putting the money into a diversified portfolio of market securities.[28] 'There was also wide agreement that the fund should be carefully managed at arm's length from government under a fiduciary mandate.' And if the provinces were to keep their priority access to the fund, 'there was a strong consensus that they should pay market rates.'[29] Disagreement was limited to smaller concerns. Could the money be invested abroad? Should it be reinvested in the communities of contributors or simply put into safe, but high-yielding, securities.

To get some expert advice, David Walker invited investment dealers and representatives from the pension fund industry to two panel sessions in Toronto that were devoted solely to the investment policy. The only outlier at those meetings was Hugh Mackenzie of the United Steel Workers of America, standing in for Canadian Labour Congress officials who were tied up at a conference. An economist who had been executive director of Ontario's Fair Tax Commission when the NDP was in power, he commented that of all the participants at the session, 'I'm the only one that doesn't have a conflict of interest in the outcome of this.'[30]

Mackenzie excepted, the sessions produced a consensus that the old 'provincial access approach' to investing the CPP fund should be scrapped. Instead, most or all of the new money should go into a 'diversified portfolio of market securities to increase returns and restore confidence in the CPP,' which was referred to as a 'market oriented approach.'[31] Most participants agreed that the fund should have one objective: to maximize returns in the interest of current and future beneficiaries, with no secondary objective to promote economic development. Once more, Mackenzie dissented. All but one (again, Mackenzie) of the participants agreed that while a diversified CPP fund would hold some provincial securities in its portfolio, provincial governments should have no preferential access to the money.

There was no dissent on the basic question of governance. The pension and investment crowd said the CPP fund 'should be governed by an independent, arm's length, board of trustees operating under a clear fiduciary mandate.'[32] Most figured the federal and provincial governments should jointly select the board. A number of participants said several large public sector pension funds – the Ontario Teachers' Pension Plan Board was cited as one example – could be used as models for governing the CPP.

The experts also talked about operational issues. Should the money be managed internally by fund officials – though not 'by government,' they insisted – or by private sector fund managers? Some wanted the fund broken into smaller separate funds to promote competition and avoid the possibility that one big fund might unduly influence the economy. Others thought one big internally managed fund would be more cost-effective. The two groups also debated the relative merits of active versus passive fund management – whether the fund should get into picking specific stocks or stick to investing in indexes that mirrored the broader market. Some said passive management would reduce both management costs and the potential for political interference. Others countered that active management would generate returns large enough to outweigh the extra management costs.

They also agreed – almost unanimously – that the fund should be able to invest in foreign securities, because that would allow for a more diversified portfolio and at the same time take pressure off Canada's small domestic capital market. To illustrate the Canadian market's limitations, one pension fund manager observed that the top 100 companies accounted for fully 80 per cent of the Toronto Stock Exchange's total capitalization. That this group of financial community heavyweights should support greater freedom to invest globally was hardly surprising. In their own activities, they were chafing under federal tax rules that prevented them from investing more than 20 per cent of their assets abroad and most wanted the ceiling raised or abolished altogether. Besides, as one actuary noted, a sound investment strategy would allow the CPP to invest in countries with different demographic characteristics than Canada.[33]

The Caledon Brawl

The public consultations featured regular disagreements, but it is doubtful that any single session could have compared with the intellectual and rhetorical brawl that broke out during another one-day 'experts' forum' run by the Caledon Institute of Social Policy in early May 1996. This one, sponsored by Finance Canada, was far different in content and tone than the Caledon roundtable eleven months earlier sponsored by Human Resources Development Canada. Structured explicitly around the *Information Paper*, the program this time featured many of the leading commentators on CPP reform and pitted left against right in what reads, a decade on, as perhaps the most pugnacious – certainly the most direct – confrontation between the two broad camps fighting in the public arena over CPP reform. Better yet, the federal Finance Department joined the fray with some analysis that – despite disclaimers that it did not represent government policy – provided valuable insight into the department's thinking.[34]

Almost every key interest group in the CPP debate had someone in the room and observers showed up from five federal departments plus the Prime Minister's Office (Finance and Human Resources Development each sent a dozen or more), four provinces, and the opposition parties in Parliament. Even Tom Kent, architect of the CPP in the 1960s, and Harvey Lazar, whose massive report had been a key feature of the Great Pension Debate in the late 1970s and early 1980s, were there.

The opening session set the tone, with the first two speakers explicitly representing the right and left. Leading off was economist Bill Robson from the C.D. Howe Institute, a conservative think tank. Four months earlier, he had produced a report comparing the CPP to a Ponzi game – a pyramid scheme in which early investors get their income not from real investments but from the money put into the pot by later investors – and arguing for the winding up of the CPP altogether.[35] At the Caledon session, he reiterated his argument that because 'the CPP is a bad deal for younger Canadians,' it was not worth keeping. 'It is no insult to our children's future compassion for the truly needy to speculate that when they are old enough to vote, they will vote for candidates –and there will be many – who promise to overturn the system.' Better to act now, he said, and 'phase the CPP out in favour of expanded private retirement saving.'[36]

First up for the left was Monica Townson, who had been chair of the Ontario Fair Tax Commission under the NDP government in the early 1990s. She took dead aim at what she saw as the failings of the *Information Paper*. 'It claims the CPP is unsustainable, but it produces no evidence to support the claim. It claims future generations will be asked to pay considerably more than their benefits are worth, but there is no explanation or analysis to substantiate this. It claims future generations will not be willing or able to pay higher contributions, but it does not tell us how it arrived at this conclusion.'[37] The 'problem,' as she saw it in quotation marks, was that 'the government is trying to push through massive changes to the CPP that will have a major impact on the financial security of the future elderly, without adequate analysis or discussion of its claims that the plan is 'unfair' or that it is 'unsustainable,' and without any analysis whatsoever of the impact of its proposals on the incomes of the future elderly.'[38]

Finance Answers the Critics

Next came Munir Sheikh, head of the Finance Department's economic studies and policy analysis division, the unit that had provided the economic rationale for fuller funding. One senses that he had been itching for a chance to respond to critics from both the left (who thought

PAYGO was sustainable) and the right (who wanted to privatize the whole system); the Caledon forum was just that opportunity. Fuller funding, he said, was a 'middle-of-the-road position [that] has been criticized by both those who think the status quo is more or less fine and those who think the system is so awful that it has to be abolished.'[39] Public servants rarely get the opportunity to engage their critics publicly in such detail. Sheikh's extensive point-by-point rebuttal of Finance's critics is probably the most complete summary on record of how the department regarded the debate outside its doors.

Among the usual arguments in favour of PAYGO funding, he first took on the idea that because people in other countries were already paying premiums of 14 per cent or higher, there was no reason to believe Canadians might rebel at such rates. The problem, Sheikh said, was that a 14 per cent premium in Canada would 'buy' a maximum pension of only $8,700 in current dollars. In France and Japan, contribution rates of 15 to 16 per cent produce an $18,000 pension, while in the United States, a 12 per cent premium would buy a pension of about $14,500. Moreover, many of those countries were already worried enough about their own pension finances that they were moving to contain pension costs – France by reducing benefits and the United States by raising the normal retirement age to 67. To the related argument that Canada's payroll taxes were low compared with elsewhere, Sheikh said it was the total tax burden that mattered – and Canada's was the third highest among G7 countries, substantially higher than those of the United States, Japan, and Britain.

As for those who said countries simply cannot pre-fund their pensions, Sheikh replied that of course they can. 'It is strange to think that different generations are totally disconnected.' Pre-funding should increase national savings and investment, which would increase future production and thus reduce future contributions. And for those who said there was no theoretical or empirical support for this rosy view of the blessings fuller funding would bring in the future, Sheikh said more assets in the CPP fund was 'exactly symmetric' to a decline in government debt. The only things that could offset 'this direct increase in national savings' would be an increase in pension benefits or a dollar-for-dollar drop in private savings as CPP contributions rise. If governments are going to solve the underfunding problem, they must not increase benefits, he argued. And economic theory and empirical evidence both supported the view that people do not fully reduce their savings when contribution rates rise. If the private sector fully offset increased savings in the public sector, he argued, there would be no point in even reducing government deficits and debt. Indeed, he added, if that argument were correct, then 'the public provision of pensions, or for that matter many other government services, could be totally futile as they would be fully neutralized by private sector behaviour.'

Some critics also argued that PAYGO could still work because wage growth would again exceed real interest rates as it had in the 1960s and 1970s. Not true, said Sheikh. The evidence – both from theory and data – was that 'the only stable situation that can persist over long periods is for real interest rates to exceed real growth,' though there might be some spells when the opposite was true. Even then, so what? 'Suppose we increase funding of the CPP and real growth miraculously takes off. Is that a problem? Not at all. We can easily lower contribution rates in the future in response to such a development.'

He also dismissed concerns that a large pension fund might be misused or be eroded by inflation; a proper institutional structure could avoid the first, and wise investment would prevent the second, he said. Next, he took on the argument that one generation would pay twice in any transition to fuller funding, a criticism he found ironic. PAYGO created the very unfunded liability that 'would make someone – it is just a question of who – pay more than their CPP benefits.' Since the double payment is unavoidable, the only way to minimize it is to move as quickly as possible away from the system that created it.

Finally, Sheikh turned on the right, specifically the proponents of a Chilean-style system of mandatory RRSPs of the kind being promoted by the Reform Party, *The Globe and Mail*'s editorial board, and conservative think tanks like the Fraser Institute and the C.D Howe Institute. Privatization, Sheikh noted, would not deal with the unfunded liability, the very point that the University of Waterloo's Rob Brown had made when Reform first came out with its plan (see chapter 8). Sheikh figured that even if the system were privatized, Canadians would have to keep paying a contribution rate of almost 6 per cent for another thirty-five years to cover the cost of the CPP's retirement benefit promises, in addition to saving for their own retirement through mandatory RRSPs. Private pensions would lose the benefits of public pensions, he added, citing pensions as an area of market failure. Governments provide national defence, laws and regulations, environmental protection, and health care because markets cannot, he argued; the same is true with 'certain types of pensions.'

A private system would also sacrifice the insurance element of the CPP – like disability and spousal benefits – and increase administrative costs. The Chilean system was not one Canadians should think to emulate, Sheikh said. There, the private annuities market was inefficient because the main buyers were people who expected to live a long time, while the main suppliers were primarily interested in selling only to people who were not expected to live very long. As a result, 'most Chileans are forced to opt for phased withdrawals of their funds when they retire' rather than buy annuities. Those who live longer than expected may run out of money before they die. The CPP insures against that possibility. And the CPP is cheap to run, Sheikh added, with costs amounting to about 0.1 per cent of the annual covered earnings of plan members. Administrative expenses in Chile and private sector plans in the United States cost six to thirty times what the CPP did.

The Language of the Left

That was just the first session. The left–right divide over the CPP was on display in the second as well. Louis Erlichman, Canadian research director of the International Association of Machinists and Aerospace Workers and a former chairman of the CPP Advisory Board,[40] accused the federal government of mounting 'a fundamental attack on the CPP,' through a 'misinformation campaign' based on 'the unbalanced *Information Paper*' and 'a parody of a consultation process.'[41] There is no financing 'crisis,' he argued, reiterating the usual argument that the CPP's projected peak rate was below that of many other countries, the very point Munir Sheikh had just addressed. Erlichman tore into the Finance working paper on the economics of the CPP as 'proof of little but the Finance department's prejudices.' The paper used 'an old trick in economics: Assume what you claim to be proving, churn out some numbers, and bury it all in jargon and equations.' He agreed that the CPP's sustainability ultimately depended on future workers' ability and willingness to pay the costs but said federal economic policy had, for the previous two decades, 'focused almost exclusively on suppressing workers' earnings and stifling the growth of employment and the economy.' This wage suppression, he added, had directly raised the CPP contribution rate and 'because of chronic high levels of unemployment and stagnant wages, made people less likely to want to transfer income to CPP beneficiaries or anyone else.'

If the language of the labour movement and social policy advocates was beginning to sound somewhat intemperate, it may have been a product of frustration. The left was losing battle after battle against deficit reduction and spending cuts across the country as governments went to work restoring their budgetary finances. Support for the federal NDP was meagre – it had won only nine seats in the 1993 election – and it was still faring badly in public opinion polls. Part of the problem was that the left in general – with its continuing support for deficit financing – 'was so discredited on fiscal issues,' as one senior federal official later put it. 'You've got to remember the mood of the country.' The left found it especially galling that no one was listening to its message at a time when economic conditions might have been expected to create a sympathetic audience. In mid-1996, the economy seemed to be bouncing back from its 1995 slowdown, but job growth had slowed and the unemployment rate was still above 9 per cent and rising again. Real income remained lower than in 1989, before the recession of the early 1990s. For the left, the message to Ottawa was simple – get the economy growing again and the CPP will take care of itself. But no one was listening to its prescriptions.

It would be wrong to leave the impression that all labour union representatives used such excessive language. An exception was Bob Baldwin, the CLC's leading pension expert. A thoughtful economist who was widely respected in the pension community even by those who disagreed with him, Baldwin told the Caledon gathering – in a low-key but tough-minded talk – that the *Information Paper*'s menu of possible changes to the CPP represented 'a remarkably perverse set of reactions' to the income security needs of Canadians:

- A cut in the CPP retirement benefit is suggested in spite of the substandard incomes of the retired population;
- A reduction in drop-out periods is suggested notwithstanding the reality that people spend more time out of active employment due to periods of unemployment, training and education, and early retirement;
- A host of 'nickel and dime' cuts to CPP disability benefits are suggested despite the fact that one of the most glaring holes in Canada's social security system is the absence of a comprehensive disability insurance program;
- Increasing the age of eligibility for CPP retirement benefits is suggested even though there is an increasing desire to leave the labour force early and, in many situations (e.g., the federal government), pressure to do so
  ...
- Reducing the YBE is suggested while there is increasing reason to be

concerned about the impact of CPP contributions on the living standards of people with low incomes as the CPP contribution rate goes up;

- Limiting indexing is proposed when increasing longevity makes indexing even more important;
- Limits are suggested for survivor benefits when the ability of survivors
  to maintain their standard of living is clearly a problem.'[42]

A Better Way?

Malcolm Hamilton, a prominent actuary who had given much thought
to the CPP and become a forceful advocate of financing reform, could
be just as tart as Baldwin in outlining his views. His take on the two
methods of CPP financing – PAYGO or fuller funding – was unique and
arresting. Funding a social insurance plan on a pay-as-you-go basis, he
said, was just a sophisticated version of 'the oldest retirement system
known to man – parents relying on their children.'[43] But the fishermen
and farmers of centuries past knew how to do it right: have lots of children, 'give them the nurturing, training, tools and support that they
need to be productive,' and support yourself for as long as possible.
The CPP was in trouble because Canadians had done none of those
things, he argued. 'We haven't had large families. We haven't successfully integrated Generation X into our economy, and we haven't asked
seniors to support themselves to the limit of their ability.' If you cannot
rely on your children, you have to rely on savings, but that works only
if you save enough and earn a decent rate of return on what you save.
But Canadians had not saved enough, he said. So the real choice lay
between counting on the kids or saving more through a better-funded,
better-invested CPP.

Hamilton rejected both PAYGO and full funding of the CPP, but he
liked some aspects of the steady-state financing proposal. His real preference, though, was the system he had helped devise for the Canadian
Institute of Actuaries' task force – conditional (or smart) funding, under
which the CPP would move back and forth between PAYGO and fuller
funding depending on the projected relationship between interest rates
and wage growth. (See the earlier reference in this chapter.) He made
his case in some detail but won no converts. (Hamilton said recently
that he was told at the time by people in Finance that the idea was a
non-starter because the key ingredients moved around too much.) His
passion for more saving in the CPP was reinforced by his view that
Canada's public debt of more than $800 billion was, like the CPP, an
intergenerational embarrassment and that both could be solved only if

Canadians saved more.[44] 'We've tried dissaving and borrowing. It produces insolvency, not growth. It's time to try something else. Save more. Borrow less. Consume less. It isn't fun. It isn't pretty. But it might work.'

Pension expert Keith Ambachtsheer contributed some advice on how a new CPP fund should work and some hard numbers for others to chew on. The CPP should invest solely for the benefit of its stakeholders, create a structure that empowers a knowledgeable board of trustees to hire skilled and motivated managers, and insist on full accountability and transparency. It would be reasonable to expect, if those three steps were taken, that a market-oriented investment policy would produce an additional 1 percentage point of returns, with another 0.25-point annual return from the 'value-adding' skills of the investment team.[45]

More Fireworks

There were more fireworks when the forum turned to the question of disability benefits. Some participants recall the outrage from various quarters that greeted two presentations in particular. A Dutch official, Dirk Beekman from the Netherlands' Ministry of Social Affairs and Employment, outlined his country's experience with allowing an explosion in disability benefits followed by a tough effort to bring them under control. During the first period, he said, the country learned that if too little is done to reintegrate people back into the job market, beneficiaries 'tend to settle into disability. It is a lifestyle of some sort, and a socially accepted one.'[46] In 1986, 778,000 people, almost 14 per cent of the working population, were disabled; by 1989, the number was heading towards 'one million disabled in an otherwise healthy country of 15 million people' when the government began its reforms, which included tougher eligibility criteria and reduced benefits for those who did qualify. His advice to Canada was to 'be strict in admitting people to the disability benefit.'

The other panelist was Dr Allan Wilson from the University of Ottawa and the Royal Ottawa Hospital Addiction Program, who said that for over twenty-three years he had clinical experience with some 50,000 patients who had alcohol and other substance dependence problems. Many of those patients were getting CPP disability pensions, and the fact that their addiction was the source of their income worked as a disincentive to overcoming their dependence on alcohol and drugs. 'Most alcohol or substance-dependent patients receiving CPP disability benefits either refuse to attempt rehabilitation or, once in treatment, cannot accept responsibility for their well-being and engage in self-defeating behaviour or exhibit learned helplessness.'[47] His advice: 'Alcohol abuse, alcohol dependence, substance abuse and substance dependence are not grounds for a disability pension under any circumstances.' That tough prescription was not popular with some in the room. One observer recalled: 'Boy, was he attacked.'[48]

In his summary of the forum, the Caledon Institute's president, Ken Battle, noted the 'profound disagreement on the nature of the problem' but still found some reason for optimism. 'Ironically, however, the discord over fixing the CPP was somewhat less deep than over what is wrong with the program. There may be the makings of a political compromise.'[49]

The Gender Issue

The Caledon Institute was not finished with the CPP. Two weeks later, it hosted another roundtable, this one sponsored by Status of Women Canada, the federal agency dealing with women's issues. The topic was the gender implications of CPP reform. No one disputed that both the CPP as it stood and the various proposals to reform the plan had and would have different impacts on women and men. Yet the gender issue never managed to muscle its way into the public consciousness in a major way. Even so, the Caledon roundtable served as a forceful reminder to policymakers not to forget women as they made their reform decisions. Officials from every province (except Quebec) and both territories, mainly from provincial agencies dealing with women's issues, attended the conference, and there is little question they fed the results back to their teams at the negotiating table.

The CPP mattered greatly to women primarily because of its many features that – though usually not designed for this specific purpose – helped to offset many of the disadvantages faced by women in building a retirement income. Monica Townson, who led off the session,[50] set those out:

- The CPP covered everyone in the workforce, regardless of which sector they worked in. Women tended to work in sectors like retail, where pension coverage was lowest; in 1993, 42 per cent were covered by an occupational pension plan, compared with 47 per cent of men.
- The CPP covered the self-employed and all paid workers, including those in non-standard employment like part-time, temporary, con-

tract, or part-year jobs. About 40 per cent of women were in non-standard jobs, compared with 27 per cent of men.

- The CPP was completely portable, so it did not work to the disadvantage of women who tended to change jobs more often than men. On average, women spent 83 months in a job, while men spent 105 months.
- The childrearing drop-out provision of the CPP accommodated women's family responsibilities. The years of little or no earnings while rearing children under 7 could be dropped from the earnings calculation on which retirement benefits were based.
- The CPP allowed for retirement anytime between 60 and 70. Women tended to retire earlier than men.
- It provided for sharing of benefits between spouses at retirement, divorce, or death. That was usually not possible in private occupational pension plans.
- It was fully indexed to inflation and so protected those who live longest. At age 65, life expectancy was twenty more years for women and sixteen for men.

There may not have been anything in the proposed reforms that would help women, but there were plenty of options that could hurt, Ken Battle, Caledon's president, argued. 'Most of the options to reduce CPP benefits would hit women harder than men, for several reasons: Women earn less than men, live longer than men and are relatively more reliant on public pensions than men.'[51] The planned acceleration in contribution rate increases would also affect women more, because most women had modest to average earnings that imposed the highest effective tax burden, he added. For example, the CPP premium for anyone earning the yearly maximum would in 1996 have been about 5 per cent of total earnings (the then 5.6 per cent rate levied on the difference between the maximum and the year's basic exemption), while someone earning double the maximum – a group in which there were proportionately fewer women – would have paid about 2.5 per cent of all earnings. That, however, would be far less damaging than the possible cuts to benefits.[52]

Ontario's Hearings

While the joint federal–provincial consultations were under way, Ontario decided to take the process one step further. Though the joint panels would touch down six times in Ontario, three of those sessions would be devoted to particular issues – the investment policy in Toronto, disability in Waterloo, and youth in Ottawa. Only three were open to all comers, one each in Toronto, Hamilton, and Thunder Bay. Queen's Park wanted to tap opinion in other centres as well, so it struck its own panel, headed by government backbenchers Ed Doyle and Tim Hudak, both of whom had co-chaired the joint sessions with David Walker.

Michael Gourley, Ontario's deputy minister of finance at the time, said that in his long experience as a public servant, he learned that no politician likes to surprise the public by solving a problem that most people do not even know exists. So as a first step, the provincial government had to explain the problem to the public. 'If we had not done that, there would have been no solution.'[53] There was also some scepticism at Queen's Park about the federal agenda. The joint consultation 'was going to be a federal process; it was their agenda.'[54] There was a practical reason as well; the provincial government wanted to tap a broader range of public opinion. During the final two weeks of April, the Ontario consultations team – in addition to helping run the three joint hearings – went to seven other communities as well, where it heard ninety-four presentations. It also received sixty-three written submissions.

Doyle and Hudak produced their report on the consultations in late June, and it reflected the same broad themes that turned up in the national consultations. Like other Canadians, Ontarians – 'the overwhelming majority' – wanted the CPP maintained. 'The panel heard very clearly that Ontarians want a Canada Pension Plan, but they want a Plan that is more efficiently and effectively managed and they do not want contribution rates to rise to a level that is unaffordable.'[55] To meet that goal, most of those at the hearings, while they 'did not necessarily wish to see benefits reduced, ... were prepared to endorse changes in some benefits.'[56]

In a sign of things to come, though few recognized it as such at the time, the report flagged one key issue, Unemployment Insurance premiums:

Several submissions suggested that an increase in CPP contributions would have much less effect on job creation and economic growth if the increase in this payroll tax were balanced with a decrease in another payroll tax, Unemployment Insurance (UI) premiums. These presenters pointed out that the federal government has been running a significant surplus on the Unemployment Insurance Program. At the current premium rate, the UI account will have accumulated a surplus of approximately $5 billion by the end of this year and $10 billion by the end of 1997. The accumulated surplus will rise to over $25 billion by the end of the century if premium rates are not reduced. This suggested the possibility of increasing CPP contributions while decreasing UI premiums and still keeping payroll taxes at a manageable rate.[57]

12 Progress and Stumbles

By June 1996, it was time to get down to the business of making some real decisions. Over the previous three months, the finance ministers – through their consultation process – had talked to hundreds of ordinary Canadians and to pension experts of all stripes. From this point on, outside voices were largely blocked out. The only thing that mattered was what happened inside the room when officials and ministers met. Paul Martin, for one, figured that when he looked around the table at a finance ministers' meeting, he had all the political diversity he needed to make a deal that would be acceptable to Canadians. Representing the provinces were Progressive Conservatives from Ontario, Alberta, and Manitoba; Liberals from Nova Scotia, New Brunswick, Newfoundland, and Prince Edward Island; New Democrats from British Columbia and Saskatchewan; and the Parti Québécois from Quebec. 'We had all the views around the table,' he said later.[1] The only party in Parliament that was not in the CPP meetings – aside from the PQ's federal surrogate, the Bloc Québécois – was the Reform Party, and Martin was not inclined to pay much attention to its call to scrap the CPP.

Finance ministers were ready to meet again, this time in Fredericton. It was the usual routine – a dinner for ministers on the evening of 17 June followed by a full day of talks on the 18th. The CPP was not the only item on the agenda – various tax issues would be discussed as well – but it was the biggest, with more than five hours set aside to talk pensions. The officials who specialized in the CPP had gotten together two weeks earlier in St John's, Newfoundland. Their deputy ministers, who typically met just before ministerial gatherings to trade views so they could brief their ministers on what to expect, had held their meeting on the 12th.

Officials at the two-day St John's meeting, which ran until about 11 p.m. on the second day, recall a tense meeting that wound up making considerable progress on the CPP. Indeed, some came away thinking a deal was all but done. 'That's where the package was wrapped up,' one provincial official recalled later.[2] 'That was the pivotal meeting.' Officials had taken the attitude that 'we had to resolve it at that meeting,' so they were willing to work late on the second day to get what he called the 'final package.' A federal official whose involvement ended shortly after when he moved to another job recalled that he 'felt okay after that meeting,' that the task was almost done. 'I felt confident that it was going to work.'

(The meeting was not all work. Several recalled fondly an afternoon break during which they were bused down the south shore from St John's to Bay Bulls for a boat trip out to see the puffins, a prime local attraction. 'That was the funnest part,' one said. Few were prepared for an outing on the chilly North Atlantic, so one federal official took them to Nonia Handicrafts, one of St John's better-known shops, where they added.woollen sweaters and jackets to their wardrobe.)

Misplaced Optimism

Their optimism was misplaced. Officials may have been happy with where the talks were going, but their ministers were not yet ready to deal. Going in to the Fredericton meeting, no one expected to come out with a final decision on the CPP, but most were hoping for enough progress that another meeting in September could wrap it up. On at least one broad point, most were agreed: they had to fix the CPP now, though Saskatchewan and British Columbia were still muttering about the need for more consultations. One problem for the meeting was that British Columbia had no one at the table who could make any commitments at all. The province's NDP government had changed leaders in February, replacing Mike Harcourt with Glen Clark as the new premier, and Clark had just won a closely contested election on 28 May, one in which he had received fewer votes, but more seats, than the opposition Liberals. On the day finance ministers were flying to Fredericton, Clark's new cabinet was being sworn in and Andrew Petter was given the finance job, one that Clark had held himself for a period under Harcourt. British Columbia was represented in Fredericton by a senior official who had just stepped in as acting deputy minister of finance and would shortly move on to another permanent post. For decision-making purposes, British Columbia wasn't really at the meeting.

Still, all the governments were willing to release the consultations report and some were even ready to endorse a set of principles for CPP reform that officials had drawn up; British Columbia's effective absence made that impolitic and that item was put off to the next meeting. On the broad outlines of a reform, Ottawa and the provinces were not quite on the same page, but they were at least getting closer. They agreed that the contribution rate should not exceed 10 per cent, that the CPP fund should be invested in the market, that some benefits should be cut, and that governance of the fund should be improved. But even within that broad consensus, there were caveats. Most accepted steady-state financing, but Alberta went further: it wanted to pay off the unfunded liability entirely over the next century. Ontario and Newfoundland hedged their support for investing the fund in financial markets; they wanted a 'modified market approach' that would give them the right of first refusal on CPP funds, though they would pay full market rates for any borrowing. (Ontario, at this point, still had a fiscal deficit of almost $9 billion, the biggest in the country relative to its gross domestic product, while Newfoundland's total debt amounted to about two-thirds of its GDP, far higher than that of any other province.)

Alberta and Ontario were the hawks in the crowd, particularly Alberta. It was willing to pay for full funding – and elimination of the entire unfunded liability – with rate increases that would be higher and benefit cuts that would be deeper than those supported by any other province. Alberta diverged from Ontario by supporting a full-blown market-oriented investment policy, and it wanted an entirely new governance structure for the CPP fund – both an arm's-length body to advise governments on how to keep a steady-state funding policy on track plus an arm's-length body to invest the funds. Ontario, for its part, wanted to go much further than just freezing the YBE; it would reduce the exemption from the 1996 level of $3,500 down to $1,000 or $2,000. Moreover, Ontario thought the *Information Paper* did not go far enough in proposing that disability pensions should go only to those who had contributed to the CPP in four of the previous six years; it wanted a tougher test. It also wanted reviews of the CPP carried out every three years instead of every five, an idea that several provinces, including Alberta, Manitoba, and Nova Scotia, supported. 'The 15th report shocked us,' one provincial official said later. 'That's one reason

we increased the frequency to three years from five for reviews.'
Ontario and Manitoba were also interested in some kind of default provision in case the projections of contributions and benefits were out of
whack in the future, something that would prevent the CPP from getting back into trouble in the long term.

Jim Dinning, Alberta's treasurer at the time, recalls being particularly
firm about three things: the 9.9 per cent cap on contribution rates in the
final deal; governance of the investment board; and benefit cuts. He figured a 9.9 per cent contribution rate was 'too God-damn high,' but if
the policymakers could create a truly independent investment board, it
could work. The provincial government was then in the midst of overhauling the governance of its Alberta Treasury Branches, a govern-
ment-owned near-bank, and was 'adamant about board-building.' As
for benefits, Dinning said, 'this "oops" style of increasing benefits
without costing them was over; we had to put the brakes on benefit
increases. We had to stop the arguments for adding baubles to the CPP
Christmas tree as had been done in the [previous two agreements]. Our
predecessors defaulted to "yes" on benefits without asking if they were
affordable ten, fifteen, twenty years from now.'[3] (Martin's reaction to
Dinning's line: 'Amen.')[4]

Saskatchewan was shaping up as the go-slow province in the room,
and its views, fittingly since it had an NDP government, reflected some
of the concerns raised by the left in the public consultations and expert
forums. It was not fully persuaded that the problem was as big as
Ottawa and most provinces thought and it was concerned about the
impact the proposals might have on women, young people, and seniors.
Nor had the province yet signed on to the need for fuller funding of the
plan. It was also thinking about carrying out more public consultations
in Saskatchewan.

Quebec Stakes Its Ground

Quebec was in an odd position, as it always is in talks about the CPP. It
is part of the amending formula for the CPP – two-thirds of the provinces with two-thirds of the population – but not part of the CPP, since
it runs the separate QPP. But both Quebec and the CPP provinces have
an interest in maintaining the parallelism of the two plans. The QPP
was facing the same pressures as the CPP, and the Quebec government
had released its own working paper on possible reforms to the QPP just
before the Fredericton meeting.[5]

The Quebec paper echoed many of the issues in the CPP *Information Paper*, but the Quebec government said clearly that it had no interest in the four potential changes to retirement benefits that the CPP paper had listed as options to reduce the cost of the program. Specifically, Quebec would not touch the 25 per cent income replacement rate; it would keep the normal retirement age at 65; all benefits would remain fully indexed to inflation; and the dropout provision for years of low earnings would be kept. Quebec did, however, support steady-state funding and the rapid increase in the contribution rate such funding would require; it was also ready to freeze the year's basic exemption beginning in 1997 and perhaps even reduce it gradually according to income so that it would fall to zero for anyone at the year's maximum pensionable earnings.

On the face of it, Quebec had just scuttled any chance of reducing the cost of retirement benefits for the CPP as well as the QPP. Realistically, however, the four options had already died during the federal–provincial CPP consultations, where three of the four had been roundly rejected and the fourth – removing some of the inflation protection from benefits – had received mixed reviews at best. All governments were facing the same feedback from their constituents. Quebec was simply the first to acknowledge that these four items were too unpopular for governments to accept.

Planks and Ramps

The language of the discussions revolved around planks and ramps, which were outlined in a table of what were called 'Planks to Decision-making on Reform Package' that all governments had already seen. Planks were the various packages or combinations of rate increases and benefit cuts that ministers would consider. In each case, Finance had calculated two possible steady-state contribution rates – one that would be achieved if the new rate were phased in over six years (the faster ramp) and the other if the new rate were phased in over eight years (the slower ramp). Plank 1, which consisted only of the new investment policy – and assuming a 3.8 per cent real rate of return a year – implied a steady-state rate of 12.2 per cent if ministers chose the faster ramp, but 12.6 per cent if they chose the slower. In effect, the new investment policy on its own would let ministers dodge the bullet of a contribution rate heading to around 14 per cent by a considerable margin.[6]

But they were still a long way from the 10 per cent rate that most thought marked the upper limit of voter tolerance for a higher contribution rate. Now it was a matter of figuring out the cluster of benefit reductions that would – bit by agonizing bit – bring the steady-state contribution rate down to the magic 10 per cent. Over the next few months, this is how officials and ministers would deal with the numbers. 'All options were viewed through the prism of reducing the contribution rate by 0.1 or 0.2 percentage points,' one provincial official recalled.

Plank 2, freezing the year's basic exemption at $3,500, would further reduce the steady-state rate to 10.9 per cent on the faster ramp and 11.1 per cent on the slower ramp. Plank 3 was a package of so-called core benefit reductions that would cut 7 per cent from the plan's total costs in 2030 and lower the steady-state contribution rate to 10.1 per cent on the faster ramp, 10.2 per cent on the slower ramp. It included elimination of the death benefit and inclusion of what the *Information Paper* had called the 'stronger labour force link' under which people could get a disability pension only if they had contributed in four of the previous six years. It also incorporated some of the technical changes to disability and survivor benefits.

They were still shy of the 10 per cent contribution rate, so the officials had put together a set of 'mix and match' benefit cuts. Plank 4A would treat differently one of the technical changes to disability benefits included in Plank 3. This change would bring the steady-state rate down to 9.9 per cent or 10 per cent, depending on the ramp, so it had considerable appeal for the obvious reason that it met the 10 per cent target. Plank 4B would raise the normal retirement age to 66 over a three-year period beginning in 2007, which would shave another 0.1 percentage points off the long-term contribution rate. Plank 4C would index all benefits to the rate of inflation minus one percentage point. That would reduce the long-term rate by another 0.8 percentage points. Planks 4B and 4C shared a fatal deficiency: Quebec had already rejected them and neither had won widespread support in the public consultations on the CPP. Then came estimates of savings from combining Planks 4A plus 4B, 4A plus 4C, and 4B plus 4C.

The 100-Year Horizon

Alberta's push for absolute full funding of the CPP was based on the belief that the CPP was in trouble mainly because all the benefit enrichments after 1966 had not been matched by the higher contribution rates needed to pay for them. As one Alberta official put it later, 'you should force on the politicians the idea that you should write a cheque to cover the costs; you don't slough it off. Full funding would impose that discipline.' Alberta, he said, 'would have bitten the bullet,' even to the point of pushing the retirement age to 72 or raising the contribution rate to 12 per cent or 14 per cent to get full funding. 'We would have done whatever it takes.'

That plan went too far for the others around the table – it would be comparable to paying down the entire federal debt. Still, it had to be taken seriously enough at least to run the numbers on how it would work. Ottawa's steady-state plan would stabilize the contribution rate but would allow the unfunded liability to keep growing so that it would be a constant multiple of the CPP fund. Federal Finance officials put the cost of full funding at one percentage point over a 100-year time horizon, an amount that would have to be added to whatever steady-state rate the ministers otherwise chose. The extra point would pay off the unfunded liability over a century, at which point the contribution rate could drop to what was called the current service rate of about 6 per cent, which was actuarially fair. Paul Martin, for one, did not think the ministers could persuade Canadians that they would have to pay an extra percentage point – at least 11 per cent – for a century just so that CPP contributors in the late twenty-first century could pay 6 per cent. And if they wanted to stick to their 10 per cent maximum on the contribution rate and opt for full funding, ministers would have to find further benefit cuts worth one percentage point on the long-term contribution rates.

The Options Narrow

Already, one option at least was off the table. The workers' compensation offset – which would to some extent have limited CPP disability benefits to those already getting WC benefits – had been found to be just too complex to be solved this time around. Provincial views differed widely and ministers figured there was no use wasting their officials' time on a fruitless quest for agreement on something that would have very little impact on the finances of the CPP. There was also general agreement on one easy matter. From now on, governments should review the CPP every three years, rather than every five years. The speed at which the recession had undermined the plan's finances had spooked ministers considerably and they were all determined to monitor the CPP more closely in the future.

As the full-day meeting got going, Martin noted that he had just received a letter from Hedy Fry and Rosemary Vodrey reminding the finance ministers to keep gender issues in mind as they reviewed the CPP. Fry and Vodrey were, respectively, the federal and Manitoba ministers responsible for the status of women. The letter originated a few weeks earlier from an agreement by all status of women ministers at a meeting in Winnipeg to press their concerns on the CPP negotiators. The finance ministers, for their part, were aware of the pressure from women's groups and their own cabinet colleagues but generally agreed that an exhaustive review of gender matters was not possible if they were going to meet any reasonable deadline for wrapping up the CPP review.

Through the morning, they ran through the proposals. David Walker reviewed the consultations process and the resulting report, which they agreed to release. Susan Peterson walked them through the 'planks' paper as a prelude to a general discussion of the options, and David Dodge followed with an outline of the officials' work on a new investment policy, for which everyone knew there was widespread public support. Indeed, the consultations had revealed a clear preference for a CPP fund that followed the principles of most pension plans. In the three decades since the CPP came into being, Ottawa and the provinces alike had reformed their legislation governing private pension plans to steer them towards a prudent portfolio approach that stressed diversification. The CPP did not fit those norms. Capital markets had also changed over that period, so that provincial governments no longer had trouble raising money in public bond markets. That was obvious because the CPP fund had been lending no new money to the provinces since 1993, when the plan's total revenue from contributions and investment income no longer exceeded expenditures.

What Kind of Fund?

Since ministers appeared to have accepted the idea of market investment for the CPP fund, the choices on the preferred investment policy now came down to two: would it take a pure or modified market-oriented approach? In other words, would the CPP fund be free to invest everything in a diversified portfolio of market securities, or would it still be required to give the provinces some kind of preferred access to at least some of the money? Whichever route they chose, ministers would still have to decide on a governance structure and an investment objective for the fund. They would need to state clearly a funding policy that would tightly link contributions and benefits, as well as provide a guide to investment decisions. To meet that test, the fund's sole objective should be to invest in the interest of CPP contributors and beneficiaries – that is, with no secondary objectives like propping up companies or industries that politicians deemed in need of aid. They also needed a proper balance between returns and investment risk.

A pure or unfettered market approach, with professional management, offered the best chance for the fund to earn the 3.8 per cent real return each year that would contribute most to strengthening the CPP's finances. It would also be consistent with the principles embedded in federal and provincial legislation governing private plans and, based on the views expressed during the consultations, be the option most likely to win public support. There were risks, of course. Such a fund would be breaking new ground; there were no real models out there of national pension funds acting in this fashion. Higher returns were not guaranteed, and year-to-year returns could be volatile. The pure approach would not cut provinces off entirely from CPP funds, but their access would be determined by the fund's board of trustees and managers, who would likely invest much in the way that private pension plan managers invested; provincial bonds would be part of the diversified fund and bought on the open markets like any other bonds.

The alternative was the modified market approach in which the CPP legislation would spell out how much the provinces could borrow, at what interest rates, over what length of maturities, and whether their borrowings would be marketable or not. Such a course might smooth the provinces' transition to a pure market approach for the CPP fund, but it had several risks, most of which were the obverse of the arguments for a pure market approach. The modified approach would be inconsistent with the principle of investing solely in the interest of plan members; it might be harder to sell to the public; and it might make the task of achieving a 3.8 per cent return more difficult.[7]

By the time the discussion was over, what they had all known at the beginning of the meeting was even more obvious: they were nowhere near ready to make substantive decisions on the CPP. The politicians had more thinking to do and – just as important – they had to get some feedback from their own cabinets on where the CPP talks were heading. The officials had plenty more work to do, especially on the new investment policy, which some ministers were still struggling to fully understand, let alone accept. Officials had hoped ministers might at least endorse a short paper they had drafted – a broad statement of what were called 'principles to guide federal–provincial decisions on the Canada Pension Plan'[8] – but that plan was discarded when it became obvious that no BC minister would make an appearance.

The Guiding Principles

The version of the 'principles' paper distributed to all ministers on the previous Friday had begun with a reassurance that governments felt they 'must put to rest the worries that Canadians have that their CPP pensions will not be there for them when they retire in the future.' They had thus agreed to 'solve the problems facing the CPP quickly,' and when they did, they would be guided by eight principles. The principles read as follows:

1. The CPP is a key pillar of Canada's retirement income system that is worth saving.
2. The CPP is an earnings-related program. Its fundamental role is to help replace earnings upon retirement or disability, or the death of a spouse – not to redistribute income. The income redistribution role is the responsibility of the income tax system, the Old Age Security/Guaranteed Income Supplement/Seniors Benefit, and other income-tested programs paid from general tax revenues.
3. The solutions to the CPP's problems must be fair across generations.
4. The CPP must be affordable and sustainable for future generations. This requires fuller funding and a contribution rate no higher than the already legislated future rate of 10.1 per cent. In deciding how quickly to move to this rate, governments must consider economic and fiscal impacts.
5. Governments must tighten administration as the first step towards controlling costs.
6. Disability and survivor benefits are important features of the CPP. However, they must be designed and administered in a way that does not jeopardize the security of retirement pensions.
7. CPP funds must be invested in the best interests of plan members and maintain a proper balance between returns and investment risk. Governance structures must be created to ensure sound fund management.
8. Governments must more regularly monitor changing economic, demo-

graphic, and other circumstances which can affect the CPP and provide Canadians with the appropriate information so they can judge for themselves that the integrity and security of the CPP is being protected.

The first two principles effectively brushed off both the right and left. They would not scrap the CPP in favour of a Chilean-style reform and they would not undermine the existing link between contributions and benefits by raising one without a parallel increase in the other. The third was a quasi-endorsement of steady-state funding, while the fourth cemented their opposition to any long-term contribution rate higher than 10 per cent. The fifth was obviously needed in light of the recent explosion in disability benefits, and Ontario, for one, had made that point a consistent line of its rhetoric on the CPP's problems. The sixth was interesting in that it gave voice to a view, held especially by provinces like Alberta, that the CPP would be better off if it stuck to retirement pensions alone. If disability and survivor benefits could not be hived off into a separate program, they would at least rank below retirement benefits in importance and, implicitly, could be sacrificed to some extent to protect the CPP's retirement promises. The seventh would clearly indicate that any new fund created by the reform would not get into the economic development business, as the left wished; it would stick to earning the best return possible for CPP members. The eighth principle might be termed a 'never again' clause, an expression of the view that the CPP should be reviewed every three years so that it could never again get this far off track.

Though the Fredericton meeting could not approve them, the principles were still very much alive and would re-emerge, with some minor revisions, a few months later when everyone was at the table.

Discord over Harmonization

But while the CPP took up most of the ministers' time in Fredericton, other issues commanded most of the attention. Indeed, the CPP was quite overshadowed by the much more dramatic conflict over the goods and services tax and a range of related provincial complaints with Ottawa. Where ministers felt a sense of shared purpose for the CPP because of their joint stewardship, the rest of the agenda was far more typical of federal–provincial meetings, which is to say they fought bitterly. 'The Fredericton meeting was so confrontational that the CPP was a sideshow,' Janice MacKinnon, Saskatchewan's finance minister, recalled later.

For some time, there had been growing discontent, mainly from the richer provinces of Ontario, Alberta, and British Columbia, over Ottawa's tendency to treat provinces differently under national programs. A month earlier, the federal government had persuaded Nova Scotia, New Brunswick, and Newfoundland to 'harmonize' their provincial sales taxes with the federal goods and services tax (GST). The deal included $1 billion in federal compensation to the three provinces for any revenue losses they might incur. Martin had tried to sign all provinces onto a harmonization deal, which – though it was probably good public policy in its own right – amounted to a face-saving device for the federal Liberals to squirm out of their unrealistic election promise to do away with the GST, but only three agreed.

Alberta Treasurer Jim Dinning had written to Martin protesting the billion-dollar payments and several other examples of what he saw as unequal treatment, such as varying federal tobacco taxes (lower in the east to combat cheaper smuggled cigarettes from the United States) and taxation of electrical utilities (higher on Alberta's privately owned utilities than on the publicly owned utilities that were common in most provinces). 'These policies set a very disturbing trend,' he said in his letter. 'It's time your government reversed these policies and committed itself to treating Canadians the same regardless of where they live in the country.'[9]

Ontario's Finance Minister Ernie Eves had a similar complaint about the federal Unemployment Insurance (UI) program, whose name would be changed to Employment Insurance (EI) only two weeks later. Ontario's employers and workers were paying $8 billion a year into the plan, while taking out only $4 billion in benefits. 'Ontario's obviously the big loser when it comes to unemployment insurance,' Eves said before the meeting. Ominously for the CPP talks, he was beginning to insist that because CPP premiums had to rise – something he had conceded months earlier – UI premiums should fall to offset the impact on business of higher CPP contributions.[10] Martin was distinctly chilly to that idea. The UI account was taking in more than it paid out in benefits and Martin needed the resulting surplus to help reduce the federal government's overall deficit. Without the UI account's $7.6 billion surplus in the 1996–7 fiscal year, Ottawa's deficit would have been $16.3 billion rather than the final reported figure of $8.7 billion.

These were not isolated gripes but part of what some provinces saw as a wider pattern in Ottawa's behaviour – the systematic use of all programs to redistribute income from richer to poorer provinces. The Unemployment Insurance program was probably the most visible example of this pattern, simply because the numbers were easier to track, but it applied more broadly. The richer provinces were beginning to grumble, and that discontent was soon to spill over into the CPP negotiations. Taxpayers in the wealthier provinces are net contributors to the federal purse, typically paying more in taxes than they get back in spending. The surpluses that the federal government runs in those provinces finance a wide range of transfers to poorer provinces. The one program explicitly designed for this purpose is equalization, which is mandated under the Constitution (section 36(2)) 'to ensure that provincial governments have sufficient revenues to provide reasonably comparable levels of public services at reasonably comparable levels of taxation.' In the mid-1990s, seven provinces – all but Ontario, British Columbia, and Alberta – received equalization payments. While the richer provinces continued to support equalization, they were beginning to object when other federal programs were also used for redistributive purposes. 'How many equalization programs do we need?' Eves asked in an interview with *The Globe and Mail*. 'Do we need one or 101?' His answer was obvious. Martin dismissed such talk as 'a lot of empty fed-bashing that should have gone out with the dodo bird,' but he had few allies. Queen's University economist Thomas Courchene, a leading authority on federal–provincial finances, warned that Ottawa would bring the equalization program into disrepute if it used every program to redistribute funds regionally.[11]

Even Saskatchewan objected to what MacKinnon calls 'back door equalization.' In her case, the flashpoint came later in the year over a proposed federal infrastructure spending program which would have tilted the benefits to provinces with high unemployment rates. Because Saskatchewan's young tend to move to Alberta if they cannot find jobs at home, Saskatchewan's jobless rate is traditionally low, and that put it in line for less infrastructure funding. On both the federal government's GST policy and UI premiums, Ontario and the Western provinces were largely on the same page, regardless of their differing partisan labels – Progressive Conservative in Ontario, Alberta, and Manitoba; NDP in British Columbia and Saskatchewan. There was also an element of contempt for the three Liberal governments on the east coast that were seen as willing to bend to the agenda of the Liberal government in Ottawa. MacKinnon summarized the attitude bluntly: 'We [in the West] regard the Atlantic provinces as client states of the federal government.'[12]

The Reform Nudges Forward

When the finance ministers emerged from their meeting, their divisions over tax and redistribution issues were fully on display, and the media, true to form, played up those divisions. As for the CPP portion of the talks, ministers said little of real substance, but it was apparent that they were largely moving in the same direction. They confirmed that there was little support for a contribution rate higher than 10 per cent, but they were prepared to move the rate to that level fairly quickly to catch the baby-boom generation in its peak earning years.[13] They also said that officials could continue to study the options for reduced benefits over the summer, though this point was couched in the usual assurances that any cuts would hit only future recipients.

For the financial press, the fact that most ministers were agreed on the wisdom of investing the CPP fund in the markets raised hopes that the hated 20 per cent foreign property rule – the tax provision that prevented most private pension plans from investing more than one-fifth of their assets outside Canada – might be lifted.[14] At least one option appeared to have died altogether, the idea of removing some of the inflation protection enjoyed by existing seniors by limiting annual benefit increases to the rate of inflation minus one percentage point. Eves called it 'probably the most difficult and controversial aspect of the CPP' and added that while everything was still formally on the table, partial de-indexation of benefits 'would have a pretty difficult road.'[15]

The Crucial Difference

The contrast between the ministers' steady work on the CPP and their battles over other issues is quite striking – amazingly so to any student of federal–provincial relations in the 1990s, when combat was common. 'There were a lot of angry ministers' at the Fredericton meeting, 'one of the nastiest meetings I've ever been in,' MacKinnon recalled later. But in calling the CPP 'a sideshow to the GST,' she put her finger on what seems to have been a crucial point about the CPP negotiations. Disagreements on other issues rarely spilled over into the CPP arena, with one major exception that will be explored in chapter 14. The finance ministers' subsequent meeting in October – again with the CPP and other issues on the agenda – was contentious too, 'but it never seemed to come back on the CPP.'

The 1995 federal budget had included deep cuts to transfer payments to the provinces, provoking sharp attacks from the provincial governments that would have to cut their own programs – and incur criticism from their own voters as a result. Ottawa followed that with its time-wasting – as MacKinnon saw it – effort to 'coerce, cajole, persuade' the provinces to harmonize their sales taxes with the GST, but the CPP 'wasn't a major preoccupation at the time.' As a historian who returned to the University of Saskatchewan to teach public policy after leaving politics,[16] MacKinnon regards the CPP reform as 'more interesting' in light of the fact that the 1995 budget and its aftermath did much to 'poison the well' of federal–provincial relations. The CPP was 'not seen as a battleground.' The politics of it were different, she argues. Ottawa would get blamed for any shortcomings in the reform – whether the higher contribution rates or reduced benefits – but the provinces, which took the political flak for their spending cuts after the 1995 budget, 'would not be out in front on the CPP.'

All finance ministers at the time prided themselves on being on the same page in terms of getting their fiscal houses in order, 'so we couldn't let the CPP just sit there. We had the capacity to do [the reform],' MacKinnon said. 'Our contribution as finance ministers was to leave Canada with better finances.' It helped that Martin and the federal Finance Department 'handled [the CPP] a lot better. They played a lot of games on the GST, but not on the CPP. They played that straight.' When the provinces asked for more consultations, 'they said fine, we'll have more consultations. When we said we want more options, they said fine, here are more options.'

(Martin takes issue with MacKinnon's view that the federal government was playing games with the GST – 'We wanted to harmonize; we failed; I don't know what games she's talking about' – and that its budget cuts poisoned the well of intergovernmental relations. He does not recall the Fredericton meeting as a nasty one.)[17]

In effect, MacKinnon argues, the provincial finance ministers had no trouble at all separating the need for federal–provincial cooperation on CPP reform from their running disputes with Ottawa over a host of other issues. They simply put the CPP reform into the same mental compartment as deficit and debt reduction, to which almost all were firmly committed. 'Better finances' would be their legacy to Canadians, and it would be delivered through prudent budgets that reduced deficits and debt and through a CPP reform that put the CPP on a sound financial footing and made it sustainable for generations.[18]

When MacKinnon's analysis was put to others involved in the reform, it invariably evoked agreement. 'Her theory makes sense,' Dinning said.[19] And though Martin contested some of MacKinnon's recollections of how the various federal–provincial policy debates played out, he too agreed on this point, adding that this approach is typical of the clubbiness and camaraderie of finance ministers generally. 'It's the same thing internationally. When I went to G7 finance ministers' meetings, the attitude was: "We are the only seven sane people in the world."'[20]

UI: The Gathering Cloud

But when the ministers left Fredericton, one other dynamic had changed dramatically, though few recognized it at the time. Ernie Eves's attempt to link higher CPP premiums to a reduction in UI premiums was no mere rhetorical flourish designed to prove his tax-cutting credentials. He was quite serious, and anyone who had paid attention to his record as Ontario's finance minister – then only one year long – should have been able to see trouble coming.

The Ontario government's opposition to taxes of all kinds was deeply felt and well-known. Premier Mike Harris and his Progressive Conservatives had been elected in 1995 largely on the strength of their opposition to high taxes, and payroll taxes figured prominently in their thinking. The new government's basic philosophy – as set out in Eves's 1996 budget – was simple: 'Tax cuts create jobs and spur growth.'

There was no question that Ontario needed both jobs and growth. The 1990–2 recession had pummelled the province more than any other. In some ways, the national tale of a contraction in economic activity followed by an achingly slow recovery was Ontario's story. In the early 1980s, Ontario and the rest of Canada followed much the same course through recession and recovery, but this time around, Ontario parted company with other provinces.

The rest of the country went through a painful, but short, recession; real GDP per head fell by just over 2 per cent in 1991 and 1992 and recovered all the lost ground in 1993. In Ontario, however, the slide had begun a year earlier, in 1990, and continued through 1993, when output per head was fully 9 per cent lower than in 1989; it took another four years, until 1997, to get back to the pre-recession peak. The job numbers were just as grim. With only two-fifths of all jobs nationally, Ontario absorbed fully three-quarters of the country's job losses – 329,000 of the 437,000 nationally. Relative to population, the employment decline in Ontario was almost double the national average. The recovery, when it came, seemed to bypass Ontario. Collectively, the rest of the country took just over a year to recover all the jobs lost in the recession; Ontario took almost five years.

The recession was especially evident in Ontario's government finances. In 1992 and 1993, Ontario shared with Alberta and Saskatchewan the dubious distinction of running the country's biggest provincial deficits relative to GDP – roughly 4 per cent. By 1995, however, tough budgeting in the two Prairie provinces had put their accounts back into surplus, while Ontario's more leisurely approach under its NDP government had produced only a small reduction in the deficit. When they got their chance, Ontario's voters bounced out the NDP – which had stretched its term to the five-year legal maximum – and replaced it with Harris's promised 'Common Sense Revolution' (CSR) of lower spending and lower taxes. The new government was utterly committed to its platform, and government officials soon learned that any policy that was not part of the CSR would simply have to wait until the CSR was fully implemented.

Eves's first budget not only made deep cuts to personal income taxes, but also took aim at two major payroll taxes. He announced a phasing out of the Employer Health tax on the first $400,000 of payroll, a move that would – over three years – wipe out the tax for almost nine of every ten Ontario companies; and it reduced the premiums that companies paid to finance the province's workers' compensation program. Those two measures, the budget said, 'will cut mandatory payroll costs and create jobs.'[21]

Payroll taxes had come to be seen as a major problem by the mid-1990s. Even the Bank of Canada got into that debate in a study published about the time the Harris government was elected. The Bank estimated that total employment would have been about 1 per cent higher in 1993 – equal to about 130,000 jobs – if payroll taxes had not increased so substantially. It said supplementary labour income – a measure of the employer's contributions to unemployment insurance, health insurance, workers' compensation, and the CPP and QPP – had increased from 10.6 per cent of total wage and salary income in 1989 to 14.1 per cent in 1994.[22]

The only purely federal payroll tax – premiums paid by workers and employers to finance Unemployment Insurance (UI)[23] – was beyond Ontario's control, and it rankled deeply. From 1989 through 1994, the federal government had raised the premiums by 57 per cent. Employees were paying $3.07 for every $100 of insurable earnings, while employers – who paid 1.4 times the employee rate – were contributing another $4.30, for a total of $7.37, up from $4.68 in 1989. In fact, the increases were even steeper because the base on which premiums were calculated – insurable earnings – climbed by 29 per cent over the same period. In 1994, the maximum annual contribution per worker was almost $3,000, more than double the limit five years earlier.

Such steep increases had been made necessary by the recession, which pushed the annual cost of regular UI benefits up from $10 billion in the 1989–90 fiscal year to more than $15 billion in 1992–3. At the time, UI premiums were reset annually to cover the cost of benefits, using a formula that was designed to drive the balance in the UI account back to zero. The 'perverse result' was that premiums fell during periods when lower unemployment reduced the need to pay benefits but tended to rise at the bottom of the business cycle, when unemployment was on the upswing. 'Hence, the pro-cyclical nature of this rate-setting process served to raise the cost of labour at a time when lower labour costs were needed to stimulate job growth and to reduce the unemployment rate.'[24] The UI account, which had enjoyed a small surplus in 1990, ran deficits in each of the next three years even as the premium rate for contributions climbed.

By mid-1996, when finance ministers were meeting in Fredericton, economic growth had reduced the annual bill for UI to less than $10 billion. But despite surpluses in the UI account from 1994 on, the federal government was slow to reduce premiums. From the 1994 peak of $7.37 per $100 of earnings, the rate was reduced to $7.20 in 1995 and $7.08 in 1996. This meagre 4 per cent reduction, when set against a decline of more than 35 per cent in benefits paid out and a growing surplus in the UI account, aroused considerable controversy and opposition. Martin was using the UI system as another source of revenue to help him with his broader battle against Ottawa's overall deficit.

One reason for Ontario's concern went to the heart of the UI program itself. As a rule, workers in primary and seasonal industries like fishing, forestry, construction, and tourism drew far more in benefits than they contributed, simply because the program was very generous to workers in those industries; a few weeks of work – and contributions – could earn an entitlement to many weeks of benefits. In 1992, for example, benefits for workers in construction and primary industries were about four times contributions.[25]

As a result, provinces that relied heavily on such industries, and which had high unemployment, drew more in benefits than they contributed. In practice, that meant the four Atlantic provinces had an unblemished record of taking in more from UI than they paid out, while Ontario, Alberta, Manitoba, and Saskatchewan in most years paid more into the UI coffers than they took out. Quebec and British Columbia had been net beneficiaries through the 1980s but had recently become net contributors.

Ontario's most recent experience was a particular irritant. From 1990 through 1992, the overall UI account had run a $3.1 billion deficit, hardly surprising at a time of rising and high unemployment. But in Ontario, at the epicentre of the recession, workers and their employers paid $19 billion into the account, $4.7 billion more than the $14.3 billion they took out. Over the next three years – 1993 through 1995 – the overall account racked up a total of $12.6 billion in surpluses, and Ontario's net contribution more than doubled to $10.6 billion – $23.6 billion in contributions versus $13 billion in benefits.[26] It was this 'federal revenue grab of Ontario taxes that most annoyed Queen's Park' and stoked the province's opposition to higher CPP premiums.[27]

Though they could never admit it publicly, many federal officials sympathized with Ontario's concerns. They recognized that the province paid far more in than it took out and that the recession of the early 1990s had been particularly tough on Ontario. Even so, Paul Martin was not about to give up – at that stage – a key source of funds that he needed to meet his deficit-reduction targets. 'I was quite open about that,' he recalled.[28]

From Ontario's perspective, then, UI had become a threat: high premiums were a payroll tax that discouraged companies from hiring more workers. No one should have been surprised that Harris and Eves were upset. But while they had absolutely no control over UI premiums, they did have some very real clout over the CPP contribution rate – Ontario's veto. If they were going to endorse a substantial increase in one payroll tax (which is how they regarded CPP premiums), they would use that veto to gain some leverage over another – the UI premiums that were solely in the federal government's domain. Eves's salvo in Fredericton was merely the first.

13 Rules for the Fund

Figuring out a new investment policy for the CPP – and an institutional structure to bring it to life – was one of the trickier tasks facing policymakers. It was complex and technical, and for that reason flew well under the radar of public and media interest throughout 1996. But the ten governments had launched their own study of the issue on 5 December 1995, at a meeting of finance deputy ministers (known as the Continuing Committee of Officials, or CCO) a week before the finance ministers' meeting that decided to go ahead with public consultations. The deputies figured they needed a working group to examine all issues surrounding a diversified, market-oriented CPP and to develop a new investment strategy for ministers to consider.

Accordingly, federal Finance pulled together what one official called 'a group of financially literate people from the provinces'[1] into what was called the working group on investment that met for the first time on 12 January 1996 at the Finance Department's offices in Esplanade Laurier in Ottawa. The CCO's broader CPP committee was also meeting to discuss the contents of the forthcoming *Information Paper*. The basic idea could be explained easily enough, but the paper, released a month later, acknowledged that investing CPP funds in the market raised several important issues, 'including how such a fund should be governed and the implications that a larger CPP fund would have for Canada's capital markets.'[2]

Probing those questions would demand plenty of effort from the new working group. The process got off to a slow – even shaky – start. 'At this point, we were just looking at options and models,' one federal official recalled. To help, Finance brought in pension consultant Keith Ambachtsheer, who had signed on in December and came to Ottawa for the 12 January meeting to share his thinking on the investment issue with the working group. Finance officials had met with him several times during 1995 as they sketched out their first thoughts on an investment policy.

The meeting did not go well. While Ambachtsheer made his flip-chart presentation, a federal official recalled, some provincial officials chatted among themselves. Even some who listened quietly regarded his talk as a lecture on things they already knew well – 'Pensions 101,' one provincial official called it. Another said Ambachtsheer's advice on governance issues was all too obvious – not much beyond a suggestion to hire competent, honest people. Federal officials regarded Ambachtsheer's advice as more helpful and asked him to develop his presentation into a more complete paper. At this point, they figured they were getting little help from the provinces in developing the investment policy.

As one federal official recalls, at least two problems blocked any real progress at the January meeting. Some provinces questioned the role of the working group itself; they thought its mandate was to examine changes around the fringes of the current investment policy of lending to the provinces, not to push into the virgin territory of creating a pension fund that would invest in public markets. Others thought the group was getting too far ahead of the broader reform discussions, where some fundamental decisions still had to be made. Clearly, they needed some direction from above – from both the broader CPP committee and from the deputy ministers on the CCO. Accordingly, officials put together a short paper setting out the terms of reference for the task facing the working group. It was duly approved by the middle of February.

The two-page memorandum[3] setting out the terms of reference was cautiously presented in language that would not alarm provinces that might still favour the status quo. The choice, the memo said, was between the current policy of lending CPP funds to the provinces and a policy that would increase returns to the fund, 'particularly if the fund grows significantly,' that is, if ministers approved a steep increase in contribution rates. The role of the working group 'is to examine key issues associated with possible changes to the investment policy to increase the return on the fund. Its work will feed into the broader CPP review process, which is dealing with benefit, contribution, and macroeconomic issues, in order to assist Ministers in making decisions on the final CPP package.' The group would prepare a report to the CCO, but that was all. 'The group will not make any decisions regarding the appropriate investment objectives for the CPP fund or the preferred investment policy approach, but will provide input and analysis that will be useful in the policy decisions taken by the CCO and Ministers.'

Those were the ground rules governing the process; the content of the group's work boiled down to examining two broad options for a new investment policy. The first, called the modified provincial access approach, would give to the provinces 'the right of first refusal to borrow their share of contributions, as under the status quo, but with modifications to the terms of access.' The second was 'a diversified market-oriented investment policy.' The issues were set out in a series of brief descriptions, accompanied by one or more questions to be answered.[4]

The modified provincial access approach raised the following issues:

- Provincial funding requirements in relation to projected CPP inflows: Will the provinces need all of the available funds to meet their borrowing requirements? Should provinces be allowed to borrow CPP funds in excess of their borrowing needs?
- Cost of CPP funds for provinces: Should the CPP interest rate be set at the provinces' own market borrowing rates (as opposed to the existing system of using the federal government's rate on twenty-year borrowings)?
- Terms of borrowings: Should the CPP expand the range of bond maturities available to provinces?
- Marketability of the securities: Should the securities purchased by the CPP fund be marketable?
- Investment policy for excess funds beyond provincial take-up: How should funds not borrowed by provinces be invested?
- Expected returns: Would the expected rate of return on the CPP be enhanced under this approach?

The market-oriented approach was explicitly based on the assumption 'that the CPP fund is to be invested to maximize returns subject to prudent management in the interests of contributors and beneficiaries.' It would examine these issues:

- Governance: Should the investment policy be determined by a board of trustees operating at arm's length from government and CPP beneficiaries, or by federal/provincial ministers through legislation? How could an independent board be selected?

- Investments in provincial securities: How much in the way of provincial securities would the CPP fund be expected to hold under an independent governance structure? Should the fund be required to hold a certain proportion of provincial securities?
- Capital markets issues raised by the potential size of the fund: What impact might a large CPP fund have on Canada's capital markets? What measures might be taken to minimize any adverse consequences? In light of the fund's size, should any investment policy constraints be placed on the CPP fund other than those applying to normal pension funds?
- Foreign property investments: Should the CPP fund be investing in foreign property, that is, in foreign stocks, bonds, and other assets?
- Transition issues: What steps or decisions would have to be taken before the CPP could begin investing in the market? How would the new policy deal with the existing non-market portfolio of provincial bonds?
- Expected returns: How much would the expected rate of return on the CPP fund be enhanced under a market-oriented approach?
- If the CPP fund were given a secondary objective to contribute to Canadian economic development and employment, what issues would this raise vis-à-vis the appropriate investment policy and governance of the fund?

Approvals in hand from the CCO, Finance Department officials in the financial sector policy division agreed to prepare a paper on these issues for discussion at the next officials' meeting, which turned out to be four months off – on 6 June in St John's. At the same time, the department asked Ambachtsheer to prepare a paper based on his flip-chart presentation.

By mid-May, Ambachtsheer had produced a study[5] that – although short – laid out the two main models that governments should consider, assuming, of course, that the governments endorsed the rapid increase in contribution rates that would build the fund from its current level of about $40 billion to perhaps $150 billion in ten years. He saw three fundamental issues:

- What investment goals and policies should such a large asset pool pursue?
- What governance structure is likely to achieve the investment goals?
- What are the implications of creating a very large pool of assets?

Investment Goals and Policies

Setting investment goals was easy, Ambachtsheer implied. Only a market-oriented, diversified investment policy would satisfy the need for intergenerational fairness, increased public confidence in the CPP, and the reduction of long-term costs. The Quebec Pension Plan already followed such a course, and the same could be done with the CPP, which 'would be consistent with treating the CPP as a true pension plan.'[6] Besides, he added in an observation apparently aimed at the provincial governments, several provinces had already moved their own public sector pension plans in that very direction. If the CPP did the same, 'it would simply be falling into line with a practice the provinces themselves have already adopted.'[7]

He dismissed the argument that the CPP should pursue secondary investment goals like economic development and job creation. Buying the bonds and stocks of Canadian companies, on its own, would accomplish that goal. Why, he asked, should a pension fund do more? If some sectors or regions have trouble raising capital, 'should the beneficiaries of the CPP Fund be forced to solve such a problem?'[8] His answer was an obvious no.

The Right Governance

The governance issue was the trickiest of Ambachtsheer's three, because it involved a host of questions that could not be answered simply. A proper governance structure would display five key characteristics:[9]

- There would be 'a clear, enforceable legal requirement to invest CPP assets solely in the best interest of CPP stakeholders,' which means the pensioners and the current and future contributors, both employees and employers.
- There would be a 'clear chain of accountability' from the fund to the stakeholders.
- The stakeholders would be able to see clearly that the governance structure was 'there to look after their best interests.'
- The fund would have 'clear, unfettered paths' to the 'best strategic and tactical investment thinking and expertise' when it decided and implemented a CPP investment policy.

- The fund would have the flexibility 'to anticipate and respond to new circumstances.'

Taking the first characteristic as a given, Ambachtsheer now laid out his two governance models that might be used to invest in the best interests of stakeholders. His 'legislated governance model' (LGM) would make the federal and provincial finance ministers directly accountable to the stakeholders for the CPP fund's investment returns; in his 'independent governance model' (IGM), ministers would delegate that job to an independent CPP fund board of trustees.

Under the LGM, the ministers would need an expert advisory committee to help them decide on the right asset mix for the fund (what proportions for Canadian stocks and bonds, foreign stocks and bonds, and other investments) and an implementation unit to carry out their decisions. Under the IGM, legislation would create an 'autonomous' CPP Investment Board governed by trustees who 'would be legally charged to establish and operate an investment process in the best interest of CPP stakeholders.'[10] The trustees would decide the asset mix policy using fiduciary standards.

Size was not an issue. By 2006, Ambachtsheer said, a CPP fund would be one of several large funds in Canada, and by 2016, it would be moving into a league of its own. But current big players like the Caisse de dépôt et placement du Québec and the Ontario Teachers' Pension Plan Board 'appear to be doing more "good" than "bad"' and had brought 'high quality, low cost, disciplined management to Canada's financial markets.'[11]

Potential Problems, Potential Rewards

Both models met the accountability test, but Ambachtsheer reckoned that the IGM had the edge in terms of public perception, access to talent, and flexibility. Its big potential disadvantages lay in the risk that it might wind up with an ineffective or dysfunctional board and that it might lose money on the parts of the portfolios where it was making active investment choices rather than following broad market indexes. The choice facing ministers, he said, was a matter of risk and reward. The LGM might be less risky, 'but it also offers fewer potential rewards in terms of perceived legitimacy, opportunities for organizational excellence, contributions to informational and operational efficiency of

Canada's stock and bonds markets, contributions to small business investing in Canada, enhanced portfolio returns and other spin-off benefits resulting from introducing a new, large, independent professional investor into Canada's capital markets. To garner those rewards, a CPP Investment Board at arms length from partisan political pressures would have to be established.'[12]

For an independent expert like Ambachtsheer, these were two wholly legitimate options, though he clearly leaned to the IGM. For any minister reading the report, only the independent governance model was even remotely realistic.[13] Politicians and their partisan advisers could all too easily construct a truly horrifying scenario under the legislated governance model. Finance ministers would face sharp questions in the Commons or their legislatures if an investment turned sour or they had sent CPP money abroad for investment in foreign markets. The thought that any minister would expose himself or herself to such certain repeated attacks over every stock pick was laughably unimaginable.

Throughout the period from February to May, federal Finance officials worked on their own paper, consulting their provincial counterparts along the way, often through bilateral contacts. It too adopted the two models as the main options facing governments; Ambachtsheer's report was an annex to the federal paper. Both papers went to the provinces in mid-May, in time for the officials' planned gathering in St John's in early June. There, two meetings proceeded in parallel. In one, the broader CPP committee worked on the big package of reforms, drawing up a statement of principles for ministers to endorse at their Fredericton meeting. The draft principles included one relating to investment: 'CPP funds must be invested in the best interests of plan members, and maintain a proper balance between returns and investment risk. Governance structures must be created to ensure sound fund management.'[14] It was still vague, but it established that the CPP fund should be market-oriented and pursue no secondary investment objectives that would get in the way of the 'best interests of plan members.'

In the other meeting, the working group on investment discussed Ambachtsheer's report and the draft paper put together by Finance. 'That's where we got the real breakthrough,' a federal official recalled. At first, the meeting bogged down in the fine points like how many directors the fund should have. As one federal official recalls, the dynamics changed when one Alberta official suggested that they step back from all the detail and set out the high-level principles they were aiming for. 'They wanted us to build on the principle agreed to by the

CPP committee and get away from the weeds,' the same federal official said. He went up to his hotel room and wrote an outline of a shorter paper based on the investment principle that the CPP committee had put together for the ministers' Fredericton meeting. Principle 7 read: 'CPP funds must be invested in the best interests of plan members, and maintain a proper balance between returns and investment risk. Governance structures must be created to ensure sound fund management.' The principle effectively discarded the modified provincial access approach; the CPP fund was now on course to become a market-oriented pool of capital. The big question now was whether the market approach would be pure or modified to leave the provinces with at least some guaranteed access to the fund at market rates of interest. The new paper did the trick. The discussion now shifted from the very detailed paper Finance had prepared in advance of the meeting to the shorter, much more focused paper that the federal official had just tapped out on his laptop computer. The meeting went smoothly after that. 'People could agree to the big principles and then go on to the details,' one official recalled. The shorter paper 'got blessed by the officials and later went to ministers.' The working group never discussed the longer draft paper again, and it was never finalized.

Though the finance ministers did not release the principles statement in Fredericton two weeks later (it was put off until October), the fundamentals of the investment policy were clearly taking shape. The idea of setting up an arm's-length investment board had gained considerable momentum as a result of the public consultations. If governments were going to sell Canadians on a big increase in the CPP contribution rate, the politicians would have to be able to assure people that their funds would be well managed. An independent investment board was no longer just a technique for managing the money; it would be a key selling point for the whole reform, an affirmation that retirement funds would not be squandered on politically convenient but economically questionable business ventures.

Dealing with the Details

Now the working group on investment had to begin fleshing out the details. In mid-July, Finance cranked up its efforts with visits to Toronto and Ottawa to talk with pension experts, investment dealers, and investment management firms. It was not the first such trip. In late March, federal Finance Department officials Wayne Foster and Charles

Seeto had met with James Pesando, a University of Toronto economist who specialized in pension issues, and John Ilkiw, a one-time Ontario government pension expert who was then in the Toronto office of U.S.-based Frank Russell Co., a firm that provided investment advice to many pension funds. They also touched base with executives at the Ontario Teachers' Pension Plan Board and the Ontario Municipal Employees Retirement System, the two biggest public sector pension plans in the province. Not surprisingly, their advice to Ottawa was to replicate their own model with a CPP fund that would run like any other big pension fund and invest in the public markets.

On their July trip, the Finance officials expanded their list of contacts. In Toronto, one of their first stops was at the office of Malcolm Rowan, a policy consultant who was, in a sense, the father of the Ontario Teachers' Pension Plan Board. A decade earlier, as a senior Ontario deputy minister, he had chaired a provincial task force on investing public service pension funds. His 1987 report – titled *In Whose Interest?* – had recommended, among other things, that public sector funds, then shackled by a requirement to buy only provincial government bonds, should operate under the same rules as private sector funds without government direction as to what kind of investments they should make. Others on the list were Koskie Minsky, a law firm that specialized in pension matters; TD Asset Management; Sobeco Ernst & Young, a firm whose niche was actuarial, benefits, and compensation advice; RBC Dominion Securities; and Watson Wyatt Worldwide. In Montreal, they spoke to officials at the Caisse de dépôt et placement du Québec, the Quebec government, brokerage firm Lévesque Beaubien, and the CN Pension Plan.

The working group met again at the end of July, when it dealt with papers Finance had prepared on three issues: provincial access, governance of the fund, and questions raised by the eventual size of the fund. It was a very good meeting. They agreed that the provinces should have some access to the fund, but still had to work out the details. They agreed that independent governance was the way to go for the fund, which would be run by a professional board, though they still had not figured out how such a board would be selected. And they agreed that the CPP's pool of capital should be kept in one fund, not split into several. Over the next six weeks, the working group narrowed the remaining areas of disagreement down to a limited number of options – there were no more meetings; it was all done by email and fax – and kicked the results up to their deputy ministers for their CCO meeting in Winnipeg on 17 September.

The deputies reached agreement on many of the issues. The board would follow a passive investment strategy, tracking broad market indexes and avoiding active stock-picking, but only for the first three years. They still had to nail down the finer points of appointing directors, but it would not be a system under which each province automatically got one director. The provinces could roll over their existing loans from the CPP fund once; one province held out on that point but later came on board.

The Policy Falls into Place

When the finance ministers met in Ottawa on 4 October, they had in front of them a three-page paper[15] blessed by their deputies – some called it the 'foundation document' – that was dated 1 October and drafted by federal Finance in consultation with the working group. The paper first set out the main considerations:

- Ministers were agreed on the key investment principle (set out in Principle 7 of the June 'Principles' document) – that CPP funds would be invested in the best interests of plan members, that investment returns and risks would be properly balanced, and that governance structures would be created to ensure sound fund management.
- Ministers were also agreed that the provinces should have some access to the fund 'at market rates consistent with this principle.'
- In the public consultations, people supported higher contribution rates and fuller funding only if the investments were to be 'professionally managed at arm's length from government, like a pension fund.'
- Since Ottawa and the provinces shared responsibility for the CPP, 'both levels of government should therefore have meaningful roles in the selection of the CPP Investment Board.'
- An effective communications strategy for the new investment policy would be an important ingredient in winning public support for the overall reforms.

Next, it outlined the framework for the new policy. New funds would be 'invested in a diversified portfolio of securities by a new independent corporation, the CPP Investment Fund Board (the "Board"), in the best interests of plan members. The Board will be governed by a qualified board of directors of about a dozen members. The Board will engage professionals to manage the new fund, and administer the old (or existing) fund. The Board will be accountable to the public and federal and provincial governments and will report its investment results regularly.'[16]

The 'new fund' – the net additions to the fund from future contributions, that is – would be 'subject to broadly the same investment rules as other pension funds' and would 'strictly follow the foreign property limit of 20 per cent which applies to other pension funds.' For the first three years, all new equity holdings in Canadian companies would be 'selected passively mirroring broad market indexes.' The investment board would then ask ministers for permission to shift to active investing for 'a small proportion' of its Canadian equities portfolio. Finance ministers would consider that proposal at their next review of the CPP, set for three years hence. Provinces would have access to a set percentage of whatever sums the board decided to invest in bonds, but at their own market rate, not that of the federal government. For the first three years, they could tap into half of that bond portfolio; after that, their share would be the 'provincial and municipal share of total bonds held by trusteed pension funds, as published by Statistics Canada (44% for 1995).' The securities would not be marketable. The old fund would have its own rules. If they wanted, provinces could roll over their existing CPP non-marketable borrowings at maturity for another twenty years at their own market rate of interest. Any funds the provinces chose not to borrow would be invested in marketable securities.

The memo laid out a process for finding directors that was cumbersome but necessary to ensure that all governments were content with how it worked. Ottawa and the nine CPP provinces[17] would appoint a nominating committee to recommend candidates for the board. The federal government, after consulting with the provinces, would pick names from the list. Finally, it listed the key lines for a communications strategy that would touch on the key themes: a 'market-oriented fund managed in the best interests of plan members, like other pension funds' and run by 'qualified professional management at arm's length from government.'

Some details became easier once the big governance issues were settled. 'You don't have to deal with all the issues if you get the right people,' one official said. The trick was to find what he called the 'fine line between interference and accountability.' Governments would be accountable for the investment board but could not interfere in its operations unless they did so collectively, with the same double two-thirds

David Anderson, 'I could even learn to enjoy this,' August 1996

majority that governed the CPP itself. Indeed, some decisions were much more easily left to the board. When the whole thing was wrapped up and put into place, for example, neither the act nor the regulations said anything about where the CPPIB's head office would be located. 'It's missing. We left it up to the board to decide,' a federal official said.

They were about to sign off on the single biggest transformation in the whole reform package. There would be plenty of critics ready to pounce on the idea of handing the management of that much money – and a major chunk of Canadians' retirement savings to boot – over to what some would regard as a government agency, notwithstanding the provisions for an arm's-length relationship. It would be an easy target for fear-mongering. At the same time, the policymakers knew that Canadians were not at all disturbed by the examples of pension funds like Teachers' and OMERS.

There were details to work out, and the whole CPP reform package was about to face its stiffest test, but the investment policy was solidly on track.

14 Autumn Obstacles

The finance ministers' planned meeting for October in Ottawa began to unravel in September when British Columbia kicked the struts out from under any chance that a deal might be struck soon. Without warning, the province's new finance minister, Andrew Petter, rolled out a new set of proposals that challenged the emerging consensus for reform.

British Columbia's reversal, which surprised and angered ministers and officials in Ottawa and the other provinces, followed a changing of the guard in the provincial government. In February, Glen Clark had replaced Mike Harcourt as leader of the governing New Democratic Party and premier of the province. Three months later, he won an election with a small majority in the legislature even though the Liberal Party won more votes. But Elizabeth Cull, who as finance minister under both Harcourt and Clark had spoken for British Columbia in the CPP talks, was defeated in her own riding. Clark replaced her with Petter, a constitutional law professor who was also minister of intergovernmental affairs. The new cabinet was sworn in 17 June, too late for Petter to get to the Fredericton finance ministers' meeting that began that evening and ran all the following day. Very shortly, the BC finance department had a new deputy minister as well, and a new person in charge of the CPP file, Bruce Kennedy, who was effectively just a notch down the hierarchy from the deputy. Kennedy already knew the CPP thoroughly, having written his PhD dissertation on it in 1989. It was a clean sweep – highly unusual in government – and over the summer, the new team took a fresh look at the province's position on the CPP.

The rest of the country got its first view of the fresh look in mid-September, when British Columbia dropped its new proposals into a meeting of finance deputy ministers in Winnipeg on 17 September. It was the usual deputies' meeting in advance of a ministers' meeting scheduled for two weeks later in Ottawa. This time, deputies hoped, the meeting would move them much closer to a deal that ministers might approve at the Ottawa meeting. British Columbia put an end to that prospect when Petter immediately went public with the province's new position. One proposal involved a complex formula under which the federal government would cut employment insurance (EI now, after the 1 July change in name) premiums to offset the planned increases in CPP contribution rates. This put Petter squarely on the side of Ontario's Ernie Eves in an odd alliance of one of the country's most left-wing provincial governments with one of its most right-wing provincial governments. Ottawa, Petter told the *Toronto Star*, was 'over-collecting on a payroll tax.' He also wanted the finance ministers to settle first on higher contribution rates and then take more time to study possible benefit cuts. 'We don't have to swallow the entire apple in one bite. We can do it a bite at a time.' He was particularly opposed to any reforms that would hit low-income workers and the disabled. 'There appears to be very little concern about the progressivity of what we are doing to a program that was designed to help those most vulnerable.'[1]

The next day, Petter escalated his attack when he told the *Financial Post* that Ottawa was trying to 'ram through' the changes and refusing to spend more time studying other possible solutions, a charge that irked not only the federal government but at least one other province as well. Manitoba Finance Minister Eric Stefanson called Petter's proposal to keep studying the CPP unacceptable. 'There has been an extensive national consultation process,' he said. 'There isn't any reason to delay making decisions. All that will do is compound the problem.' Still, Stefanson agreed with Petter's (and Eves's) position on EI. 'Our assessment shows that there is an opportunity to reduce EI premiums and that has to be directly related to any upward adjustment to CPP contributions.' British Columbia alone could not block an agreement, but Martin was reluctant to press ahead against the protests of a major province. The *Post* quoted an unnamed senior Liberal official as saying that Martin thought 'this is a sufficiently important file that all provinces have to buy in. He doesn't believe there is any room for acrimony from any province on this file.'[2]

British Columbia's New Stance

There was more to the BC plan than foot-dragging and cuts to EI premiums. Two versions of a BC position paper spelled out the details.[3] The province fully supported the federal government's proposal for a rapid increase in the contribution rate to a steady-state level and the creation of a fund to manage the money (Plank 1), though it preferred the slower ramp to get there. But it opposed the Plank 2 idea of freezing the year's basic exemption at $3,500 because low-income workers would face proportionately larger increases in their contributions than those further up the earnings scale. That meant a YBE freeze would adversely affect women and lower-income workers, something this NDP government could not support. It also rejected both the Plank 3 benefits cuts that would mainly affect the disabled and survivors, 'a very vulnerable group of people' and most of the other benefit cuts in Plank 4. There was one exception: it would cut the death benefit in half to 5 per cent of the YMPE.

The provincial paper included an 'alternative reform plan' that began with the 12.1 per cent long-term contribution rate in Ottawa's Plank 1 and worked the rate down from there. It endorsed a variety of small provincial proposals but needed two further major changes to reduce the long-term rate to under 10 per cent. Its proposal to use some of the surplus in the EI account to subsidize the CPP would cut the long-term CPP rate by 0.7 percentage points. But the real kicker was British Columbia's final suggestion – an increase in the year's maximum pensionable earnings level to $50,000 from $35,400. Earnings above the maximum were not subject to CPP contributions, so this proposal meant that CPP premiums would be collected on up to an additional $14,600 of the annual earnings of every worker who earned more than $35,400, which would substantially increase the CPP's total revenues. The province figured this measure alone would reduce the long-term contribution rate by 1.37 percentage points, enough to bring the overall rate to less than 10 per cent. The usual rebuttal to this idea was that it would break the link between contributions and benefits, since many – though not all – such proposals envisioned the collection of higher revenues without a corresponding increase in benefits.

The BC idea was different: as well as collecting higher premiums, it would also increase benefits, but do so only by phasing the new benefits in over a very long period. No one would collect a full benefit on the additional contributions for another forty-seven years, which would make the proposal actuarially sound. The extra revenues would get the CPP through the baby boom; after that, benefits would once more come into line with contributions. 'The financial lift to the CPP would have maximum impact during the first few decades after implementation, just when the demographic pressures caused by the retirement of the baby-boom are most acute,' the provincial paper said. Moreover, the change could be delayed for a decade to 'allow enough time for private pension arrangements to anticipate the changes.'[4] For politicians in other provinces, and in Ottawa, however, the BC proposal had a big drawback. The CPP contributions of someone earning $50,000 – hardly rich by any measure – would rise by more than 40 per cent, but the matching benefit would not be available for several decades. Politically, it could all too easily be characterized as an attempt to cure the CPP by forcing the middle class to bear most of the burden. Their additional contributions would spare those further down the income scale from bigger contribution increases.

For Petter, the CPP issue was a welcome break from what he later called 'that other whirlwind,' the fallout from the provincial government's pre-election budget. Just after he took over the finance portfolio in June, Petter had re-introduced in the legislature the same budget tabled two months earlier by his predecessor, Elizabeth Cull. It said British Columbia had run a surplus in the 1995–6 fiscal year, but when Petter discovered a few weeks later that the numbers were wrong – and that the government had actually run a deficit – he immediately told the media. That set off a massive controversy over what became known as the 'fudge-it budget.' The government spent months scrambling to repair the damage, with Petter in the middle, where he was very much preoccupied with budget management and the spending cuts needed to bring the government's finances back into line with the budget's projections.

As he recalls, the government's new position was put together by Bruce Kennedy, though Petter was only too happy to promote it. 'There was a real changing of the guard at that point – new premier and government, new finance minister, new deputy and Kennedy was new.'[5] Petter wanted 'a position that was aligned with our broader views.' While he was cutting spending on provincial programs, he could demonstrate his continuing commitment to NDP principles through the CPP. 'The fact that we had an important issue like the CPP was useful. I could speak from a social democratic point of view, so I welcomed it. There were choices that reflected some good research and policy work. I could take a strong political position.'

Pugnaciousness and Perplexity

Even so, some thought British Columbia's new CPP policy was more a reflection of Glen Clark's general chippiness – even with his own ministers – and his pugnacious attitude to federal–provincial relations. Clark always gave the impression that he relished any opportunity to do battle with distant Ottawa, and British Columbia's about-face on the CPP appeared to be part of his broader approach. Its natural ally in the CPP talks should have been Saskatchewan, but Janice MacKinnon recalled being perplexed by the change in British Columbia. She described Elizabeth Cull, the previous minister, as very responsible, a politician who had left-wing views but who was very collegial and a very powerful minister in the Harcourt government to boot. She could 'take a position and be confident that the government would support her. Petter was saddled with proposals that you wondered if he was comfortable with.'[6] (Nevertheless, Saskatchewan allied itself fully with British Columbia's new position in the final stages of the CPP talks.)

Petter himself was diplomatic when such comments were put to him, but Vaughn Palmer, the *Vancouver Sun*'s well-connected veteran political columnist, recalled that Clark and his closest advisers had hoped to finesse their way through the budget problem. As a former finance minister himself, Clark tended to listen to his own advisers when it came to issues that were normally handled by the finance minister and was known, on occasion, even to call in finance department officials, without their minister's knowledge, for private briefings. After Petter went public so quickly with the real deficit numbers, Clark's people no longer really trusted him, Palmer said. They viewed Petter as a woolly academic who did not know politics, so Clark tended to undermine him. Petter did not dispute this interpretation of his relations with Clark during this period, but his discretion slipped a bit during an interview when he recalled the day in 1998 when he left finance for another portfolio he much preferred – advanced education. He cheerfully – and approvingly – mentioned that one newspaper account of the swearing-in ceremony after the shuffle said Petter 'looked like the happiest person in the room.'

The Federal Counterattack

With just over a week to go until the finance ministers' October meeting, the federal government counterattacked the BC plan through the media. Federal officials and politicians gave interviews to the major newspapers and wire services slamming the BC proposal, both for its content and timing. *The Vancouver Sun* reported that federal officials were angry at British Columbia for possibly killing a CPP deal. 'The federal government views the BC stand with suspicion, calling it a political gesture for domestic consumption that could kill growing expectations of a CPP breakthrough at the meeting,' the story said. Even so, Ottawa still hoped for British Columbia's endorsement of a reform package. The *Sun* quoted a senior federal official as saying, 'I don't think anybody wants to isolate any province, but obviously we're a little bewildered. Our sense is that things were going well. We hope this doesn't scuttle what's really important, and we trust they [the BC government] know just how important the sustainability of the pension system is to Canadians.'[7]

David Walker returned to the battle (Martin was out of the country on other business) to criticize British Columbia's 'shoot from the hip' protest that he said had come too late to prevent an agreement. Where Martin had previously regarded unanimity as essential for CPP reform, Walker now warned that Ottawa did not need British Columbia's signature to press ahead. 'One always hopes that Canadians will come to a consensus, but I don't think a consensus requires unanimity ... I think that most people would consider that saving the CPP would be the highest priority if they had to choose between unanimity and seeing the CPP review put to bed this year.' He characterized the proposal to raise the YMPE to $50,000 as an 'additional tax on the middle class' amounting to $600 a year; the idea had already been considered and rejected as 'not a serious proposal.' In a final snipe, he said CPP reform is 'very, very complicated work. That's why we were surprised when BC, which didn't put its proposal in front of us ever, has suddenly had strong views about what would and would not work.'[8] A BC official said recently that the federal government's 'surprise' was overdone. British Columbia's concerns were well-known through meetings of the federal–provincial CPP committee of officials (actually, the sub-committee of the Continuing Committee of Officials, which was the deputy ministers' group), he recalled. 'There were no proposals in the September or October BC position papers that would have been unfamiliar to members of the CPP committee or [the CCO]. I don't recall whether or not courtesy copies of the public position papers were distributed in advance to Ministers.'[9]

Walker went even further in another interview, accusing the BC government of 'putting themselves in the same bed as the [right-wing] Fraser Institute and all these people who say governments can't fix programs. Just get out of it.' The very conservative Fraser Institute was among those pushing governments to shut down the CPP in favour of a Chilean-style system of individual retirement accounts. 'There is a whole constituency out there in the right wing across this country who would say, "See I told you so, the feds and the provinces can't get together."'[10]

The federal government got some comfort from an editorial in *The Vancouver Sun*, which called Petter's plan 'downright amusing' in light of his own government's record on financial matters. 'Bluntly put, a lack of credibility attends Mr. Petter's idea for boosting CPP premiums – yet his approach could stall the implementation of important changes to the plan because Finance Minister Paul Martin hopes to achieve consensus. If Mr. Martin has enough support from the rest of the country, he should go ahead. Ignoring Mr. Petter on this matter is unlikely to cost the Liberals any votes in BC.'[11]

The following Monday, four days before the finance ministers were scheduled to meet, the federal government got a bit of a public relations gift from Michel Bédard, the EI program's chief actuary at Human Resources Development Canada. The EI account had gone into deficit during the recession of the early 1990s but had recovered to the point where an expected 1996 surplus of about $4.6 billion would bring the accumulated EI reserve to more than $5 billion. Even so, Bédard advised the government to build a fund of between $10 and $15 billion, enough to get through another recession without raising premiums or cutting benefits. At that point, the EI fund was expected to add another $4.5 billion in 1997, so the actuary's target could be met quickly. Even though the EI 'fund' was nothing more than an accounting entry in the public accounts, and any surplus was actually used to reduce the overall federal deficit, Bédard's report bolstered Martin's claim that it was not yet time to cut EI premiums.[12]

The EI actuarial report was the third interjection into the CPP debate from a federal agency in the days leading up to the finance ministers' meeting. On 24 September, the National Council of Welfare, an advisory body to the Minister of Human Resources Development, issued an angry report that accused the federal and provincial governments of excessive secrecy in reforming the CPP. It slammed them for 'the poor quality of the research that went into the CPP consultation paper' and 'the cavalier approach by governments when it comes to decisions about the CPP.'[13] It described the *Information Paper* as 'misleading and manipulative and a disservice to the governments who commissioned it. It is a faint shadow of the useful and thoughtful work on pension reform done by governments in the early 1980s.' The Council was dismayed by the fact that the paper 'outlined a variety of cuts in CPP benefits and not one single improvement.' In addition, the *Information Paper* 'uses scare tactics to manipulate Canadians into supporting sharp increases in the CPP contribution rate in the short term to avoid a long-term rate of 14.2 per cent.' Since Finance apparently had no interest in 'improving the Canada Pension Plan for the benefit of Canadians,' the Council urged the prime minister to 'remove the Finance Department as the federal government's lead Department on the Canada Pension Plan and replace it with the Department of Human Resources Development.'[14]

Two days later, Auditor General Denis Desautels released a damning report on the record of the CPP's disability component over the previous decade.[15] The cost of disability benefits had more than tripled in the decade to $2.8 billion in the 1995–6 fiscal year from $841 million in 1986–7. The number of CPP disability beneficiaries had almost doubled over the same period, while the number of Quebec Pension Plan disability beneficiaries had remained flat. The auditor found cases in which people received unemployment insurance and CPP disability benefits at the same time (not allowed under the rules) and cases in which CPP officials granted benefits based on scant medical evidence of disability, sometimes only the word of the applicant. He also found lax follow-up verification procedures to track beneficiaries whose health might have improved to the point where they could return to work. None of this was new to the government. HRDC had found many of the same things in a study of its own, a study frequently cited in the auditor general's report. In its formal reply to the auditor general's report, the department said it was already working to solve many of the problems. Nevertheless, Desautels's report once more put the public spotlight on the disability question.

Going into the final stages of their negotiations over the CPP, the federal and provincial governments – Ottawa especially – were being buffeted from all sides with conflicting advice that was raising the public profile of the CPP and making for headlines that aroused concerns from all sides of the political spectrum.

Dicey Outlook

As Martin prepared for the Friday meeting with his provincial counterparts, a deal looked dicey. British Columbia had set off on its own track, with Saskatchewan – the other social democratic provincial government – largely following in its wake; Janice MacKinnon agreed that the governments should take more time to work out a deal. But four prov-inces – Ontario, British Columbia, Manitoba, and Saskatchewan – were now lined up on the side of forcing Ottawa to reduce EI premiums as an offset to higher CPP contributions. Martin was adamant in his opposi-tion. As far as he was concerned, EI was a purely federal program and its surplus would not be used to prop up the finances of a joint federal–provincial program, especially not when he needed the money to meet his deficit-reduction targets.

Going into the meeting, however, everyone knew that – setting aside the EI question – most of the pieces for a CPP reform had fallen into place for a deal. Deputies had discussed the details one last time on 29 September – the Sunday before the ministers' meeting – and the main points lined up this way:

- The contribution rate would rise to a new steady-state rate over seven years (a compromise between the six-year fast ramp and the eight-year slow ramp). It would climb from the current 5.6 per cent by 0.4 percentage points in 1997 and 1998, another 0.6 points in 1999, and a further 0.8 points in 2000, 2001, and 2002. This would bring it to 9.4 per cent in 2002. In the seventh year – 2003 – it would rise by whatever residual was needed to reach the steady-state rate.
- New funds would be invested in the public markets, but for the first three years, all such investments would be passive, meaning the new board running the CPP fund would invest to mimic broad market indexes rather than make their own choices. After that, the board could make proposals to the governments for a more discretionary investment policy. Provinces would be allowed one rollover of their existing CPP debt; any borrowings could be renewed for another twenty years when they expired. For the first three years, half of the new CPP funds allocated to bond purchases would be invested in the bonds of the provinces; after that, the provincial bond share would be floated at the same proportion as that for all private trusteed pension funds, which was then 44 per cent.
- Two provinces wanted the Year's Basic Exemption of 10 per cent of the YMPE to be left indexed to wage inflation, while seven wanted it frozen at the current level (then $3,500, because it was always rounded to the nearest $100), which would gradually reduce it over time relative to total earnings as inflation chipped away at its real value. Quebec wanted it frozen for the duration of the seven-year ramp and then phased out for workers with average or above-aver-

age earnings. A possible compromise would be a freeze with a review at the end of the seven-year ramp.

- There appeared to be general agreement to reduce the death benefit from 10 per cent of the YMPE – then with a maximum of $3,540 – to $2,000 and then freeze it.
- CPP members would be eligible for disability benefits only if they had contributed in four of the previous six years, as proposed in the *Information Paper*. Eight provinces agreed on this point; two were silent.
- There was still no resolution of the more technical question of bringing the retirement pensions of the disabled more in line with those of other Canadians.
- They still needed to balance the package by doing something to reduce the growth of current retirement pensions; most provinces had trouble with the idea of changing disability pensions without touching retirement pensions. There were three options, all of which involved the removal of some inflation protection (known as partial de-indexing). In each, the retirement pension would increase annually by the rate of inflation minus one percentage point. Seven provinces supported partial de-indexing for ten years, ending at age 75 at the latest. Five provinces would probably accept partial de-indexing until the age of 70, but the others were silent on that point. The same five could support five years of partial de-indexing if the overall rate stayed below 10 per cent; the rest were silent.
- Everyone supported a three-year review for the CPP with annual reporting to Parliament and the provinces and a new default provision under which all benefits would be frozen if the provinces could not come to an agreement at each review.

Decisions on Investment

Also in front of ministers were the conclusions of the working group on investment on the institutions and rules needed to make the new investment policy work. New CPP funds would be managed by a new independent corporation – tentatively called the CPP Investment Fund Board – that would be governed by a qualified board of directors of about a dozen members. They in turn would hire professionals to manage the new fund and administer the old fund. The board would be accountable both to the public and to the stewards of the CPP – the federal government and the governments of the nine provinces that were

At the federal Finance Department, deputy minister David Dodge (left) and minister Paul Martin (right) pushed hard to bring financial sustainability to the CPP. Both worried about Canadians' lack of confidence in the CPP – and in the ability of governments to resolve difficult issues. This photo was taken in 2000, when the government had just named Dodge to be Governor of the Bank of Canada.

Bernard Dussault, the federal government's chief actuary for the CPP, wrote the 15th actuarial report on the CPP – the one that launched the finance ministers' review of the plan that led to its reform. His report was a bombshell with its projection that substantially higher contribution rates were needed to prevent the CPP from running out of money.

Finance ministers Elizabeth Cull of British Columbia (left) and Janice MacKinnon of Saskatchewan (right), seen here at a federal–provincial finance ministers' meeting in December 1995, both argued in favour of holding public consultations on the future of the CPP. The other ministers agreed and the consultations began four months later.

Flanked by provincial and territorial finance ministers, federal finance minister Paul Martin briefs the media on the finance ministers' meeting in February 1996 that released a consultation paper on the CPP that would become the basis for public consultations. The ministers, from left to right, were John Ostashek (Yukon), Edmond Blanchard (New Brunswick), Martin, Jim Dinning (Alberta), Ernie Eves (Ontario), and Bernard Landry (Quebec).

At the public consultations run by MP David Walker (right centre, from behind), citizens and interest groups were seated around a table as they made their presentations and then were encouraged to discuss their views with each other. This format – seen here at a session in Hamilton, Ontario, on 16 April 1996 – forced people to debate their positions with others who held different opinions.

David Walker, the Liberal MP for Winnipeg-North Centre, headed the public consultations on the CPP that visited eighteen cities in all ten provinces and both territories. He had been Paul Martin's parliamentary secretary at Finance and was 'sulking' about a recent shift to chairing a Commons committee when the offer came to head out on the road and talk about pensions with Canadians. He was later appointed one of the first directors of the Canada Pension Plan Investment Board.

Rob Brown figured prominently in the CPP debate. He was especially popular with the media, because he could speak clearly and knowledgeably about the complex issues involved. As a professor of statistics and actuarial science at the University of Waterloo, he had published extensively on pension issues, and as a former president of the Canadian Institute of Actuaries, Brown was deeply involved in preparing several key reports by the CIA on retirement issues.

Monica Townson, a leading pension expert with a left-of-centre tilt, spoke often and forcefully about retirement incomes for women. She argued that they were especially disadvantaged because their lifetime earnings were well below those of men, which reduced their benefits from the CPP's earnings-based pensions.

Economist Bob Baldwin, the Canadian Labour Congress's leading pension expert, was widely respected in the pension community even by those who disagreed with him. His presentations were typically thoughtful, clear, and tough-minded. He argued that the federal and provincial governments' menu of possible changes to the CPP represented 'a remarkably perverse set of reactions' to the income security needs of Canadians.

Ken Battle, president of the Caledon Institute of Social Policy, and one of Canada's leading social policy analysts, played a key role in fostering expert debate on the CPP issues in addition to his own contributions to the discussion. The Caledon Institute hosted a series of expert round tables and seminars on various aspects of the CPP, one of which turned into a memorable intellectual brawl among people with sharply opposing views.

Malcolm Hamilton was a prominent actuary and forceful advocate of CPP financing reform. His quiet demeanour belied his willingness to take on anyone he thought was wrong on the issues. A pay-as-you-go CPP, he argued, was just a sophisticated version of 'the oldest retirement system known to man – parents relying on their children.'

Pension consultant Keith Ambachtsheer wrote a key study of the investment and governance issues involved in setting up a large fund of CPP money that would be invested in public financial markets rather than loaned to the provinces, which had been the rule in the CPP's first three decades.

British Columbia finance minister Andrew Petter, who took over from Elizabeth Cull in the middle of the CPP negotiations, produced an entirely new proposal for reform that angered both Ottawa and many other provincial governments.

Preston Manning's Reform Party advocated replacing the CPP over time with a system of mandatory private savings accounts similar to registered retirement savings plans. When the CPP agreement was announced, he said the increase in contribution rates would 'light a fire under the long-suffering Canadian taxpayer.' It never materialized.

Alberta treasurer Jim Dinning was a strong advocate of arm's length governance for the CPP fund. He also played a key role in bridging the divide between federal finance minister Paul Martin and Ontario finance minister Ernie Eves when they were arguing over premium reductions for the Employment Insurance program, an issue that held up the final agreement.

Michael Gourley, Ontario's deputy minister of finance, was a key player in the CPP reform – one of four people in the room at the Langevin Block in Ottawa when Ontario and the federal government made the breakthrough that led to the final agreement a week later.

Ontario finance minister Ernie Eves (left) startled other ministers at a meeting in October 1996, when he insisted that Ottawa cut its Employment Insurance premiums to offset planned increases to CPP contributions. Federal finance minister Paul Martin (second from right) resisted, arguing that he needed those revenues to reduce his deficit. Between them, at this ministers' meeting in February 1996, was Susan Peterson, assistant deputy minister for federal–provincial relations and social policy in the federal Finance department. At right is human resources development minister Lloyd Axworthy.

Prime Minister Jean Chrétien and his senior policy adviser, Eddie Goldenberg, seen here in a 1998 photo, both talked to Ontario premier Mike Harris during a Team Canada trade mission to Asia in January 1997. Harris's agreement to support anything endorsed by his finance minister, Ernie Eves, helped break the logjam and clear the way for an agreement.

part of the CPP. The board would report its results regularly. It would also be subject to broadly the same investment rules as other pension funds, which included the 20 per cent foreign property limit on investments that applied to all pension funds. This would disappoint Bay Street, which hoped to eliminate the 20 per cent rule altogether and had hoped the CPP fund might be the catalyst for just such a change.[16]

The governments knew it was vital to get one item right the first time – how to ensure that the investment fund board was truly independent and not under the thumb of governments. There were plenty of Canadians suspicious of the biggest thumb of all – that of Ottawa – and would be looking for evidence that the board was truly at arm's length from all governments. The answer to that question lay in a cumbersome process for appointing directors. The finance ministers of Canada and the nine CPP provinces would first appoint a nominating committee, which would then produce a list of candidates for the board. That list would go back to the ministers. The federal finance minister, after consulting with the provincial ministers, would then choose board members from the list. There was no specific requirement for regional balance, though this was implicit, and no requirement at all that specific groups in society – labour unions, for example – should be represented; indeed, the governments wanted to avoid that altogether.

The details of where governments stood at that point made it clear that they were close to an agreement on the CPP per se. If the discussion had stuck to the glide path ministers and officials had been following for almost a year, a deal might have been struck reasonably quickly. They still had their differences, to be sure, but these were relatively small. Only British Columbia was off the map as far as Ottawa and the other provinces were concerned, and most were ready to press ahead without British Columbia's support.

In the final days leading up to the Friday, 4 October, finance ministers' meeting, Martin and several provincial ministers talked to the media about their expectations, often taking pot shots at each other. Martin aimed most of his remarks at Petter. 'What is important is that we don't do what in fact has been done by politicians for the last 15 years, and that is simply defer the matter, refuse to face up to the choices that have to be made,' Martin told reporters in Ottawa. 'Because the net result of that is that the right wing is going to win, and that the CPP is going to be in difficulty.'[17] At the same time, the federal minister appeared to have accepted the obvious – that no deal was possible just now – and Finance officials were already trying to arrange another meeting for December. Martin was now hoping merely to 'advance the yardsticks' on Friday. MacKinnon argued for more time to study the BC plan, which was 'worth significant analysis.' In a line that would have been anathema to Martin, who worried about losing momentum for a deal, MacKinnon added that 'there's no arbitrary deadline. The federal government could extend this discussion for another six months, eight months, another year if it had to.' The Manitoba finance minister, Eric Stefanson, dismissed MacKinnon's view: 'The worst thing is to tinker and delay.'[18]

Stumbling Blocks

On Friday morning, as the meeting was about to begin, the newspapers were filled with the last-minute musings of the ministers. Martin was floating a new idea to accommodate the recalcitrant provinces – a second round of CPP talks to follow a quick deal on all the elements that appeared to be already settled. 'In Round 1, what we have to solve now is to put in place those measures which will ensure future generations of Canadians that their CPP is financially sound and will be there for them,' Martin told *The Globe and Mail*. 'That's what we've got to accomplish now. Round 2 is for other things on the CPP that I think we should be dealing with.' Round 2, then, could look at the BC proposal and another proposal from Manitoba to examine the impact of the CPP on retired women.[19] There was a limit to Martin's conciliatory tone. In another interview, he said pointedly of the BC plan: 'I first learned of this proposal in the newspapers. I've never seen a piece of paper on it.'[20]

The account that best put the whole affair in perspective came from the *Financial Post*, whose reporter, John Geddes, had been following the talks closely. 'Finance Minister Paul Martin wanted to make overhauling the Canada Pension Plan a model for federal–provincial co-operation. But as he prepared to meet today in Ottawa with his provincial counterparts, the process was in danger of going down as another rancorous chapter in the history of strained relations between the two levels of government.' Martin said he was 'going to do everything I can to get a consensus,' but failing that, 'I guess we're going to move.'[21]

To almost everyone – especially those on the outside – it looked as if the BC proposal was the biggest stumbling block to a deal. It wasn't. When Petter made his presentation, the other ministers gave him a polite hearing, but that was all. 'We gave him his day in court,' one provincial official recalled. 'We ignored him and moved on. BC was going in the wrong direction.' Jim Dinning, Alberta's treasurer, recalled that because this was Petter's first meeting, he was still something of an outsider in the finance ministers' club. It would be going too far to say he had not earned his stripes, Dinning said, but 'we'd been through enough battles at that point as finance ministers that there was a pretty strong chemistry around the table.' The other ministers felt some solidarity with each other: 'All of us were in the same boat.'[22]

Then came the shocker. Ontario's Ernie Eves dug in his heels on the question of EI premiums, startling many of those around the table. The position he had set out in Fredericton four months earlier was not just a bit of posturing. The major task for the meeting was to make the benefit cuts necessary to get the contribution rate down under 10 per cent, but Eves was not prepared to talk about CPP cuts unless Martin was willing to reduce EI premiums. British Columbia had some small inkling that this might be coming; just before the meeting began, a BC official recalls an Ontario official walking over to tell him quietly that 'Eves would have a surprise that we would find interesting.' Martin may also have been ready for Eves's tough line, since the two had talked by phone the day before.

Certainly, Martin was ready with arguments to address Eves's position. He was only too willing to promise that the EI rate would come down over time and those reductions would help to ease the pain of higher CPP premiums on both workers and employers. But he would not commit himself to a firm schedule of EI premium cuts until he saw how quickly the federal government was eliminating its overall fiscal deficit. He had in hand one argument that might appeal to finance ministers worried about their own provincial budgets: if Ottawa did not meet its deficit target, interest rates were likely to rise and that would throw the provinces off their fiscal tracks as well. And if he did not have EI surpluses to help meet his deficit targets, he could pointedly ask for their advice on what he should do instead – cut transfers to the provinces even further? Cut transfers to seniors? Since he would only know year by year how much fiscal room he would have to cut EI premiums, he could not agree to a six- or seven-year schedule of EI reductions. Besides, he could argue, if you're so keen on offsetting payroll tax cuts, why don't you reduce your workers' compensation premiums or your special health and education payroll taxes? The latter argument could hardly have cut much ice with Eves, who had done exactly that in his most recent budget five months earlier.

A Scrap of Progress

The ministers did manage to salvage one thing out of the meeting – the statement of principles that had been ready to go in Fredericton four months earlier but postponed because of British Columbia's absence. What they agreed to and released in Ottawa was a slightly amended version of the Fredericton version. (See chapter 12 for the original eight principles.)

Principle 3, which said 'the solutions to the CPP's problems must be fair across generations,' was expanded by adding the words 'and between men and women.' This would be their symbolic response to calls for greater gender equity. A new line, inserted as Principle 7, was meant to underscore their determination never again to endorse benefit enrichments that were not paid for with matching increases in the contribution rate: 'Any further benefit improvements must be fully funded.' The old Principles 7 and 8 were renumbered as 8 and 9. The final principle was strengthened to force future ministers to act quickly to solve any emerging problems and to require more transparency. It now read (with the new words italicized): 'Governments must monitor changing economic, demographic, and other circumstances which can affect the CPP, and *act to respond to these changing conditions. Annually, Ministers of Finance should* provide Canadians with the appropriate information so they can judge for themselves that the integrity and security of the CPP is being protected.'[23]

When the finance ministers emerged from the meeting, they did what ministers usually do in these circumstances: try to put the best possible face on failure. Even so, media coverage was uniformly negative.

The Canadian Press story, the one that found its way into many of the country's newspapers, opened by saying that a CPP deal 'appears farther away than ever.' The declaration of shared principles was seen as little more than an attempt to put a positive spin on the meeting. 'Yet the vast majority were rehashes of points that have long been accepted. In the end, the ministers couldn't even agree on when to meet next.' The only thing new in terms of a CPP deal was an agreement that premiums would rise no higher than 10.1 per cent. But though the BC proposal had been thought to be the biggest block to a deal, Martin's 'biggest hurdle' was now Ontario's insistence on a federal commitment to reduce EI premiums.[24]

Eves's hard line on EI had simply brought progress on a CPP reform package to a halt. Ministers had already agreed they wanted a contribution rate of less than 10 per cent. To get there, they would need to cut benefits, but they had not yet agreed on which benefits to cut or even how big a package of cuts they would need. But until the federal government yielded on EI premiums, Eves insisted, he would not discuss benefit cuts. 'I still think that for quite a few provinces, not just the province of Ontario, the ultimate issue comes down to payroll taxation,' Eves said. 'From the province of Ontario's point of view, we kept reiterating the principle that we're not prepared to talk about reducing benefits until we talk about what we're going to do to reduce UI premiums. And I keep coming back to the fact that a payroll tax is a payroll tax is a payroll tax.'[25]

For the media, Martin simply reiterated his long-standing position that he would bring the EI rate down as quickly as his own finances permitted but would not commit himself to the multi-year schedule of cuts that so many provinces (Quebec had now joined Ontario, British Columbia, Saskatchewan, and Manitoba on this point) wanted. Martin and Eves, one Western provincial official observed, were 'ships passing in the night. Their attitude to each other was – "You just don't get it."'

Disaster or Not?

So the meeting was a disaster. Or was it? For anyone paying close attention, it seemed clear that the EI issue was now the only thing standing in the way of a CPP deal. That does not minimize its importance – it was a very large roadblock – but it was increasingly looking like the only one. Ottawa and the other provinces were obviously ready to do a deal without British Columbia and Saskatchewan if need be. Only Ontario could, on its own, stop the reform, because it had more than one-third of the population. Yet here was Ernie Eves saying that if Martin yielded on the EI question, a CPP deal could be done quickly: 'I think you could come to some resolution before the end of the year, but that depends on what develops or doesn't develop.'[26] He was clearly holding out a deal.

Martin, who had already said he would reduce the EI premium for employees from the 1996 rate of $2.95 per $100 of earnings to $2.90 in 1997, was not just facing down the provincial finance ministers on the issue. The week after the finance ministers' meeting, *The Globe and Mail* reported that Martin's officials in the Finance Department were pressing him to reduce the EI premium even more. The bureaucrats put forward three arguments that would have been music to the ears not only of provincial finance ministers, but business organizations, labour unions, and many economists as well. They were recommending a cut of 15 to 20 cents, rather than 5 cents, for three reasons: 'it would promote job creation; it would help offset the economic impact on the economy of heavy government spending cuts that will kick in over the next year; and it would also help offset the plans to increase Canada Pension Plan contributions as part of a reform of that program, as has been demanded by Ontario and several other provinces.' Martin, determined not to miss his deficits targets, was resisting. 'The more he has been pressed by his department in recent weeks, the more he has pushed back,' *The Globe* quoted sources as saying.[27]

Perhaps the makings of a deal were there, though there was a cloud in the form of the personal relationship between Martin and Eves, also reported by *The Globe*. Its weekly column of political gossip included a fascinating tidbit from the finance ministers' meeting a week earlier. 'As the meeting broke up, Mr. Martin, who prides himself on his good personal relations with the other ministers, invited Mr. Eves upstairs for a private chat. The gesture of conciliation failed to elicit the desired result. Mr. Eves spoke his mind to the press and then left without a further word, leaving a red-faced Mr. Martin standing alone at the altar.'[28]

The problem went beyond Martin and Eves and beyond the payroll tax issue embodied by the CPP and EI. Persistent sniping had become the overriding dynamic in dealings between Ottawa and Queen's Park shortly after the election of the Mike Harris government in June 1995. Less than ten months later, the animosity had already begun to attract attention. The *Toronto Star*'s Shawn McCarthy wrote a long feature on the deteriorating relationship in which he detailed the gripes of each government about the other.[29] Ottawa complained that Ontario was frustrating the federal government's desire for action on a wide range of issues involving the provinces, like taxation, training, internal trade, and regulatory reform; Queen's Park retorted that the lack of cooperation was all on the federal side. 'The truth is, we've accommodated the federal government far more than they've accommodated us,' Harris said. In a direct jibe at Eves personally, Terrie O'Leary, Paul Martin's executive assistant, said the finance minister appeared to have too much on his plate, since he was also the government's house leader in the legislature, a time-consuming task, and deputy premier. 'Finance officials were also dismayed at the pre-Christmas federal–provincial finance ministers' meeting, when Eves appeared to be unprepared to deal with the discussion on the Canada Pension Plan,' the *Toronto Star*'s story said, though it added that Ontario officials 'complained that

Ottawa appeared to be in too much of a hurry and was driving the agenda faster than not only Ontario, but other provinces, were comfortable with.' Queen's Park came off worse in the article, since the only outside commentators quoted came down on Ottawa's side. 'Ontario has got a very full agenda and this federal–provincial aspect doesn't seem to rank in any sense,' Bill Robson, of the C.D. Howe Institute, said. 'These are important things and many of us would like to see more co-operation.'

Jim Dinning speculated in an interview that the sour relations between Ottawa and Queen's Park reflected the partisan politics of the day. Ontario was a major electoral battleground for the federal Liberals, unlike Alberta, where their support was slender. Dinning said he and Martin got along well. 'I didn't have the same kind of fights with Martin that Ernie did,' probably because 'Martin and Chrétien never saw the west as fertile territory for them politically, so there was no point in scoring political points off us. We were not going head-to-head the way the federal Liberals were with the Conservatives in Ontario.'[30]

Figuring out Eves

Ministers and officials from the other provinces had always had a hard time reading Eves, who was something of an enigma to most. At finance ministers' meetings, he stayed to himself and read from prepared scripts, rarely engaging in the give-and-take discussions, one federal official recalled.[31] Martin was apparently unconcerned about this behaviour, though it upset some members of his team. Don't worry about it, he would tell them; How are you getting along with his officials?

That, as it happened, was a problem, for both federal and provincial officials alike. In interviews, many recalled their frustrations in dealing with Ontario during that period. One federal official said they had problems in getting a provincial response to new proposals because Ontario officials appeared to have trouble getting feedback from Eves. An official from one Western province used much the same language: 'Ontario was strange; my Ontario counterparts said Eves was unclear [in his directions to them]; he was not engaged in the issue.' Yet another Western official had the same recollection: 'Ontario's stance was kind of confusing. They [the officials] were working in a vacuum. They were not close to their masters. We'd ask them what their minister thought and they often did not have an answer; they'd have to get back to us.'

That slowed the whole process down, he said. This approach puzzled officials in places like Alberta, where Jim Dinning was fully involved in the CPP file and gave his own officials, headed by his immensely capable deputy minister, Al O'Brien, full clearance to speak to other governments. One federal official said Ontario was 'not really engaged' in the process, that Eves was never very strong as a minister and did not play as big a role as might have been expected from such a key province. His recollection is that 'Eves felt he was operating on orders from Harris not to be co-operative.'

Eves's personal style also rankled some, who regarded him as a bit of a showboat. 'He was there to get his sound bite and go home. He made his point and he'd say it on TV,' said one. Occasionally, he would arrive late for meetings, a habit that one person from another province called a form of psychological warfare. A federal official recalled having the sense 'that he was mad that he had to be there at all and that it was imposed on him. He was not there to be helpful.' Andrew Petter referred to Eves 'showing up late and being Ernie.'

Michael Gourley, Eves's deputy minister at the time, brushed such comments aside. There was no trouble getting feedback from Eves as issues arose, he said, and no problem with clearance to talk to other governments. But Eves wanted to manage both the message going back to Ottawa and the timing of its delivery, so that it would never interfere with something else the provincial government was doing. If Eves appeared impatient at meetings or arrived late, it was because he regarded most meetings of any kind as 'not a good expenditure of time.' Tardiness was not an attempt to engage in psychological warfare. If he often read from a text, it was because leaks to the media were inevitable and 'he wanted to be consistent in public and in the private ministers' meetings.'[32]

Eves was a bit of a puzzle on the policy front as well when it came to the CPP. Given the reputation of both Harris and Eves on economic issues, Ontario was never as conservative on CPP issues as one might have expected. One federal official recalled that Ontario was always pushing for reform but never for benefit cuts as deep as Alberta wanted, while an Ontario official said that Eves once inquired about the idea of privatizing the CPP along the lines suggested by the Reform Party, but utterly lost interest after getting a note from his finance department explaining the implications. Although he was very much an architect of the Harris government's anti-tax 'Common Sense Revolution,' and although he never wavered from his general opposition to higher payroll taxes, he had from the beginning of the CPP talks accepted the need for higher contribution rates. The furthest he went was to warn that too-steep increases were likely to hurt the economy and should be resisted. As far as David Walker was concerned, Eves was on side all along with the kind of reform that eventually emerged. He recalled Eves saying at the Fredericton meeting that 'we've got to solve this.'[33]

Keeping Up the Pressure

Through the rest of 1996, Eves kept up the pressure on Martin to cut EI premiums. 'By 1999, there will be $20 billion accumulated surplus,' he told one interviewer. 'It's supposed to be an Employment Insurance fund, not a cash cow so government can balance its books.'[34] Whether it was Eves's doing or repeated calls from business groups for lower EI premiums, the balance in the public relations battle seemed to be tilting away from Martin as the media grew more sceptical of his stance. One newspaper article noted that while Martin said he needed an EI surplus to avoid raising premiums in the event of another recession, 'he won't say how much of a surplus he requires, nor why such a large one is needed if, as he predicts, the economy is in for a long period of sustained growth.' And while he once attacked payroll levies as a 'tax on jobs,' he 'now points to evidence that lower payroll taxes don't necessarily lead to job creation.'[35]

In late November, Martin (jointly with Pierre Pettigrew, the new Human Resources Development minister) officially announced what everyone expected – that the EI premium would fall·by 5 cents to $2.90 per $100 of earnings. Though they sweetened the news with a two-year $250 million premium holiday for small businesses hiring new employees, they were attacked from all sides for the growing surplus in the EI reserve. Business wanted even lower premiums while organized labour wanted Ottawa to restore previous cuts to EI benefits. From Queen's Park, Eves added his voice to the chorus by repeating his earlier 'cash cow' line, of which he had obviously grown fond. Once more, Martin rejected any linkage to the CPP, which he said had to stand on its own. 'It is not related to either unemployment insurance or in fact to provincial health taxes or workmen's compensation.'[36] A few days later, Eves spelled out the kind of EI premium reductions he had in mind – 20 cents a year for the following three years. Even with cuts that big, he said, Ottawa would still run surpluses in the EI account. He even expressed some solidarity with the country's two NDP governments, adding that changes should not be pushed through over the objection of British Columbia and Saskatchewan: 'I can't see hammering two or three dissenting provinces. I'd like to think that when we're fixing the Canada Pension Plan, we're fixing it for all Canadians.'[37]

The 'Deadline' Passes

By now, Martin's year-end deadline for a deal appeared to be out of reach. David Walker professed optimism that a breakthrough might occur before Christmas, but others were sceptical. Employers wanted to know soon how much they should deduct from their employees' paycheques as of 1 January 1997 – the 5.85 per cent rate mandated under the existing legislation or a new higher rate that would come out of a deal – and talks continued among officials, though they remained confidential. Eves had not changed his position, but a spokeswoman said 'many other issues' were in play.[38] That was perhaps the first public clue to what else was going on; Ontario had a number of complaints with Ottawa – irritants, really – that the province wanted to talk about as well.

Martin and Eves met privately on 27 November but got nowhere. By early December, Martin too appeared to have given up hope of a deal before the end of the year and was ready to announce the 5.85 per cent CPP rate for 1997. 'I am ... quite optimistic that we will arrive at a solution,' he said in the House of Commons. 'I would have preferred to have [a deal] done by January 1. We may go beyond that, but I believe there is good will on all sides to arrive at a solution.'[39]

Just before Christmas, the veil lifted slightly on what Ottawa might have in mind to break the impasse. Giles Gherson, Southam News' well-connected columnist, reported that the federal government was quietly talking about

> handing Ontario and B.C. more federal money for immigration in return for a CPP deal. The idea is that this would remedy a long-standing, legitimate complaint from both provinces that they are being badly short-changed compared to Quebec, which benefits handsomely from a special immigration deal. Currently Quebec takes 12 per cent of Canada's immigrants and gets 30 per cent of federal immigration money. Ontario receives the same amount of money to settle 50 per cent of the country's immigrants. B.C. settles one-quarter of Canada's immigrants and receives 12

per cent of funding. Fixing the immigration imbalance would be costly. But, if successful, the overture would remove a serious provincial grievance and put CPP reform back on the rails.[40]

But as the year ended, the CPP remained mired in the mutual stubbornness of Paul Martin and Ernie Eves and the governments they represented. Both men wanted a deal, but both had their price and it revolved around EI premiums. A BC official said later it was a 'scary interlude.' Much as British Columbia objected to the reform package on the table, no reform at all would have been a 'disaster' for both British Columbia and Saskatchewan; the country's two social democratic governments would have been tagged with threatening the collapse of a prized and much-loved social program.

Gourley, Eves's deputy, agreed it was scary in that 'hopes were up and everyone wanted to preserve the atmosphere of getting a deal.' The problem was that 'no one could figure out how to bring it together in a way that was a win for all the parties involved.' Ontario and Ottawa 'were stick-handling at centre ice, with not much offense and not much defence.' Both Eves and Martin were still in combat posture. Gourley described Eves as 'a tough negotiator. If he's still posturing, he doesn't think you're ready to deal. If he thinks you'll deal, he can shift into deal-making mode quickly.'[41]

Through all this period, officials continued to talk and Martin kept in touch with his provincial counterparts. Everyone knew a deal was there for the taking, but the spark to make it happen eluded them all.

15 The Deal Is Done

The needed spark for a deal was struck in, of all places, Asia. On 8 January 1997, Prime Minister Jean Chrétien took off on a trade mission for two weeks in South Korea, the Philippines, and Thailand with 400 businesspeople, officials, and nine of the ten provincial premiers in tow. Designed to do business with three key countries in Asia, the so-called Team Canada trip was also a chance for federal and provincial politicians to do some informal business with each other.

In his 2006 memoirs, Eddie Goldenberg, Chrétien's senior policy adviser, revealed two conversations from that trip that helped break the logjam on the CPP. Just before they left Ottawa, Goldenberg got a worried call from Finance Minister Paul Martin. If Ontario did not agree soon to the CPP reforms, Alberta's approval for the emerging deal might disappear. Alberta was heading for an election soon and Jim Dinning would not be running again. His likely successor as finance minister, Stockwell Day, could not be counted on to maintain Alberta's support, so it was important to get Ontario's endorsement before Dinning left. 'Can you and the prime minister do something with [Mike] Harris on your trip?' Goldenberg quotes Martin as asking.[1] Martin recalled it slightly differently. He said Eves wanted to go ahead with the CPP reform, but Harris occasionally stopped Eves from doing what he wanted to do. Knowing that Chrétien and Harris often clashed, Martin wanted to be sure that they got along during the trip. 'We didn't need Harris to push Ernie; we just needed no one to get Harris's back up.'[2]

Goldenberg says he buttonholed Harris for a chat one morning in the lobby of a Seoul hotel. Harris reiterated his opposition to tax increases of any kind but said he would leave the CPP to Eves; if Eves agreed, Harris would not overrule him. Goldenberg, he added, should talk to

David Lindsay, Harris's chief of staff, when they returned to Canada. Later that morning, Harris confirmed this directive in a thirty-second conversation with Chrétien.[3]

Even before the Team Canada crew got back to Canada, Eves was hinting publicly that a deal was at hand. Going into a caucus meeting on 18 January, he told reporters that Ottawa and Queen's Park were negotiating an agreement under which the surplus in the Employment Insurance account would be capped, with the savings used to put a lid on CPP premiums. 'I think we're fairly close,' *The Globe and Mail* quoted Eves as saying. 'We're still talking, which is always a good sign. Nobody has given up on either side and I think that we're moving towards an accommodation.'[4]

The Langevin Meeting

Once back in Canada, Goldenberg called Lindsay, and the two agreed to meet in Ottawa, along with the two deputy ministers of finance: David Dodge for the federal government, Michael Gourley for Ontario. It was a hopeful sign. Dodge and Gourley got along well, and since neither Goldenberg nor Lindsay had been directly involved in the CPP talks to date, they both had plenty of room to manoeuvre. The meeting took place in Goldenberg's boardroom in the Langevin Building across Wellington Street from Parliament Hill; it began shortly after noon on Friday, 7 February,[5] and lasted until past seven that evening.

Recollections of the meeting vary considerably. Lindsay recalls only that he was there. It was his only involvement with the CPP reforms, but his presence signified Harris's approval of whatever Gourley, representing Eves, would endorse. Dodge's recollections are sketchy – mainly that the Chrétien–Harris discussion in Seoul 'broke the logjam,' and 'while things were tough after that, they were doable.' It was their job, as officials, to nail down the details. To him, the Langevin session was a plain, ordinary meeting. 'The orders were to get on with it.' It was a matter of 'get the deal done, suck in your tummy and don't use niggly details to oppose it,' he said, something officials are very good at once the politicians have given them clear marching orders.[6]

Goldenberg and Gourley have more complete memories of the meeting, but clashing interpretations of how it went. Goldenberg, in his memoirs, says that the Ontario team 'brought to the table a smorgasbord of issues that had nothing to do with the public pension system. They included matters relating to student loans, the collection of the retail sales tax at the border, infrastructure, employment insurance premium rates, and federal spending on immigration in Ontario.' He and Dodge, he says, found it 'irritating' that critical reforms to make the CPP sustainable could be held hostage to 'such totally irrelevant matters' as the ones on Ontario's list. 'Dodge didn't hide his disgust and impatience and, at one point, was ready to walk away,' but both understood that they had little choice but to dicker. Without tying their hands or setting precedents, he says, they agreed to enough of Ontario's list to allow Eves to sign on to the CPP deal. In his office after the meeting, Goldenberg reminded Dodge 'that in the first meeting we had in 1993 [after the election that brought the Liberals to power], he had briefed Chaviva Hosek and me on the urgency of taking action to ensure the long-term safety of public pension plans.'[7]

Gourley says it was a meeting of 'two teams of good cops and bad cops' and Goldenberg should have balanced his account by indicating that Gourley 'was equally disgusted at the federal government's position of not being willing to offset what was surely an increase in a payroll tax by an agreement to roll back the unconscionable and indefensible level of the EI premiums. History certainly has vindicated Ontario's view of the EI tax. No one will ever be able to say how many jobs were lost as a result of the increase in CPP premiums or how many were lost from the protracted delay in reducing EI premiums.' The list of irritants 'that plays so prominently in Goldenberg's version completely underplays the presentation of the EI issue as delivered by Ontario. It was clear to all that this was the only issue of substance and Minister Eves had said as much publicly. Going into a "bilateral" meeting, it was a bad-cop tactic to add a few legitimate issues to the list of negotiable items.'[8]

In an interview, Goldenberg said the CPP negotiations had reached a point where 'it needed a closer' and at the Langevin meeting 'that's what we did.' He said Gourley was very prickly in the first half of the meeting, which made the session very difficult for a while. 'Then it was apparent they were there to make a deal,' and it went much better. There were arrangements we would announce, he said without elaboration, but they would not be explicitly related to the CPP, and EI premiums were going down anyway.[9] Gourley's rejoinder: 'If I was "prickly" during the first half of the discussions, I would say that Eddie was rebarbative and arrogantly uncooperative during the first half. With the full benefit of hindsight, I can say that it sometimes takes a prickly bad cop to encourage a deal.'

Gourley recalls the other issues on the table as irritants, not deal breakers. Ontario had a veto on changes to the CPP, but such a powerful tool could be used only with great care and a 'very good explanation,' he said. Ontario was well aware of the risks: if the CPP had been destroyed, Ontario would have been blamed and 'all the problems of the CPP would fall into [our] lap.' But he said there was no grand epiphany in the meeting, no 'eureka' moment when the deal fell into place. Martin and Eves found it difficult to bend from their positions but were willing to leave the matter to officials 'to do what they could without offending anybody.' Gourley said Mike Harris did not get in Eves's way. Harris wanted the CPP fixed 'because it was an element of government that was broken and that he could help fix.' But he worried that the fix would be seen mainly as a tax increase – contrary to his 'Common Sense Revolution' stance – that did not solve the CPP problem.

'Crucial in an odd way'

The Langevin meeting, Gourley said, 'was crucial in an odd way: There was no confrontation; there were no accusations. We had the PMO [Prime Minister's Office] and the Premiers' Office there. Sometimes, that's all you need – no objections: I can play with this; I can be a father of it [CPP reform]. We came out saying, "We're going to do it; let's start putting together the announcement and the press releases," but it still could have been stopped.' It was a low-key meeting in which both sides were saying, 'Can we do a little more? There was no one saying, "I must have this now." We were saying, "I'm seeing the possibility of a deal and it's not such a bad thing. Maybe it's a good thing. I can live with this because I don't like the alternatives."' It probably helped, he added, that the CPP was not central to the political ambitions of either Martin or Eves (both later became leaders of their respective parties, Martin as prime minister and Eves as premier of Ontario), so getting a CPP deal would not give either of them some great political advantage. It also helped that 'no other dispute arose while the compromise was at its most delicate stage.' The deal was done in a very Canadian way, Gourley suggested. Ontario had a good run at making its point, and had gotten some of what it wanted, like a contribution rate under 10 per cent, and the result looked like a fix that might endure.

In an interview, Gourley said there was no undertaking – even of the wink-and-nod variety – that Ottawa would cut EI premiums. But several months later, in December 2007, he said in a speech that there was 'no linking but lots of winking.'[10] Goldenberg, in an interview, agreed that the deal involved no explicit linkage, but that a wink was involved. This may simply be a matter of interpretation. Martin had said consistently that he would bring EI rates down as fast as he could once Ottawa's books were in better shape. It may be that in the Langevin meeting, Dodge and Goldenberg were more persuasive about that commitment or that Gourley and Lindsay were more inclined to accept it as genuine or a bit of both. In any event, Martin followed through on his broad promise. From its 1997 rate of $2.90 per $100 of covered earnings, the EI premium for employees fell to $2.70 in 1998 and – at this writing – in every year since. In 1999, 2000, and 2001, the decline was 15 cents in each year.

That Ontario came to the Langevin meeting ready to make a deal reflected – in Ottawa's view, anyway – one other factor. At some point in the weeks before the meeting, Jim Dinning called Ernie Eves to persuade him to press ahead with an agreement. Martin said Dinning was the go-between with Eves: 'I asked Dinning to talk to Eves.'[11] Dinning himself was modest about his role but acknowledged in an interview that he probably played the role of broker near the end: 'I guess we did.' Dinning had been given a list of questions about the CPP talks before the interview, but though they did not 'spark a flood of memories,' he remembered some of the battles between Martin and Eves: 'I got in the middle of that.' Dinning had a good relationship with Martin, who asked Dinning to talk to Eves 'when things got hot.' He recalled that he told Eves: 'We're doing what we were sent here to do. This is the best fix to come along in a long time. It was good on benefits and good on the investment board.' Eves was receptive, Dinning said. The Ontario finance minister was willing to 'play silly bugger' on EI premiums and his list of other irritants, but on the CPP reforms themselves, 'he was not that far from the consensus view.' He is unsure when that conversation took place: 'My chat with Ernie at the end must have accelerated it, but I can't recall the timing.'[12]

Gourley had another observation with which Dodge agreed: 'Although the Langevin meeting was important in testing the waters of each side's determination in sticking to its publicly stated positions on matters of substance, i.e., CPP rates and EI rates, I believe more credit should be given to finance ministers Martin, Eves, and Dinning for keeping the rhetoric down to a dull roar, thus enabling a soft landing for the CPP rate issue.'

In the week after the Langevin meeting, there was a flurry of phone calls and fax messages between Ottawa and the provincial capitals as the finishing touches were put on the CPP agreement. Martin's sense of urgency when he called Goldenberg before the trade mission was fully justified in one respect. On Tuesday, 11 February, four days after the Langevin meeting, Alberta Premier Ralph Klein called an election for 11 March, after which Dinning would no longer be finance minister.

Sealing the Deal

By Thursday night, the deal was sealed. British Columbia and Saskatchewan withheld their support, but eight provinces with more than 83 per cent of the population had signed on, comfortably over the two-thirds, two-thirds requirement. The next day, Friday, 14 February 1997, Martin announced the agreement and tabled in the Commons a draft version of the legislation needed to implement it.

The agreement was an amalgam of provisions that were expected, not-terribly-surprising, and utterly novel. (See table 15.1.) Most governments had shied away early from raising the retirement age, which remained at 65. Most were leery of reducing benefits for existing seniors, so the debate among governments over partial de-indexing of pensions ended with a decision to stick with the status quo; all CPP benefits would remain fully indexed to inflation. Indeed, anyone getting CPP benefits of any kind would not be affected by the deal. The contribution rate would rise to 9.9 per cent by 2003, putting it – to use the terminology of the negotiators – on a seven-year ramp that was a compromise between the six-year fast ramp and the eight-year slow ramp discussed earlier. Anyone familiar with government decision making could have seen that one coming. Employers were already deducting on the basis of the 5.85 per cent rate announced in December, but the rate for 1997 would be 6 per cent, with the unpaid balance collected in early 1998, when tax returns were filed. Once reached in 2003, the 9.9 per cent rate would be permanent. (See figure 15.1.)

The revenue stream from the higher contribution rates would put the CPP back into the black on an annual basis so that the accumulated fund would begin to grow again, eventually reaching a level equal to five years worth of benefits. The CPP would not be fully funded – an idea pushed by Alberta in the early stages of the talks, but later abandoned. It would remain primarily a PAYGO plan, counting on contribu-

Table 15.1 Comparison of existing CPP and new CPP proposals

- All retired CPP pensioners or anyone over 65 as of 31 December 1997 are not affected by the proposed changes. Anyone currently receiving CPP disability benefits, survivor benefits, or combined benefits, is also not affected.
- All benefits under the CPP will remain fully indexed to inflation.
- The ages of retirement – early, normal, or late – remain unchanged.

	Existing CPP	New CPP proposals
Reserve fund	Equal to two years of benefits and declining	Growing to five years of benefits
Contribution rates	Rising to 10.1% by 2016 Projected to increase to 14.2% in 2030	Rising to 9.9% by 2003, then held steady Will not rise above 9.9%
Year's basic exemption	Currently $3,500 indexed to wages	Frozen at $3,500
Year's maximum pensionable earnings (YMPE)	Indexed to wages	No change
Investment policy	Invested in non-negotiable provincial bonds	New funds invested in a diversified portfolio of securities
Provincial borrowing	Provinces borrow at federal rates	Limited provincial borrowings at their own market rates
New retirement pensions and earnings-related portion of disability and survivor benefits	Based on average of last 3 years' maximum pensionable earnings (YMPE)	Based on average of last 5 years' YMPE in line with majority of private plans
Normal retirement	Age 65	No change
Early retirement	Starting at age 60	No change
Late retirement	Up to age 70	No change
Eligibility for disability benefits	Must work and contribute in 2 of last 3 or 5 of last 10 years	Must work and contribute in 4 of last 6 years
Retirement pensions for disability beneficiaries	Based on year's maximum pensionable earnings (YMPE) when recipient turns 65, then indexed to prices	Based on YMPE at disablement with subsequent price indexing

Table 15.1 (*Concluded*)

	Existing CPP	New CPP proposals
Combined survivor-disability benefits	Ceiling equal to maximum retirement pension plus larger of two flat-rate components	Ceiling is one maximum disability pension
Combined survivor-retirement benefits	Ceiling equal to maximum retirement pension	No change to ceiling
All benefits	Fully indexed	No change
Death benefit	6 months retirement benefits, maximum of $3,580 grows with wages	6 months retirement benefits to maximum of $2,500 and frozen

Note: In this table, released on the date of the deal, Finance Canada fell into the same error that many made and that we have noted before. The contribution rate was projected to increase to 13.9 per cent in 2030 and 14.2 per cent in 2040. It was the PAYGO rate that was projected to rise to 14.2 per cent in 2030.

Source: Finance Canada news release 1997–010, 'Draft Legislation to amend the Canada Pension Plan Tabled, Ottawa, February 14, 1997.'

tions to finance most of its annual benefits, but the five-year reserve marked a significant move towards fuller funding of the plan. The larger CPP fund would be 'prudently invested in a diversified portfolio of securities in the best interest of contributors and beneficiaries. This new policy is consistent with the investment policies of most other pension plans in Canada and the QPP. Prudent assumptions indicate investing the fund in the market could generate an average real return of 3.8 per cent per year – i.e., a return of 3.8 per cent above the rate of inflation.' The money would be 'managed professionally at arm's length from governments' by a new CPP Investment Board (CPPIB) run by 'a qualified board of directors of up to 12 members,' the governments said in a paper explaining the agreement.[13]

For at least the first three years, 'all of the Board's domestic equity investments will be selected passively, mirroring broad market indexes.' Provinces would be allowed to roll over their existing borrowings from the fund at least once and would pay their own market rates for those loans. Of the portion that the board decided to invest in bonds, the provinces would have first crack at half those funds for the first three years; after that, the provincial share of the CPPIB's bond portfolio would be

Figure 15.1 CPP contribution rate schedules: Contributions as a per cent of contributory earnings

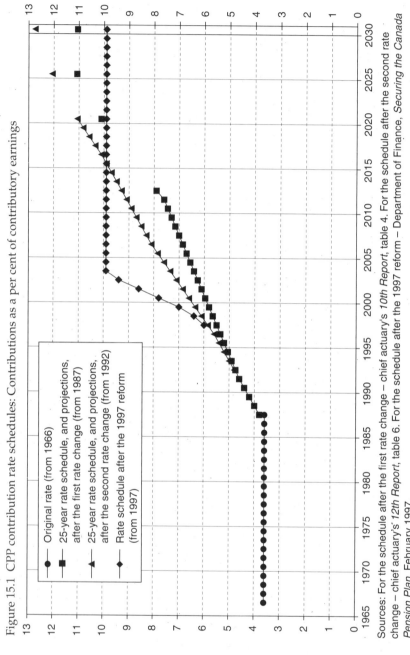

Legend:
● Original rate (from 1966)
■ 25-year rate schedule, and projections, after the first rate change (from 1987)
◀ 25-year rate schedule, and projections, after the second rate change (from 1992)
◆ Rate schedule after the 1997 reform (from 1997)

Sources: For the schedule after the first rate change – chief actuary's *10th Report*, table 4. For the schedule after the second rate change – chief actuary's *12th Report*, table 6. For the schedule after the 1997 reform – Department of Finance, *Securing the Canada Pension Plan*, February 1997.

equal to the average of other pension funds.[14] It was straight out of the official's memo in early October that summarized the consensus of the working group on investment before the October meeting of finance ministers.

In broad terms, there were no real surprises here; most of this had been long telegraphed to the public. The provision for passive investment in Canadian stocks was a bit of a refinement. Earlier public statements had made only general references to limiting the CPPIB to a passive investment strategy for the first three years, but now it was clear that the board could take a more active role when it came to other investments.

The policymakers had also taken great care to ensure that the CPPIB would be as far removed from government influence as possible. 'We pushed for the most arm's length model we could find,' one official recalled later.[15] They began with the rules governing the Bank of Canada, which operates with almost complete independence from the government, and then went further: 'In every area we could think of, we put more distance between the government and the CPPIB.' The CPPIB would be a Crown corporation, but its board of directors would appoint the chief executive officer, with no right of veto for Ottawa; it would not even be subject to federal hiring guidelines for such positions. This alone made it unlike any other Crown corporation. Most such companies (like the Royal Canadian Mint and Canada Post) are explicitly agents of the Crown, and all their obligations are guaranteed by the government; non-agent Crowns have no such financial backing.

It was politically important as well for another reason. As one federal official put it, the new investment policy – investing solely for the benefits of CPP members, an arm's-length board, and strong governance rules – 'was the idea that gave Dinning the ability to sell it in Alberta; it also made the deal acceptable to Harris.'

Visible Cuts – and Stealthy Cuts

The most visible benefit cuts in the agreement involved the disabled, but the amendments were so technical that few outside the circle of pension experts and advocacy groups understood them. What registered with the public was the fact that the cuts had centred on the CPP's disability provisions, source of the biggest increases in CPP expenditures in recent years. Disability benefits would go only to those who had worked and contributed to the CPP in four of the past six years (and only if their earnings had been at least equal to the YBE), not two of the last three or five of the last ten. The retirement benefit for people already getting a disability pension would move to a new base, though the specific proposal made in the *Information Paper* was rejected. Those with disabilities would continue to get a bigger pension than most Canadians, but the differential would be smaller.

The governments' paper explained once again what Ottawa had been saying for months: the administration of disability benefits, so much criticized by the auditor general, had already been tightened considerably. The governments also agreed that those eligible for both survivor and disability benefits would find their benefits capped at the maximum disability pension. But there would be no change to the rules for people who qualified for both survivor and retirement benefits.[16]

Two more provisions were reasonable outcomes. First, the year's basic exemption would be frozen at its current level of $3,500, which had been the consensus around the time of the October finance ministers' meeting. This was a powerful change, one capable of trimming about 1.4 percentage points off the long-term contribution rate. It amounted to what is often called a 'stealth' cut; it appears small at the beginning but grows in value over time. The year's maximum pensionable earnings (the ceiling) would continue to grow in line with wages, but since the exemption was frozen, the earnings subject to contributions – the amount between the ceiling and the exemption – would grow at a faster rate than the ceiling.

Originally, some provinces wanted to go further by either eliminating the YBE altogether or reducing it substantially and then freezing it. But that was opposed by British Columbia and Saskatchewan. Some officials recall that the freeze at $3,500 was a compromise designed to win the support of British Columbia and Saskatchewan. 'They both won compromises from the other provinces on benefits and then did not go along with the final package,' one federal official said later. 'We froze the YBE to keep them onside when some provinces wanted it reduced over time. That stuck in my craw.' A senior Alberta official recalled feeling similar annoyance.

The second such change involved the death benefit, which was reduced from its current maximum of $3,580,[17] where it was growing in line with wages each year, to $2,500, where it was frozen. This measure combined a very direct and immediate reduction with yet another stealth cut; the real value of the $2,500 benefit would dwindle over time into near insignificance with inflation.

The Five-Year Base

The biggest stealth measure of all, however, was one that had never been discussed publicly. Once the governments had rejected removing some of the inflation protection from rising CPP benefits, they needed another cut to reduce the steady-state contribution rate to under 10 per cent. They found it in a provision that evoked almost no public comment when the deal was announced. Put simply, retirement benefits[18] had been based on an average of the last three years of earnings; they would now be based on an average of the last five years. 'Most private plans use a five-year average,' the governments' agreement paper said blandly.[19]

The provision was actually more complex than that,[20] but the officials who understood the CPP knew that the impact of this change would be far greater than most people outside government noticed. Over time, it would make a very large difference in the cost of pensions compared with what they would otherwise have been. 'It was very last-minute,' according to one Quebec official of the day, who said he and his colleagues learned of it only the weekend before the deal was announced. It was the brainchild of Réal Bouchard, the federal finance official who had worked on the CPP file for most of the previous twenty-five years. He put the suggestion forward at a meeting of Finance Department officials, all of whom immediately grasped its significance. When he came up with that idea, one said later, 'we all clapped. We thought Réal should have gotten a big bonus.' One Ontario official recalled the shift to five years of earnings as the final measure that 'brought us under the 10 per cent.' No province complained. 'I thought it was a winner,' he said. 'It was big enough and benign enough to get [the job] done.' That described the proposal perfectly: it packed a powerful punch in terms of reducing the CPP's long-term costs, but no one was likely to notice such an arcane provision. And if someone did, it was not a flag around which anyone could rally a strong protest.

News of the deal broke before Martin stood up in the Commons to make his announcement. *The Globe and Mail*'s Edward Greenspon, quoting unnamed sources, reported in that morning's paper that 'Martin has given ground on the demand of Ontario Treasurer Ernie Eves to accompany CPP reforms with cuts to unemployment-insurance premiums,' despite his previous rejection of any linkage. 'To win over Ontario, Mr. Martin is to announce in Tuesday's budget a UI premium reduction of 10 cents on every $100 of insurable earnings, to take effect next Jan. 1, the sources said. However, they added that there will not be any federal acknowledgment that the measure on UI is linked with the CPP issue.' The story added that Ottawa would address other Ontario grievances as well, 'including complaints that the federal government rebates corporate-tax revenue to the province only once a year, sitting on a pile of cash that the province says rightfully should be in its hands from the time it is collected.'[21]

The EI announcement came through as promised in the 1997 budget, though the 10-cent cut to $2.80 for 1998 was characterized merely as an assumption for planning purposes. In any case, the rate was actually reduced by 20 cents in 1998 to $2.70 and by another 15 cents in each of the three following years. Although Martin continued to deny that the extra EI premium reduction was a tradeoff for Ontario's CPP support, he said that 'in all likelihood in November we would have announced a 10-cent drop in EI premiums for next year, anyway. Ontario wanted us to announce it now.'[22]

Never Again

Another handful of stipulations in the deal might be called the 'never again' provisions. The policymakers had learned a thing or two from their recent experience. 'There must be improved stewardship of the CPP to avoid again putting the sustainability of the CPP at risk,' the agreement paper said. 'Economic and demographic realities have changed significantly over the years without adequate response. Enrichments to benefits have repeatedly been made without proper adjustments to contributions. Administrative procedures have strayed from the intent of the legislation. And the period of time between statutory reviews may have allowed long-term projections of revenues and expenditures to get off-track without speedy corrective action.'[23]

In plainer language, it could be rendered as: the world changed and we did not notice; we were bad financial managers and bad program administrators; and we failed to monitor the CPP closely enough to correct the problems as they developed. It helped that they were talking about their predecessors rather than themselves, but even so, it was a startlingly candid admission of the policy and decision-making failures of the 1970s, 1980s, and early 1990s. Politicians never like to admit they are wrong, but here was a group of senior ministers almost grovelling in the court of public opinion to forgive a quarter-century of blundering. It would not happen again, they vowed. From then on, the CPP would be reviewed once every three years rather than every five, and if a significant problem was found, Canadians would again be consulted before any changes were made. In a direct lift from the guiding principles released in October, 'any future benefit improvements must be fully funded.' (The principle was easily stated, but it took most of the next decade for the experts to figure out exactly how to make this pledge operational.)[24] The full-funding requirement would also make any substantial benefit improvements very difficult since they would quickly push the 9.9 per cent steady-state rate to over 10 per cent. Indeed, the full-funding provision can be viewed as a bit of an oddity: though proud of their new steady-state approach to funding, ministers were implicitly suggesting that they had enough of a lingering attachment to the full-funding approach in general that they would apply it to future incremental benefits.

The ministers also strengthened the default provisions in the CPP. The 1985 agreement had said that if they could not agree on a new contribution rate schedule at each five-year review, the new twenty-five-year schedule of rate increases would be adjusted according to the complex fifteen-year formula under which rates would always aim to bring the reserve fund back to two years' worth of benefits. Now they went much further, with a new fail-safe mechanism that would kick in 'if, in any future statutory review of the CPP, the chief actuary calculates the CPP is not sustainable at the steady-state rate, and ministers cannot reach a consensus on actions to sustain the CPP. In the unlikely event that no agreement can be reached, an extra increase in the contribution rate will be phased in over three years, and benefits will be frozen until the subsequent review.' The impact would be split roughly evenly between the two. If the 1985 provision put a gun to their heads, this one put a cannon. From now on, the consequences of policy failure would not just be higher contribution rates but benefits that would be stripped of all protection from inflation until balance was restored. Since the politicians had just rejected even a partial de-indexing of CPP benefits as too dangerous politically – seniors would be outraged to lose even one percentage point of inflation protection – this was breathtakingly audacious. If their successors were even tempted to defer tough solutions, this proviso would be likely to stop them cold.

To these new stewardship arrangements were added some new accountability requirements as well. Ottawa would send out to individual contributors regular statements of their pension status, moving to annual statements 'as soon as feasible.' The CPP Investment Board would publish quarterly financial statements and annual reports on the performance of the assets under its control; it would also 'hold public meetings at least every two years in each participating province.' The annual CPP reports to Parliament 'will be more complete in the information they provide, and will in particular explain how administrative problems are being addressed.'[25]

Réal Bouchard, who retired from the Finance Department in 2007 after a career spent mostly on the CPP, has singled out those provisions as some of the most important in the deal. 'The 1997 reforms put in place robust tools to deal with unexpected future events – because we know the future is uncertain,' he told a Washington conference in 2006. 'More frequent actuarial reporting would bring problems to light earlier, new default provisions would ensure rapid policy action to address problems should they arise, and the new full funding provisions for benefit enrichments would ensure that the cost of enrichments would no longer be passed to future generations. As a result of these governance changes, the CPP should be able to weather the uncertain future.'[26]

Predictable Reaction

Reaction to the agreement was predictable. The right attacked the rise in contribution rates while the left attacked all cuts to benefits. Those in the middle, like actuaries, served up a more nuanced blend of praise and criticism.

The Reform Party blasted the changes as a tax grab that would kill jobs and put too great a burden on younger workers. 'No matter how you slice it, this is a tax increase,' Reform MP Ian McClelland said. His party stressed that the increase in the contribution rate worked out to a rise of more than 70 per cent. The premium hike would take money from working Canadians and employers would have less money to hire new workers: 'Just watch the unemployment rate once this kicks in.' He said the Liberals resisted deeper benefit cuts because they feared a backlash from seniors in the months leading to a federal election, something everyone was expecting soon. 'Seniors vote, and seniors' grandchildren don't,' he said.[27]

Reform Party leader Preston Manning was almost gleeful in his criticism of the proposed changes. 'What we needed was something to light a fire under the long-suffering Canadian taxpayer and Martin just lit the match,' he said the following week. 'What Martin did on Friday is the equivalent of what [former prime minister Brian] Mulroney and [former finance minister Michael] Wilson did with the GST [goods and services tax],' he said. 'They have stuck a goad into the taxpayers that will turn this CPP premium increase into the equivalent for the Liberals what the GST was for the Conservatives.' Manning's grasp of the details of the proposed changes to the CPP was shaky. He claimed that the eight provinces supported the higher contribution rates because they had a vested interest in preserving their access to CPP funds at low interest rates; this ignored the agreement's provision that limited the provinces to one rollover of their existing loans and, in any case, required them to pay full market rates. Martin dismissed Manning's comments: 'The position of the Reform party as far as the Canada Pension Plan is concerned is very clear. They want to blow it up. They want to see it destroyed.'[28] Within weeks, the Reform Party rolled out a series of newspaper advertisements blaring, 'Get Ready for the Biggest Tax Hike of Your Life.'[29] (No one, it appears, mentioned that CPP contributors can claim a non-refundable federal tax credit on their contributions. Ken Battle of the Caledon Institute later estimated that when provincial income tax savings are included, the average CPP tax credit is worth about 24 per cent of contributions.)[30]

The two dissenting provinces captured most of the arguments from the left. In a press release, BC Finance Minister Petter called the reform 'a straight fairness issue. The federal government has followed the hard-line conservative provinces and put the burden for CPP change onto lower-income people, on older women and on the disabled. Everyone agrees on the need for changes but there are other, fairer options available that would have been just as effective in putting the CPP on a sound financial footing without hitting these groups.'[31] From Saskatoon, Janice MacKinnon, Saskatchewan's finance minister, accused Ottawa of fixing the CPP on the backs of seniors, the disabled, and low-income Canadians. 'The people who are going to be hit the hardest in the changes are the disabled, elderly senior women and low income earners. From our point of view, these are people who need more protection.' The deal was contrary to what she called practical proposals put forward by British Columbia and Saskatchewan. 'A number of different proposals came out of the consultations, but the federal government never showed a willingness to study these alternatives.'[32]

Eves's Vindication

Ontario's Ernie Eves claimed vindication for his tough stance on EI premiums. 'I think it's a victory for Canadians. We had a lot of support at the table, there was no doubt of that. We had many other provinces supporting our position.'[33] Eves won some unusual praise from the *Toronto Star*, no fan of the Harris government. In an editorial, the *Star* said Eves's 'stubbornness paid off' in pressing for reductions in EI premiums. Though he did not get everything he wanted, 'he gave Canadians a welcome bit of help in their battle against the shrinking paycheque.'[34] In Quebec, Employment Minister Louise Harel said she was 'joyous' that CPP premiums would not rise above her own 10 per cent target, and she noted that the CPP changes reflected Quebec's own proposals.[35]

Among actuaries, the group best positioned to understand the arithmetic of the fix, the reviews were generally favourable. One former president of the Canadian Institute of Actuaries, Kit Moore, said he was 'personally quite happy.'[36] The CPP was already one of the best plans in the world, he said, and 'the changes were done in a way that is politically acceptable and address the problems of financial inequity between generations.' Another former CIA president, Paul McCrossan, gave the revamped CPP an 'A' grade because it made the three repairs needed to put the CPP on a sound footing – higher rates, control over runaway disability benefits, and stock market investment of the reserve fund.[37] Malcolm Hamilton, of William Mercer Ltd., who had been so prominent in the CPP debate, had wanted to see a provision for partial indexing so that current seniors would foot part of the bill for a reform but still gave the governments a score of eight out of ten for the deal. 'We're putting it in a more sustainable form but only by compelling future generations to contribute more than they should,' he said. 'The government should basically admit they're sticking it to young people, who are still being asked to pay twice what the benefit is worth to pay for the free ride their parents and grandparents have taken.'[38] Another Mercer actuary, Allan Tough of Calgary, said the 9.9 per cent contribution rate 'sounds definitely better for my children than going to 14 per cent later.' He repeated the mantra of pension experts everywhere: 'With any problem, it's better to face up to it now than later. The longer you delay, the worse it gets.'[39]

The CPP reforms made a cameo appearance in the Alberta provincial election campaign that was then underway. The Canadian Taxpayers' Federation, an Alberta-based anti-tax lobby, attacked Premier Ralph Klein for signing on to the CPP reform package and urged him to withdraw his endorsement. Klein replied that he did not like the higher contribution rate, but it was necessary: 'I don't support it. But you have to at some time make the plan actuarially sound.' The tax group said it would try pressuring Manitoba and Ontario to withdraw their support as well, noting that if two of the three changed their minds, the CPP overhaul would fail. Klein dismissed that idea bluntly: 'I think they're dreaming in technicolour.'[40]

Counting the Cuts

Missing from the documents released in Ottawa, but not from the coverage, was the overall impact of the benefit cuts over the long term. Officials told the media that when the reforms reached full maturity the benefit reductions would knock 9.3 per cent off the annual costs of the CPP. The switch to the five-year base for pensions did not go entirely unnoticed. *The Globe*'s Greenspon inquired about the impact before writing that 'the biggest measure on the benefit side is a virtually silent one.' He quoted officials as saying the measure 'would trim benefits by $144 a year at the maximum income level of $35,800 a year.'[41] In 1997, the maximum annual retirement pension was $8,842, so that would work out to a reduction of just over 1.6 per cent.[42] In the end, however, the provision was as benign as the policymakers had hoped. None of the major critics of the reform package picked up on the point and tried to make an issue of it.

There was one other quiet spin-off from the Langevin meeting between Ottawa and Queen's Park. Three weeks after the CPP deal was announced, Southam News columnist Giles Gherson reported that Ontario would be getting more federal funding to help it with the task of settling immigrants in the provinces:

> It will amount to a 30-per-cent increase that should go a long way to answering Ontario's bitter complaint that in recent years the province has received only 35 per cent of federal immigration money even though it takes in more than 50 per cent of the nation's immigrants – while Quebec gets the same amount to handle 13 per cent of the immigrants. The beauty of the immigration deal is that behind the scenes it was a key factor in ending Ontario Finance Minister Ernie Eves' refusal to sign on to Paul Martin's Canada Pension Plan reform package, without which it could not proceed.[43]

Why Did It Work?

Those involved in the extensive negotiations over the CPP have reflected on the reasons they got to a deal in the end.

Gourley puts it down to a combination of the natural inclinations of all the politicians involved and good work at the officials' level. The politicians did not want 'to be part of failure,' and the deal averted that outcome. 'At the end, we thought of those people living only off the CPP and being able to say to them, "Yes, you're okay."' The officials' long involvement in the issue also helped; most had known each other – and their provinces' views – for twenty years. 'We kept calm. Officials did not fly off the handle,' he said. 'If you're going to fly off the handle at the staff level, you'll never get anywhere.'

Bob Christie, Gourley's assistant deputy minister at the time, says the federal and provincial officials involved 'were long-time pension professionals' who worked well together – 'the hard slogging through the details' – until they were comfortable with the result. 'If staff is comfortable with it, people will be less likely to talk it down.'[44]

Réal Bouchard, in his 2006 Washington speech, observed that for all its importance in the Canadian retirement income system, the CPP was still not a very big program, and that helped. 'The relatively modest nature of the benefit, as well as the strong sense that the plan was first and foremost a retirement plan with benefits that should be linked to contributions, likely made reform easier. In public pension programs that attempt to address a number of objectives, and with higher [income] replacement rates, reform may be more difficult.'[45] CPP spending, he noted, amounts to only 2.4 per cent of gross domestic product, compared with 4.3 per cent for the U.S. Social Security program. A key reason is that Social Security has a much greater role in redistributing income, a task that in Canada is left to the Old Age Security program. OAS, with its Guaranteed Income Supplement, is very much aimed at those with low incomes. All told, however, the Canadian system is much more generous to very poor seniors. A single senior with average pre-retirement earnings of $10,000 would get a retirement income of about $15,000 in Canada from OAS-GIS and the CPP, compared with only $8,000 in the United States.[46]

A former colleague of Bouchard's made much the same point in an interview. What the United States delivers in the way of benefits is funnelled through a single program, Social Security; Canada does the same through two separate programs – OAS/GIS and the CPP. 'We do not put all our eggs in one basket,' this official observed. In countries whose pensions replace much more than the CPP's 25 per cent of pre-retirement income, 'people see that they have a bigger stake in the outcome of any changes, so it's an upside, in a sense, to diversify your portfolio. The irony is that because [Canada's system] is so complex, people don't really know what's going on. So they take the attitude that if it doesn't affect my OAS or my RRSP or my occupational pension plan, I can go back to sleep.'

BC pension expert Bruce Kennedy, who was deeply involved in the talks and has studied the CPP as an academic, offers another fascinating observation – that the first calculation of the CPP's unfunded liability – in the chief actuary's sixth report in 1978 – may have been 'the most significant single event in the whole story.' Walter Riese, as the CPP's chief actuary in the 1970s and 1980s, made that first calculation at the behest of the auditor general, despite his own doubts that it was appropriate for a social insurance plan (see chapter 3). Kennedy argues that the unfunded liability notion 'implicitly set pre-funded private pension plans as the point of reference for the CPP,' something that was not done for other public programs like OAS and medicare. 'It was this shift in framework, or mental models, that subsequently made it easy for finance ministers to bring their budget deficit thinking (and testosterone) to the CPP.' Health care is PAYGO financed in that people on average are 'net contributors throughout their working lives, but draw heavily on the system late in life. Analyzed in the same way, it has enormous unfunded liabilities and intergenerational transfers. We don't pre-fund it, and we don't expect it to be pre-funded, or recognize any liability,' Kennedy said. 'The choice of mental models matters a lot. The CPP inevitably incurred the analytical framework that it did because governments since 1966 presented it as something analogous to a private pension plan.'[47]

All Over but the Shouting

This is one of those cases where it is tempting to fall back on the cliché that it was all over but the shouting once the federal and provincial governments had announced their agreement. There was plenty of shouting, especially when the legislation was going through Parliament in the fall of 1997. But aside from several more months of quiet work by federal and provincial officials to make the CPP Investment Board operational – no easy task, but one devoid of public interest – the CPP reform was indeed over. The governments had made their deal and they would stick to it.

The rules of the game for reforming the CPP are unlike those for any other policy instrument in Canada. The requirement that all changes must be approved by two-thirds of the ten provinces with two-thirds of the population is unique. Even the Constitution requires the support of only two-thirds of the provinces with 50 per cent of the population to make changes, a hurdle low enough to prevent any single province from having a veto. Constitutional negotiations are notoriously difficult in Canada; two attempts to amend the Constitution failed in the late 1980s and early 1990s when they were unable to win that level of approval. Yet the CPP talks, facing a stiffer test for adoption, had produced an agreement in a remarkably short period. Less than two years passed between the report from the CPP's chief actuary in February 1995 and the agreement struck in February 1997.

One senior federal official reflected recently that it is easy to forget – since the reforms have worked out so well – just how tough the 1995–7 negotiations really were. 'The two-thirds, two-thirds formula is either a curse or a blessing. It's a curse because you have to go through hours and hours of negotiating to reach a compromise,' the official said. 'But it's a blessing because it involves governments of all parties and it is finance ministers who are responsible. They all devoted a lot of time to this. They knew the issues and the compromises and they took both the issues and compromises to their cabinets. So when you get an agreement, it is hard to get a groundswell of opposition to it. When you get out the other side, the result is strong.'

It was a perceptive observation. For federal MPs and provincial legislators who would like to tinker with this or that provision, the amending formula has been as much of a frustration as it was to the MP in the 1960s who complained that the Commons committee studying the original CPP legislation was merely a 'rubber stamp.'[48] As long as the federal government enjoys a majority in Parliament, the CPP is impregnable to changes the federal government opposes. And as long as four provinces (even one, if that province is Ontario) or any group of provinces with at least one-third of the population oppose it, a given proposal for change cannot pass. The CPP is, in short, an extraordinarily sturdy vehicle.

The Report Card

There was plenty of talk to come, but it had to wait until after the 2 June 1997 election, which the Liberals won with a reduced majority of 155 seats in the 301-seat House of Commons. As a campaign issue, the CPP had been a bit player, but when Parliament resumed in September, it was at the top of the government's order paper. Bill C-2, introduced on 25 September, carried a splendid, if somewhat cumbersome, title: 'An

Table 15.2 The math of the deal

(All figures as a percentage of contributory earnings)	
15th actuarial report: Costs in 2030 (PAYGO rate)	14.2
would be financed by	
investment income from the CPP fund	0.3
and a contribution rate of	13.9
1997 agreement: 2030 contribution rate would be	9.9
a reduction in the long-term contribution rate of	4.0
Sources of the 4-point reduction	
Accelerated contributions + new investment policy (CPPIB)	1.5
Freezing the Year's Basic Exemption (YBE)	1.4
Reduced benefits	1.1

Source: Chief Actuary's *16th Report.*

Act to establish the Canada Pension Plan Investment Board and to amend the Canada Pension Plan and the Old Age Security Act and to make consequential amendments to other Acts.' Its short title was more manageable: 'Canada Pension Plan Investment Board Act.' The CPP Act itself needed only amending; to set up the new CPP Investment Board, the government needed a whole new piece of legislation.

Accompanying the legislation was a new set of projections from the CPP's chief actuary, Bernard Dussault. Under the CPP legislation, the chief actuary is required to produce a report whenever the government introduces a bill to amend the CPP. This *16th Actuarial Report*[49] gave the finance ministers what they needed – a clean bill of health for the reform package they had put together. The higher contributions meant that the CPP account would begin growing again almost immediately and keep doing so until 2018. By then, the accumulated fund – then worth $40 billion – was projected to reach $379 billion, about 4.85 times the annual cost of all expenditures on benefits and administration.

The actuary provided his own breakdown of how the policymakers had brought down the projected long-term contribution rate, using 2030 as the benchmark year. That was when, under the *15th Report*'s projection, the PAYGO rate would have reached 14.2 per cent and the contribution rate would have climbed to 13.9 per cent.[50] Getting from there to the 9.9 per cent steady-state rate involved a four percentage point change, which the actuary helpfully decomposed. (See table 15.2.) The combined effect of the accelerated contribution rate schedule and the new investment policy accounted for 1.5 percentage points of the difference.[51] The freeze in the year's basic exemption reduced the steady-state rate by another 1.4 points and the benefit cuts by a further 1.1 points.[52] In effect, then, the split between higher contributions and reduced benefits was about three to one. The actuary also figured that over the long term the benefits he had earlier projected for 2030 would, because of the new provisions, be reduced by 9.1 per cent.[53] The switch to the five-year basis for benefits – the last-minute proposal that one official had called 'big and benign' – was large enough to reduce the PAYGO rate by 0.44 points. It was about equal to the impact of all the measures designed to tighten disability benefits and triple the effect of reducing and then freezing the maximum death benefit.[54]

The report provided further fodder for the CPP debate to come in Parliament. The CPP agreement had – at a stroke – reduced sharply the plan's unfunded liability, the figure that those on the right liked to cite as evidence of the plan's fundamental weakness and that those on the left (and many actuaries) dismissed as irrelevant for a social insurance program. Dussault said it had reached $588 billion by the end of 1996 (up from $488 billion in 1993) but would now be only $457 billion, down 22 per cent, primarily because of the higher investment returns expected under the new investment policy.[55] He explicitly assumed a real return of 3.8 per cent annually on future net cash flows to the CPP account.[56]

Dussault also had new estimates of how different generations would fare under the CPP in terms of the real (after-inflation) return they would get in retirement pension income on the money they had paid in contributions. Those already retired would be unaffected; anyone born in 1911 could still expect a 22.5 per cent real rate of return, while those born in 1929 could expect a 10.1 per cent return. The baby boomers would lose out from the reforms. The real return for the 1948 cohort would fall to 4.9 per cent from 5.1 per cent, while that for those born in 1968 would now be 2.5 per cent rather than 2.9 per cent. Later generations would still be the unluckiest of the lot but would do better under the new CPP than the old. Those born in 1988 could expect a real return of 1.9 per cent rather than 1.6 per cent, while those who would be born fifteen years hence – in 2012 – would get a 1.8 per cent real return rather than 1.5 per cent.[57] Those numbers would get a workout once the CPP legislation got to committee.

. Another report – this one on the gender implications of the deal – was also available at this time but curiously was not made public for another seven months, when it was given to members of the Commons Finance Committee, who asked if such a study had been done. Its conclusions were almost diametrically opposed to the prevailing view that women were singularly disadvantaged under the CPP and especially by the changes to the plan.[58] The report, released under the name of the federal, provincial, and territorial governments, reiterated the major general advantages of the CPP for women – a list that could have been lifted directly from the one put forward in May 1996 by Monica Townson at the Caledon conference on gender issues (see chapter 11). The CPP covered everyone, was fully portable, accommodated women's family responsibilities through the childrearing drop-out provision, permitted early retirement, allowed pension splitting, and was fully indexed to inflation. The government paper added another advantage: even though women lived (and collected CPP retirement benefits) longer than men, both women and men paid the same contribution rate.

The paper acknowledged that women get smaller retirement benefits than men but said that was because they had traditionally earned less than men – and the CPP was, after all, an earnings-based pension plan. They earned less for several reasons: they had spent fewer of their working-age years in paid jobs; many worked part-time and in low-paying occupations; women were more likely to head single-parent families and more likely to provide the bigger share of unpaid family care, which kept them out of paid work. The paper also noted that women relied more on public pensions (CPP and OAS-GIS) for their retirement income. In 1994, 48 per cent of the income of women 65 and older came from the public pension system and only 11 per cent from employer pensions and private retirement savings; for men, the figures were 34 per cent and 21 per cent, respectively. This, however, would change in the future because more women were now working, the 'lifetime earnings patterns of men and women are becoming more alike,' and families were having fewer children, resulting in fewer breaks in employment for women.[59]

None of that would have surprised anyone familiar with the details of the pension issue. What was new, however, was a cluster of numbers on contributions and benefits, most of which showed that the long-term impact on men and women from the changes were about the same. In 2030, CPP contributions under the reformed CPP would be 20.2 per cent lower than under the old CPP for women, but 21.9 per cent for men. Benefits in 2030 would be 9.7 per cent lower for women and 8.9 per cent lower for men under the new CPP.[60] Most striking of all, however, was the paper's estimate of the CPP's 'value for money.' Under the existing CPP, an 18–year-old in 1997 could expect to get back $1.83 in lifetime benefits for every $1 of lifetime contributions. For women, the figure was $2.62; for men, it was $1.34. Under the reformed CPP, the benefit-contribution ratio would be 1.82 for everyone – but 2.56 for women and 1.36 for men. In other words, women might get lower benefits in total than men for all the earnings-based reasons set out, but relative to what they put into the CPP, women got far more out of it than men. They lived longer (and collected retirement pensions for an average of almost five years more than men), made greater use of the childrearing drop-out provision, and were the usual recipients of survivor benefits because they outlived their husbands.[61]

When it was finally released, the paper must have had some impact. The periodic complaints of the previous two years over the lack of gender-based sensitivity in the reforms almost disappeared.[62]

The government wanted to get the legislation through Parliament by the end of the year, so it moved briskly. The bill was brought forward for second reading – approval in principle – on 7 October and debated for only a day before the government introduced a motion to allocate the remaining time for debate, a form of closure that prompted MPs from the Reform Party and the New Democratic Party to protest by walking out of the chamber. On 9 October, Bill C-2 passed easily by a vote of 202 to 69. The Reform and New Democratic parties both voted against it – for very different reasons – but both the Bloc Québécois and the Progressive Conservatives (reflecting the views of their partisan allies in the provincial governments) joined the Liberals in supporting the bill.[1]

The bill then went to the Commons Finance Committee, chaired by Liberal Maurizio Bevilacqua, for detailed study and the hearing of witnesses. Considering that a key element of the bill involved investing tens of billions of Canadians' money in the stock market, the timing of the committee's first hearing – 28 October 1997 – was hardly auspicious. The previous day, stock markets around the world had fallen in a mini-crash that reduced the Toronto Stock Exchange's benchmark index of 300 stocks by 6.2 per cent.

Most parties sent their big hitters to the hearing, a two-hour evening session that began with set-piece speeches by the main party representatives and ended with a series of lively exchanges between Martin and three Reform Party MPs.[2] Martin brought along Human Resources Development Minister Pierre Pettigrew. Preston Manning was no longer just leader of the Reform Party but Leader of the Official Opposition as well. His party had placed second to the Liberals in the June election, even though his predicted bonfire of taxpayer revolt failed to materialize. NDP leader Alexa McDonough and Progressive Conservative Party leader Jean Charest were also on hand, while Bloc Québécois leader Gilles Duceppe yielded his spot to Paul Crête, his finance critic.

In his opening statement, Martin largely repeated the lines he had honed over almost two years of talking about the CPP. He emphasized the joint nature of the proposed reforms: 'The federal government and eight provinces were determined not to shirk our responsibility to act now.' He recited the now-familiar statistics: eight working-age Canadians for every senior in 1966, five now and three in 2030; longer life expectancies that meant Canadians would be collecting pensions for twenty years, compared with fifteen in the CPP's early years; escalating costs that would push the contribution rates from under 6 per cent to over 14 per cent – 'an increase of over 140 per cent for future generations' – if governments did not act. He stressed the public consultations that had been part of the reform process: 'The clearest message that we heard is that Canadians want, Canadians need and Canadians count on the Canada Pension Plan. They told us that they want the CPP fixed now and they want it fixed right – not left to [drift],[3] not privatized and not scrapped, as some have suggested. They told us to fix it in a way that does not pass on an unbearable cost burden to future younger generations.'

New Ground for Martin

But Martin moved onto some new ground as well on the issue of intergenerational fairness. The 9.9 per cent steady-state rate, he said, would 'cover an individual's own benefits plus a uniform fair share of the burden of the plan's unfunded liability which has been built up over the years because we have not been paying our way. This is the fairest way to honour our outstanding obligations. The costs of the pensions will be spread evenly and fairly across generations.' He had previously defended the 9.9 per cent rate primarily because it would prevent a contribution rate of 14.2 per cent later on. The new spread-the-burden message had a partisan twist too. The committee hearings would offer all parties a platform for their positions and Martin could use the intergenerational argument to take on both the New Democratic and Reform parties – 'two minority views,' he called them.

He tackled the left first. The NDP, and the left in general, had argued that there was no real problem with the CPP, that all could be solved by letting the contribution rate rise steadily towards 14 per cent in the future. 'Those who claim that there is nothing wrong with the Canada Pension Plan must live on another planet.' Martin said. For the past decade, governments in Canada had 'ignored the warning signs for the CPP, preferring to leave the problem for others to deal with,' and now 'the only responsible thing to do is to make sure that people like me and the baby boomers in this room start paying more now, while we are still working, so that our children are not stuck with a truly punishing bill.'

Next, he turned on the right, attacking the Reform Party's proposal to replace the CPP with mandatory RRSPs, through which Canadians would be required to invest through their own individual retirement savings plans. 'Canadians ... do not want all of their basic retirement pension to be dependent on a fluctuating stock market. I would simply ask you to think of the insecurity, the volatility that we saw just yesterday and understand the consequences that that could lead to.' Mandatory RRSPs could not replace all the benefits of the CPP at a lower cost, he insisted. First, the CPP's new investment policy would generate returns equal to those of any private investor, with the added advantage that the federal government 'stands behind the defined benefit.'[4] Second, the CPP's administrative costs would be 'considerably lower than the costs associated with millions of individual plans.' Third, the CPP pays disability and death benefits and 'protects the pensions of parents who take time out of the workforce to care for young children,' something RRSPs could not do.

Then he highlighted the key weakness in the Reform Party's approach – one that actuarial expert Rob Brown of the University of Waterloo had noted two years earlier when Reform first released its position on the CPP – the failure to deal with the unfunded liability (see chapter 8). The Reform Party, Martin said, was 'ignoring the very real cost of honouring outstanding commitments under the CPP, commitments not only to today's seniors but to those who have been paying into the CPP for years and who are counting on a pension when it is their turn to retire.' If Manning's party was not going to renege on these commitments, they should explain who would pay the bill. 'Which taxes will they raise and by how much? Fuzzy talk about recognition bonds is simply not good enough, because no sleight of hand is going to take care of that $600 billion.'

Manning's Four Questions

Next in line was Manning, who raised what he called his 'four big questions: the fairness question, the rate-of-return question, the job question and the alternatives question.' His fairness question drew on the chief actuary's calculation[5] of the declining return from their CPP contributions for later generations – from the 22.5 per cent real return for those born in 1911 to the 1.9 per cent return for those born in 1988 to the 1.8 per cent return for 'every child born after that.' How could Martin 'defend that kind of intergenerational unfairness?' Then he tackled Martin's promise that the revamped CPP investment fund would earn a return of 3.8 per cent, far too low by Manning's reckoning, based again on a comment by the chief actuary that the QPP had earned 4 per cent annually since its inception and private sector plans earned 5 per cent. The job question was simple: How many jobs would be lost from the rise in payroll taxes as a result of the higher contribution rate? Finally, he asked Martin what alternative new ideas for pension reform he had studied; had he, for example looked at new proposals in the United States, Britain, Chile, and Singapore? Manning promised his own plan: 'Some time relatively soon my colleagues and I would like the opportunity to present an approach to pension reform which is an alternative to that presented by the [government].'

On intergenerational fairness, Martin and Manning were simply talking past each other. Martin figured that spreading the load of the unfunded liability trumped Manning's worry that later generations would get a smaller return than earlier ones. Neither addressed the other's main point. Martin dismissed as a quibble Manning's complaint about the 3.8 per cent return: it might be too low, but it was a prudent assumption and if the investment managers beat that target, the CPP could enhance benefits or reduce premiums. Their debate over payroll taxes was old and sterile. Though his department had studied the negative impact on job creation of payroll taxes, a category in which it included CPP premiums, Martin refused to refer to the premiums as taxes because the money did not go into the government's coffers but into a separate fund where it was clearly linked to benefits paid.[6] And yes, the government had looked at alternatives, he said. If his description of the Reform Party's pension policy was 'inadequate, unfinished or incompetent, it's because that's all they have given us. After two years of debate across the country, when all the provinces have come to the table [and] set their ideas out [and] the federal government has set its ideas out, all we've got [from the Reform Party] are sound bites in the House of Commons. We have not got a decent plan. For the Reform Party leader to say that he will put one forth at some eventual date ... We've been hearing that for two years.'

NEST EGG —

CPP

Dale Cummings, 'Nest egg,' 9 September 1997

The BQ's Paul Crête supported the legislation – 'I believe this is a good bill' – but pressed Martin to reduce Employment Insurance premiums. Jean Charest for the Progressive Conservatives reminded Martin of the Tories' election position that other taxes should be cut to offset the effect of rising CPP premiums. He also took a swipe at Manning for failing to address the unfunded liability. 'Frankly, I think you said it correctly, Mr. Martin ... that the issue for the Reform Party and Mr. Manning boils down to one simple question: show us the money ... Its $600 billion hole is a pretty big hit on Canadians. Young Canadians will pay a heck of a lot of money for their grandparents' [pensions]. They will also have to pay for their parents' and [sufficient] for their own, and that's a serious issue that cannot be compensated with TV clips.'

McDonough brought the views of the two provincial dissenters – the NDP governments of British Columbia and Saskatchewan – into the hearing room, with references to provisions that she said would affect women disproportionately – reduced survivors' benefits, tighter eligibility criteria for disability benefits, and the freeze on the year's basic exemption that would punish low-income earners, most of whom were women. 'So my question to the minister is what specific gender impact analysis has in fact been carried out, and will the minister tonight commit to tabling with this committee any such studies that have been carried out?' It may have surprised her when Martin blithely replied that a gender analysis had indeed been prepared and 'I would be delighted to table it with this committee and make a copy available to the Leader of the NDP.'

Heated Exchanges

The most heated exchanges of the evening began after Reform MP Monte Solberg told Martin that higher premiums were 'an unjust burden on millions of Canadians.' He chided Martin for failing to offer other tax relief to offset the CPP increase. Martin retorted: 'Every other political party at this table understands the issue. All of the provincial governments, without an exception, of all political stripes, understand the issue. The issue is that there is a $600 billion liability ...' Solberg interjected: 'You can't answer.' Martin continued: '... and unless you're prepared to renege on that liability, it has to be dealt with.'

Moments later, Martin resumed his attack with some genuinely new information – the cost of covering the unfunded liability by raising other taxes rather than CPP premiums. 'Now, if you're not prepared to deal with it in the CPP, then you are prepared to accept a 25 per cent increase in income taxes, because that's what it would cost; or you're going to accept a doubling of the GST, because that's what it would cost; or you will accept a much larger increase in a different way ... The problem ... is the $600 billion liability, which exists. It's there. You can't ignore it. I think the hearts of all of us go out to ... Canadians who are going to have to pay this, and I wish governments had dealt with it in the past. But Mr. Solberg, blowing up the CPP and reneging on a $600 billion liability is not the answer.'

Another dust-up followed when Reform MP Diane Ablonczy pressed Martin on why he rejected the kind of reforms being carried out in other countries. She did not specifically mention Chile, the country on which the Reform Party had modelled its pension proposals, but Martin did. Most countries that had adopted compulsory RRSPs, he said, had much younger populations than Canada, which made it 'much easier to make the transition. That doesn't mean there aren't problems. In the case of Chile, for example, they are starting to run into great problems with their annuity system, simply because people are jumping from one annuity to another and they are living longer.'

The 9.9 Per Cent Breakdown

To underline its case against the Chilean system, the government distributed, both to MPs and the media – a memo[7] to Martin signed by Scott Clark, who had replaced David Dodge as deputy minister of finance in August.[8] Written by finance official Réal Bouchard, the memo said that if proponents of mandatory RRSPs used the same assumptions about investment returns as the chief actuary, 'the cost of mandatory RRSPs can be *no lower* than the CPP for the *same* retirement and other benefits.' Indeed, 'once the higher investment, administrative and annuity costs of private plans are taken into account, providing CPP-type benefits through private means would cost at least a full percentage point more, that is, *at least 15 per cent more*, than providing the same benefits through the CPP.'[9]

The memo broke the 9.9 per cent contribution rate down into its component parts, a decomposition that made the burden of the CPP's generosity to its first large cohort of retirement beneficiaries all too clear. (See table 16.1.) Fully 3.8 percentage points were needed just to meet the CPP's commitments made in the thirty-one years since the plan began. The remaining 6.1 percentage points covered everything else –

Table 16.1 Breakdown of the 9.9% rate

Retirement pensions	4.3
Insurance (disability, widows, orphans)	1.7
Administration	0.1
Unfunded liability	3.8
TOTAL	9.9

Source: Scott Clark memo to Paul Martin

4.3 points for all future retirement benefits, 1.7 points for the insurance items in the CPP (1.1 points for disability benefits and 0.6 points for survivors, orphans, and the death benefit), and 0.1 points for all administrative costs.

In effect, if policymakers were working with a clean slate, they could have delivered the same menu of benefits for a contribution rate of only 6.1 per cent, a figure sometimes referred to as the actuarial fair cost; that is what it would cost Canadians 'to provide CPP-type benefits in the future – whether through the CPP or private plans – if there were no unfunded liability.' The other 3.8 points represented the drag of history. Private plans could expect to earn investment returns no better than a properly invested CPP fund, the memo argued, and the costs of running such plans would be far higher. The CPP's operating costs would be in the order of 0.1 per cent of assets, on a par with those of the major public plans in Ontario and Quebec, far lower than the 2 per cent commonly charged for individual RRSPs. In addition, Chile had already experienced high marketing costs – paid by individuals – as private pension providers tried to induce Chileans to switch from one plan to another. Quite simply, the cost of administering 'millions of small pension plans' would be far higher than the cost of running the CPP. All told, the fair cost of privatized individual pensions would be 'at least 7.1 per cent ... to provide what the CPP provides for 6.1 per cent.' As for covering the cost of the unfunded liability, the memo laid out the estimates Martin had already unveiled for the committee – raising the GST to 14 per cent or raising personal income taxes by 25 per cent over thirty years.

Martin and his officials had a strong incentive to beat back the notion that a Chilean-style system might have some merit. In Alberta, Stockwell Day, Jim Dinning's successor as treasurer, was talking about taking Alberta out of the CPP and setting up an Alberta Pension Plan, which might draw on the Chilean model for inspiration. Dinning recalled that

Martin wanted him to appear before the parliamentary committee to support the CPP reform, but 'I said no, I'm out of politics.' The chatter from Alberta was worrying in that the province had yet to pass the cabinet order that would legally cement its approval of the deal. So it was important to give no quarter when it came to suggestions that there might be alternatives better than the CPP.[10]

The federal government had been keeping an eye on the Chilean example throughout the reform process. Officials were aware that it had many proponents in Alberta and would be given new life if the CPP reform efforts had flagged. As one put it in an interview, the idea 'would have had a lot of traction if we had failed' to reform the CPP. 'It was the default option that everyone realized was out there.'[11] No one wanted to finance retirement pensions through any kind of ordinary taxes, where it would be part of the budgetary tax base.

Dealing with the Liability

At the committee's second hearing the next evening,[12] the same issues got another workout when officials from Finance and HRDC appeared. By now, MPs had had some time to absorb the Finance Department's memo, but it was clear that the Reform Party's biggest difficulty in coming to terms with the CPP legislation continued to be the components of the contribution rate and the workings of the unfunded liability. Reform was fixated on the idea that younger Canadians – 'at some point,' as Ablonczy put it – would figure out what a raw deal they were getting and 'simply ... not be willing to make the contribution necessary to keep the scheme going.'

Finance officials – mainly Susan Peterson, the assistant deputy minister for federal–provincial relations and social policy – repeatedly argued that the unfunded liability could not be avoided and that financing it through CPP premiums was the best alternative available. The new CPP would not eliminate, or even reduce, the unfunded liability that had scared so many people for so long; only a fully funded plan would accomplish that objective. 'To pay it off or to pay it down over the next number of years would mean that the CPP contribution rates would have to go above 9.9 per cent,' Peterson said. 'That would mean that one or two generations would pay more than successive generations, so the provinces and the federal government ended up agreeing that the fairest way to deal with the unfunded liability is to make sure all generations pay an equal amount towards carrying that burden.' The unfunded liability would continue to grow in absolute terms, but it would remain roughly constant in relation to total CPP expenditures. If the weight of the unfunded liability were not carried in that 3.8 percentage point levy on earnings, 'it has to be paid for in some other way,' Peterson said. The 3.8 points 'is the way to spread out that burden forever as opposed to having one or two generations really hit hard with it. So you may say that this is not as good as you would like it to be. But it's as good as it gets if you're not going to discount or renege on the unfunded liability.'[13] She noted that Chile, the Reform Party's model for a retirement income plan, had begun with a clean slate in 1980 when it switched to its new system of mandatory individual retirement accounts, but did so by devaluing the old plan's obligations to its members through inflation; in effect, Chile had reneged on its liability.

Investing the Money

MPs also raised questions about the new CPP investment policy, a subject that had received little attention in public commentary since the deal was signed eight months earlier. The NDP's Lorne Nystrom wanted to know if the investment board would be truly independent and if it would invest 'at least certain proportions [of the fund] in different regions of the country.' Had policymakers given any thought 'to some of the social concerns like employment and so on, investing in certain companies so they can create more jobs?' Bob Hamilton, the Finance Department's assistant deputy minister for financial sector policy, was reassuring on the first point and blunt on the second. 'One of the important factors that was pointed out to us as we talked to people about the proposed changes to the Canada Pension Plan was that the investment board would be independent, and we've gone to quite great lengths to ensure that as much as possible. The objectives of the board will clearly be to invest in the best interests of the beneficiaries and contributors of the plan. There is no secondary objective.'

Monte Solberg was also concerned about the board's independence, but for the opposite reason. What would prevent the investment board's directors, 'who are chosen by the provinces and are somewhat beholden, I guess, to the provinces, from pumping money into things that specifically benefit those provinces? ... Ultimately, is there any mechanism that will stop them from investing money into, for instance, if you're in B.C., B.C. Hydro, or into Sprung greenhouses in Newfound-

Brian Gable, 'Cat food futures,' 20 June 1996

land,[14] or some of the regional development things that have gone on in the past – the sorts of things that have caused taxpayers no end of heart-ache?' It was a sensitive point; almost every province had, at some point, made a well-intentioned government investment that went terribly – often embarrassingly – wrong. How, Solberg asked, could Hamilton be sure that the CPP Investment Board would have no secondary economic development objective? 'It is provided in the legislation,' Hamilton replied:

> We've made it as clear as we possibly can in the legislation that this is not part of their mandate. Their mandate is explicitly to make investments that will operate to the best interests of the beneficiaries and contributors and maximize the returns, subject to them being prudent. There is no mechanism in here to allow them to invest for reasons other than that, by having transparent policies and forcing them to be accountable publicly. We felt that was the best mechanism to try to make sure that the board had a clear mandate and that it would be well known to everyone what are their policies, and for which they'd be held accountable.

Hamilton returned to the investment issue later in response to a question from Conservative MP Jim Jones, who – concerned that the investment fund might become too big – inquired if it 'could be split in two, three or possibly four different entities, totally independent of one another,' either now or in the future, so that investment returns and management could be compared. Hamilton acknowledged that the CPPIB 'would be a large fund,' though only one of several 'other funds close to that size.' He said the government 'had paid close attention to these questions' and consulted investment and pension plan advisers and major funds like the Ontario Teachers' Pension Plan Board and the Caisse de dépôt et placement du Québec. 'We really sought their views, because they are large pension funds operating in the economy.' Their advice was reflected in the legislation, beginning with the CPPIB boards' limited mandate to invest only in the best interests of CPP members. 'We've tried to have rules and accountabilities in place to ensure that they deliver on that and that what they are doing and what their policies are is transparent in the reporting.' The board would also have to begin by investing passively in broadly based market indexes. 'The board won't be picking individual stocks over the first three-year period, at least ... That will be reviewed after three years.'

The Interest Groups Speak – Again

Over the next three weeks, the committee held eight more meetings and heard thirty-three witnesses – from business and organized labour, from think tanks on the right and left, from professional groups with expertise but no ideological agenda, from academics, and from a few individuals with varying concerns.

The Canadian Chamber of Commerce came to praise the arm's-length investment strategy, but opposed both the inclusion of disability benefits in the CPP and the contribution rate increase.[15] The Canadian Institute of Actuaries showed up to support Bill C-2, which it figured met almost all the concerns it had raised in its task force studies of the CPP.[16] The Council of Canadians with Disabilities came to protest that the cuts to disability pensions would be devastating 'to a great many disadvantaged and vulnerable individuals.' Legal counsel Harry Beatty cited projections in the chief actuary's *16th Report* showing that by 2005, CPP spending on disability pensions would be reduced by over $1 billion, but on retirement and other benefits by only $700 million. 'Since the disability program is only about one-fifth of the total CPP, this means that on a proportional basis it is being cut much more than any other component.'[17]

The Canadian Labour Congress sent Nancy Riche, its executive vice-president, who delivered a fiery critique of the legislation. 'Neither the contents of Bill C-2 nor the process that led to it are satisfactory,' she said.[18] The government had produced no analysis of the impact of the proposed changes on different groups of affected Canadians, only information that supported its preferred position. 'This is ... a thoroughly corrupt interpretation of its obligation [to provide information] that reflects utter disrespect for a serious debate of public policy.' The CLC's position could not have been clearer: 'The combination of unwarranted benefit cuts, a regressive change in the contributory earnings base, and an illegitimate process for developing proposed changes to the CPP means that Bill C-2 has to be opposed.'

The conservative think tanks – like the Fraser Institute, the C.D. Howe Institute, and the Atlantic Institute for Market Studies – said the CPP reform was a step in the right direction, but their fondness for Chilean-style mandatory individual RRSPs was undimmed. 'I expect that certainly within my working lifetime we will see a system of personal retirement accounts in this country,' said Bill Robson of the C.D.

Howe Institute. 'I expect that in fact debate is going to heat up the moment this legislation passes, if it passes.'[19]

Actuary Malcolm Hamilton of William M. Mercer Ltd., a leading figure in the whole CPP debate, thought a debate over mandatory RRSPs would be useful, but he was sceptical of the Chilean example. 'It's very hard to compare pension systems in different countries.' Chile's reform worked for Chile, he said, but might not work in Canada. 'They did it at a time when they had a lot of nationalized industries they could sell off. They did it in a very different economic and industrial environment than we have in this country. They had extraordinary returns on their capital markets. We've already had those. I'm not sure we can expect another 10 or 20 years of them. So I think it would be dangerous to assume that just because it worked well in Chile it would work well here.'[20]

The Pension Industry's Assessment

Consultant Keith Ambachtsheer, who had advised the federal–provincial negotiators on pension fund issues, told the MPs that governance was one of two key factors that would determine the success of the CPPIB. 'This is no longer just an opinion. A major study we have just completed involving 80 major U.S. and Canadian pension funds established a statistically significant link between organizational performance and organizational design. The most important organizational design driver turned out to be the quality of the board of governing fiduciaries.' But he also had an answer to the earlier questions about whether the CPP's pool of cash should be kept together or split into two or more funds for investment. The second determinant of fund success identified in his study was size: 'Larger funds produce higher risk-adjusted net returns than smaller funds. Thus pension fund management is an industry where "bigger is better."'[21] Robert Bertram, senior vice-president for investment at the Ontario Teachers' Pension Plan, one of the country's largest funds, endorsed the idea of a single board. 'By having multiple funds, you simply increase the chance of earning average returns at a higher cost of management than if you have a single fund – or a fund that's managed by a single entity, at least – at the least possible cost.'[22]

Don Walcot was there to speak for the Pension Investment Association of Canada (PIAC), which had created the first pension fund governance model in the world, one that had 'received widespread recognition and acceptance.'[23] In drafting Bill C-2, the government had consulted PIAC, whose 123 members represented 47 public pension funds and 76 corporate pension funds. Walcot set out PIAC's criteria for sound fund management. The fund should first 'understand the pension promise involved in the plan provisions.' Then, 'the stewards of the pension plan must recognize who the stakeholders in the plan are and what accountabilities and benefits are owed to each.' (He said this line twice because he thought it so important.) Next, the stewards should focus on four key governance features: 'one, board [of] trustee selection and organization; two, power sharing between the board of trustees and management; three, effective monitoring of management's performance; four, continual reassessment and modification of the overall governance process itself.'

Clear governance rules of this kind would 'create an organization that manages the total pension fund organization effectively,' Walcot said, but it should be strengthened with another element: 'A clearly written investment policy statement will assist in the prudent management of the investment of the assets.' Such a policy would include nine components:

a description of who the stakeholders are and general plan objectives; a measure of risk tolerance based on creditor volatility; identification of the approved asset classes in which to invest; asset mix ranges, for example 30 per cent to 50 per cent for equities, 20 per cent to 40 per cent for debt, and 0 per cent to 20 per cent for cash; performance objectives that are simple, investment-related, and quantifiable; reporting requirements – monthly, quarterly, etc. – and contents; structures and ways to take corrective actions; specific policies such as on securities lending or derivatives; and very importantly, a code of ethics.

Proper investment policies and process were now standard and had been used widely for about a decade, Walcot said. 'I believe with a clear governance model and a realistic investment policy statement, all types of pension funds can be successfully managed to the satisfaction of all stakeholders.' His assessment of Bill C-2: 'I would like to take this opportunity to commend the government for incorporating much of this philosophy into the CPP investment structure.' The finance ministers and their officials could ask for no stronger endorsement.

On one point, everyone from the investment and pension community was agreed. The provision that limited the foreign investments of all Canadian investors – including pension funds – to 20 per cent of their portfolios should be dropped; the CPPIB would be a good place to start.

All told, the transcripts of the Finance Committee hearings make for some fascinating reading – a crash course in the complexities of the CPP. During Martin's appearance, the session was dominated by partisan sparring; there was even a degree of edginess to the MPs' dealings with officials from the Finance Department. With the witnesses, however, the discussions were substantive, serious, and largely non-partisan. MPs sought support for their views, to be sure, but they treated their guests with far more respect than their political opponents.

One witness injected what might have been an unwelcome thought, but none of the MPs picked up on it. Garth Whyte, vice-president of the Canadian Federation of Independent Business (CFIB), opened his presentation by noting that the CFIB was more concerned those days with the threat of an imminent postal strike than with the CPP. 'We did not apply to appear before this committee because essentially we see [the CPP reform] as a done deal ... It's been signed off by the provinces and the federal government. There's little tinkering that can be done without going back there.'[24]

Back to the Commons

He was right. On 20 November, the committee took only two hours and twenty minutes to carry out its clause-by-clause examination of the bill. All opposition amendments were defeated and all government amendments – all of them technical in nature – were passed. Just before noon, the committee passed Bill C-2 and sent it back to the Commons. Debate on the report stage of the legislation, when amendments are considered, began the following week. Diane Ablonczy promised 'a very gripping debate,' and perhaps it was for a small group of observers. The first day of debate concentrated on the accountability provisions that would apply to the CPPIB and on the 20 per cent foreign property rule, a peculiar focus for MPs who usually worry more about the day-to-day financial issues that preoccupy their voters – like contribution rates and benefits. The second day meandered off into an extended discussion of regional economic conditions that was triggered by proposals to let the provinces keeps their preferred-rate borrowings, require the CPPIB to invest for economic development purposes, and reduce Employment Insurance premiums.

For the government, that was enough. Having failed to win an all-party agreement on a timetable for the debate, it once more imposed time allocation and once more heard, as Hansard recorded it, some honourable members cry, 'Shame.' That was a Friday; the next Monday, the bill was debated further and cleared the report stage by a vote of 171 to 75. The Conservatives, who had supported Bill C-2 in principle on second reading, joined the Reform and New Democratic Parties in opposition.

On Thursday, 4 December, the Commons wrapped up its debate on Bill C-2. Martin was not in the House, so his parliamentary secretary, Tony Valeri, presented the government's final pitch for the legislation. Most of the debate consisted of reiterating positions explained many times before. Progressive Conservative leader Jean Charest did, however, explain his party's change of position. He supported the bill on second reading to get it into committee, where 'we could have a real debate about the impact of this legislation. We did it assuming that the government would be listening ... We were wrong, very wrong. The government ... did not listen, it did not pay attention.' Charest said the premium increase could not be 'allowed to happen without offsetting ... tax reductions, in particular with reductions in other payroll taxes such as employment insurance premiums.'[25]

Chile's pension plan returned to the debate when Reform MP Ted White referred to a recent television program which interviewed Chileans, who 'said what a significant change it was and how good that had been for the pension plans of Chile. With that plan now almost 20 years old, the benefits to pensioners have been phenomenal.' Robert Nault, the parliamentary secretary to the human resources development minister, replied that he was quite aware of the Chilean experience. 'The Reform Party does not tell Canadians that on top of the 10 per cent contribution rate that Chileans pay, they must pay another 3 percentage points for administration fees and other benefits,' compared with one-tenth of one per cent under the CPP. 'Chile is the worst example [one] could use.' Reform MP Monte Solberg, who had sparred with Martin in the Finance Committee meetings, jumped in to point out that Chile at least offered people a choice. 'When they had a choice, 90 per cent got out of the corrupt public system and went into a private system because it provides better returns.'[26]

At 5:15 p.m., the debate ran out of its allotted time and MPs voted. The result: 167 in favour, 73 opposed, and 16 MPs who did not vote because they were paired with absent members. Just before 5:45, the

Commons speaker declared that the motion had carried; Bill C-2 was read for the third time and passed.

And On to the Senate

Fifteen minutes later, the bill was given first reading in the Senate; second reading debate began the following Monday, with Liberal Senator Michael Kirby speaking for the government on the bill. The heat was now on the Senate. The government wanted the bill passed by the end of the year and time was running out. The Senate is often called the house of sober second thought, but for Bill C-2, it sometimes looked more like the house of wounded pride and gratuitous personal insults. Always sensitive to slights based on their unelected status, senators regularly bristle if they think they are being pushed around, and this was a case in point. On the second day of debate, a miffed Progressive Conservative Senator David Tkachuk said Bill C-2 would have Canadians 'simply shovelling our hard-earned money into the greedy hands of Paul Martin.' He balked at the deadline. 'The minister says that he needs the bill now to satisfy an agreement with the provinces. I have heard of no agreement ... We have not heard one province asking us to abandon our parliamentary responsibilities and rush this bill through by January 1 on the threat that they will cancel their agreement ... Merry Christmas, Canada. Let us give Canadians a Christmas present by defeating this bill. Let us kill the bill.'[27]

Over the next few days, the senators kept talking about the bill, but added little of substance to what had already been said in the Commons. On 10 December, after only two days of talking about Bill C-2, the government gave notice that it would bring in a motion to limit debate just as it had done in the Commons. But that threat was dropped on 16 December, when Kirby announced that if the bill passed briskly, the Senate would get one more kick at the government's plans for the CPPIB. Paul Martin would not bring the bill's main clauses regarding the investment board into force until the Senate's Standing Committee on Banking, Trade and Commerce 'has had an opportunity to study them, and the regulations governing investment policy.'[28] Kirby was chairman of the committee, which was already engaged in a broader examination of pension fund issues, so it was well prepared to take on the task. But clearly, there was a deal here to speed passage of the bill. Within moments, the legislation passed second reading and was referred not to an ordinary Senate committee, but to Committee of the Whole. In effect, the whole Senate would, for a time, meet as a committee, which would allow them to conduct business a bit differently.

Martin Appears Once More

Mainly, it would let them hear – and question – Paul Martin, who appeared the next day. His presentation was familiar to anyone who had been following the issue; indeed, some of his lines were lifted straight from his statement to the Commons Finance Committee a few weeks earlier. But he added a stronger attack on proponents of compulsory RRSPs; the Reform Party had no senators, but some Progressive Conservative members of the upper house had spoken favourably about the idea.

'Ultimately, replacing the CPP with some sort of mandatory RRSP would hit [Canadians] with a triple whammy,' Martin said. 'They would be forced to honour the obligations to their grandparents, seniors currently earning pensions. They would have to honour the obligations to their parents, paying them the pensions they have been counting on for years and which they expect to receive when they retire. In addition, they would be expected to set up and contribute to their own RRSP accounts. Furthermore, if they wanted the same protection as the CPP provides, they would also have to pay for private disability and life insurance. The cost of all of this would be staggering.'[29]

The first thing Progressive Conservative John Lynch-Staunton, the opposition leader in the Senate, wanted from Martin was confirmation 'that the clauses dealing with the board will not be proclaimed until the Senate has had the opportunity to make recommendations following hearings.' He got it – assuming the Senate could move quickly enough – when Martin replied: 'I am prepared to confirm that those provisions of the legislation will not come into force until April 1.'[30]

One issue that had popped up occasionally, both in the Commons and Senate debates, was the question of size – should the CPP's pool of capital be kept in one fund or split among several? Senator Jerry Grafstein raised it again. 'The legislative history of banking and financial institutions in Canada was based on a simple thesis that economic power, financial power, should be divided, dispersed, competitive, and accountable ... [so that] no one source of economic power could predominate or challenge or dilute the power of Parliament or the power of the people or such institutions as the Bank of Canada ... What are your thoughts, having in mind the size and scope of the investment fund that this legislation proposes?'

Martin had obviously been thinking about this question, because his answer was more detailed and nuanced than in the past. He said he shared the concern over a fund's power, but 'there is less of a danger of [CPP] funds being used for political purposes ... [because] not only will the federal government be involved – in other words, one government – but 10 [provincial] governments and two territories, and, if you look at the political scene in Canada today, three political parties. That does provide a certain measure of protection.'

He and the provincial finance ministers had been very conscious of the size issue, he added, but there was a major advantage to having one big fund: 'The administrative costs of competing funds are quite large, and there is a major saving in having one fund.' Projections suggested that within a decade, the CPP fund would be about the same size as both the Ontario Teachers' Pension Plan and Quebec's Caisse de dépôt, and slightly larger than the Ontario Municipal Employees Retirement System. 'In other words, it will be one of the five largest funds in the country, but it will not be the dominant giant at that point. That having been said, the federal government and the provinces will have triennial reviews. The dangers which you raised are very real. If they, in fact, come to pass or are anticipated, then it will be within the powers of the various governments to split the fund into competing funds.'

Law of the Land

The Senate wrapped up its work, moving the bill back out of Committee of the Whole to the Senate sitting in its normal mode. The next day, the senators talked about how the banking committee would handle the chore it had just been assigned and then gave the legislation its third and final reading. The whole process took less than twenty minutes.

The government's year-end deadline had been met. It was Thursday, 18 December 1997, and Parliament was about to take its Christmas break. Indeed, the House of Commons had ended its fall session a week earlier, but resumed briefly for the day's formalities. Shortly after 5 p.m., MPs were invited to the Senate chamber, where Governor General Roméo LeBlanc gave royal assent to Bill C-2. It was the last piece of parliamentary business done in 1997. The legislation was now law.

17 Launching the CPP Investment Board

Federal and provincial officials had been far from idle through 1997 while Parliament worked on the legislation. They had to set up the new Canada Pension Plan Investment Board and write the regulations that would govern it. The first task was to find a board of twelve people to organize and oversee the new fund. Since they had written into their agreement a cumbersome process of board selection, that took some time.

On 23 October, Martin announced the make-up of the nominating committee that would seek out directors for the CPPIB. Heading the committee was Michael Phelps, chairman and chief executive officer of Vancouver-based Westcoast Energy Inc. Phelps knew his way around business and government alike, having been a top ministerial aide in Ottawa in the early 1980s, when he was executive assistant to then–energy minister Marc Lalonde. The nine provinces that would be the CPPIB's joint stewards along with Ottawa[1] got one member each. Alberta, like the federal government, found a businessman for the job – Brian MacNeill, president and chief executive officer of IPL Energy Inc. (now Enbridge Inc.), a leading Calgary-based pipeline company. New-foundland named a former finance minister, Winston Baker, to the committee, and the other seven assigned senior public servants – usually from their finance departments – to the task.

Not everyone was pleased with the choices. When Martin appeared before the Senate in December, Progressive Conservative Senator Gerry St Germain of British Columbia asked Martin to defend the Phelps appointment. Though he described Phelps as 'a very competent, experienced and capable British Columbian [with] ... a proven track record in both the public and the private sectors,' he noted that Phelps 'has had longstanding and strong ties to the Liberal Party.' Since perception is important in political matters, 'appointments such as this are perceived as pure patronage appointments.' Martin replied that it was difficult for him to see a patronage issue here. 'Mr. Phelps is simply the chair of a federal–provincial committee. The provincial governments, the majority of which ... are not Liberal, named their representatives. Those representatives, in turn a non-partisan group, will name 20 people. From those 20 people, the federal Minister of Finance, in consultation with the provinces, will choose 12.'[2]

Alberta was not thrilled with the composition of the nominating committee. 'I don't think we felt the spirit of the deal was adhered to. We thought the deal was that the provinces would put a credible person on the nominating committee,' one Alberta official said.[3] Ottawa and Alberta followed that model with their appointments, but the others did not. 'Instead, most provinces named a former minister or deputy minister.' It left a sour taste and a concern that other provinces might not be fully committed to naming solid investment professionals to the CPPIB board. 'I felt we had been suckered again; we were the poor country bumpkins. You only need one minister who wants to put in a party hack to undermine this.'

Senators at Work

The Senate Banking Committee had its own assignment – a study of all the issues raised by the creation of the CPPIB. Between mid-February and mid-March of 1998, it held seven meetings in five cities and heard from twenty-eight people, a mix of familiar faces from the pension and investment industries, organized labour, and think tanks plus a few independent academics. The first session was held in Toronto, in the heart of the financial district, but the first witnesses were Finance Department officials who were there to explain the government's plans for the board and to answer questions.[4]

An early question, for example, involved protection for the CPPIB's independence from government, one of the more sensitive issues. Bob Hamilton, the department's assistant deputy minister for financial sector policy, said the board would be protected by 'the clear statement of the object in the legislation.' The CPPIB 'is responsible to invest in the best interests of the plan ... if it decides to invest in something that is not in the best interests of the plan, because the Department of Finance or some government thinks that that is the right [thing] to do for a particular reason, then it is not carrying out its fiduciary duty.'

Finance had released draft regulations the previous week, so the officials were in a better position than earlier to clarify the rules they were considering. Bob Hamilton[5] said the key elements in the regulations were taken from provisions in the Pension Benefits Standard Act, provisions that applied to all pension funds and adapted to the CPPIB. Usually, the rules were the same, but in some cases, 'it means tweaking those rules slightly, to recognize the special circumstances.' Like all pension funds, the CPPIB would be subject to the rule that no fund could invest more than 10 per cent of its assets in one investment vehicle and no fund could own more than 30 per cent of the common shares of a company. Unlike other pension funds, however, the regulations would prevent the CPPIB from using financial derivatives to get around the 20 per cent ceiling on foreign investments.

Reality Intrudes

Bob Hamilton also noted that as with the CPP legislation, the regulations needed the support of two-thirds of the participating provinces with two-thirds of the population before they came into effect.[6] 'Therefore, as we move toward finalizing the regulations, we are required to talk to the provinces and make sure that we have sufficient support.' Progressive Conservative Sen. David Angus, a Montreal lawyer, picked up on that point. What would Finance do with a change recommended by the committee? 'Can you give us some assurance on the record that this exercise is not futile and a waste of money?' Bob Hamilton was diplomatic, but firm. Any recommendations by the senators would be valuable, 'but, ultimately, any change must be approved not only by ourselves but also by two-thirds of the participating provinces ... So that part is clear.' Angus pursued the issue: What would Finance do if the committee issued a unanimous report that was adopted by the full Senate? 'I am not sure how much assurance I can give you,' Bob Hamilton replied.

Soothing words, to be sure, but the reality was that the entire Senate initiative was largely irrelevant. 'The provinces have no respect for the Senate – none, zip,' another federal official of the day said in an interview. 'We couldn't go back to the provinces with objections from the Senate.'

Active or Passive?

The committee then turned to its expert witnesses, many of whom had already appeared before the Commons Finance Committee or spoken elsewhere on CPP issues. Malcolm Hamilton and Keith Ambachtsheer, both with long experience in advising pension funds, sparred over the issue of active versus passive investment. The draft regulations – based on the February 1997 agreement – would require the CPPIB, when buying publicly traded Canadian stocks, to replicate broad market indexes. This passive domestic equity strategy would remain in place for at least the first three years, at which point it would be reviewed.

Malcolm Hamilton triggered the debate when he suggested that if the CPPIB earned average market returns, that would be good enough and probably the best that could be expected. Because the CPP would never be more than 20 per cent funded and because the ups and downs could be amortized over such a long period, big gains or big losses would have very little effect on the CPP's financial health. 'I have a concern that this is dismally understood by the Canadian public. I have a concern that people will think that if you appoint the right panel of wizards, and if they go out and invest as effectively as Warren Buffet, all this nation's pension problems are behind it. And that is just not the case. This is not a big enough fund to create that kind of potential.' What's needed, he said, is simply a fund run by 'a competent group getting market returns.'

Ambachtsheer disagreed. There is a right balance between passive index-based investing of the kind Malcolm Hamilton proposed and active investing that could wring extra returns out of the market; the CPP Investment Board could find that right balance by giving the best professionals incentives to find it. 'Why would we want to take away from the CPP Investment Board that opportunity to create an excellent investment organization?' A good investment organization 'can produce about 50 basis points a year of risk-adjusted net value added.' On a fund of $100 billion, that would represent $500 million a year. 'Why [would] we want to leave $500 million a year on the table if we have an opportunity to create an organization to take that off the table?' Malcolm Hamilton replied: 'I just do not think it is in the cards that you are going to beat the markets by 50 basis points ... In the long-run, beating the markets is not as easy as people think. There is a reason why those guys who really do it make a lot of money, and the reason is that it is awful hard to do ... So I am comfortable with passive.'

Advice on the Board

The committee next listened to the chief executive officers of two of the country's biggest pension plans. Claude Lamoureux of the Ontario Teachers' Pension Plan Board had some straightforward advice for the senators: 'Firstly, create a strong board with qualified members and give them a clear mandate. Secondly, give the new investment fund freedom to operate; let them make mistakes. Thirdly, hire top quality people, and pay them market rates. Lastly, do not ignore your liabilities, but rather, think of matching your assets and liabilities.'

Lamoureux had some comforting words for senators who worried that directors of the CPPIB might be named solely from motives of political patronage and thus constitute a weak board too ready to take directives from politicians. His own board is appointed partly by the Ontario government and partly by the teachers' unions. 'If you came to listen to one of our board meetings you would not know who is represented by whom ... Everyone on our board knows that he or she is there to act in the best interests of the teachers of the province, and their beneficiaries. We have never had an issue that was decided with one side opposing the other.' Dale Richmond of the Ontario Municipal Employees Retirement Board recounted the same experience with his own board – half appointed by employers and half by the employees' unions. 'If you were a fly on the wall, you could not determine which side is represented by whom. Further, there have never been any close votes, which is quite remarkable.'

From there, the committee moved on to hearings in Calgary, Vancouver, Halifax, and Ottawa. In Calgary, the senators heard a plea that the CPP's capital pool be broken into several funds. Philip Heimbecker, a former chair of the Alberta branch of the Investment Dealers Association of Canada, advocated 'multiple funds, managed by experienced regional investment managers who are accountable to the pension board.' This would ensure that the fund 'would be more attuned to regional opportunities,' which would be less likely under 'a highly centralized investment structure.'[7] Michael Walker, executive director of the Fraser Institute, wanted multiple funds for a different reason. He appeared in Vancouver to propose the creation of '10 funds, one for each province.' At some point, individual CPP members would be allowed 'to choose which of those funds would hold their deposits.' He had 'an ulterior motive' for this proposal: 'it provides the first step toward the eventual privatization of the Canada Pension Plan,' something he had consistently advocated.[8]

Another witness at the Vancouver hearing was Michael Brown, president of Ventures West and a self-described 'pitch man for venture capital.' He wanted to 'to ensure that, when this fund is set up, provision is made for this type of investment compared to simply investing in the TSE index, or whatever is presently contemplated.'[9]

Selecting the Board

The committee stumbled on some new insights into the appointment of the CPPIB's first board of directors when it met in Halifax with Peter Van Loon, director of investments in the Nova Scotia department of finance. Van Loon was one of the ten members of Michael Phelps's nominating committee that had been working for the previous five months on finding the first twelve directors for the CPPIB. Helpfully, he told the senators what instructions the federal Finance Department had given them on the qualifications they should seek. 'First, they stressed the need for a competent, professional and independent board, with a core group of qualified investment professionals. Second, since this will be the first CPP Investment Board, public confidence in CPP policy will be significantly influenced by the credibility of the board members. This suggests the need for at least a certain number of directors who possess a significant degree of prominence and public respect among Canadians. Third, and lastly, they stressed the need for regional representation on the board.'[10]

The committee, Van Loon assured the senators, had followed those guidelines closely. It hired a management consulting firm to help draw up a list, and each member was asked to produce names from their own province. Nova Scotia wound up nominating two men with 'extremely good investment backgrounds ... [who] had actually applied to serve on the board.' At its first meeting in Vancouver in November, only a month after the committee was struck and a month before the legislation had cleared Parliament, the group began with a list of 160 candidates and pared that down to 35 in half a day. It then asked for further 'biographies of the 35 people left on the list and, at the second meeting [in Winnipeg during December], we were able to pare the list down to 20.' That list, already submitted to Paul Martin, 'contains many prominent Canadians and very qualified investment professionals.' (Van Loon's evidence was interesting for what it said about the timeline: Martin and the provincial ministers had the nominating committee's recommendations in hand by mid-March 1998, yet it would be another seven months before they announced the names of those on the CPPIB's first board.)

When Senator Catherine Callbeck asked Van Loon if there were any women on the list, Van Loon said it included 'a number of ladies who have distinguished service, having served on other pension boards.' There had been some bumps along the road, he revealed, centring on the conflict of interest question. At the first meeting, he said, Phelps 'broadened the rules about the potential conflict of interest so widely that there was no investment professional on the list.' That was soon sorted out: 'It says right in the legislation that there could be potential conflicts of interest with some of the board members, and it states that they are to withdraw themselves from those processes and not vote on those processes.' Conflicts, he added, were likely to arise: 'There will undoubtedly be one or two situations that will affect certain members.'[11]

The Senators Report ...

In the end, the senators issued a report with nineteen recommendations. It urged the government to take the time to do a proper job of launching the CPPIB. William Robson of the C.D. Howe Institute had told the committee at one hearing that 'the conduct of the CPP Investment Board will be a key determinant of public confidence in the plan,' and the senators agreed. 'The Committee has stressed that public confidence must be restored, and views the establishment, operations, and policies of the Canada Pension Plan Investment Board as key to achieving this goal. The appointment of Canada Pension Plan Investment Board directors, establishing transparency and accountability, and selecting the proper investment strategy, among other issues, are critically important as we try to "get it right."'[12]

... and the Government Replies

The government's response to the committee's report can easily be read as a polite brush-off. A draft of its short reply noted that 'stewardship of the CPP is the joint responsibility of the federal government and the provinces,' so a response to the committee had been delayed while federal finance officials consulted their provincial counterparts.[13] 'The federal government considered such consultation to be highly important.' The government acceded easily to recommendations on minor points to which no reasonable person could object. It agreed, for example, to a recommendation to make public the results of any special audits and special examinations; these would be included in the CPPIB's annual report, which was already required to be tabled in Parliament.

The response noted that there was plenty of common ground between the Senate committee and the government. The committee wanted to ensure full transparency in both appointments to the CPPIB and in the board's own operations. 'The government agrees fully that the governance and accountability provisions applicable to the Investment Board should be at the cutting edge of pension industry practice, and pension experts, including those appearing before your Committee, have confirmed that this is the case. As the Committee recommends, all aspects of investment and governance policy will be open to scrutiny during the triennial reviews.' It confirmed that 'the nominating committee [for CPPIB directors] will be a standing committee and all director appointments will be made from its list.' To the committee's desire for CPPIB directors with expertise and a broad range of other skills, the government replied with an almost weary 'this is and will continue to be the case.' To reinforce the point, it said 'the criteria used by the nominating committee will be released at the time of announcing the names of the first board of directors.'

There were other suggestions that would be left until the first triennial review of the CPP, three years hence. The committee's suggestion for fifteen directors, rather than twelve, evoked some enthusiasm from the federal government ('merits serious consideration'), but that would require a change in the legislation and there was not yet enough provincial support for such a move. The committee's recommendation that the CPPIB switch to more active investing after only two years instead of three 'was already slated for the first review' (i.e., after three years). Ministers would also have plenty of chances to consider whether to split the CPP fund into multiple funds, another item the senators suggested was worth further study.

Other recommendations would be left for the CPPIB itself to implement, if it chose. But the government noted that the legislation already pointed in some of the directions highlighted by the senators. The senators wanted the board to develop performance standards and report on how it measured up to them. The legislation already required the board to report publicly on its objectives and 'on the extent to which it has met its objectives.' The board was already required not only to meet the legislation's 'own stringent conflict provisions,' but enhance them: 'the Board must establish and publish procedures to identify and resolve conflicts, and establish a committee to monitor the application of these procedures.'

Finally, there were recommendations the government did not accept. The senators wanted the federal finance minister to appoint the CPPIB's auditor. That, replied the government, 'would be inconsistent with both the independence of the Board and the joint federal–provincial stewardship of the CPP, as well as with the practice of other major independent pension funds.' The senators wanted future regulations governing the CPPIB to be vetted by Parliament before going into effect. The government said there was no reason to go 'beyond the procedures that already exist for public and parliamentary scrutiny of regulations.'

Dussault Is Dumped

Following the Senate report at the end of March 1998, there was a long spell in which the federal and provincial governments were quietly trying to reach agreement on which directors to appoint. In public, the CPP disappeared from the media until September, when Canadians learned that the federal government had fired Bernard Dussault a month earlier. What followed was a captivating, though short-lived, drama. Dussault was in the midst of preparing the *17th Actuarial Report* on the CPP, which would have been the first full review since the reform had gone through. It would use actual data to the end of 1997 and fully updated assumptions as the basis of its new projections. Immediately, there was intense speculation that the report would reveal that the 9.9 per cent contribution rate was too low, which would mean a further rate increase or further benefit cuts. Indeed, Dussault said in an interview that while his work was not complete, he was heading towards a conclusion that the real steady-state rate should be 10.1 per cent.[14]

The chief actuary's office is part of the Office of the Superintendent of Financial Institutions (OSFI), which said Dussault's departure was the result of 'management differences' between Dussault and his boss, Superintendent John Palmer: 'It has nothing to do with the report ... This is not a political decision.'[15] As the controversy swirled, OSFI underlined that point: 'These differences have been over issues of management style, and do not in any way touch on the professional work of Mr. Dussault or his staff on any actuarial projections or opinions, including the upcoming report on the Canada Pension Plan.'[16]

Palmer later called a press conference to insist that 'there was no political interference in my decision to ask him to leave.' Dussault was an excellent actuary, he said, but one with problems as a manager: 'Everything was a battle.' On the same day, Dussault said Palmer had asked him twice 'to change a figure [in his report] because it would embarrass the minister of finance.'[17] Palmer demanded an apology and told his lawyers to sue Dussault for defamation. Martin, forced to answer a barrage of questions in the Commons, said he learned of the firing only after it happened. The matter dragged on for three years and was finally settled out of court. All parties agreed not to discuss the terms, but one item could not be kept secret. A payment to Dussault of $364,387 as 'compensation for wrongful dismissal' was duly recorded in the Public Accounts of Canada for 2001–2.[18]

To complete Dussault's unfinished report, the government brought in Toronto actuary Michael Hafeman, who figured the CPP could actually be sound with a long-term contribution rate of 9.8 per cent. Hafeman said there had been 'absolutely no interference' in his work and 'never any pressure to change any assumption,' but Reform Party MP Diane Ablonczy called for an assessment from the federal auditor general.[19] Instead, the government appointed a panel of three outside actuaries to review the *17th Report*.[20] Their conclusion, released in 1999, was that the 9.8 per cent rate was just fine. They thought Hafeman had been too optimistic in his assumptions about immigration, but that was cancelled out by two of his economic assumptions, which they thought too conservative.[21]

One item in the *17th Report* is worth noting: the assumption regarding disability. The *15th Report* that triggered the whole CPP review had assumed that there would be 5.5 disability cases per 1,000 eligible workers. That rate contributed significantly to Dussault's projections of trouble ahead for the CPP, and some argued at the time that it was too high (see chapter 7). In his *16th Report*, released along with the CPP legislation in September 1997, Dussault scaled that assumption back to 5 cases per 1,000 and suggested it might go down to 4 per 1,000 in the next full report. The *17th Report*, under Hafeman, assumed a rate of 3.5,[22] and subsequent actuarial reports pulled that down to 3.25.

In the summer of 1999, the government hired a new chief actuary for the CPP, Jean-Claude Ménard, who had been with the Quebec Pension Plan for eighteen years, the last four as chief actuary.

Publication of the *17th Report* effectively sealed the debate on whether the reforms had worked. The *16th Report* had been – to a considerable extent – an extension of the *15th Report* that had launched the reform process. The *17th* was entirely new, and its projections for the key numbers illustrate the impact of the reforms on the outlook for the CPP. The cost of the program, rather than rising to 14.2 per cent of contributory earnings in 2030, was now expected to go no higher than 11.2 per cent. The CPP fund, rather than falling to zero in 2015, would now hit a low of just under two years' worth of benefits in 1999 before rising to about five years of benefits by 2020 and six years in the late twenty-first century. Contributions would exceed expenditures until 2020, generating a positive cash flow of money that could be added to the CPP fund, which by then would reach $371 billion. After 2020, the cash flow would turn negative, but by then investment earnings on the fund would be substantial enough that a portion of them could be used to pay for CPP benefits.[23] The projected returns to all generations of CPP members were also higher than shown in previous reports. Dussault had estimated in his *16th Report* that the cohort born in 2012 would receive a real return on their contributions of 1.5 per cent annually under the previous version of the CPP and 1.8 per cent under the amended plan.[24] Hafeman's *17th Report*, which included estimates only for those born in years ending with a zero, put the return at 2.0 per cent for anyone born in 2010.[25]

Finding Board Members

While the Dussault dispute was underway, Martin and the provincial ministers were near the end of their dickering over which directors to choose for the new CPP Investment Board. Since the senators on the banking committee knew that the CPPIB nominating committee had completed its work long ago, some got impatient. In early June, two asked when the government was going to actually appoint directors to the CPPIB, but they did not get a response until late September, when the government offered a bland reply. The act required the federal finance minister to 'consult with his provincial counterparts prior to naming the directors. This consultation process, though well underway, is not yet complete.'[26]

Most provinces would have pushed hard for one of their own to sit on the first board. There would have been no such parochial flak from Alberta. Jim Dinning had been adamant about getting a board made up of people who knew their way around investments. 'Our position was that we want the best and if they're all from Ontario, that's okay,' one Alberta official recalled. 'We did not want this two-per-province routine. We said a lot of the investment expertise is in Ontario.' Another of his colleagues from that period went further: 'Dinning said that if the best board is six women from Bay Street, so be it.' Asked about that line

Figure 17.1 CPP costs (PAYGO): Before and after the reform, as a per cent of contributory earnings

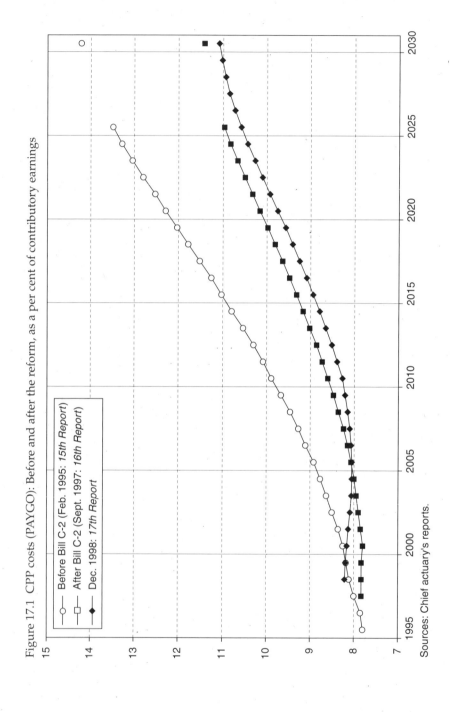

Before Bill C-2 (Feb. 1995: *15th Report*)
After Bill C-2 (Sept. 1997: *16th Report*)
Dec. 1998: *17th Report*

Sources: Chief actuary's reports.

Figure 17.2 Fund/expenditure ratio, expressed in years' worth of benefits

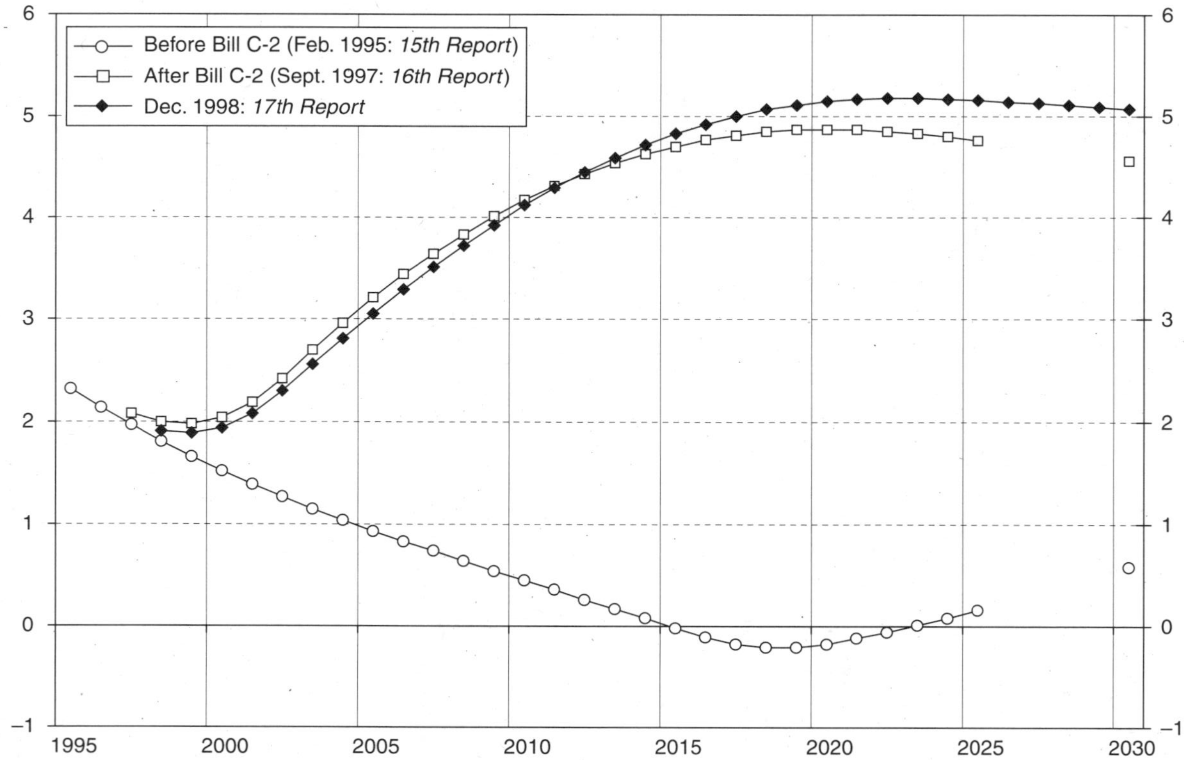

Legend:
—○— Before Bill C-2 (Feb. 1995: *15th Report*)
—□— After Bill C-2 (Sept. 1997: *16th Report*)
—◆— Dec. 1998: *17th Report*

Sources: Chief actuary's reports.

in an interview, Dinning was puzzled: 'I don't think I would have said that.'[27] Perhaps he didn't, but it would not have been out of character. He had something of a reputation among his officials for corny 'Yogi Berra-isms,' and it was exactly the kind of thing he might have said to underline his insistence that when it came to naming directors for the CPPIB, expertise mattered most.

Paul Martin's recollection – which he acknowledges is sketchy – is that it took some time to sort out how many directors would be named from which provinces.[28] Ontario, with half of the population of the CPP's participating provinces, wanted six of the dozen directors; Martin drew the line at five, but mollified Ontario by choosing a chair for the board from Ontario.

That left seven to be divided among nine provinces – nine because Martin wanted one director from Quebec to reflect the portability of the CPP and QPP; some workers would move into and out of Quebec during their careers. Also, Quebec represented almost one-quarter of the Canadian economy, so the federal government thought it would be helpful to have one director who had some direct knowledge of the province. The eight remaining CPP provinces would get six. The real fight among ministers over directorships, Martin said, arose because not every province would get a seat. In the end, because two seats went to British Columbians, three provinces were left off the first board – Saskatchewan, Newfoundland, and Prince Edward Island.

On 29 October 1998, Martin finally announced the board. It would be chaired by Gail Cook-Bennett of Toronto, a management consultant with a PhD in economics whose long résumé included stints as an academic, think-tank executive, and corporate board member. She was then a member of six boards and had previously served on the boards of the Bank of Canada, Toronto-Dominion Bank, and – most relevant for this job – of the Ontario Teachers' Pension Plan Board, so she knew her way around pension plans.

There were four other directors from Ontario. Susan Carnell had retired two years earlier as vice-president, director, and chief economist at the brokerage firm Richardson Greenshields of Canada. Helen Meyer was president of her own firm, Meyer Corporate Valuations Limited, and had held senior positions at Merrill Lynch Canada, Morgan Bank of Canada, and Dominion Securities Limited. Joseph Regan had been chair of the Pension Commission of Ontario from 1990 until 1994 after retiring from the Royal Bank of Canada, where he had ended a forty-year career as senior executive vice-president for strategic initiatives. He was also a member of the Ontario Pension Board. Richard Thomson had just retired after eighteen years as chairman and chief executive officer of the Toronto-Dominion Bank, where he had worked since 1957.

Four directors came from the West. Mary Arnold (later Mary Ritchie) of Edmonton was a management consultant and chartered accountant who was a director of several corporations as well as of social, artistic, and charitable organizations. Jacob (Jack) Levi of Vancouver was an actuarial consultant who specialized in pensions and workers' compensation. For many years, he had been the external actuary for four major public sector pension plans in British Columbia and the BC Workers' Compensation Board. Dale Parker, also of Vancouver, was a corporate director and consultant but had a long history in business, especially in the financial sector, where he had been chairman and CEO of the British Columbia Financial Institutions Commission, president and CEO of the Bank of British Columbia, and executive vice-president of the Bank of Montreal. He was also on the boards of several companies and active in charitable organizations. David Walker was the only director with a history of active politics. After all his work on the CPP from 1995 through 1997, he had been defeated in the 1997 election and was back in Winnipeg running his own consulting firm. Martin said recently that his good relations with Manitoba's Progressive Conservative government, especially Finance Minister Eric Stefanson, made that appointment possible.

The Atlantic provinces had two spots on the new board. Gerard La Forest of Fredericton had been a leading legal scholar before his appointment to the New Brunswick Court of Appeal in 1981 and then to the Supreme Court of Canada, from which he had recently retired. Richard McAloney of Halifax, a chartered accountant and financial analyst, was chief executive officer of the Nova Scotia Association of Health Organizations Pension Plan. Before that, he had been executive director of investments, pensions, and treasury services with the Nova Scotia finance department. He had also been a member of the Pension Investment Association of Canada's pension plan governance committee.

Finally, there was one member from Quebec – Pierre Michaud of Montreal, chairman of Réno-Dépôt Inc. and Provigo Inc. and a member of several corporate boards.

'I am very proud of the well-balanced and highly qualified board we have put together,' Martin said in his news release. Funds would begin flowing to the board in early 1999, giving the directors time to set up the board's operations, he added.

The opposition parties in Parliament barely registered the announcement. It took several days before Progressive Conservative MP Scott Brison objected in the Commons that five of the twelve directors had made 'substantial contributions to the Liberal party either personally or through their own companies' and asked: 'Is this another example of Liberal political interference in the Canada pension plan?' Jim Peterson, answering for Paul Martin, said no director was appointed 'unless they had provincial approval. If the member has a difficulty, maybe he should take it up with the provinces.'[29] The next day, when Martin was in the House, Brison repeated his question. Martin called the charge of interference 'absolute nonsense.' The appointments were made jointly and 'the vast majority of these people were recommended by the provinces ... All of these people have outstanding qualities. It does no good to the Canada Pension Plan or to Canadians for the honourable member to demean some very high quality Canadians.'[30]

About two weeks after being named, the board gathered in Ottawa for its first meeting. Paul Martin showed up at a reception the evening before the meeting – he drank Scotch, one attendee recalls – and the next day, Finance official Bill Mitchell made a presentation to the new directors covering the reform process, the board's mandate, and a variety of other issues facing the group.[31] The board met every month after that until spring – cadging space from its legal firm or, if the meeting were held on a Sunday, at the Royal York Hotel in Toronto. As Cook-Bennett put it almost ten years later, the twelve directors had 'no offices, no staff ... and no small mandate.' Her own responsibilities included 'scouting out office space for an organization that didn't yet exist and whose size we couldn't predict,' she told a conference marking the reform's first decade. 'I'm making light of this but the fact is we knew the size of the task at hand and were well aware that we were operating in a goldfish bowl.'[32]

The directors knew from the first meeting that they might get cash flow from CPP contributions as early as February 1999 and recognized the risks at hand. Some people were sceptical at the very existence of the CPPIB, and all contributors were facing the pain of a steep increase in contribution rates. The board quickly had to come up with an investment strategy and a plan to manage the funds. 'And what would happen if the portfolio declined in value during the first few years of our management? ... A misstep by us or a market correction now could be fatal. Surely there would be a public (or political) outcry to change our mandate and undo this experiment before more money was lost. In this respect – and in our view at the time – there was every bit as much riding on the first 100 dollars we invested as there would be on the 100 billionth dollar.'[33]

By February, they had hired external fund managers to help manage the investments, and in March 1999, the first transfer of funds for investment arrived – a cheque for $12.1 million. Relative to the almost $123 billion fund now[34] managed by the CPPIB, it was a tiny sum – one dollar for every $10,000 in early 2008 – but it was a start.

18 Lessons Learned

Many of the key players in this chapter of Canada's public policy history have reflected on the reform of the Canada Pension Plan and almost all have fond memories of – and no little pride in – the outcome, if not the hard work and tough negotiating that went into getting there. In a recent discussion of the CPP reforms, Paul Martin said, 'you are really glossing over how tough these negotiations really were.'[1] One of his former officials had made much the same point in an earlier conversation.

The pride of the CPP reformers is evident, especially a decade on, when the latest actuarial report has verified that the CPP remains sustainable at the 9.9 per cent contribution rate.[2] The reformers were part of a major policy overhaul that worked. They began with an extraordinarily popular national program that, while not in crisis, was deeply troubled and needed fixing. Its problems were financial and political, but so intertwined that they could not be separated. The simple arithmetic said the CPP could be kept going indefinitely – could be 'sustainable,' in the jargon of the debate – with higher contribution rates and no benefit cuts. That was the chief actuary's default projection made on the basis of a formula agreed to in 1985. But the politicians were horrified by the prospect of asking future Canadians to pay contribution rates of 14 per cent of their earnings for a package of benefits that were worth only 6 or 7 per cent.

The arithmetic might work in an abstract world, but the politics would not. The CPP had begun with an act of intergenerational generosity – a cohort that suffered depression and war got substantial benefits that it did not pay for. Subsequent cohorts, including the baby boomers, had footed the bill easily because there were plenty of them and few seniors. But they were not saving enough to pay for their own future benefits. Unchecked, the CPP would force their children to pay those bills. But they had produced so few children that the burden would be much heavier for the next generation. They were about to inflict an intergenerational penalty on their kids, who in that future era of only two workers for every senior would each have to pay half the pension of one senior while saving for their own retirement. 'Sustainability is essentially political,' actuary Malcolm Hamilton observed. 'It was technically possible to keep raising contribution rates to keep paying the bills, but if the rates can't be sustainable politically, you can't sustain [the CPP].'[3] Indeed, he found it almost immoral that some people – those on the left – argued that while current workers could not afford to pay a contribution rate much higher than 6 per cent or so, future workers would contentedly pay 14 per cent. Hamilton was perhaps better at the politics of the future than the present. He consistently argued that benefits should be reduced for existing seniors so that all generations would share the burden of the CPP's earlier intergenerational errors, but no politician would embrace that.

Still, Hamilton's view was shared by many policymakers. One Quebec pension official from those days recalls arguing the need for a long-term consensus on pension issues at a time when the premier, Robert Bourassa, was not known for long-term thinking. 'My point at the time was that if we think the C/QPP is important, we should look for a sustainable rate. If we are not willing to suffer, why should we ask people in the future to suffer? There is no right time to do it.'[4]

It is human nature for many to claim credit for a policy success and for those involved to recall their own contributions with special clarity. But many of those involved credit Alberta, and especially Treasurer Jim Dinning, with a crucial role in the talks. The very fact that Alberta pushed hard for benefit reductions from the beginning doubtless influenced the outcome. Ontario came to that position more slowly, after it became clear that the long-term contribution rate could be held to under 10 per cent only if benefits were reduced.

One federal official figures Alberta's tough position, far from making a deal more difficult, was actually a key driver of the deal. 'We had Alberta on one side and the NDP governments on the other, with Ontario pushing hard for reform but a bit more in the middle. There was a very useful dynamic here. Alberta wanted more benefit cuts, while the Atlantic provinces were not so much in favour, so all had to make concessions and give ground. We had the more aggressive and the less aggressive. The softer provinces could not get Alberta on side and vice versa. It all left plenty of room for compromise.' Other provinces knew that Dinning was 'in a difficult position, probably the most difficult of all the provinces,' because some people in Alberta were willing to blow up the CPP altogether. 'Dinning really played a key role here. It was not easy in that province and he had to convince his colleagues. His position helped with the other provinces. He helped to balance those on the left and those in the Atlantic provinces who were nervous about cuts to benefits.' In effect, they had to swallow cuts they did not really like to accommodate the political realities of Alberta.

The Alberta perspective differs. One official there recalls that the possibility of a separate Alberta Pension Plan did not gain any real steam until after the deal was done and after Dinning had left politics. He figures his minister broke the logjam by consistently saying 'let's do what's right.' Dinning and Martin built a friendship around the idea of 'don't do the same old stuff,' he recalled. Still, everyone on the federal team gives major credit to Dinning for the outcome, Martin in particular: 'My great ally at the table was Jim Dinning.' Ernie Eves and Andrew Petter were the toughest to deal with – for very different reasons – but the general attitude, Martin says, was, 'Let's fix this thing; there was great good will at the table.'[5] Despite Eves's stubbornness over EI premiums, he adds, the Ontario minister was very good to work with in selling the final package, especially when some critics suggested separate provincial plans.

In a 2007 speech, Martin singled out three provincial ministers for their roles – Eves, MacKinnon, and Dinning. 'Ernie Eves could have killed the reform, because Ontario had an effective veto, but when the time came to get the deal done, he got it through Queen's Park. Janice MacKinnon was constrained by her party's views on a wide range of social issues and indeed Saskatchewan did not support the final arrangement. Nonetheless, she was a constructive force for positive change throughout the negotiation and I always had the feeling that if at the end we had needed her province's vote she would have gotten it. Finally Alberta. Let me simply say that in every federal–provincial negotiation I've been in, there are one or two provincial leaders who step forward and while fighting hard for their province's perspective, they speak as well for the national interest. Alberta did well for having Jim Dinning at the table, but so did Canada.'[6]

Today, Martin is extremely proud of what was done in the mid-1990s. Some of his officials through the late 1990s and early 2000s, however, recall that he was slow to take credit for the reforms, or even to list the CPP as among his major accomplishments. Martin does not recall things quite that way, but says he had seen too many economic forecasts and budget projections go awry to stake too much on the first couple of reports from the chief actuary on the reformed CPP. 'I wasn't going to declare victory until I was sure.'[7]

Federal officials, not surprisingly, give much of the credit to their own minister. Once seized of the issue, Martin pushed it hard, even when it meant supporting a significant increase in CPP rates just before an election. One of Martin's great strengths as finance minister was his ability to sell tough financial medicine to the Canadian public. He did it with his seminal deficit-cutting budgets and he did it with the CPP, battling with equal fervour against the Reform Party's simplistic and costly Chilean-style proposals and the NDP's continued advocacy of a status quo solution for the CPP. In both cases, his message was much the same: we have a problem and we need to fix it with reduced spending and higher taxes, but our solution will get us out of this hole we have dug for ourselves. There was a pithier way to put it – short-term pain for long-term gain – but that line had been used by the Progressive Conservatives during their abbreviated spell in government in 1979, a taste of power cut short by the Liberals who had mocked the notion.

The officials who had worked the CPP vineyard for years were also ready for a major overhaul, perhaps more than the politicians, many of whom were new to the file. They had slogged through two sets of talks and produced two agreements, in 1985 and 1991, that fertilized the sickly vines with rate increases, but failed to prune the plants with benefit cuts. Now, in 1995, they were facing an even worse outlook. Many of them shared a sense of failure: a properly rejigged CPP would not need these repeated fixes; if they did not carry out a more fundamental reform this time around, they would be back at the negotiating table in 2000 and 2005 facing the same issues yet again. One Alberta Treasury official recalled that Dinning 'would keep asking us, "why are we doing the same-old, same-old?"' Officials in Ottawa and the provinces were of the same mind.

Bob Christie, a senior Ontario official who worked the file, says much of the credit for the CPP reform must go to middle-level officials in Ottawa and the provinces whose names will never be widely known. 'If there are any heroes in this – it will sound precious – it's the people who worked on this year after year and never became cynical and when the time came, were able to work together and do it.'[8] Paul Martin made much the same comment: 'When the time came, they were ready with ideas, with options and with the firm determination to get it right.'[9]

Martin singled out David Dodge ('one of Canada's great public servants') and other finance officials like Susan Peterson and her team. 'This was the federal public service at its best and I know the same can be said of the provincial teams who were their counterparts.'[10] Michael Gourley credits Dodge in particular with pushing the whole process along. 'Dodge would have phone calls with hundreds of people across the country. That's what kept this thing going. He's one of the heroes of this.'[11] Dodge's own officials in Finance recall the same pattern internally – that at meeting after meeting he was constantly driving his officials for progress on the CPP file.

Janice MacKinnon, in an observation that perhaps reflects her training as a historian, figures there might be no particular heroes or villains. 'You find a compromise that suits none of the ideologues, but it gets the job done.'[12] It is a more mundane view of the process, but one that others endorse too. 'There wasn't any kind of white knight riding a charger through the conference room. There was not a lot of drama' in the federal–provincial meetings, Christie said.[13] Jim Dinning thinks the fact that many of the governments were in their first terms in office helped: 'We didn't know what couldn't be done.' But he never sensed at the time that he and the others were in the middle of a unique process. 'I don't recall feeling that we were making history at that point, and this is not the "aw, shucks" modesty shtick I'm doing now. It was good, it was worth the effort, but that's all.'[14] Martin had the same feeling, 'but I also knew the importance of what we were doing.'[15]

With the benefit of hindsight, many now look back fondly on the CPP negotiations – tough as they were at the time. 'In terms of all the intergovernmental stuff I've been involved with, it may have been the best in terms of both process and outcome,' Christie said. 'Not all intergovernmental endeavours wind up with a level of enduring agreement. This one was different. Both the staff and the political level came together to do something that a lot of people would have bet against.'[16]

A Final Assessment

Canadians are all too familiar with the federal–provincial battles that seem never-ending. They are part not just of our history but of our present as well, ingrained so deeply in the political life of this country that they can appear in the oddest and most unexpected places. The smaller disputes often appear silly, narrow, and unnecessary. The bigger ones are simply dispiriting – major clashes that finally end with a resolution of some kind, but leave a bitter taste in the mouth and a sense that our elected officials could have handled their disagreements differently.

The CPP reforms of the mid-1990s *were* handled differently. The question is why. There were probably four broad reasons – good luck, good people, a good package, and good communications.

Good Luck

First, there was 'a confluence of events,' to borrow the phrase used by one person interviewed. This may be another way of saying the policy-makers got lucky: the political and economic environment of the day favoured reform. Timing may not be everything, but in politics and in negotiations, it is a very important thing. Three events were crucial.

Event Number One: public opinion on broad fiscal issues changed significantly in the middle half of the 1990s – especially from about 1993 on. After a generation of deficits and rising debt, Canadians quite suddenly and quite remarkably turned on a dime to support lower government deficits, even surpluses. No government in Canada was immune to that pressure. Perhaps no one truly understands this country's sudden conversion to fiscal probity, but it has been extraordinarily durable. To this day, Canadians have remained quite bloody-minded on this question, almost uniquely so. Other countries also reversed their deficit positions in the second half of the 1990s, notably the United States and Britain. But most fell back into deficit in the first half of this decade and stayed there. The United States and Britain have been prominent back-sliders, with persistent deficits since 2001 and rising government debt ratios. Canada has maintained its surpluses and its debt ratio has continued to fall. Why have we been so different? A single answer is elusive. But there is little question that this sudden turn in public opinion figured prominently in the reform of the CPP. Canadians had grown mistrustful of governments, questioning their very ability to manage the financial affairs of the public sector. Some argue that this loss of confidence on the part of the public constituted the CPP's real crisis, more so than the underlying finances of the CPP itself. The politicians had to demonstrate to Canadians that they understood this new mood and could respond to it with concrete action.

Event Number Two: the luck of the calendar. In the 1985 agreement, the federal and provincial governments put the CPP review process on a tight rein, with reviews every five years that were triggered by the report from the chief actuary. This time around, the actuarial report came out in February 1995, just a few days before the turnaround 1995 federal budget. At the same time, several provincial governments had already moved strongly in the direction of fiscal virtue – Saskatchewan, Alberta, and New Brunswick were leading examples – and others were heading in the same direction. The calendar delivered the next five-year CPP review at a time when many governments had already committed themselves to reducing deficits and debt. It was easy to transfer that thinking to the CPP and unfunded liabilities.

Janice MacKinnon observed that finance ministers simply thought about the CPP differently than they thought about other issues discussed at the federal–provincial table. Ottawa and the provinces had many disputes during this period, but most finance ministers mentally put the CPP, with its deficits and its unfunded liability, into the same intellectual box that contained fiscal deficits and fiscal debt. That made a huge difference. This was not a zero-sum game like federal fiscal transfers to the provinces or dividing up federal spending on infrastructure projects – where a provincial win was a federal loss or where one province's win was another province's loss. The CPP was 'our win' or 'our loss' as finance ministers. It was just as much a legacy issue for them as sound budgetary finance – something with huge future dividends once the current pain was absorbed. No one wanted to be associated with a failure. Many of the ministers and officials interviewed thought MacKinnon's interpretation was valid. Had the CPP cycle come two years earlier or later, that same momentum among so many governments might have been missing, or they might have been so preoccupied with their own affairs that they did not want to upset their voters with another big money issue. Jim Dinning thinks the absence of partisanship helped. 'The CPPIB model and the returns it's earning today and the stability of the CPP today shows that when you remove partisan politics from such things, good things flow and the country benefits quietly.'[17]

Event Number Three: the chief actuary's dire projection for the CPP and the ensuing realization by federal and provincial policymakers of what it meant. If they could not agree on a genuinely sustainable long-term financing formula that held the contribution rate to a level they deemed acceptable, then, by default, contributions would go onto an escalator to the dreaded 14.2 per cent level by 2040. The projection was rooted in the 1985 review, when the governments of the day agreed on how to handle the subsequent five-year reviews. The legislation from the 1985 agreement said they must either agree to a new schedule of contribution rate increases or accept the chief actuary's projected increases using the fifteen-year rule. The rule, in turn, dictated that rate increases had to be large enough to generate a fund worth two years of benefits after fifteen years. The policymakers of 1985 had put a gun to the heads of their 1995 successors: they would either find an acceptable solution or face the policy failure of moving to 14.2 per cent based on the automatic formula contained in the existing legislation. That was a powerful incentive; no politician likes to admit failure quite so nakedly.

Good People

The confluence of events was a matter of luck. But getting lucky does not advance the file very far if no one is ready, willing, and able to take advantage of the circumstances that were favourable to reform. The second reason the CPP reform succeeded in the mid-1990s is that Canada had in place a group of officials and politicians who were all three. Many officials had grown increasingly uncomfortable over the failure – their own and that of their political masters – to resolve the CPP's financing problems in the 1980s and early 1990s.

From 1966 to 1985, the stewards of the CPP left contribution rates frozen while enhancing benefits. The 1985 review increased rates but also enriched some benefits substantially. The 1991 review increased rates again but left benefits almost unchanged. There was a trend at work here – and it led right to the 1997 reform of higher rates and reduced benefits – but it was unfolding at an agonizingly slow pace. This time, the officials and politicians alike wanted to get the mix right in terms of the CPP's long-term sustainability and credibility.

Canadians were lucky to have a diverse group of public servants and politicians who cared about the program and were willing to put in the huge effort involved to come up with a long-term solution. Perhaps they could have cobbled together yet another easy-way-out agreement that would have avoided a 14 per cent contribution rate or sloughed it off as something to be resolved another day, when the economy was stronger. They did not; they seized the day that was given to them.

Another factor was at work here – the legislative constraint on their decision making. The Canadian Constitution and the CPP's own history dictated their rules of engagement: Ottawa and the provinces needed each other in a way they do not need each other when they deal with other federal–provincial issues. They were and are *joint* stewards of the CPP; none can act alone or even in concert with just a few others. The federal government and two-thirds of the provinces with two-thirds of the population must agree to any deal, so they automatically need Ontario. This meant Ottawa really had to work with the provinces and vice versa. The federal government could not be heavy-handed – the usual provincial complaint – and the provinces could not shuck off their responsibility for national policymaking – a common federal complaint. If they could not come up with a solution, they would fully share in the failure of a popular program over which many Canadians were deeply concerned. That fact doubtless affected the dynamic of their talks.

Good Package

The negotiators also came up with a good package. It accomplished the goal they had set for themselves and it did so in a balanced fashion. They wanted to put an end to three decades of tinkering with the CPP that had too often featured enhanced benefits without the contribution rate increases needed to finance them. That aspect of the CPP's history angered Jim Dinning and Paul Martin in particular, and they – perhaps more than any of the other ministers – were determined to put the CPP on a sustainable financial footing. The deal did just that. As Dinning put it when lobbying Ernie Eves just before the deal was struck, 'we're doing what we were sent here to do. This is the best fix to come along in a long time.'[18]

It was in some ways a narrow answer to the broader issue of retirement income in general, but that too was probably a reason for success. Ken Battle argues that it was part of a process in which governments – stung by 'the failure of past efforts at big-bang reforms' – were turning away from 'grand new designs' for social policy in favour of 'relentless incrementalism,' which he said consisted of 'strings of reforms, seemingly small and discrete when made, that accumulate to become more than the sum of their parts.'[19] Many, he conceded, would not characterize the CPP reforms as incremental, but many, one can argue, would have preferred a much grander policy thrust to solve the overall problem of income security for the elderly. The very focus of the CPP reform effort contributed to the outcome.

The agreement was also in tune with public opinion. It responded to Canadians' newly acquired passion for fiscal responsibility that produced so much public support for deficit-cutting. It also fit the message that had come back from Canadians during the public consultations: fix the CPP; raise contribution rates if you must, but invest the money wisely; and go easy on benefit cuts. The package featured a three-to-one ratio of higher rates and reduced benefits. The deal was very Canadian in another sense. It was a middle-of-the-road solution that pleased neither left nor right. Ottawa and the assenting provinces rejected both the pressure to enhance the CPP yet again and the calls to scrap it in favour of mandatory RRSPs. Neither of those options ever really made it onto the agenda of the talks in a serious fashion, but even among the remaining choices, ministers discarded solutions they knew would make it harder to sell the reform, like raising the age of entitlement for retirement pensions.

Good Communications

The fourth reason for success was that policymakers carried out a model exercise in public communications and consultation. Some would challenge this assessment. Some would have preferred a broader consultation that covered the entire retirement income system – OAS/GIS and RRSPs as well as the CPP – and others would have preferred a CPP debate (launched with an utterly neutral discussion paper, unlike the actual *Information Paper*) whose options ranged from doubling the CPP to killing it altogether. But consultations of either kind would have gone nowhere; the weight of their own implausible or unaffordable options would have dragged them down. Either would have become a royal commission in all but name and produced an interesting report but no deal. Instead, the governments came up with a consultation process that was designed and run to produce a federal–provincial deal, not a report destined to gather dust.

The public consultations run by David Walker were extraordinarily focused. To a considerable extent, the governments loaded the dice in favour of their preferred outcome – not in the details, to be sure, but in the broad direction of a reform with higher contribution rates, reduced benefits, and a new investment policy. As one provincial official commented: 'Don't ask the question if you don't know the answer.'[20] It may sound cynical and be somewhat manipulative, but it is the kind of consultation that not only airs the issues but also gets things done. The *Information Paper* laid out the facts – a version of the facts, some would say – very simply. It laid out the choices – a few of the choices, some would say – in very clear terms. It forced those who took part in the process to address the issues and talk about the trade-offs. Because it was focused, it prepared public opinion for the mix of contribution rate increases and benefit cuts that comprised the final deal and laid the foundation for what in early 2008 was an almost $123 billion investment fund.

The choices put forward in the public consultation were very real. The options were the same ones the governments were considering, so in that sense the process was very honest. Governments had already discarded other alternatives. These were the ones they were dickering over and these were the ones they asked the public to consider. Canadians can make shrewd and quite tough decisions if they think they are being given straight information and asked to choose among real options. The resulting feedback, from a negotiator's viewpoint, was a gift – a very clear message: save the CPP, yes; raise rates if you must, but get a good return on the cash generated and do not let politicians mess with the money; cut some benefits if you must, but go easy. Governments knew just where the public stood and could negotiate a deal on that basis. And when they did the deal, it stuck. Canadians may not have liked parts of it, but they understood why it was done that way. There was no groundswell of opposition to it. The widespread protest that Preston Manning so confidently predicted simply did not materialize. Good policy is easy to communicate. Canadians are more than capable of understanding complex policy issues if they are well thought through and if they are presented in clear language.

A Transferable Model?

If the key ingredients of success were good luck, good people, a good package, and good communications, does that combination make the CPP a model for resolving other federal–provincial disputes? The answer, alas, is almost certainly no. It is far too simplistic to suggest that when the right conditions appear, officials and politicians should seize the moment, press ahead, and deploy a good communications strategy to win the day.

The problem is that the Canada Pension Plan is unique. It is not just the CPP itself that is a child of the 1960s; so too are all the mechanisms for changing it. Pensions are a matter of shared jurisdiction. It took a constitutional amendment in 1951 to allow the federal government to launch Old Age Security and another constitutional amendment in

1964 to allow Ottawa to set up the CPP with benefits for the non-aged, like disability, spousal, and death benefits. Ottawa and the provinces work together as stewards of the CPP because – and perhaps only because – they are constitutionally required to work together.

One point bears repeating: the amending formula for the CPP is tougher than the general amending formula for the Canadian Constitution. The CPP formula requires seven provinces with 67 per cent of the population; the formula for the Constitution requires seven provinces with only 50 per cent of the population. There has not been a major overhaul of the Constitution since 1982. The last two attempts – the Meech Lake Accord and the Charlottetown Accord – were such political disasters that almost every politician since then has put constitutional change on the bottom of the priority list. Yet the CPP has undergone many small changes since 1966 and three substantial revisions since 1982, the last being a major reform.[21]

National programs have been proposed in other major policy areas where joint action would be needed from the federal and provincial governments – pharmacare and child care, to name just two. But there is no constitutional pressure on governments to work together because jurisdiction is not shared. Governments are not compelled to work together, so they do not work together.

Securities regulation could be added to this list. It is ironic that the question of setting up a national securities regulator – still unresolved – was a live issue in 1996 at the same finance ministers' meetings that worked on the CPP. Canada is almost alone in leaving that task to its provinces. During the Asian trade mission in January 1997, Jean Chrétien and the premiers sketched out just such a deal. But the agreement fell apart after the first ministers returned to Canada. The CPP would appear to be a good model for such an arrangement – the creation of a national body to regulate the country's financial markets. Securities regulation is widely viewed as being entirely under provincial jurisdiction; much as Ottawa would like to put it on a national footing, it has nothing more than the power of persuasion at its disposal. It is tempting to conclude – because, at this writing, the issue is still unresolved – that the two orders of governments have not worked together to find a solution because nothing compels them to. This view of provincial jurisdictional paramountcy is not unanimous, however. Some constitutional experts believe that the federal government has a clear role in securities regulation through its constitutional powers over interprovincial trade. Accordingly, some observers of the issue continue to feel that the CPP is indeed a good model for securities regulation. The problem, in this view, lies not in the Constitution but in the federal government's unwillingness to assert the constitutional rights it already possesses.

The CPP model is extraordinarily robust for its own purposes. The negotiations of the mid-1990s were not a cakewalk. They were a very tough set of talks. There was – to use the phrase of one provincial official – a very scary period near the end when success was not at all assured. The deputy finance minister, David Dodge, did not think a deal was in the bag until the deal really was in the bag. In the end, governments were forced to agree by the constraints imposed on them both by the Constitution and by the rules agreed to in 1964 and 1965. The 1960s are very much alive every time the federal and provincial governments sit down to talk about the CPP. The rules agreed to in 1985 were no less important, but even they had their roots in those earlier arrangements.

That is a key lesson from CPP reform. Getting a deal was very difficult. But as one official suggested, the agreement that emerged was much stronger for it. Once those governments had made their pact, the 1997 reform could not be touched by any MPs, senators, or provincial legislators who would have liked to chip in their own improvements. This is how 1960s-style executive federalism worked in the 1960s – to the dismay of some people in those days – and it is the way federalism still works when it comes to the CPP. This is a good thing. The CPP is an example of how Ottawa and the provinces can develop and maintain a truly national program through a process in which each respects the interests and powers of the other but in which all work together to produce results.

Aftermath

Tom Kent's reflections on the creation of the CPP in 1965, cited in chapter 2, seem as apt today as they were in 1988, when he noted how quickly the arguments over the pension plan died once the CPP was in place. 'Indeed, it is hard to think of anything of comparable significance to people about which there has been so little subsequent controversy.'[22] The same can be said of the CPP reforms that went into effect in 1997.

The CPP reforms have worn their first decade well. The latest projections from the chief actuary show that the CPP should remain sustainable for the next seventy-five years at a steady-state contribution rate of

9.82 per cent, marginally lower than the actual rate of 9.9 per cent. The projections show assets of $235 billion by the end of 2015, up from $114 billion at the end of 2006.[23] Contributions are expected to exceed expenditures until 2019, when assets will have grown to $312 billion. By then, the baby-boom generation will be roughly 55 to 75 years of age, and a rapidly increasing proportion will have retired. To pay their pensions from 2020 on, the CPP will need to draw cash from the fund managed by the CPPIB. By then, however, the fund will be earning enough income on its investments that it will be able not only to cover its share of the annual bill for CPP benefits from only a portion of its investment income, but to keep growing as well. At most, the CPP will never need more than about one-third of the annual investment returns, or 2 per cent of the entire fund, to keep paying its bills.

It is a remarkable result, an example of what Canada's fractious governments can accomplish when they work together for the national good. All too often, politicians have trouble seeing beyond the next election, and long-term problems fester until they become crises that are far more difficult to resolve than they would have been if they had been tackled earlier. For three decades, that is how Canada's politicians treated the Canada Pension Plan. In the middle of the 1990s, they did something quite different – they fixed the future.

Appendix: Summary of Canada Pension Plan Provisions

In each major report, the chief actuary of the CPP includes a summary of the provisions of the CPP. This is an edited version of the summary found in the *23rd Report*, released in October 2007.*

I. Introduction
The Canada Pension Plan (CPP) came into force on 1 January 1966. Since that time, it has been amended several times.

II. Participation
The CPP includes virtually all members of the labour force in Canada, including both employees and self-employed persons between the ages of 18 and 70 with employment earnings, other than those covered by the Quebec Pension Plan (QPP). The main exceptions are persons with annual earnings lower than $3,500 (the Year's Basic Exemption, defined below), members of certain religious groups, and other persons who qualify under excepted employment. The CPP covers all members of the Canadian Forces and the Royal Canadian Mounted Police, including those who live in Quebec. Those getting CPP retirement or disability pension are not required to contribute.

III. Definitions

A. Year's Maximum Pensionable Earnings (YMPE)
The YMPE for a calendar year is the limit to which employment earn-

---

* Office of the Superintendant of Financial Institutions, *Actuarial Report (23rd) on the Canada Pension Plan, as at 31 December 2006.*

ings are subject to contributions for purposes of the Plan. The YMPE increases each year by an amount based on the percentage increase, in June of the preceding year, in the twelve-month average of the Industrial Aggregate (Statistics Canada's measure of Average Weekly Earnings). If the amount so calculated is not a multiple of $100, the next lower multiple of $100 is used (although the exact amount forms the basis for the following year's calculation). Under no circumstances is the YMPE allowed to decrease from one year to the next. The YMPE is set at $43,700 in 2007.

B. Year's Basic Exemption (YBE)
The YBE for a calendar year is the minimum employment earnings necessary to participate in the CPP. As well, contributions are waived on earnings up to the YBE. Before 1998, the YBE was calculated as 10 per cent of the YMPE and rounded, if necessary, to the next lower multiple of $100. For each year after 1997 the YBE is $3,500.

C. Contributory Period
The contributory period is the number of months from reaching age 18 (or from 1 January 1966, if later) to the earliest of the month in which the contributor dies, the month before the one in which the retirement pension commences and the month before the one in which the contributor reaches 70 years of age, less the number of months during which the contributor received a CPP or QPP disability benefit (including the three-month waiting period), or during which the contributor had at least one eligible child under seven years of age and had earnings for that year lower than the YBE.

D. Pension Index
The Pension Index for a given calendar year is equal to the Consumer Price Index averaged over the 12-month period ending with October of the preceding year; however, the Pension Index of a given year may not be less than the previous year's Pension Index.

IV. Contribution Rates
Contributions are required during the contributory period in respect of the contributory earnings of each contributor. From 1966 to 1986, the annual rate of contribution applicable to contributory earnings was 1.8 per cent for employees (and the same amount for their employers) and 3.6 per cent in respect of self-employed earnings. This combined

employer–employee contribution rate of 3.6 per cent was subject to an annual increase of 0.2 percentage points for 1987 to 1996, attaining 5.6 per cent in the last year of this period. The rate rose to 6.0 per cent in 1997, 6.4 per cent in 1998, 7.0 per cent in 1999, 7.8 per cent in 2000, 8.6 per cent in 2001, 9.4 per cent in 2002, and 9.9 per cent in 2003, where it remains.

The legislation gives the federal and provincial ministers of finance the authority to make changes in contribution rates through regulation, in connection with a triennial review. However, year-over-year contribution rate increases cannot exceed 0.2 per cent; beyond that, legislation is required.

If a triennial actuarial report projects a minimum contribution rate in excess of the scheduled rate and the Ministers cannot agree upon appropriate changes, the regulation concerning the calculation of default contribution rates would apply. The contribution rate would then be increased in stages and a temporary freeze on inflation adjustments to benefits in payment would apply.

V. Retirement Pension

A. Eligibility Requirements
A person aged 60 or over becomes eligible for a retirement pension upon application, provided contributions have been made during at least one calendar year. For a retirement pension to become payable before age 65, an applicant must have wholly or substantially ceased to be engaged in paid employment or self-employment. A person may not contribute to the CPP after a retirement pension becomes payable or, in any event, after age 70.

B. Amount of Pension
The initial amount of monthly retirement pension payable to a contributor is based on his or her entire history of pensionable earnings during the contributory period. The retirement pension is equal to 25 per cent of the average of the YMPE for the year of his or her retirement and the four previous years, referred to as the Maximum Pensionable Earnings Average (MPEA), adjusted to take into account the contributor's pensionable earnings. For this purpose, the contributor's pensionable earnings for any given month are indexed by the ratio of the MPEA for the year of retirement to the YMPE for the year to which the given month belongs.

Some periods with low pensionable earnings may be excluded from the calculation of benefits by reason of pensions commencing after age 65, disability, childrearing for a child less than 7 years of age, and the 15 per cent drop-out provisions. The maximum monthly retirement pension in 2007 is $863.75.

C. Adjustment for Early or Postponed Retirement

The retirement pension is subject to an actuarial adjustment that depends on the contributor's age at commencement of the retirement pension. The retirement pension is permanently adjusted downwards or upwards by 0.5 per cent for each month between age 65 and the age when the pension commences or, if earlier, age 70.

VI. Disability Benefit

A. Eligibility Requirements

A person is considered disabled if he or she is determined to be suffering from a severe and prolonged mental or physical disability. A disability is considered severe if by reason of it the person is regularly incapable of pursuing any substantially gainful occupation; a disability is considered prolonged if it is likely to be long-continuing and of indefinite duration or likely to result in death.

A person who becomes disabled prior to age 65 and is not receiving a CPP retirement pension is eligible for a disability benefit provided that contributions have been made, at the time of disablement, for at least four of the previous six calendar years, counting only years included wholly or partly in the contributory period. With the introduction of Bill C-36, contributors with twenty-five or more years of contributions to the Plan can meet the eligibility requirement with contributions in three of the last six years. Contributions must be on earnings that are not less than 10 per cent of the YMPE rounded, if necessary, to the next lower multiple of $100.

B. Amount of Pension

The amount of monthly benefit payable is the sum of a flat-rate portion ($405.96 in 2007) depending only on the year in which the benefit is payable and an earnings-related portion equal, when it commences, to 75 per cent of the retirement pension that would be payable at the onset of disability if the contributory period ended on that date and no actuarial adjustment applied.

The automatic conversion at age 65 of a disability benefit into a retirement pension is based on the pensionable earnings at the time of disablement and price indexed to age 65. In other words, the indexing from disablement to age 65, which determines the initial rate of the retirement pension, is in line with increases in prices rather than wages. The maximum monthly disability benefit in 2007 is $1,053.77.

VII. Survivor Benefit

A. Eligibility Requirements
A legal spouse, a separated legal spouse not cohabiting with a common-law partner, or a common-law partner of a deceased contributor is eligible for a survivor benefit if the following conditions are met as at the date of the contributor's death:

- The deceased contributor must have made contributions during the lesser of ten calendar years, or one-third of the number of years included wholly or partly in his or her contributory period, but not for less than three years.
- If the surviving spouse is the separated legal spouse of the deceased contributor, there must be no cohabiting common-law partner at the time of death. If the surviving spouse is the common-law partner of the deceased contributor, they must have cohabited for not less than one year immediately before the death of the contributor. If the common-law partner is of the same sex as the deceased contributor, the death must have occurred on or after 17 April 1985.
- The surviving spouse or common-law partner must have dependent children, be disabled, or be at least 35 years of age. A surviving spouse or common-law partner with dependent children means a surviving spouse who wholly or substantially supports a child of the deceased contributor where the child is under age 18, aged 18 or over but under age 25 and attending school full-time, or aged 18 or over and disabled, having been disabled without interruption since attaining age 18 or the time of the contributor's death, whichever occurred later.

B. Amount of Pension
The amount of the monthly survivor benefit depends on the age of the survivor at the date of the contributor's death, the survivor's disability status, and the presence of dependent children. If a surviving spouse or

common-law partner is receiving a retirement pension or a disability benefit, the monthly amount of the surviving spouse's benefit may be reduced. (The chief actuary's report sets out five cases that are relevant in the calculation; they cover various combinations based on age, disability, and whether dependent children are involved.)

VIII. Death Benefit

A lump-sum benefit is payable to the estate of a deceased contributor if the eligibility rules for survivor benefits are met. The amount of the death benefit is equal to six times the monthly amount of retirement pension accrued or payable in the year of death, adjusted to exclude any actuarial adjustments, subject to a maximum of $2,500.

IX. Child Benefits

Each child under age 18 and each full-time student aged 18 to 25 who is dependent on a contributor eligible for a CPP disability benefit or was dependent on a deceased contributor satisfying the contribution requirement for a survivor benefit is entitled to a flat-rate monthly benefit ($204.68 in 2007). Furthermore, where applicable, a child may receive more than one child benefit simultaneously.

X. Inflation Adjustments

All monthly benefits payable are increased in accordance with inflation each year. Benefits are multiplied on 1 January of each calendar year by the ratio of the Pension Index applicable for that calendar year to the Pension Index for the preceding year.

XI. Credit-Splitting

Pensionable earnings may be split between divorced or separated couples (legal or common-law partners) for each year the couple lived together. Pensionable earnings are used to establish eligibility for CPP benefits and to calculate the amount of benefits. Contributors may obtain a credit split even if they have remarried. However, pensionable earnings cannot be split for any month in which the earnings allocated to each spouse would be less than 1/12 of the YBE.

XII. Pension Sharing

Couples (legal or common-law partners) in an ongoing relationship may voluntarily (at the request of one of them) share their CPP retirement pensions in proportion to the number of years during which they cohabited. This applies provided both spouses have reached the minimum age requirement to receive a retirement pension. Sharing is possible even if only one of the spouses has participated in the Plan. Pension sharing ceases upon separation, divorce, or death.

Notes

1. Gloomy Canada

1 *Maclean's*, 8 June 1992, 18.
2 'Manning is first to tap concern over national debt,' *Toronto Star*, 31 March 1993.
3 Edward Greenspon and Anthony Wilson-Smith, *Double Vision: The Inside Story of the Liberals in Power*, 271.
4 *Wall Street Journal*, 12 January 1995, A14.
5 'Budget moment of truth for Martin: Investors require deficit credibility,' *The Globe and Mail*, 27 February 1995.
6 'Deficit numbers larger than life: Conservative forecast means Ottawa may overshoot rather than underperform targets,' *The Globe and Mail*, 28 February 1995.
7 Janice MacKinnon, *Minding the Public Purse: The Fiscal Crisis, Political Trade-offs, and Canada's Future*, 218.
8 Greenspon and Wilson-Smith, *Double Vision*, 256.
9 Interview with the author, 17 February 2008.
10 Eddie Goldenberg, *The Way It Works: Inside Ottawa*, 146–7.
11 Interview with the author, 17 February 2008.
12 Department of Finance, *Budget Speech*, 27 February 1995, 20.
13 Human Resources Development Canada, *Evaluation Report: Phase 1 of the Evaluation of the Canada Pension Plan (CPP)*, 14.
14 Statistics Canada, *Canada's Retirement Income Programs: A Statistical Overview (1990–2000)*. Calculated from data in table 1-1, p. 13.
15 This section draws heavily on Bob Baldwin, *Pension Reform in the 1990s: What Was Accomplished, What Lies Ahead?*
16 Statistics Canada, *Canada's Retirement Income Programs*, table 1-1, p. 13.

17 Ibid., tables 1-2 and 1-3, pp. 15–17. Calculations of all figures as a share of GDP were based on the 1995 GDP of $810.4 billion from Statistics Canada's National Accounts.
18 Robert Brown, 'Canada Pension Plan: Financing.'
19 In the opening scene of the 2002 film *About Schmidt*, Jack Nicholson, as actuary Warren Schmidt, is counting down the minutes until 5 p.m. sharp, at which moment his forty-year career will end and he will be retired.
20 Geoff Bowlby, 'Defining Retirement,' 16–17.
21 Bob Baldwin, 'Overview of the Retirement Income System,' in Caledon Institute of Social Policy, *Roundtable on Canada's Aging Society and Retirement Income System, June 5, 1995*, 22.
22 Ken Battle, *Sustaining Public Pensions in Canada: A Tale of Two Reforms*, 28–9.

2. The Creation of a Pension Plan

1 The website of the Canadian Museum of Civilization includes a history of Canadian pensions that offers a wonderful overview of aging, poverty, and pensions since Confederation. Much of the material in this section is drawn from that account.
2 Paul Martin, Sr, the father of Paul Martin, was deeply involved in pension issues as minister of national health and welfare from 1946 to 1957.
3 Canadian Museum of Civilization, *The History of Canada's Public Pensions*, 'Reducing Poverty 1952–1967,' p. 8, http://www.civilization.ca/hist/pensions/1952-1967_e.pdf.
4 The best accounts of the 1965 creation of the Canada Pension Plan can be found in four very different books. This section draws on all of them. Peter Newman's *The Distemper of Our Times*, published in 1968, is a journalist's vivid telling of the Pearson government's five turbulent years. Richard Simeon's classic study, *Federal–Provincial Diplomacy: The Making of Recent Policy in Canada*, first published in 1972, was reissued in 2006 with a new afterword. The other two are the works of insiders to the negotiations. Judy LaMarsh, the minister of national health and welfare at the time, recounted her version of events in *Memoirs of a Bird in a Gilded Cage* in 1968, while Tom Kent, a key Pearson adviser, covered the CPP story in his memoirs, *A Public Purpose*, in 1988.
5 Kent, *Public Purpose*, 256.
6 Newman, *Distemper of Our Times*, 306.
7 Kent, *Public Purpose*, 256.
8 Ibid., 220.
9 Simeon, *Federal–Provincial Diplomacy*, 45.

10 Ibid., 46.
11 Bruce Richard Kennedy, 'Intra-cohort Redistribution Using Longitudinal Microsimulation,' 40.
12 Simeon, *Federal–Provincial Diplomacy*, 46.
13 Kent, *Public Purpose*, 258.
14 Ibid.
15 Ibid., 260.
16 Ibid., 262.
17 Ibid., 263.
18 Ibid.
19 Cited in Simeon, *Federal–Provincial Diplomacy*, 50–1. Simeon commented in a footnote: 'The vehemence of this attack could well have backfired.'
20 Ibid., 53.
21 Kent, *Public Purpose*, 274–5.
22 Newman, *The Distemper of Our Times*, 309. Duff Roblin and Joey Smallwood were premiers of Manitoba and Newfoundland respectively.
23 Simeon, *Federal–Provincial Diplomacy*, 56.
24 Kent, *Public Purpose*, 277–8.
25 Ibid., 279.
26 Simeon, *Federal–Provincial Diplomacy*, 58.
27 Kent, *Public Purpose*, 281.
28 It was $600 for employees and $800 for the self-employed; the two were made equal in the 1970s.
29 Kent, *Public Purpose*, 282.
30 Ibid., 283.
31 Newman, *The Distemper of Our Times*, 314–15.
32 Kent, *Public Purpose*, 285–6.
33 Simeon, *Federal–Provincial Diplomacy*, 61.
34 Kent, *Public Purpose*, 286.
35 Ibid., 289.
36 Simeon, *Federal–Provincial Diplomacy*, 62–3.
37 Kent, *Public Purpose*, 290–1.
38 Cited in Alan Michael Jacobs, 'Governing for the Long Term: Democratic Politics and Policy Investment,' unpublished PhD thesis, Department of Government, Harvard University, Cambridge, MA, 2004, 246fn302.
39 Ibid., 248–9.
40 Ibid., 252.
41 Kennedy, 'Intra-cohort Redistribution,' 42.
42 Department of National Health and Welfare, *The Canada Pension Plan: Actuarial Report*, tables 9–11, pp. 25–7.

43 Kennedy, 'Intra-cohort Redistribution,' 45.
44 Kent, *Public Purpose*, 255.

3. The Desultory Decades

1 This chronology is taken mainly from Robert D. Anderson, 'Canada and Quebec Pension Plans,' 33–4.
2 Initially, the GIS was to be phased out in 1976, when full CPP pensions were to be paid; this never happened.
3 The Year's Maximum Pensionable Earnings level, which at first grew by 2 per cent annually, was also raised substantially during this period to match wage increases.
4 Kennedy, 'Intra-cohort Redistribution Using Longitudinal Microsimulation,' 45.
5 Department of Insurance, *Canada Pension Plan Actuarial Report as at December 31, 1969*, 50–1.
6 Kennedy, 'Intra-cohort Redistribution,' 46.
7 Department of Insurance, *Canada Pension Plan Actuarial Report as at December 31, 1969*. Table 3 on p. 35 shows that contributions were projected to exceed costs in 1980 but would fall short of costs in 1985. The report does not contain data for the intervening years.
8 Ibid.
9 Department of Insurance, *Canada Pension Plan Actuarial Report No. 2 as at December 31, 1972.*
10 Department of Insurance, *Canada Pension Plan Actuarial Report No. 3 as at December 31, 1973.*
11 There were four separate projections for each fund, the existing plan under each of the two inflation assumptions and the proposed (Bill C-224) plan under each of the two inflation assumptions. For the sake of simplicity and clarity, we will focus on only one version of each fund, the one that uses the higher inflation assumption and the one for the proposed plan under Bill C-224, since that bill became law.
12 Department of Insurance, *CPP Actuarial Report No. 2*, 4.
13 Department of Insurance, *CPP Actuarial Report No. 3*, 7.
14 Kennedy, 'Intra-cohort Redistribution,' 46.
15 Department of Insurance, *CPP Actuarial Report No. 3*, table 2, p. 11.
16 Kennedy, 'Intra-cohort Redistribution,' 47.
17 Department of Insurance, *CPP Actuarial Report No. 3*, table 2, p. 11.
18 Ibid., 7.
19 Ibid., 21.

20 The fourth and fifth reports dealt with issues that had no substantive effect on the projections.
21 Department of Insurance, *Canada Pension Plan Actuarial Report No. 6 as at December 31, 1977*, 3.
22 Ibid., 4.
23 Ibid., 11.
24 Cited in *Report of the Royal Commission on the Status of Pensions in Ontario*, vol. 5, *Ontario and the Canada Pension Plan*, v.
25 Ibid., vi–vii.
26 Ibid., Appendix D, 61–3.
27 Emails to the author, 7 and 9 September 2007.
28 This first estimate of the unfunded liability may deserve more attention than it usually gets. See Bruce Kennedy's comments in chapter 15.
29 To put this number in perspective, the debt of the federal and provincial governments (more properly, their net financial liabilities, as measured in Statistics Canada's national balance sheet accounts) was almost $49 billion.
30 The seventh report, in early 1981, was a short assessment of a small technical change in the CPP.
31 According to the Parliament of Canada website, 'the term white paper is ... commonly applied to official documents presented by Ministers of the Crown which state and explain the government's policy on a certain issue' (see http://www2.parl.gc.ca/Parlinfo/Pages/WhitePapers.aspx). A green paper is defined as 'a statement by the Government not of policy already determined but of propositions put before the whole nation for discussion' (see http://www2.parl.gc.ca/Parlinfo/Pages/GreenPapers.aspx).
32 Interview with the author, 27 June 2007.
33 Interview with the author, 28 February 2007.
34 All of these reports are cited and referenced in Louis Ascah, 'Recent Pension Reports in Canada: A Survey.'
35 Ibid., 416.
36 Ibid.
37 *The Globe and Mail*, 24 February 1981, 6.
38 National Council of Welfare, *Pension Reform: A Report by the National Council of Welfare* (1990), 1. This report, which called for its own sweeping improvements to public and private pensions, was published, ironically, in February 1990, on the eve of the 1990–1 recession.
39 Ibid., 1.
40 Ibid., 1–2.
41 National Council of Welfare. *Pension Reform: A Report by the National Council of Welfare* (1984), 31.

42 Michael J. Prince, *Wrestling with the Poor Cousin: Canada Pension Plan Disability Policy and Practice, 1964–2001*, 36.
43 National Council of Welfare, *Better Pensions for Homemakers: A Report by the National Council of Welfare*, 1.

4. Finally, Some Action on Financing

1 Interview with the author, 28 February 2007.
2 See figure 3.1.
3 Department of Insurance, *Canada Pension Plan Actuarial Report No. 8 as at December 31, 1982*, 3.
4 Ibid., 4.
5 Ibid., 20.
6 'Governments agree: Big rate rise coming for Canada Pension,' *The Globe and Mail*, 16 January 1985, p. 1.
7 'Wilson wrong on CPP rise, Grossman says,' *The Globe and Mail*, 18 January 1985, p. 5.
8 '"Boots-to-granny" budget has Wilson in hot water; Pension flap gives Tories reputation of taxing poor to help rich,' *The Gazette* (Montreal), 8 June 1985, p. B5.
9 The GIS for low-income seniors was 'super-indexed' to offset the reduction in inflation indexing of the OAS benefit, but not until after the 1985 budget.
10 '"You lied to us," pensioner tells Mulroney in sudden confrontation,' *The Gazette* (Montreal), 20 June 1985, p. A1.
11 'Tories revive idea of pensions for housewives,' *Ottawa Citizen*, 19 September 1985, p. A3.
12 Canada, *The Canada Pension Plan: Keeping It Financially Healthy.* The quote is taken from the Preface, signed by Michael Wilson as minister of finance and Jake Epp as minister of national health and welfare.
13 Ibid., 3.
14 Ibid., 5.
15 Ibid.
16 Ibid., 5–6.
17 Ibid., 6–7.
18 Ibid, 8–9.
19 Ibid., 9–10.
20 Ibid. 11.
21 Ibid., 11–12.
22 Ibid., 12.
23 Ibid., 18–21.

24 Interview with the author. The official, who is still a public servant, spoke on a not-for-attribution basis.
25 The chief actuary's *8th Report* put the figure at $102 billion (66).
26 Interview with the author, 19 June 2007.
27 'Pension plan premiums to be increased,' *Ottawa Citizen*, 14 December 1985, p. A1.
28 Interview with the author, 12 December 2006.
29 Notes by Réal Bouchard on an early draft of this volume, 14 March 2008.
30 Interview with the author, 20 June 2007.
31 'Paying for the nation's golden years,' *Ottawa Citizen*, 17 December 1985, p. A8.
32 Bruce Kennedy, 'Intra-cohort Redistribution Using Longitudinal Microsimulation,' 53.
33 Department of Insurance, *Canada Pension Plan Statutory Actuarial Report No. 10 as at December 31, 1985*, table 4, p. 9.
34 Bruce Kennedy, 'Refinancing the CPP: The Cost of Acquiescence,' 40.

5. Finance Takes Over the File

1 Interview with the author, 12 December 2006.
2 Battle left the National Council of Welfare in 1992 to found the Caledon Institute of Social Policy, which has since become one of Canada's leading social policy think tanks. Torjman is vice-president of the institute.
3 Ken Battle and Sherri Torjman, *How Finance Re-Formed Social Policy*, 6–7.
4 Interview with the author, 19 June 2007. The former official spoke on a not-for-attribution basis.
5 Gail Armitage, interview with the author, 20 June 2007.
6 The *9th Report*, in 1986, was a four-page assessment of a small technical change.
7 Department of Insurance, *Canada Pension Plan Statutory Actuarial Report No. 10 as at December 31, 1985*, 19.
8 Office of the Superintendent of Financial Institutions, *Canada Pension Plan Eleventh Statutory Actuarial Report as at December 31, 1988*, 7, main table 1A.
9 Ibid., 17.
10 Ibid., 8, main table 1B.
11 Canadian Press Newswire story on the finance ministers' meeting, 28 January 1991.
12 Both officials, who are still public servants, spoke on a not-for-attribution basis.

13 Office of the Superintendent of Financial Institutions, *Canada Pension Plan Twelfth Statutory Actuarial Report, October 1991,* 7, main table 1A.
14 Sherri Torjman, *The Canada Pension Plan Disability Benefit,* 26–7. The total average disability payment (there was an earnings-related payment in addition to the flat-rate payment) increased from $371 to $554 a month.
15 Michael J. Prince, *Wrestling with the Poor Cousin: Canada Pension Plan Disability Policy and Practice, 1964–2001,* 41.
16 Ken Battle, *Relentless Incrementalism: Deconstructing and Reconstructing Canadian Income Security Policy,* 26.
17 Torjman, *The Canada Pension Plan Disability Benefit,* 27.
18 Battle, *Relentless Incrementalism,* 26.
19 The *13th Report,* in April 1992, had assessed the impact of Bill C-57.
20 Office of the Superintendent of Financial Institutions. *Canada Pension Plan Fourteenth Actuarial Report as at 31 December 1991,* 3.
21 Ibid., 6, main table 1.

6. Public Fears, Proposed Solutions

 1 Sherri Torjman, *Social Programs: Tail or Dog,* 2. The phrase and the description came from an influential 1990 report from the Economic Council of Canada, *Good Jobs, Bad Jobs: Employment in the Service Economy* (Ottawa: Minister of Supply and Services).
 2 'Are Pensions Safe?: Why Canadians cannot count on government to secure a golden retirement,' *Maclean's,* 2 March 1992, p. 24.
 3 'Can you afford to retire?' *Ottawa Citizen,* 16 May 1992, p. J1.
 4 'Financial fears about retirement boosting RRSP savings, survey says,' *Toronto Star,* 23 January 1993, p. C3.
 5 Auditor General of Canada, *1993 Report,* chapter 18, paragraph 18.59.
 6 Susan Crompton, 'Facing Retirement.'
 7 Ibid., 37–8.
 8 Abdul Rashid, 'Seven Decades of Wage Changes.'
 9 To 23.2 per cent from 11.6 per cent.
10 'Pension, health systems in peril; Statscan urges restructuring,' *The Globe and Mail,* 8 April 1993, p. A1.
11 'Deputy Minister calls for reforms,' *Calgary Herald,* 6 May 1993, p. A18.
12 'Actuaries get it partly right on pension plan,' *Toronto Star,* 15 November 1993, p. A19.
13 Interview with the author, November 2007. The official, who is still a public servant, spoke on a not-for-attribution basis.
14 Email to the author, 11 November 2007. The former official communicated on a not-for-attribution basis.

15 'Canada Pension Plan reforms urged,' *The Globe and Mail*, 23 September 1993, p. B8.
16 'Fears over CPP called overblown: Actuaries outline modifications,' *Financial Post*, 12 November 1993, section 2, p. 17.
17 Canadian Institute of Actuaries, *Canadian Retirement Income Social Security Programs, Report of the Task Force on Social Security Financing*, 16.
18 More precisely, the figure was 24.1 per cent in 1993.
19 Canadian Institute of Actuaries, *Canadian Retirement Income Social Security Programs*, 13.
20 Ibid., 14.
21 Jason Siroonian, 'A Note on the Recession and Early Retirement.'
22 The estimates do not add to the totals because of rounding.
23 Doreen Duchesne and Hubert Frenkel, 'An Interview with Laurence E. Coward.'
24 'Will we still feed them, when they're 64?' *The Globe and Mail*, 15 November 1993, p. A15.
25 'No handouts for seniors, thanks,' *The Globe and Mail*, 30 November 1993, p. A23.
26 'Paying for pensions,' *The Globe and Mail*, 9 December 1993, p. A28.
27 'Canada's other national debt: The tension in pensions,' *The Globe and Mail*, 15 August 1994, p. A9.
28 'How the CPP can be fixed,' *The Globe and Mail*, 16 August 1994, p. A6.
29 'Let's create a nation of savers,' *The Globe and Mail*, 17 August 1994, p. A5.
30 'CPP dilemma soon: Pensioners overtaking taxpayers,' Vancouver *Province*, 24 August 1994, p. A30.
31 'Put pension plan out of misery,' Halifax *Daily News*, 5 September 1994, p. 15.
32 'Gray Power,' Montreal *Gazette*, 2 July 1994, p. B1.
33 Human Resources Development Canada, *Improving Social Security in Canada: A Discussion Paper*.
34 My thanks to Jennifer Arnold for her extensive research assistance on this section.
35 World Bank, *Averting the Old Age Crisis, Policies to Protect the Old and Promote Growth, A World Bank Policy Research Report*.
36 World Bank, 'Averting the Age Old Crisis for the Old.'
37 World Bank, *Averting the Old Age Crisis*, 370 and 224.
38 'Oversold: The World Bank changes its tune on Latin America's privatized pensions,' *The Economist*, 25 September 2004, p. 92.
39 Since published: Indermit Gill, Truman Packard, and Juan Yermo, *Keeping the Promise of Social Security in Latin America* (Stanford: Stanford University Press, 2005).

40 'Oversold,' *The Economist*, 25 September 2004, p. 92.
41 Alberto Arenas de Mesa and Carmelo Mesa-Lago, 'The Structural Pension Reform in Chile: Effects, Comparisons with Other Latin American Reforms, and Lessons,' 149.
42 Sheetal K. Chand and Albert Jaeger, *Aging Populations and Public Pension Schemes.*
43 Deborah Roseveare, Willi Leibfritz, Douglas Fore, and Eckhard Wurzel, *Ageing Populations, Pension Systems and Government Budgets: Simulations for 20 OECD Countries.*
44 Nicholas Barr, 'Pensions: Overview of the Issues,' 3.

7. The Bombshell Report

1 Réal Bouchard, interview with the author, 12 December 2006.
2 Office of the Superintendent of Financial Institutions, *Canada Pension Plan Fifteenth Actuarial Report as at December 31, 1993*, 3.
3 Canada, *The Canada Pension Plan: Keeping It Financially Healthy*, 8.
4 Though many Canadians found the idea of a 14.2 per cent contribution rate quite disturbing, the fact is that no one would ever pay a contribution amounting to 14.2 per cent of their earnings. For one thing, most earners would split the cost with their employers at 7.1 per cent each, just as they split the 1995 rate of 5.4 per cent at 2.7 per cent each. Even that overstates the case, because contributions were paid not on a person's full earnings, but only on what were called contributory earnings, the amount between the Year's Basic Exemption (YBE) and the Year's Maximum Pensionable Earnings (YMPE); the latter was the ceiling. To take the contribution rate of the day as an example, 5.4 per cent was levied on a person's contributory earnings, the amount between the YBE of $3,400 and the YMPE of $34,900, or $31,500. That worked out to an annual contribution of $1,701 (5.4 per cent of $31,500), which means the ceiling on contributions was only 4.87 per cent of the $34,900 YMPE. A self-employed person whose earnings were exactly the YMPE would pay that full amount, an employee half that. Anyone earning more than the YMPE would pay an even smaller percentage of their earnings; with earnings of double the YMPE, for example, the total contribution by the employee and employer would amount to 2.44 per cent of actual total earnings. So the numbers were less scary than they looked on the surface, a point that people like Bob Baldwin of the Canadian Labour Congress often made. In either case the scale of the increase in proportionate terms was much the same.

5 Office of the Superintendent of Financial Institutions, *CPP Fifteenth Actuarial Report*, 58.
6 Ibid. The U.S. OASDI program is more commonly known as Social Security.
7 Ibid.
8 Ibid., 4.
9 Ibid., 100.
10 *Financial Post*, 25 February 1995, p. 5.
11 *The Globe and Mail*, 25 February 1995, p. B1.
12 *Winnipeg Free Press*, 25 February 1995.
13 *The Vancouver Sun*, 25 February 1995.
14 Department of Finance, *Budget Speech*, 20.
15 'The Federal Budget: Ottawa aims to shrink deficit,' *The Globe and Mail*, 28 February 1995, p. A1.
16 'Pension reform to hit boomers: Martin assures New York audience deficit targets will be met,' *Calgary Herald*, 4 March 1995, p. A3.
17 'Will you still need me, Will you still bleed me, When I'm 65,' *The Vancouver Sun*, 21 March 1995, p. A15.
18 'Toward a renewed pension system,' *The Globe and Mail*, 11 March 1995, p. D6.
19 'Ottawa hid fact CPP's future is not so grim,' *Calgary Herald*, 15 September 1995, p. A1.
20 'Documents show CPP not as badly off as Ottawa said,' *The Gazette* (Montreal), 15 September 1995, p. D3.
21 'Let's face it, pension plan could run out of money,' *The Gazette* (Montreal), 4 October 1995, p. B2.
22 Caledon Institute of Social Policy, *Roundtable on Canada's Aging Society and Retirement Income System*, 74.
23 'Ottawa aims to end abuse of disability pensions,' *Toronto Star*, 3 April 1994, p. A3.
24 'Canada Pension Plan: Probe finds 4,000 get disability payments, but don't qualify,' *Ottawa Citizen*, 15 September 1995, p. A4.

8. The Outside Debate

1 Robert Brown, 'Who's going to pay?' *Financial Post*, 11 March 1995, p. 23.
2 'The second national debt,' *The Globe and Mail*, 23 January 1995, p. A14.
3 'Pension "delay" sparks anger,' *The Hamilton Spectator*, 11 January 1995, p. C12.
4 Notes by Réal Bouchard on an early draft of this volume, 14 March 2008.

5 'Quebec Referendum: Bouchard claims pensions on Ottawa's chopping block,' *The Windsor Star,* 29 September 1995, p. A7.
6 'Pensions won't be cut: PM; But eligibility age could be raised,' *The Gazette* (Montreal), 29 September 1995, p. A1.
7 Interview with the author, 29 May 2007.
8 Interview with the author, 23 May 2007.
9 Canadian Institute of Actuaries, *Troubled Tomorrows – The Report of the Canadian Institute of Actuaries' Task Force on Retirement Savings.*
10 Caledon Institute of Social Policy, *Roundtable on Canada's Aging Society and Retirement Income System, June 5, 1995.*
11 Canadian Institute of Actuaries, *Troubled Tomorrows,* 8.
12 The G7 countries were the United States, Germany, Japan, France, Britain, Italy, and Canada.
13 Canadian Institute of Actuaries, *Troubled Tomorrows,* 9.
14 Caledon Institute of Social Policy, *Roundtable,* 2.
15 Ibid., 1.
16 Ibid., 3.
17 Ibid., 8.
18 Canadian Institute of Actuaries, *Troubled Tomorrows,* 24.
19 'Apocalypse Soon? Ominous forecasts about our graying population and the next recession, Report warns of huge future costs to support the elderly,' *Toronto Star,* 21 January 1995, p. C1.
20 'Actuaries' report sees dark days for C/QPP,' *Financial Post,* 21 January 1995, p. 43.
21 Caledon Institute of Social Policy, *Roundtable,* 9–14.
22 Ibid., 15–26.
23 Ibid., 27–30.
24 Ibid., 59–71; emphasis in original.
25 'Reform offers "super-RRSP" as pension plan alternative,' *Edmonton Journal,* 12 October 1995, p. A3.
26 'Super-RRSP as renewal of Canada Pension Plan,' *Canada AM,* CTV network, 11 October 1995.
27 'Super-RRSP,' *Edmonton Journal,* 12 October 1995, p. A3.
28 'Let us hope Reform Party's pension proposal perishes,' *Toronto Star,* 17 September 1995, p. D8.
29 'Canada Pension Plan must change or face collapse, MP Brown warns,' *Calgary Herald,* 9 December 1995, p. A13.

9. The Reform Takes Shape

1 Much of this chapter is based on interviews with former and current federal and provincial officials, most of whom spoke on a not-for-attribution basis. Accordingly, such comments will not be footnoted further.

2 House of Commons Standing Committee on Finance, 29 October 1997. The transcript is available at http://cmte.parl.gc.ca/cmte/Committee Publication.aspx?SourceId=49426.

3 Mintz later carried out a major study of business taxation for the Finance Department. From 1999 to 2006, he was president of the C.D. Howe Institute, and in 2007, he became the first head of the School of Policy Studies at the University of Calgary, where he holds the Palmer Chair in Public Policy.

4 Interview with the author, 13 February 2008.

5 Interview with the author, 10 May 2007. Subsequent Martin quotes, unless otherwise noted, are from this interview.

6 Paul Martin, speaking notes, C.D. Howe Institute Policy Conference, 'The Canada Pension Plan Reforms Ten Years After: Lessons and Prospects,' 10 December 2007, p. 3.

7 In 2008, Sheikh was appointed Chief Statistician at Statistics Canada.

8 Steven James, Chris Matier, Humam Sakhnini, and Munir Sheikh, *The Economics of Canada Pension Plan Reforms.*

9 Ibid., 6.

10 Ibid., 7.

11 Ibid., 8.

12 Ibid., 24.

13 Ambachtsheer still runs his consulting business and is the founding director of the International Centre for Pension Management, a research centre affiliated with the Rotman School of Management at University of Toronto, where he is an adjunct professor of finance.

14 Keith Ambachtsheer, 'Saving Canada's Social Security System: A Bold Proposal.'

15 Under a DB plan, plan members know exactly what benefit they will receive in retirement; contributions while they work are adjusted to deliver that benefit. In a DC plan, they make specified contributions each year while they work, but their eventual pension is based on how big a personal retirement fund they have earned over the years and on the investment return they can get from it during their retirement years.

16 Ambachtsheer noted in a recent email (15 February 2008) that there is an implicit assumption – that should be made explicit – in his observation that

the operating costs of DB pension systems are lower than those of DC systems. The assumption is that (as in the Chilean case and in the case of most of Canada's own RRSP assets) the DC/RRSP systems are sold and managed by external for-profit institutions. In contrast, this is not true in the case of a $435 billion non-profit co-op such as TIAA-CREF in the United States, which describes itself as 'the leading retirement system for people who work in the academic, research, medical and cultural fields.' Ambacht-sheer noted that TIAA-CREF, which offers a DC option, runs at fee levels that compare favourably with those of large DB plans. So the 'sold and managed by external for-profit institutions' assumption is important in characterizing DC arrangements as generally 'high cost.'

17 Interview with the author, 8 February 2007.
18 Email to the author, 25 January 2008.
19 'Quebec opposes CPP age rise to 67,' *The Globe and Mail*, 12 December 1995, p. A1.
20 Ibid.
21 'Ministers warn CPP must change to survive,' *Financial Post*, 14 December 1995, p. 5.
22 'Provinces squabble over funding,' *The Globe and Mail*, 14 December 1995, p. A1.
23 Interview with the author, 10 April 2007.
24 Interview with the author, 10 May 2007.
25 'Provinces squabble over funding,' *The Globe and Mail*, 14 December 1995, p. A1; and 'Ministers warn CPP must change to survive,' *Financial Post*, 14 December 1995, p. 5.
26 Ken Battle, *Sustaining Public Pensions in Canada: A Tale of Two Reforms*, 33.

10. Clarifying the Choices

1 'Martin says CPP to stay, though it may cost more and pay less,' Canadian Press Newswire, 9 February 1996.
2 Canadian Press Newswire, no title, 9 February 1996.
3 'Canada Pension Plan: Ministers agree to seek public input on reforms; Higher premiums, reduced benefits remain bottom line,' *Ottawa Citizen*, 10 February 1996, p. A3.
4 Department of Finance, *An Information Paper for Consultations on the Canada Pension Plan* (hereafter *Information Paper*).
5 Ibid., 3.
6 The discussion was never carried out in terms of dollars, always as percent-

ages of contributory, or covered, earnings, which is the amount between the year's basic exemption (YBE) and the year's maximum pensionable earnings (YMPE) ceiling.

7 *Information Paper*, 3.
8 Ibid., 4.
9 Ibid., 7.
10 Ibid., 7–8.
11 Ibid., 17.
12 Ibid., 19.
13 Ibid., 20.
14 Ibid., 21.
15 Ibid.
16 Ibid., 22.
17 Ibid.
18 Ibid., 23–4.
19 Ibid., 24.
20 Ibid., 53–4.
21 Ibid., 53.
22 Ibid., 54.
23 Ibid., 27.
24 Ibid. Further technical details on steady-state financing were spelled out in Annex C, on pp. 55–60 of the *Information Paper*.
25 Ibid., 28.
26 Ibid.
27 Ibid., 28–9.
28 Ibid., 29.
29 Ibid., 30.
30 Ibid.
31 Some of this chapter is based on interviews with former and current federal and provincial officials, most of whom spoke on a not-for-attribution basis. Such comments will not be noted further.
32 *Information Paper*, 30.
33 The Year's Maximum Pensionable Earnings was set to be roughly equal to the average industrial wage.
34 *Information Paper*, 30.
35 Ibid.
36 Ibid.
37 Steven James, Chris Matier, Humam Sakhnini, and Munir Sheikh, *The Economics of Canada Pension Plan Reforms.*

38 *Information Paper,* 31.

39 Ibid.

40 Ibid., 33.

41 Ibid., 34. All material in this section on retirement pensions is drawn from pp. 34–7.

42 Since the Year's Maximum Pensionable Earnings was roughly equal to the average industrial wage, the 25 per cent rate meant the CPP replaced about one-quarter of the average industrial wage.

43 A CPP member earns the maximum benefit if he or she has worked forty years. The formula is 65 years (the 'normal' retirement age) minus 18 (the age at which contributions begin) times 0.85 (after dropping out 15 per cent of non-working or low-income years from the earnings record.)

44 *Information Paper,* 35. The reader should bear in mind that the CPP does not have a mandatory retirement age. The plan's notional – or reference – retirement age is 65, with benefits adjusted downward or upward by 6 per cent a year for people who retire earlier or later. As one provincial pension expert pointed out in an email to the author, 'if the reference point is increased to 66, then regardless of what age you retire at, you simply get a 6 per cent smaller pension than you would with the reference point at 65. In other words, there is no difference mathematically between raising the 'retirement age' by one year and simply cutting pensions by 6 per cent. There is a huge difference in communications potential, however, between these two equivalent formula. Many who argue in favour of increasing the retirement age to 66 wouldn't openly advocate an across-the-board 6 per cent cut to new CPP pensions.'

45 *Information Paper,* 37.

46 Ibid. All material in the section on disability benefits is drawn from pp. 37–40.

47 Ibid., 38.

48 Ibid., 39.

49 Ibid.

50 Ibid., 40. All material in the section on survivor benefits is drawn from pp. 40–1.

51 Ibid., 42.

52 Ibid., 45–7.

53 Interview with the author, 8 February 2007.

54 Interview with the author, 28 February 2007.

55 'Reid-Southam poll: Canadians warn against elimination of pension plans,' *Ottawa Citizen,* 29 February 1996, p. F12.

11. Consultations – Of All Kinds

1 'Savvy Liberal takes on thankless task: Reforming pension plan demands optimism,' *Financial Post*, 16 April 1996, p. 19.
2 Department of Finance, 'Chief Federal Representative to Consultations on Canada Pension Plan Named.'
3 The official spoke on a not-for-attribution basis, as did other former and current federal and provincial officials cited in this chapter. Such comments will not be noted further.
4 Interview with the author, 17 February 2008.
5 'Seniors defend CPP before federal committee,' Canadian Press Newswire, 18 April 1996.
6 Federal/Provincial/Territorial CPP Consultations Secretariat, *Report on the Canada Pension Plan Consultations* (hereafter *Consultations*).
7 Ibid., 13.
8 Ibid., 14.
9 Ibid., 14–16.
10 Ibid., 16–17.
11 Ibid., 18–19.
12 Ibid., 19.
13 Ibid., 30.
14 Ibid., 22–4.
15 Ibid., 22.
16 Interview with the author, 8 July 2007.
17 *Consultations*, 23–4.
18 Ibid., 28–9.
19 Ibid., 31–2.
20 Ibid., 35.
21 Ibid. See also Canadian Institute of Actuaries, *Report of the Task Force on the Future of Canada/Québec Pension Plans*.
22 *Consultations*, 37.
23 Ibid., 38–9.
24 Ibid., 44–5.
25 Ibid., 45–6.
26 Ibid., 46–50.
27 Ibid., 51.
28 Ibid., 55.
29 Ibid., 56.
30 Ibid., 57.

31 Ibid.
32 Ibid.
33 Ibid., 59.
34 Caledon Institute of Social Policy, *Experts' Forum on Canada Pension Plan Reform.*
35 William B.P. Robson, *Putting Some Gold in the Golden Years: Fixing the Canada Pension Plan.*
36 Caledon Institute, *Experts' Forum*, 22–6.
37 Ibid., 29.
38 Ibid., 33.
39 Ibid., 39. The next section on Sheikh's presentation is largely taken from pp. 39–43 and will not be footnoted further. One exception is the reference to real interest rates exceeding real growth, which is found on p. 37.
40 This was an advisory body to the Minister of Human Resources Development that produced periodic reports on the operations of the CPP.
41 Caledon Institute, *Experts' Forum*, 49. Erlichman's entire presentation is on pp. 49–52.
42 Ibid., 69. Baldwin's entire presentation is on pp. 65–70.
43 Ibid., 54. Hamilton's entire presentation is on pp. 53–64.
44 According to the Statistics Canada *Daily* of 3 May 2007, the combined debt of all Canada's governments was $837 billion, equal to 102 per cent of gross domestic product, at the end of March 1996. That was the recent peak for the debt ratio.
45 Caledon Institute, *Experts' Forum*, 45–7.
46 Ibid., 78. Beekman's entire presentation is on pp. 77–84.
47 Ibid., 95. Wilson's entire presentation is on pp. 93–5.
48 Interview with the author, 27 February 2007. The observer, a senior federal official, spoke on a not-for-attribution basis.
49 Ibid., 1.
50 Caledon Institute of Social Policy, *Round Table on Canada Pension Plan Reform: Gender Implications.* This summary is drawn from Townson's presentation on pp. 21–6.
51 Ibid., 31.
52 Ibid., 31–2.
53 Interview with the author, 17 July 2007.
54 Ibid.
55 Ministry of Finance (Ontario), *Ontario Report on Public Consultations on the Canada Pension Plan*, 7.
56 Ibid., 11.
57 Ibid., 8–9.

12. Progress and Stumbles

1 Interview with the author, 10 May 2007.
2 The official spoke on a not-for-attribution basis, as did other former and current federal and provincial officials cited in this chapter. Such comments will not be footnoted further.
3 Interview with the author, 16 April 2007.
4 Interview with the author, 17 February 2008.
5 Régie des Rentes du Québec, *For You and Your Grandchildren: Guaranteeing the Future of the Quebec Pension Plan: A Reform of the Quebec Pension Plan.*
6 It is worth reiterating the point made in chapter 7. The 14.2 per cent rate that stuck so firmly in the minds of everyone involved in the CPP debate was the projection for the *cost* of the plan in 2030, i.e., the PAYGO rate. The projected contribution rate for that year was 13.9 per cent, the difference from 14.2 per cent being made up from earnings on the CPP investment fund. Many people referred to 14.2 per cent as the projected contribution rate in 2030. Coincidentally, that was the projected contribution rate for 2040.
7 The entire investment issue will be explored in more detail in chapter 13.
8 Department of Finance, *Principles to Guide Decisions on the Canada Pension Plan*, draft, 14 June 1996.
9 'Discord over GST on agenda for talks; Finance ministers not in harmony,' *The Globe and Mail*, 17 June 1996, p. A1.
10 Ibid.
11 Ibid.
12 Interview with the author, 10 April 2007.
13 'Higher CPP premiums on way: 10 per cent ceiling on deductions, cuts in pension benefits discussed to keep plan solvent,' *The Globe and Mail*, 19 June 1996, p. A1.
14 'CPP Reform may end 20% rule,' *Financial Post*, 19 June 1996, p. 1.
15 'Pensions to cost more: Premiums to double but benefits to drop,' *Toronto Star*, 19 June 1996, p. A1.
16 In 2008, she was also chair of the board of the Montreal-based Institute for Research on Public Policy.
17 Interview with the author, 17 February 2008.
18 Interview with the author, 10 April 2007.
19 Interview with the author, 16 April 2007.
20 Interview with the author, 10 May 2007.
21 Ontario, *Budget Paper A*, 5 and 27.
22 Ron Parker, 'Aspects of Economic Restructuring in Canada, 1989–1994,' 32.

23 The name was changed to Employment Insurance on 1 July 1996.
24 Kevin B. Kerr, *Employment Insurance Premiums: In Search of a Genuine Rate-Setting Process.*
25 Kevin B. Kerr, *Unemployment Insurance Financing: Selected Issues.*
26 These figures, which come from Statistics Canada's Provincial Economic Accounts, are on a calendar-year basis, so they differ from those reported in the Public Accounts, which are on a fiscal-year – April through March – basis.
27 John Ibbitson, *Loyal No More: Ontario's Struggle for a Separate Destiny.*
28 Interview with the author, 10 May 2007.

13. Rules for the Fund

 1 Most interviews for this chapter were with federal and provincial officials who spoke on a not-for-attribution basis.
 2 Department of Finance. *An Information Paper for Consultations on the Canada Pension Plan,* 30.
 3 Department of Finance, 'Working Group on Canada Pension Plan (CPP) Investment Policy, Terms of Reference,' undated.
 4 What follows is almost an exact transcript of this section of the memo; it has been lightly edited for clarity.
 5 Keith P. Ambachtsheer, *Moving to a 'Fiduciary' CPP Investment Policy: Two Possible Paths.*
 6 Ibid., 4.
 7 Ibid., 5.
 8 Ibid.
 9 Ibid., 6.
10 Ibid., 8.
11 Ibid., 17.
12 Ibid., 21.
13 It is likely that no minister ever read Ambachtsheer's report. Paul Martin, in a 17 February 2008 interview with the author, said he has no recollection of the legislated governance model as a serious option. By the summer of 1997, there appears to have been a consensus that if governments were going to adopt a market-oriented investment policy, they would adopt some form of the independent governance model.
14 Department of Finance, *Principles to Guide Decisions on the Canada Pension Plan,* draft, 14 June 1996.
15 *New CPP Investment Policy,* Draft, 1 October 1996.

16 Obviously, they had not quite settled on a name for the board – would it be the CPP Investment Board or CPP Investment Fund Board? – but that was a small matter.

17 Quebec is a 'province' for amendments to the CPP itself, but not for this task.

14. Autumn Obstacles

1 'Use UI surplus to offset pension costs, Martin told,' *Toronto Star*, 19 September 1996, p. A15.

2 'BC could scupper CPP reform,' *Financial Post*, 20 September 1996, p. 1.

3 Ontario, Ministry of Finance and Corporate Relations, *Reforming the Canada Pension Plan: British Columbia's Position*, 23 September 1996. A later version of the paper, with the same title but dated 15 October 1996, is less technical but offers more in the way of explanations aimed at a wider audience. It was apparently made public, but not widely distributed.

4 Ibid., 9.

5 Interview with the author, 18 June 2007.

6 Interview with the author, 10 April 2007.

7 'BC's pension reform plan angers Ottawa: Federal officials are trying to overhaul the system to prevent a fiscal crisis in the future,' *The Vancouver Sun*, 24 September 1996, p. A1.

8 'No retreat on CPP Reform, Ottawa says: BC's objections too late to stop changes, Liberals contend,' *Financial Post*, 25 September 1996, p. 1.

9 Email to the author, 3 January 2008.

10 'Ottawa attacks BC over plans to change CPP: Proposals would raise taxes on those earning middle incomes, MP warns,' *The Globe and Mail*, 25 September 1996, p. A4.

11 'Been there, done that: Saving for the future? Surely you jest, Mr. Petter,' *The Vancouver Sun*, 25 September 1996, p. A14.

12 'Bigger EI surplus sought,' *Financial Post*, 1 October 1996, p. 1.

13 National Council of Welfare, *Improving the Canada Pension Plan: A Report by the National Council of Welfare*, 31.

14 Ibid., 32–4.

15 1996 September Report of the Auditor General of Canada, *Chapter 17 – Human Resources Development Canada – Canada Pension Plan: Disability*, http://www.oag-bvg.gc.ca/internet/English/aud_ch_oag_199609_17_e_5048.html.

16 As finance minister, Martin subsequently raised the foreign property limit

to 25 per cent in 2000 and 30 per cent in 2001; it was eliminated altogether in 2005 when Martin was prime minister and Ralph Goodale was finance minister.

17 'Ottawa ups ante in pension talks: On the eve of federal–provincial meetings on CPP, Martin warns that the "right wing" wants to replace it with a private system,' *The Vancouver Sun*, 2 October 1996, p. A3.

18 Southam News wire service, 2 October 1996.

19 'Ottawa may explore CPP expansion Martin willing to discuss BC idea if current financial woes sorted out first,' *The Globe and Mail*, 4 October 1996, p. A4.

20 Southam News wire service, 3 October 1996.

21 'Wrestling with reform: British Columbia is the odd man out on a CPP reform package carefully built during eight months of talks,' *Financial Post*, 4 October 1996, p. 8.

22 Interview with the author, 16 April 2007.

23 Department of Finance. *Principles to Guide Decisions on the Canada Pension Plan*, [final] 4 October 1996.

24 'Finance ministers strike out in bid for new pension plan: Paul Martin leaves meeting empty-handed as Ontario and BC reject his compromises,' *The Vancouver Sun*, 5 October 1996, p. A3.

25 'Governments hit CPP logjam: Provinces want Ottawa to lower UI premiums,' *Toronto Star*, 5 October 1996, p. A32.

26 Ibid.

27 'Martin fights attempts to cut UI premiums: Small savings for individuals would mean major setback in efforts to reduce deficit,' *The Globe and Mail*, 12 October 1996. p. A4.

28 'National notebook,' *The Globe and Mail*, 12 October 1996, p. A4. Michael Gourley, Ontario's deputy finance minister at the time, said in a 2007 interview that such accounts were overly dramatic. 'It's not that much of a soap opera.'

29 'Can Queen's Park and Ottawa get together? Federal officials complain they can't make headway in talks with Ontario but the provincial Tories say the feds are the problem,' *Toronto Star*, 7 April 1996, p. D1.

30 Interview with the author, 16 April 2007.

31 The official spoke on a not-for-attribution basis, as did others interviewed for this chapter.

32 Interview with the author, 17 July 2007.

33 Interview with the author, 4 December 2006.

34 'Liberals responsible for protecting the federal flab,' *Financial Post*, 7 November 1996, p. 19.

35 '"Job killers" on trial: Payroll taxes are under attack amid claims they cut employment,' *Toronto Star*, 12 November 1996, p. D1.
36 'UI premium reduction assailed: Business, labour united in attacking Ottawa's modest cut,' *The Globe and Mail*, 20 November 1996, p. B1.
37 'Eves holds firm on CPP deal,' *Toronto Star*, 27 November 1996, p. B2.
38 '11th hour push for CPP deal: Ottawa is scrambling to get an agreement on Canada Pension Plan reform before Christmas but Ontario is hanging tough and employers need time to adjust 1997 payroll contributions,' *Financial Post*, 23 November 1996. p. 1.
39 'Martin hopeful on CPP,' *The Globe and Mail*, 6 December 1996, p. B4.
40 Southam News (no headline), 19 December 1996.
41 Interview with the author, 17 July 2007.

15. The Deal Is Done

1 Eddie Goldenberg, *The Way It Works: Inside Ottawa*, 316.
2 Interview with the author, 10 May 2007.
3 Goldenberg, *The Way It Works*, 317.
4 'Deal near on UI link, Eves says,' *The Globe and Mail*, 19 January 1997, p. A7. (*The Globe and Mail* persisted in referring to Employment Insurance by its old name of Unemployment Insurance long after the name had officially changed.)
5 Goldenberg says only that it was a Friday in early February, but this is the only date that fits. The CPP deal was announced Friday, 14 February, so 7 February was the only Friday earlier than that in the month.
6 Interview with the author, 17 March 2008.
7 Goldenberg, *The Way It Works*, 318–19.
8 Unless otherwise noted, all quotes from Gourley are either from an interview with the author on 17 July 2007 or from an email to the author on 11 March 2008.
9 Interview with the author, 29 May 2007.
10 Michael Gourley, *Ontario and Reform of the Canada Pension Plan 1995–2007; Did Ontario Get What It Wanted?*
11 Interview with the author, 10 May 2007.
12 Interview with the author, 16 April 2007.
13 Department of Finance, *Securing the Canada Pension Plan: Agreement on Proposed Changes to the CPP*, 13.
14 Ibid.
15 The official spoke on a not-for-attribution basis, as did other federal and provincial officials cited in this chapter.

16 Department of Finance, *Securing the Canada Pension Plan: Agreement on Proposed Changes to the CPP*, 15–16.
17 This was the 1997 maximum benefit, up from the previously cited 1996 maximum rate of $3,540.
18 This provision applied also to the earnings-related portion of disability and survivor benefits.
19 Department of Finance, *Securing the Canada Pension Plan*, 14.
20 The full description in the agreement, on p. 14, says that new pensions 'will now be based on a contributor's average career earnings updated to the average of the year's maximum pensionable earnings (YMPE) in the last five years, instead of the last three years, prior to the commencement of benefits.' When benefits are calculated, every year's earnings are viewed as a percentage of that year's YMPE. For example, if at the age of 25 you earned 30 per cent of that year's YMPE, your earnings for that year would be counted as 30 per cent of the YMPE in the latest year. All earnings are updated in that fashion, and the three- or five-year average is calculated from those numbers.
21 'Martin strikes CPP deal; Ottawa gives ground to Ontario on UI premiums to get province's support,' *The Globe and Mail*, 14 February 1997, p. A1.
22 'We'll all pay more to keep CPP afloat,' *The Hamilton Spectator*, 15 February 1997, p. B1.
23 Department of Finance, *Securing the Canada Pension Plan*, 17.
24 The requirement for full funding of any benefit improvements was put into operation through Bill C-36, which received royal assent on 3 March 2007 and came into force on 3 May 2008. According to the chief actuary's *22nd Actuarial Report*, dated 28 November 2006, the bill provided 'for the calculation and the public reporting of the full funding costs, as well as the integration of these costs into the process for setting the contribution rate.' In a 14 March 2008 email to the author, Chief Actuary Jean-Claude Ménard said that his office began using the full-funding actuarial methodology as early as 2001, but it was extremely difficult to express in legislative or regulatory language. Bill C-36 was the first post-reform change to the CPP containing benefit improvements that needed the application of the full-funding rule. That forced the actuaries, policymakers, and lawyers charged with drafting the legislation finally to put the methodology into legal language.
25 Department of Finance, *Securing the Canada Pension Plan*, 17.
26 Réal Bouchard, *Canada Pension Plan: An Examination of the 1997 Reforms*, 24.
27 'Grits hike pension premiums: Finance minister's changes could mean increase of $690,' *Calgary Herald*, 15 February 1997, p. A1.

28 'Manning forecasts tax revolt: CPP premium hikes will "light fire": Reform chief,' *Toronto Star*, 18 February 1997, p. A11.

29 'Conflicting Visions: The Reform party pits its fiscal and social plans against the options it sees in practice,' *Calgary Herald*, 26 February 1997, p. A15.

30 Ken Battle, *Relentless Incrementalism: Deconstructing and Reconstructing Canadian Income Security Policy*, 43.

31 'B.C.: Unfair to the poor,' *The Vancouver Sun*, 15 February 1997, p. A23.

32 'Disabled, senior women hit hard by CPP revision: MacKinnon,' *The Star-Phoenix* (Saskatoon), 15 February 1997, p. A1.

33 'Pension plan premiums to jump; Canadian workers to pay more as governments build up reserves to cover future retirements,' *The Globe and Mail*, 15 February 1997, p. A1.

34 'Eves wins pension reform standoff,' *Toronto Star*, 17 February 1997, p. A16.

35 'Pension premiums going up to 9.9%,' *The Gazette* (Montreal), 15 February 1997, p. A1.

36 'CPP surgery puts plan back on feet,' *Financial Post*, 22 February 1997, p. 48.

37 Ibid.

38 Ibid.

39 'Grits hike pension premiums: Finance minister's changes could mean increase of $690,' *Calgary Herald*, 15 February 1997, p. A1.

40 'Tax group blasts Klein on CPP,' *Edmonton Journal*, 27 February 1997, p. B7.

41 'Pension plan premiums to jump,' *The Globe and Mail*, 15 February 1997, p. A1. The $35,800 was the YMPE for 1997, up from $35,400 in 1996.

42 Based on the $736.81 maximum monthly retirement pension in 1997. See table 1 in Social Development Canada, Canada Pension Plan Benefit Rates, 2008, http://www.hrsdc.gc.ca/en/isp/statistics/cppbenrates.shtml.

43 'Pre-election Liberals never had it so good,' *The Vancouver Sun*, 7 March 1997, p. A4.

44 Interview with the author, 23 January 2007.

45 Bouchard, *Canada Pension Plan*, 24–5.

46 Ibid., 6–7.

47 Email to the author, 6 March 2008.

48 See chapter 2.

49 Office of the Superintendent of Financial Institutions, *Canada Pension Plan: Sixteenth Actuarial Report, September 1997.*

50 The 0.3 percentage point excess of costs over revenues would have been covered by investment income on the CPP fund.

51 Disentangling the two was another matter altogether, something that will

doubtless be apparent only to actuaries and others with advanced mathematical training. When the actuary calculated the impact of the investment policy in isolation, it came to 0.3 points, to which was added a 1.2-point impact from the higher contribution rate. When he calculated the effect of the new contribution rate in isolation, it worked out to 0.5 points, to which was added a 1.0-point impact from the new investment policy. In both cases, this added to 1.5 percentage points. See p. 5 of the *16th Actuarial Report*.

52 Ibid., 5.
53 The 9.3 per cent estimate that officials shared with the media seven months earlier was slightly high.
54 *16th Actuarial Report*, 6–8.
55 Ibid., 14.
56 Ibid., 10.
57 Ibid., 14.
58 Department of Finance, *Gender Implications of Changes to the Canada Pension Plan*, released by the Federal, Provincial and Territorial Governments of Canada.
59 Ibid., 2.
60 Ibid., 5–6. The benefit reductions in 2030 came to 9.3 per cent for both men and women; this estimate by federal finance officials at the time of the deal was later reduced to 9.1 per cent by the chief actuary in his *16th Report*.
61 Ibid., 3 and 6.
62 Poverty data from Statistics Canada indicate that the financial position of elderly women has continued to improve since the mid-1990s. Based on after-tax incomes, the proportion of unattached women 65 and older living under StatsCan's low-income cut-off (LICO) fell from 57.1 per cent in 1980 to 26.7 per cent in 1995 and then to 17 per cent in 2004. For all elderly women, the proportion under the LICO dropped from 26.7 per cent in 1980 to 12.2 per cent in 1995 and 7.3 per cent in 2004.

16. Parliament Gets Its Say

1 House of Commons Debates, 8 October 1997, http://www2.parl.gc.ca/ HousePublications/Publication.aspx?Language=E&Mode=1&Parl= 36&Ses=1&DocId=2332717&File=0.
2 House of Commons Standing Committee on Finance, Meeting 30, 28 October 1997. References to this first day of the hearings will not be noted further. The transcript is available at http://cmte.parl.gc.ca/cmte/ CommitteePublication.aspx?SourceId=49426.

3 The Finance Committee transcript uses the word 'drip,' but this is certainly an error. Martin's notes for remarks to the committee use the word 'drift.' See Finance Department news release 1997-095, dated 28 October 1997, http://www.fin.gc.ca/news97/97-095e.html.

4 Martin's suggestion that the government 'stands behind' the CPP's defined benefit was not strictly correct. The clear understanding of the federal and provincial governments, as laid out in the agreement and in the legislation, was – and remains – that the CPP is fully self-financing with no contributions from government revenue. Indeed, the deal explicitly provided default provisions under which contributions would be raised and benefits frozen (with the impact roughly split evenly between the two measures) if governments could not resolve a future financing problem. Politically, however, Martin had a point. He believed that if some unimaginable future disaster utterly undermined the CPP – a prospect with an almost zero probability – Canadians would expect the federal government to step in and future politicians would have to respond to such pressure.

5 In Office of the Superintendent of Financial Institutions, *16th Actuarial Report*.

6 Whether or not CPP contributions constitute a payroll tax or not is a continuing debate. The defining characteristic of a tax is that it is imposed by government – i.e., it is compulsory – and CPP contributions clearly meet that test. Unlike most taxes, however, today's contribution is closely tied to future benefits for most members of the CPP; also, the funds are kept in a separate account and governments cannot use them for other purposes. Nevertheless, most employers and individuals who pay CPP premiums regard them as a payroll tax, as do most analysts of the impact of payroll taxation on the economy, including researchers in government and the Bank of Canada.

7 'Costs of Replacing CPP with a System of Mandatory RRSPs,' memorandum from C. Scott Clark to the Minister of Finance, 22 October 1997.

8 A few months earlier, the Finance Department had released a far more detailed analysis of a whole spectrum of options for pension plans ranging from the status quo to full privatization. See Steven James, *A Public versus a Private Canada Pension Plan: A Survey of the Economics*.

9 Emphasis in the original.

10 Talk of an Alberta Pension Plan has revived periodically since 1997. During one such period, the University of Alberta's Institute for Public Economics invited several scholars to examine the question. They concluded that Alberta should stick with the CPP. See Paul Boothe, ed., *A Separate Pension Plan for Alberta: Analysis and Discussion*.

11 The official, interviewed by the author, spoke on a not-for-attribution basis, as did other federal and provincial officials cited in this chapter.
12 House of Commons Standing Committee on Finance, Meeting 33, 29 October 1997. References to this hearing will not be noted further. The transcript is available at: http://cmte.parl.gc.ca/cmte/CommitteePublication.aspx?SourceId=49426.
13 As one provincial pension expert noted in an email to the author, it can be argued that the reform did renege on a part of the unfunded liability. Since the CPP's liabilities are synonymous with benefits owed to current plan members in the CPP's rules, 'any benefit cut, unless it protects earned (vested) entitlements and applies only to future service, as is generally required in private sector pension plans, reneges on plan liabilities.'
14 In the 1990s, Sprung was a popular metaphor for a government investment gone bad. In the late 1980s, the Newfoundland government invested $18.5 million in a hydroponic greenhouse operation of that name that produced 8.5 acres of dead cucumber plants.
15 House of Commons Standing Committee on Finance, Meeting 44, 4 November 1997, http://cmte.parl.gc.ca/cmte/CommitteePublication.aspx?SourceId=49385.
16 Ibid.
17 House of Commons Standing Committee on Finance, Meeting 47, 5 November 1997, http://cmte.parl.gc.ca/cmte/CommitteePublication.aspx?SourceId=49395.
18 House of Commons Standing Committee on Finance, Meeting 48, 6 November 1997, http://cmte.parl.gc.ca/cmte/CommitteePublication.aspx?SourceId=49395.
19 Ibid.
20 House of Commons Standing Committee on Finance, Meeting 50, 7 November 1997, http://cmte.parl.gc.ca/cmte/CommitteePublication.aspx?SourceId=49401.
21 House of Commons Standing Committee on Finance, Meeting 51, 17 November 1997, http://cmte.parl.gc.ca/cmte/CommitteePublication.aspx?SourceId=49341.
22 Ibid.
23 Ibid.
24 House of Commons Standing Committee on Finance, Meeting 52, 18 November 1997, http://cmte.parl.gc.ca/cmte/CommitteePublication.aspx?SourceId=49343.
25 House of Commons Debates, Thursday, 4 December 1997, http://www2.parl.gc.ca/HousePublications/Publication.aspx?Language=E&Mode=1&Parl=36&Ses=1&DocId=2332748#LINKT6#LINKT6.

26 Ibid.
27 Debates of the Senate (Hansard), 9 December 1997, http://www.parl.gc.ca/
    36/1/parlbus/chambus/senate/deb-e/028db_1997-12-09-E.htm?
    Language=E&Parl=36&Ses=1.
28 Debates of the Senate (Hansard), 16 December 1997, http://www.parl
    .gc.ca/36/1/parlbus/chambus/senate/deb-e/033db_1997-12-16-E.htm?
    Language=E&Parl=36&Ses=1.
29 Debates of the Senate (Hansard), 17 December 1997, http://www.parl.gc
    .ca/36/1/parlbus/chambus/senate/deb-e/034db_1997-12-17-E.htm?
    Language=E&Parl=36&Ses=1.
30 There is a fine legal point here. Legislation becomes law when it receives
    royal assent. But a new law does not go into force until it has been pro-
    claimed. This gives the government time to write any regulations that are
    needed to ensure that the more general provisions in the legislation are
    clear. Laws can be proclaimed piecemeal, and this is what was planned
    here. The sections involving the CPPIB would not be proclaimed until 1
    April 1998, but the provisions involving only the operation of the CPP –
    contribution rates and benefits, for example – would go into effect immedi-
    ately.

17. Launching the CPP Investment Board

 1 The Quebec government was not part of the group, since QPP funds were
    invested through the Caisse de dépôt et placement du Québec. For the pur-
    pose of monitoring the CPPIB, only the nine provinces in which the CPP
    operated would be involved. The amending formula, however, remained
    the same for the nine. Changes to the CPPIB and any directions given to it
    would have to be approved by the federal government and two-thirds of
    the nine provinces with two-thirds of their total population.
 2 Debates of the Senate (Hansard), 17 December 1997, http://www.parl
    .gc.ca/36/1/parlbus/chambus/senate/deb-e/034db_1997-12-17-E.htm?
    Language=E&Parl=36&Ses=1.
 3 The official spoke on a not-for-attribution basis, as did several other federal
    and provincial officials interviewed for this chapter.
 4 Proceedings of the Standing Senate Committee on Banking, Trade and
    Commerce, Toronto, Tuesday, 17 February 1998, issue no. 8, http://
    www.parl.gc.ca/36/1/parlbus/commbus/senate/com-e/bank-e/08cv-e
    .htm?Language=E&Parl=36&Ses=1&comm_id=3.
 5 There were two Hamiltons at that day's hearing – Bob from the Finance
    Department and Malcolm from William M. Mercer Ltd. I will include first
    names in all references to avoid confusion.

6 For the CPP itself, this means two-thirds of the ten provinces; for the CPPIB, it means two-thirds of the nine provinces that participate in the CPP.

7 Proceedings of the Standing Senate Committee on Banking, Trade and Commerce, Calgary, Wednesday, 18 February 1998, issue no. 9, http://www.parl.gc.ca/36/1/parlbus/commbus/senate/com-e/bank-e/09cv-e.htm?Language=E&Parl=36&Ses=1&comm_id=3.

8 Proceedings of the Standing Senate Committee on Banking, Trade and Commerce, Vancouver, Thursday, 19 February 1998, issue no. 10, http://www.parl.gc.ca/36/1/parlbus/commbus/senate/com-e/bank-e/10cv-e.htm?Language=E&Parl=36&Ses=1&comm_id=3.

9 Ibid.

10 The CPPIB Act specifically said, in Section 10(4), that 'the Minister shall have regard to the desirability of having directors who are representative of the various regions of Canada and having on the board of directors a sufficient number of directors with proven financial ability or relevant work experience such that the Board will be able to effectively achieve its objects.' The full text of the act may be found at http://laws.justice.gc.ca/en/ShowFullDoc/cs/C-8.3//en/en?command=search&caller=SI&fragment=Canada%20pensio n%20plan%20act&search_type=all&day=10&month=1&year=2008&sear ch_domain=cs&showall=L&statuteyear=all&lengthannual=50&lengt h=50&noCookie.

11 Proceedings of the Standing Senate Committee on Banking, Trade and Commerce, Halifax, Wednesday, 18 March 1998, issue no. 14, http://www.parl.gc.ca/36/1/parlbus/commbus/senate/com-e/bank-e/14cv-e.htm?Language=E&Parl=36&Ses=1&comm_id=3.

12 Standing Senate Committee on Banking, Trade and Commerce, *The Canada Pension Plan Investment Board: Getting It Right*, Report of the Standing Senate Committee on Banking, Trade and Commerce, March 1998.

13 Canada, *Response by the Government of Canada to the Report of the Senate Committee on Banking, Trade and Commerce on the CPP Investment Board Act and Draft Regulations (March 31, 1998)*. This undated document is a draft supplied to the author; it is not clear when a final version was sent to the Senate committee; this draft is near-final.

14 Interview with the author, 28 May 2007.

15 'Ottawa fires CPP watchdog: Chief actuary was writing report that could challenge Martin's pledge on premiums,' *The Globe and Mail*, 18 September 1998, p. A1.

16 'Pension chief fights dismissal,' *Toronto Star*, 19 September 1998, p. A15.

17 'Don't "embarrass" Martin: Fired actuary says boss twice asked him to alter CPP numbers,' *Financial Post*, 1 October 1998, p. 3.

18 Receiver General for Canada, *Public Accounts of Canada 2002, Volume II, Part II, Additional Information and Analyses*, p. 10.4.

19 'CPP report calls for premium rate of 9.8%,' *Financial Post*, 17 December 1998, p. C1.

20 Office of the Superintendent of Financial Institutions, *Canada Pension Plan: Seventeenth Actuarial Report as at 31 December 1997*.

21 Office of the Superintendent of Financial Institutions, *Review of the Seventeenth Actuarial Report on the Canada Pension Plan*.

22 *Seventeenth Actuarial Report*, 23.

23 Ibid., table II.2, p. 13.

24 Office of the Superintendent of Financial Institutions, *Canada Pension Plan: Sixteenth Actuarial Report*, 14.

25 *Seventeenth Actuarial Report*, 194.

26 Debates of the Senate (Hansard), 22 September 1998, http://www.parl.gc .ca/36/1/parlbus/chambus/senate/deb-e/077db_1998-09-22-E.htm? Language=E&Parl=36&Ses=1.

27 Interview with the author, 16 April 2007.

28 Interview with the author, 25 January 2008.

29 House of Commons Debates, 2 November 1998, http://www2.parl.gc.ca/ HousePublications/Publication.aspx?Language=E&Mode=1&Parl=36& Ses=1&DocId=2332853.

30 House of Commons Debates, 3 November 1998, http://www2.parl.gc.ca/ HousePublications/Publication.aspx?La nguage=E&Mode=1&Parl=36&Ses=1&DocId=2332854.

31 Gail Cook-Bennett, in a 6 February 2008, conversation with the author, recalled Mitchell as being especially helpful during the board's initial months.

32 Gail Cook-Bennett, 'Notes for Remarks,' 3.

33 Ibid., 4.

34 As at 31 March 2008. Canada Pension Plan Investment Board, 'CPP Fund Totals $122.7 Billion,' 22 May 2008, http://www.cppib.ca/News_Room/ News_Releases/nr_05220801.html.

18. Lessons Learned

1 Telephone conversation with the author, 30 November 2007.

2 Office of the Superintendent of Financial Institutions, *Actuarial Report (23rd) on the Canada Pension Plan, as at 31 December 2006*.

3 Interview with the author, 10 January 2007.

4 The official spoke on a not-for-attribution basis, as did other federal and provincial officials cited in this chapter.

5 Interview with the author, 10 May 2007.
6 Paul Martin, speaking notes, 2.
7 Interview with the author, 10 May 2007.
8 Interview with the author, 23 January 2007.
9 Paul Martin, speaking notes, 2.
10 Ibid.
11 Interview with the author, 17 July 2007.
12 Interview with the author, 10 April 2007.
13 Interview with the author, 23 January 2007.
14 Interview with the author, 16 April 2007.
15 Interview with the author, 10 May 2007.
16 Interview with the author, 23 January 2007.
17 Interview with the author, 16 April 2007.
18 See chapter 15.
19 Ken Battle, *Relentless Incrementalism*, 50–1.
20 Gail Armitage, retired Alberta official, in an interview with the author, 20 June 2007.
21 Since the 1997 reform, the process of federal–provincial cooperation has generated further small revisions to both the CPP itself and to the regulations governing the CPPIB.
22 Kent, *Public Purpose*, 255.
23 Office of the Superintendent of Financial Institutions, *23rd Actuarial Report*, 10.

Bibliography

Ambachtsheer, Keith. 'Saving Canada's Social Security System: A Bold Proposal.' *The Ambachtsheer Letter* 157 (12 April 1995).
– *Moving to a 'Fiduciary' CPP Investment Policy: Two Possible Paths.* June 1996. The paper was made public a year later with a new foreword written in June 1997.
Anderson, Robert D. 'Canada and Quebec Pension Plans.' In *Canada's Retirement Income Programs: A Statistical Overview (1990–2000)*, catalogue no. 74-507-XIE. Ottawa: Statistics Canada, 2003.
Arenas de Mesa, Alberto, and Carmelo Mesa-Lago. 'The Structural Pension Reform in Chile: Effects, Comparisons with Other Latin American Reforms, and Lessons.' *Oxford Review of Economic Policy* 22, no. 1 (2006): 149–67.
Ascah, Louis. 'Recent Pension Reports in Canada: A Survey.' *Canadian Public Policy* 10, no. 4 (1984): 415–28.
Auditor General of Canada. *1993 Report.* Chapter 18. Ottawa. http://www.oag-bvg.gc.ca/domino/reports.nsf/html/ch9318e.html.
Baldwin, Bob. 'Overview of the Retirement Income System.' In *Roundtable on Canada's Aging Society and Retirement Income System, June 5, 1995.* Ottawa: Caledon Institute of Social Policy, 1996.
– *Pension Reform in the 1990s: What Was Accomplished, What Lies Ahead?* Canadian Labour Congress Research Paper 30, April 2004. http://canadianlabour.ca/updir/canadapensionen.pdf.
Barr, Nicholas. 'Pensions: Overview of the Issues.' *Oxford Review of Economic Policy* 22, no. 1 (2006): 1–14.
Battle, Ken. *Relentless Incrementalism: Deconstructing and Reconstructing Canadian Income Security Policy.* Ottawa: Caledon Institute of Social Policy, September 2001. http://www.caledoninst.org/Publications/PDF/1%2D894598%2D87% 2D3%2Epdf. Originally published in Keith Banting,

Andrew Sharpe, and France St-Hilaire, eds., *The Review of Economic Performance and Social Progress. The Longest Decade: Canada in the 1990s*. Montreal and Ottawa: Institute for Research on Public Policy and Centre for the Study of Living Standards, 2001.

– *Sustaining Public Pensions in Canada: A Tale of Two Reforms*. Ottawa: Caledon Institute of Social Policy, July 2003. http://www.caledoninst.org/Publications/PDF/43ENG%2Epdf.

Battle, Ken, and Sherri Torjman. *How Finance Re-Formed Social Policy*. Ottawa: Caledon Institute of Social Policy, April 1995. http://www.caledoninst.org/Publications/PDF/474ENG%2Epdf.

Boothe, Paul, ed. *A Separate Pension Plan for Alberta: Analysis and Discussion*. Edmonton: University of Alberta Press, 2000.

Bouchard, Réal. *Canada Pension Plan: An Examination of the 1997 Reforms*. Paper presented to an international conference on social security reform, 24 February 2006. Washington, DC: Urban Institute. http://author.urban.org/toolkit/conference-papers/international-pensions/upload/RBouchard2.pdf. The accompanying slides are at: http://www.urban.org/toolkit/conference-papers/international-pensions/upload/RBouchard.ppt.

Bowlby, Geoff. 'Defining Retirement.' *Perspectives on Labour and Income* 8, no. 2 (February 2007): 15–19. Ottawa: Statistics Canada. http://www.statcan.ca/english/freepub/75-001-XIE/75-001-XIE2007102.pdf.

Brown, Robert. 'Canada Pension Plan: Financing.' In *Roundtable on Canada's Aging Society and Retirement Income System, June 5, 1995*. Ottawa: Caledon Institute of Social Policy, 1996.

Caledon Institute of Social Policy. *Roundtable on Canada's Aging Society and Retirement Income System, June 5, 1995*. Ottawa, 1996.

– *Experts' Forum on Canada Pension Plan Reform, May 1, 1996*. Ottawa, 1996.

– *Round Table on Canada Pension Plan Reform: Gender Implications, May 17, 1996*. Ottawa, 1996.

Canada. *The Canada Pension Plan: Keeping It Financially Healthy*. Ottawa: 1985.

– *Response by the Government of Canada to the Report of the Senate Committee on Banking, Trade and Commerce on the CPP Investment Board Act and Draft Regulations (March 31, 1998)*. Undated.

Canada. Department of Finance. *Budget Speech*, 27 February 1995. Ottawa.

– *An Information Paper for Consultations on the Canada Pension Plan*, issued in the name of the Federal, Provincial and Territorial Governments of Canada. Ottawa: February 1996. http://www.fin.gc.ca/cpp/maindoc/toce.html.

– 'Chief Federal Representative to Consultations on Canada Pension Plan Named,' news release 1996-029, 28 March 1996.

– *Principles to Guide Decisions on the Canada Pension Plan, Draft*, 14 June 1996.

[The note was drafted by a committee of federal and provincial officials and this version was distributed to ministers by the Department of Finance prior to their 17–18 June meeting in Fredericton.]

– *Principles to Guide Decisions on the Canada Pension Plan,* 4 October 1996. [Final]. http://www.fin.gc.ca/cpp/princips/principe.html.

– *Securing the Canada Pension Plan: Agreement on Proposed Changes to the CPP.* Ottawa: February 1997. http://www.fin.gc.ca/cpp/sec/secure.pdf.

– *Gender Implications of Changes to the Canada Pension Plan,* released by the Federal, Provincial and Territorial Governments of Canada. Ottawa: February 1997.

– 'Costs of Replacing CPP with a System of Mandatory RRSPs.' Memorandum from C. Scott Clark to the Minister of Finance, 22 October 1997.

Canada. Department of Finance. Federal/Provincial/Territorial CPP Consultations Secretariat (1996). *Report on the Canada Pension Plan Consultations.* Ottawa: Department of Finance, June 1996. http://www.fin.gc.ca/cpp/finrep/toce.html.

Canada. Department of Insurance. *Canada Pension Plan Actuarial Report as at December 31, 1969.* Ottawa: 1970. http://www.osfi-bsif.gc.ca/osfi/index_e.aspx?DetailID=499.

– *Canada Pension Plan Actuarial Report No. 2 as at December 31, 1972.* Ottawa: 1973. http://www.osfi-bsif.gc.ca/osfi/index_e.aspx?DetailID=499.

– *Canada Pension Plan Actuarial Report No. 3 as at December 31, 1973.* Ottawa: 1974. http://www.osfi-bsif.gc.ca/osfi/index_e.aspx?DetailID=499.

– *Canada Pension Plan Actuarial Report No. 6 as at December 31, 1977.* Ottawa: 1978. http://www.osfi-bsif.gc.ca/osfi/index_e.aspx?DetailID=499.

– *Canada Pension Plan Actuarial Report No. 8 as at December 31, 1982.* Ottawa, 1984. http://www.osfi-bsif.gc.ca/osfi/index_e.aspx?DetailID=499.

– *Canada Pension Plan Statutory Actuarial Report No. 10 as at December 31, 1985.* Ottawa: 1986. http://www.osfi-bsif.gc.ca/osfi/index_e.aspx?DetailID=499.

Canada. Department of National Health and Welfare. *The Canada Pension Plan: Actuarial Report,* 6 November 1964. Ottawa: Queen's Printer, 1965. http://www.osfi-bsif.gc.ca/osfi/index_e.aspx?DetailID=499.

Canada. Human Resources Development Canada. *Improving Social Security in Canada: A Discussion Paper.* Catalogue no. SC-035-09-94E. Ottawa: HRDC, 1994. http://www.canadiansocialresearch.net/ssrdiscussionpaper.htm.

– *Evaluation Report: Phase 1 of the Evaluation of the Canada Pension Plan (CPP).* Ottawa: HRDC Strategic Policy, July 1995. http://www.hrsdc.gc.ca/en/cs/sp/sdc/evaluation/sp-ah008e/prb.pdf.

Canada. National Council of Welfare. *Better Pensions for Homemakers: A Report by the National Council of Welfare.* Ottawa: Minister of Supply and Services Canada, 1984.

– *Pension Reform: A Report by the National Council of Welfare*. Ottawa: Minister of Supply and Services Canada, 1984.
– *Pension Reform: A Report by the National Council of Welfare*. Ottawa: Minister of Supply and Services Canada, 1990.
– *Improving the Canada Pension Plan: A Report by the National Council of Welfare*. Ottawa: Minister of Supply and Services Canada, Autumn 1996.
Canada. Office of the Superintendent of Financial Institutions. *Canada Pension Plan Eleventh Statutory Actuarial Report as at December 31, 1988*. Ottawa, 1990. http://www.osfi-bsif.gc.ca/osfi/index_e.aspx?DetailID=499.
– *Canada Pension Plan Twelfth Statutory Actuarial Report, October 1991*. Ottawa, 1991. http://www.osfi-bsif.gc.ca/osfi/index_e.aspx?DetailID=499.
– *Canada Pension Plan Fourteenth Actuarial Report as at 31 December 1991*. Ottawa, 1993. http://www.osfi-bsif.gc.ca/osfi/index_e.aspx?DetailID=499.
– *Canada Pension Plan Fifteenth Actuarial Report as at December 31, 1993*. Ottawa, 1995. http://www.osfi-bsif.gc.ca/osfi/index_e.aspx?DetailID=499.
– *Canada Pension Plan: Sixteenth Actuarial Report, September 1997*. Ottawa, 1997. http://www.osfi-bsif.gc.ca/app/DocRepository/1/eng/oca/reports/CPP/cpp16_e.p df.
– *Review of the Seventeenth Actuarial Report on the Canada Pension Plan*, conducted by the CPP Actuarial Review Panel, 31 March 1999. http://www.osfi-bsif.gc.ca/app/DocRepository/1/eng/oca/reviews/reporte_e.pdf.
– *Actuarial Report (23rd) on the Canada Pension Plan, as at 31 December 2006*. Ottawa, 18 October 2007. http://www.osfi-bsif.gc.ca/osfi/index_e.aspx?DetailID=499.
Canada. Parliament. House of Commons Debates (Hansard). Various dates.
Canada. Parliament. House of Commons Standing Committee on Finance. Various dates.
Canada. Parliament. Standing Senate Committee on Banking, Trade and Commerce. *The Canada Pension Plan Investment Board: Getting It Right, Report of the Standing Senate Committee on Banking, Trade and Commerce*. March 1998. http://www.parl.gc.ca/36/1/parlbus/commbus/senate/com-e/bank-e/rep-e/rep11mar98-e.htm.
Canada. Parliament. Standing Senate Committee on Banking, Trade and Commerce. Proceedings. Various dates.
Canada. Receiver General. *Public Accounts of Canada 2002, Volume II, Part II, Additional Information and Analyses*. Ottawa: Minister of Public Works and Government Services Canada, 2002. http://epe.lac-bac.gc.ca/100/201/301/public_accounts_can/2002/v22pa02-e.pdf.
Canadian Institute of Actuaries. *Canadian Retirement Income Social Security Programs, Report of the Task Force on Social Security Financing*. November 1993.

– *Troubled Tomorrows – The Report of the Canadian Institute of Actuaries' Task Force on Retirement Savings*. Ottawa: January 1995.
– *Report of the Task Force on the Future of Canada/Québec Pension Plans*. May 1996.
Canadian Museum of Civilization. *The History of Canada's Public Pensions*. http://www.civilization.ca/hist/pensions/cpp1sp_e.html.
Chand, Sheetal K., and Albert Jaeger. *Aging Populations and Public Pension Schemes*, International Monetary Fund, Occasional Paper no. 147, December 1996. http://www.imf.org/external/pubs/nft/op/147/index.htm.
Cook-Bennett, Gail. 'Notes for Remarks.' C.D. Howe Institute Policy Conference, 'The Canada Pension Plan Reforms Ten Years After: Lessons and Prospects,' 10 December 2007, p. 3. http://www.cppib.ca/files/PDF/speeches/2007_December10_GCB_C DHowe_CPP10YearsLater.pdf.
Crompton, Susan. 'Facing Retirement.' *Perspectives on Labour and Income* 5, no. 1 (Spring 1993): 31–8. Ottawa: Statistics Canada. http://www.statcan.ca/english/studies/75-001/archive/e-pdf/e-9314.pdf.
Debates of the Senate (Hansard). Various dates.
Duchesne, Doreen, and Hubert Frenkel. 'An Interview with Laurence E. Coward.' *Perspectives on Labour and Income* 5, no. 4 (Winter 1993): 22–32. Ottawa: Statistics Canada. http://www.statcan.ca/english/studies/75-001/archive/e-pdf/e-9344.pdf.
Goldenberg, Eddie. *The Way It Works: Inside Ottawa*. Toronto: McClelland and Stewart, 2006.
Gourley, Michael. *Ontario and Reform of the Canada Pension Plan 1995–2007; Did Ontario Get What It Wanted?* Presentation to 'The Canada Pension Plan Reforms Ten Years After: Lessons and Prospects,' a conference sponsored by the C.D. Howe Institute, 10 December 2007. http://www.cdhowe.org/pdf/ConferencePresentations/MichaelGourley.pdf.
Greenspon, Edward, and Anthony Wilson-Smith. *Double Vision: The Inside Story of the Liberals in Power*. Toronto: Doubleday Canada, 1996.
Ibbitson, John. *Loyal No More: Ontario's Struggle for a Separate Destiny*. Toronto: HarperCollins, 2001.
Jacobs, Alan Michael. 'Governing for the Long Term: Democratic Politics and Policy Investment.' PhD thesis, Department of Government, Harvard University, Cambridge, MA, 2004.
James, Steven. *A Public versus a Private Canada Pension Plan: A Survey of the Economics*. Department of Finance Working Paper 97-04, June 1997.
James, Steven, Chris Matier, Humam Sakhnini, and Munir Sheikh. *The Economics of Canada Pension Plan Reforms*. Department of Finance Working Paper 95-09. Ottawa: November 1995.
Kennedy, Bruce Richard. 'Intra-cohort Redistribution Using Longitudinal Microsimulation: The Impact of Potential Changes to Canada's Public Pen-

sion System.' PhD thesis, School of Public Administration, University of Victoria, Victoria, BC, 1989.

– 'Refinancing the CPP: The Cost of Acquiescence.' *Canadian Public Policy* 15, no. 1 (March 1989): 34–42. http://economics.ca/cgi/jab?journal=cpp&view=v15n1/CPPv15n1p 034.pdf.

Kent, Tom. *A Public Purpose*. Montreal and Kingston: McGill-Queen's University Press, 1988.

Kerr, Kevin B. *Unemployment Insurance Financing: Selected Issues*. Ottawa: Library of Parliament, October 1994. http://dsp-psd.pwgsc.gc.ca/Collection-R/LoPBdP/BP/bp389-e.htm.

– *Employment Insurance Premiums: In Search of a Genuine Rate-Setting Process*. Ottawa: Library of Parliament, December 2005. http://www.parl.gc.ca/information/library/PRBpubs/prb0341-e.htm.

LaMarsh, Judy. *Memoirs of a Bird in a Gilded Cage*. Toronto: McClelland and Stewart, 1969.

MacKinnon, Janice. *Minding the Public Purse: The Fiscal Crisis, Political Trade-offs, and Canada's Future*. Montreal and Kingston: McGill-Queen's University Press, 2003.

Martin, Paul. Speaking notes. C.D. Howe Institute Policy Conference, 'The Canada Pension Plan Reforms Ten Years After: Lessons and Prospects,' 10 December 2007. http://www.cdhowe.org/pdf/ConferencePresentations/PaulMartin Speech.pdf.

Newman, Peter C. *The Distemper of Our Times*. Toronto: McClelland and Stewart, 1968.

Ontario. *Budget Paper A*. 1996. http://www.fin.gov.on.ca/english/budget/ontariobudgets/1996/.

Ontario. Ministry of Finance. *Ontario Report on Public Consultations on the Canada Pension Plan*, Toronto: Queen's Printer for Ontario, 27 June 1996. http://www.fin.gov.on.ca/english/publications/1996/cpp_eng.pdf.

Ontario. Ministry of Finance and Corporate Relations. *Reforming the Canada Pension Plan: British Columbia's Position, September 23, 1996*.

Ontario. *Report of the Royal Commission on the Status of Pensions in Ontario*, vol. 5: *Ontario and the Canada Pension Plan*. Toronto: Government of Ontario, 1981.

Parker, Ron. 'Aspects of Economic Restructuring in Canada, 1989–1994.' *Bank of Canada Review* (Summer 1995): 23–34. http://www.bankofcanada.ca/en/review/1995/r953a.pdf.

Prince, Michael J. *Wrestling with the Poor Cousin: Canada Pension Plan Disability Policy and Practice, 1964–2001*. For The Office of the Commissioner of Review Tribunals, Canada Pension Plan/Old Age Security, Government of Canada, 12 June 2002. http://www.bctr.gc.ca/dapdep/r032002/index-eng.html.

Quebec. Régie des Rentes du Québec. *For You and Your Grandchildren: Guaranteeing the Future of the Québec Pension Plan: A Reform of the Québec Pension Plan.* June 1996. http://www.rrq.gouv.qc.ca/NR/rdonlyres/3C1162DC-11D4-440B-BB29-368C331BF053/0/rrq_livvert_en.pdf.

Rashid, Abdul. 'Seven Decades of Wage Changes.' *Perspectives on Labour and Income* 5, no. 2 (Summer 1993): 9–21. Ottawa: Statistics Canada. http://www.statcan.ca/english/studies/75-001/archive/e-pdf/e-9321.pdf.

Robson, William B.P. *Putting Some Gold in the Golden Years: Fixing the Canada Pension Plan.* Toronto: C.D. Howe Institute Commentary no. 76, January 1996.

Roseveare, Deborah, Willi Leibfritz, Douglas Fore, and Eckhard Wurzel. *Ageing Populations, Pension Systems and Government Budgets: Simulations for 20 OECD Countries.* Economics Department Working Papers, no. 168. Paris: Organization for Economic Co-operation and Development, 1996. http://www.olis.oecd.org/olis/1996doc.nsf/LinkTo/NT00000D8A/$FILE/09E60838.PDF.

Simeon, Richard. *Federal–Provincial Diplomacy: The Making of Recent Policy in Canada.* Toronto: University of Toronto Press, 1972.

Siroonian, Jason. 'A Note on the Recession and Early Retirement.' *Perspectives on Labour and Income* 5, no. 4 (Winter 1993): 9–11. Ottawa: Statistics Canada. http://www.statcan.ca/english/studies/75-001/archive/e-pdf/e-9341.pdf.

Statistics Canada. *Canada's Retirement Income Programs: A Statistical Overview (1990–2000).* Catalogue no. 74-507-XIE. Ottawa: Statistics Canada, 2003.

Torjman, Sherri. *Social Programs: Tail or Dog.* Ottawa: Caledon Institute of Social Policy, February 1994. http://www.caledoninst.org/Publications/PDF/895796164%2Epdf.

– *The Canada Pension Plan Disability Benefit.* Prepared for the Office of the Commissioner of Review Tribunals. Ottawa: Caledon Institute of Social Policy, February 2002. http://www.caledoninst.org/Publications/PDF/553820053%2Epdf.

World Bank. *Averting the Old Age Crisis, Policies to Protect the Old and Promote Growth, A World Bank Policy Research Report.* New York: Oxford University Press, 1994. http://www-wds.worldbank.org/external/default/WDSContentServer/WDSP/IB/ 1994/09/01/000009265_3970311123336/Rendered/PDF/multi_page.pdf.

– 'Averting the Age Old Crisis for the Old.' *World Bank Policy Research Bulletin* 5, no. 4 (August-October, 1994). http://www.worldbank.org/html/dec/Publications/Bulletins/PRB vol5no4.html.

Illustration Credits

Photos

Ashley & Crippen Photography: Keith Ambachtsheer, 31 May 2005
Michael Baldwin: Bob Baldwin, 19 April 2008
Canada Pension Plan Investment Board Annual Report: David Walker, May 2007
CP Images: British Columbia Finance Minister Elizabeth Cull and Saskatchewan Finance Minister Janice MacKinnon, 13 December 1995; Reform Party leader Preston Manning, 16 September 1996; Alberta Treasurer Jim Dinning, 6 May 1993; Prime Minister Jean Chrétien and his top adviser Eddie Goldenberg, 3 December 1998
Bernard Dussault: Bernard Dussault, December 2000
The Globe and Mail: Malcolm Hamilton, 8 June 1996
Michael Gourley: Michael Gourley
Hamilton Public Library Archives: Federal–provincial consultations on the future of the CPP, 16 April 1996
Chris Jardine: Monica Townson, 2002 or 2003
Rick Madonik: Federal–provincial meeting of finance ministers, 14 December 1995
Diana Nethercott: British Columbia Finance Minister Andrew Petter, 25 March 1997
Ottawa Citizen: Ken Battle, 2000
Reuters: Canadian Finance Minister Paul Martin and Bank of Canada Governor David Dodge, 20 December 2000; Federal Finance Minister Paul Martin with provincial counterparts John Ostashek (Yukon), Edmond Blanchard (New Brunswick), Jim Dinning (Alberta), Ernie Eves (Ontario), Bernard Landry (Quebec), 9 February 1996
University of Waterloo Graphics: Robert Brown, 24 October 1994

Cartoons

The Globe and Mail: Brian Gable, 'Pension mirage,' 12 April 1993; Brian Gable, 'Pension Fund collapse,' 19 January 1996; Brian Gable, 'There is no Easter Bunny,' 8 February 1996; Brian Gable, 'Cat food futures,' 20 June 1996; Anthony Jenkins, 'Pairs competition,' 12 February 1996

Library and Archives Canada: David Anderson, 'I could even learn to enjoy this,' August 1996; Thomas Boldt, 'Parachute,' 1996; Dale Cummings, 'Nest egg,' 9 September 1997; Duncan Macpherson, 'Psst ... the fix is in,' 1964 (with permission from the estate of Duncan Macpherson); Danny Pritchard, 'Just checking to see how big it is,' 1991

Alan King: Alan King, 'Oops, sorry,' 1 May 1994

Index

consultations on CPP, 167; and
Quebec, 187; and recession, 87; in
reformed CPP, 241, *242*
retirement income system in Canada:
1984 budget reforms to, 54–5;
beginnings of, 23–4; compared to
United States, 254–5; and explanation of retirement, 19–20; importance of CPP in, 162–3; media
criticism of, 88–9; three tiers of,
16–19, 92–3, 95, 143
Riche, Nancy, 273
Richmond, Dale, 285
Riese, Walter, 42, 45–7, 48–51, 255
Robarts, John, 25–9, 33–5
Robertson, Gordon, 30
Roblin, Duff, 29
Robson, William (Bill), 172, 231, 273–
4, 287
rolling twenty-five-year schedule, 15,
63, 65, 70; in need of revision, 97
'Rowan, Malcolm: *In Whose Interest?*,
210
Royal Commission on the Status of
Pensions in Ontario (1981), 52

Saskatchewan: 1991 opposition to
pension increases, 73; on access to
CPP fund, 28; and CPP investment
board, 294; in making CPP decisions, 183, 235, 304; on new CPP
agreement, 266; reverses support
for CPP reforms, 229, 241; and
unemployment insurance, 201,
223; wants to go slow, 184, 186; on
Year's Basic Exemption, 246. *See
also* MacKinnon, Janice
Sauvé, Maurice, 30–1
schedule of premium increases, 15–
16

Schellenberg, Grant, 116
Seeto, Charles, 209–10
self-employed, 29, 32, 69, 179–80,
323n28, 330n4
Senate, 278–80, 281; expert witnesses,
283–7; lack of power, 279, 283,
349n30; public consultations on
CPP, 282–3; report, 287–9
Seniors Benefit, 91, 109, 126; precur-
sor to, 14
Sheikh, Munir, 127, 172–5
Simeon, Richard, 29, 31, 33
Singapore and super-RRSPs, 120
Smallwood, Joey, 29
Sobeco Ernst & Young, 210
social assistance, 75
Social Credit opposed CPP, 35
Solberg, Monte, 266–7, 270, 272,
277
Southam News, 104, 159, 234,
253
Special Senate Committee on Retirement Age (1979), 52
Spousal Allowance, 16. *See also* Guaranteed Income Supplement (GIS)
Standard & Poor's, 9, 12
Statistics Canada, 81–2, 87, 329n22
Status of Women, 162, 179–80
steady-state financing/contribution
rate: 1996 consensus approaching,
185, 193, 223; 1996 proposals for,
187–9; 1997 projections of, 258; BC
on, 217; Dussault's projection of,
289–91; explanation of, 129–30;
how to sell, 131; proposals for calculating, 148–51; in public consultations on CPP, 165, 177; Quebec
on, 187; in reformed CPP, 247, 249,
257, 262, 310–11, 335n24. *See also*
contribution rates; CPP Invest-